# Lecture Notes in Computer Science 3950

*Commenced Publication in 1973*
Founding and Former Series Editors:
Gerhard Goos, Juris Hartmanis, and Jan van Leeuwen

Jörg P. Müller   Franco Zambonelli (Eds.)

# Agent-Oriented Software Engineering VI

6th International Workshop, AOSE 2005
Utrecht, The Netherlands, July 25, 2005
Revised and Invited Papers

Springer

Volume Editors

Jörg P. Müller
Technische Universität Clausthal
Institut für Informatik
Julius-Albert-Str. 4, 38678 Clausthal-Zellerfeld, Germany
E-mail: joerg.p.mueller.ext@siemens.com

Franco Zambonelli
University of Modena and Reggio Emilia
Facoltà di Ingegneria, Sede di Reggio Emilia
Dipartimento di Scienze e Metodi dell'Ingegneria
Via Allegri 13, 42100 Reggio Emilia, Italy
E-mail: franco.zambonelli@unimore.it

Library of Congress Control Number: 2006924852

CR Subject Classification (1998): D.2, I.2.11, F.3, D.1, C.2.4, D.3

LNCS Sublibrary: SL 2 – Programming and Software Engineering

| | |
|---|---|
| ISSN | 0302-9743 |
| ISBN-10 | 3-540-34097-1 Springer Berlin Heidelberg New York |
| ISBN-13 | 978-3-540-34097-3 Springer Berlin Heidelberg New York |



Springer is a part of Springer Science+Business Media

springer.com


Printed in Germany

Typesetting: Camera-ready by author, data conversion by Scientific Publishing Services, Chennai, India
Printed on acid-free paper SPIN: 11752660 06/3142 5 4 3 2 1 0

# Preface

New technology developments, such as Ambient Intelligence, the Internet of Things, the Grid, and Autonomic/Organic Computing, impose new requirements on the engineering of software systems. Nowadays, software is to be based on open architectures that continuously change and evolve to accommodate new components and meet new requirements. Software must also operate on different platforms, without recompilation, and with minimal assumptions about its operating environment and its users. Furthermore, software must be robust and autonomous, capable of serving a user with a minimum of overhead and interference.

Agent and multiagent concepts provide a number of interesting properties to respond to these challenges. They offer higher level abstractions and mechanisms which address issues such as knowledge representation and reasoning, communication, coordination, cooperation among heterogeneous and autonomous parties, perception, commitments, goals, beliefs, and intentions all of which need conceptual modeling. The implementation of these concepts can lead to advanced functionalities, e.g., in inference-based query answering, transaction control, adaptive workflows, brokering and integration of disparate information sources, and automated communication processes. At the same time, successful research is being performed to provide links between the modeling of agent systems and state-of-the-art software modeling techniques and tools, such as the Model-Driven Architecture$^{TM}$, or the Unified Modeling Language.

Like its very successful predecessors of the years 2000 to 2004 (*Lecture Notes in Computer Science*, Volume 1957, 2222, 2585, 2935, and 3382), the AOSE 2005 workshop sought to examine the credentials of agent-based approaches as a software engineering paradigm, and to gain an insight into what agent-oriented software engineering will look like, and what its benefits will be.

AOSE 2005 was hosted by the 4th International Joint Conference on Autonomous Agents and Multiagent Systems (AAMAS 2005) held in Utrecht, The Netherlands, in July 2005. The workshop received 35 paper submissions. After a round of reviews where each paper received at least three reviews from independent reviewers, 13 papers were selected for regular presentation at the workshop, plus seven additional papers for short presentation. The workshop program included an invited talk, technical sessions in which the accepted papers were presented and discussed, and a closing plenary session. It congregated more then 50 attendees among researchers, students and practitioners, who contributed to the discussion of research problems related to the main topics in AOSE. After the workshop, the authors of the accepted papers were asked to review their papers based on both the reviewers' comments and the outcomes of the workshop discussion. Then, after a second round of reviews, 18 papers made it into this book, in which we are confident the readers will find a comprehensive high-quality overview of the state of the art in agent-oriented software engineering.

This book is organized into five sections, each dealing with various very important aspects of multiagent systems development: Modeling Tools, Analysis and Validation Tools, Multiagent Systems Design, Implementation Tools, and Experiences and Comparative Evaluations.

## Section 1: Modeling Tools

The first section focuses on the issue of modeling multiagent systems, and includes three papers.

The first paper, titled *Operational Modeling of Agent Autonomy*, by Weiß et al., focuses on the concept of autonomy, which is a central one in AOSE. The authors correctly discuss that, while there has been considerable progress in the theoretical aspects related to the autonomy concept, little has been done so far into transforming autonomy into a practical software property. To this end, the authors proposes ASL (Autonomy Specification Language) as a first step in this direction. ASL helps modeling autonomy in terms of the degrees of freedom left to the agents for the execution of their activities, and allows for the precise identification of the activities to be carried on by a set of agents.

The starting point of the paper authored by Cheong and Winikoff and titled *Hermes: Designing Goal-Oriented Interactions* is that interactions between agents are traditionally specified by using notations such as Petri Nets, AUML, etc., which – being message-centric – hardly fit autonomous goal-oriented agents. Also, since interaction protocols typically prescribe how interactions must be carried out by agents, they may limit the flexibility of interactions and the overall robustness of a multiagent system. Based on these assumptions, the authors present a new goal-oriented approach to practically model interactions, Hermes, which includes a methodology for designing goal-oriented interactions, failure-handling mechanisms, and a process for mapping design artifacts into an executable implementation.

The third paper, *Modeling Social Aspects of Multiagent Systems: the AML Approach*, by Cervenka et al., outlines the need for any modeling tool to provide suitable ways for representing the social aspects of multiagent systems, including the social structure of a multiagent system, the social behavior driving the overall dynamics of the system, and the social attitudes of the individuals in the system. In this context, the authors propose a new Agent Modeling Language (AML) to model social aspects. The paper specifically focuses on analyzing those aspects of AML related to social structure modeling and to role modeling, and evaluates the effectiveness of AML with the help of application examples.

## Section 2: Analysis and Validation Tools

This section focuses on the important issue of analyzing and validating multiagent systems.

The starting point of the paper *Requirements Elicitation for Agent-Based Applications*, authored by Fuentes Fernandez et al., is that the analysis of requirements and, specifically, requirements elicitation is a key stage for the development of complex multiagent systems. Given the need for proper tools to support requirements elicitation, the authors propose a new tool based on activity theory and social sciences, the Requirements Elicitation Guide. The guide empowers teams devoted to developing multiagent systems with the necessary knowledge and experience required to succesfully perform requirements elicitation.

In their paper titled *Formalization and Analysis of the Temporal Dynamics of Conditioning*, Bosse et al. outline that it is very important for AOSE techniques and for AOSE analysis to be able to properly incorporate learning mechanisms into agent systems. By focussing on the specific learning mechanism of classical conditioning, the authors point out that traditional modeling mechanisms – based on dynamical systems theories – mismatch with the traditional way of modeling software systems (and multiagent systems), typically based on logical languages. Accordingly, the authors explore a new logical approach to model classical conditioning, which may be more suitable for integration into current AOSE techniques.

In the last paper of this section, titled *Incorporating Committment Protocols into Tropos*, Mallya and Singh attempt synthetizing two trends in the engineering of agent systems. On the one hand, modern methodologies focus on the key phases of agent development, but tend to miss properly modeling flexible interactions. On the other hand, committment protocols are deeply studied to model flexibly behaviors and interactions, but are not properly integrated into an engineering framework. The proposal of the paper is thus that the analysis phase of a multiagent system should incorporate committment protocols as a primary concern, at the same level of goals and agents, and the authors show how this can be done with regard to the Tropos methodology.

## Section 3: Multiagent Systems Design

This section consists of four papers that investigate different aspects of the design of multiagent systems.

The first paper, titled *Zooming Multi-Agent Systems*, by Molesini et al., proposes a new technique for a multi-layered description and analysis of multiagent systems called *zooming*, and describes how the SODA methodology for agent-oriented software engineering can be extended to include a simple zooming mechanism. A case study concerning the management of a university course Internet website is provided to demonstrate the applicability and potential benefits of the new technique.

The second paper, authored by Hill et al., deals with *Improving AOSE with an Enriched Modeling Framework*. The authors observe that existing agent-oriented methodologies neglect (or, e.g., in the case of Tropos, only provide rudimentary support for) the case of early requirements gathering and analysis. Their contribution targets conceptual knowledge modeling to be used in early requirements engineering. The paper proposes a MAS design framework that provides *conceptual graphs* as a modeling notation. Based on these, a transaction-based architecture is described which enables model verification during the requirements gathering phase. To allow their approach to leverage the capability of other AOSE methodologies and agent development environments, the description of a mapping of a conceptual graph model to AUML is included in the paper.

The third paper in this section, titled *Dealing with Adaptive Multi-Agent Organizations in the Gaia Methodology*, by Cernuzzi and Zambonelli, investigates factors, parameters and requirements for designing multiagent systems with view to adaptability. In particular, the paper analyzes the GAIA agent methodology with regard to its suitability in supporting and facilitating changes in the organization of a multiagent system. By means of a conference management example, the authors show how the above-mentioned factors and concepts can be taken into account when modeling a MAS using Gaia. The authors compare other methodologies with Gaia regarding their support for adaptation. They argue that while older methodologies (such as Roadmap, Prometheus, or MaSE) require MAS organizations to be derived in a more or less implicit way from the identification of roles and their interactions, the more recently proposed approaches (such as MASSIVE or Tropos) explicitly address the requirement of *design for change* to some degree.

The last paper in this section addresses the problem of providing transformations from verifiable formal goal-based specifications of agents to implementation models, so-called behavior automata. Simon and Flouret describe an approach that is based on an agent design model called goal decomposition tree (GDT), allowing designers to specify agent behaviors in a temporal logic formula (a subset of TLA). A proof system is given to enable verification of agent behaviors specified in GDT. The focus of the paper is the description of an implementation model that is based on automata, which can be automatically generated from the verified GDT agent model. In this implementation model, the behavior automaton of an agent is constructed by combining elementary automata using so-called *automata composition patterns*. These patterns are associated with the goal decomposition operators as specified in the GDT language.

## Section 4: Implementation Tools

The papers in this section describe up-to-date research efforts on the development of tools for developing agent and multiagent systems and applications.

In their paper titled *An Approach to Dynamically Generated User-Specified MAS*, Jayaputera et al. present an approach for designing multiagent systems relying on the concept of what they call *missions*. A mission is the description of a goal plus associated (partial) plan on how to achieve the goal. Given a mission, a set of agents (mobile or stationary) are created to work on the misison. The authors claim that introducing this abstraction allows them to focus on the application rather than on individual agents. Using the mission concept, the authors describe and empirically evaluate the eHermes platform that creates the (appropriate number of) agents required for a mission at run-time 'on demand.' The dynamic features of their approach provide an increased robustness of the system if the environmental conditions change during execution, and the ability to maintain state and data of the mission so that it can bc suspended and resumed at a later stage and at a different location.

The second paper in this section — *Supporting the Development of Multi-Agent Interactions via Roles* — by Cabri et al. starts from the assumption that the modeling of interactions between agents by roles can simplify the development of multiagent systems. The authors introduce the BRAIN framework for developing agent systems; the key elements of BRAIN are threefold: (i) a semi-formal model of a role (defined as a set of capabilities and its expected behavior); (ii) the XRole language, an XML-based notation for roles; and (iii) interaction infrastructures building on the XRole notation and the role model. The focus in this paper is on how roles in BRAIN can be employed in different phases of applications development, covering analysis, design, and implementation, thus establishing a central repository of information usable throughout the whole application development lifecycle. The concepts are illustrated by using an application example.

The third paper, *Automating Model Transformations in Agent-Oriented Modeling*, by Perini and Susi, advocates the usage of OMG's Model-Driven Architecture (MDA$^{TM}$) to provide a model-based approach for the analysis and design of multiagent systems. In particular, the paper discusses the role of model transformations in agent-oriented software engineering. Using the Tropos methodology, the paper discusses how MDA concepts can be applied to the different phases of agent systems development. In this context, the authors describe a model-to-model transformation from a Tropos plan decomposition model to a UML 2 activity diagram. Also, the paper describes a set of tools that the authors created for supporting the use of the Tropos methodology according to the MDA paradigm by re-engineering the TAOM Tropos modeler in the Eclipse platform. The results of this are two Eclipse plug-ins, the *TAOM4e model* implementing the Tropos meta-model, and the *TAOM4e* platform implementing the modeler functions required for building and managing Tropos models.

A similar problem is dealt with by García-Ojeda et al., the authors of the fourth paper in this section. In *Paving the Way for Implementing Multiagent Systems: Integrating Gaia with Agent-UML*, they describe a MAS development process that incrementally refines a design made using Gaia by applying agent-oriented extensions of UML (in particular Agent-UML). The authors claim that by combining Gaia with Agent-UML, a MAS design can be made more concrete. Technically, this is achieved by mapping the core models of Gaia (Interaction Model, Roles Model, Organizational Structure Model, Service Model, and Agent Model) into the three layers of the agent interaction protocols as defined in Agent-UML. Thus, it is possible to extend the representation of protocols and interaction models, agents, and organizational structures in Gaia with the corresponding concepts in Agent-UML. The applicability and potential benefits of the authors' work are illustrated by using a sample scenario involving the design of a conference management system.

In the last paper in this section, titled *Applying Multi-agent Concepts to Dynamic Plug-in Architectures*, Duvigneau et al. apply concepts of agent orientation to the plug-in-based architecture which are currently being developed in software engineering research. The work described in this paper aims at plug-in frameworks like Eclipse or NetBeans. The main goal of this research is to pull the design of plug-in-based applications up to a conceptual modeling level. The authors use their MULAN architecture, to build a conceptual model of a plug-in-based system. The core idea is to achieve extensibility by the idea of nested platform agents and to support this concept by message-based horizontal and vertical communication between the agents representing the components in the system. Based on the conceptual model, a plug-in system using the Renew platform is described, which enables dynamic configuration of the plug-in system.

## Section 5: Experiences and Comparative Evaluations

In this last section, three papers are included that report interesting experiences and evaluations of specific AOSE-related issues.

The paper *Using the Analytic Hierarchy Process for Evaluating Multiagent Systems Architecture Candidates*, by Davidsson et al., starts from the consideration that, although a number of different multiagent systems architectures are being proposed and implemented, little has been done so far to systematically evaluate them. In particular, the authors argue that – when developing a multi-agent system – it is important to evaluate possible architecture candidates with respect to their suitability to the specific application scenario. In this context, the authors focus on the problem of load balancing in intelligent networks, and they evaluate four different architectures that can be used to handle this task. These architectures are then studied via simulations, and metrics measurements are recorded and analyzed using the analytic hierarchy process, which is proposed as a useful analysis tool for deciding which architecture candidate is the most appropriate in different situations.

The paper *Estimating Costs for Agent-Oriented Software*, by Gomez-Sanz et al., focuses on software economics and on the need to carefully evaluate the costs involved in developing agent-oriented software systems. The authors correctly claim that there is a lack of shared experience in evaluating the costs associated to the development of multiagent systems, and provide some results related to this. Specifically, the authors exploit data collected from real agent-based projects, and give hints for the application of existing software cost estimation models – e.g., the well-assessed COCOMO model – and for what would be appropriate metrics for agent-based software development. These results can assist agent developers to elaborate tentative estimations of how much effort they should dedicate to their projects and determine their costs.

The last paper of this section and of the book, *Aspects in Agent-Oriented Software Engineering: Lessons Learned*, by Garcia et al., focuses on the issue of modularity in multiagent systems. The paper shows that several concerns in the development of multiagent systems cannot be represented in a modular way, since they crosscut several system modules and do not easily fit into the traditional abstractions of agent-oriented software engineering. Thus, the authors argue that is is important to systematically verify whether emerging development paradigms support improved modularization of the crosscutting concerns relative to multiagent systems. The paper then reports some lessons learned based on their experiences in using aspect-oriented methods and techniques to address these problems. In the light of these lessons, the authors also discuss related work in the area and are able to discuss a number of promising future research directions.

We believe that this thoroughly prepared volume is of particular value to all readers interested in key topics and the most recent developments in the very exciting field of agent-oriented software engineering.

February 2006

Jörg P. Müller
Franco Zambonelli

# Organization

## Organizing Committee

Jörg P. Müller (Co-chair)
Clausthal University of Technology, Germany
Email: `mueller@in.tu-clausthal.de`

Franco Zambonelli (Co-chair)
Universitá di Modena e Reggio Emilia, Italy
Email: `franco.zambonelli@unimo.it`

## Steering Committee

Paolo Ciancarini, University of Bologna, Italy
Gerhard Weiß, Technische Universität München, Germany
Michael Wooldridge, University of Liverpool, England

## Program Committee

Federico Bergenti (Italy)
Carole Bernon (France)
Giacomo Cabri (Italy)
Paolo Ciancarini (Italy)
Massimo Cossentino (Italy)
Scott DeLoach (USA)
Bruce Edmonds (UK)
Alessandro Fabricio Garcia (Brazil)
Paolo Giorgini (Italy)
Marc-Philippe Huget (France)
Michael Huhns (USA)
Carlos Iglesias (Spain)
Matthias Jarke (Germany)
Catholijn Jonker (Netherlands)
Thomas Juan (Australia)
David Kinny (Australia)
Manuel Kolp (Canada)
Juergen Lind (Germany)
Sehl Mellouli (Canada)
Andrea Omicini (Italy)
Van Parunak (USA)
Anna Perini (Italy)
Michael Rovatsos (Germany)
Brian Henderson Sellers (Australia)
Onn Shehory (Israel)
Gerhard Weiß (Germany)
Michael Winikoff (Australia)
Mike Wooldridge (UK)

# Table of Contents

## Modeling Tools



## Analysis and Validation Tools



## Multiagent Systems Design

## Implementation Tools



## Experiences and Comparative Evaluations

# Operational Modelling of Agent Autonomy: Theoretical Aspects and a Formal Language

Gerhard Weiß[1], Felix Fischer[1,2], Matthias Nickles[1], and Michael Rovatsos[3]

[1] Department of Informatics, Technical University of Munich, 85748 Garching, Germany
{weissg, nickles}@in.tum.de

[2] Department of Informatics, University of Munich, 80538 Munich, Germany
fischerf@tcs.ifi.lmu.de

[3] School of Informatics, The University of Edinburgh, Edinburgh EH8 9LE, United Kingdom
mrovatso@inf.ed.ac.uk

**Abstract.** *Autonomy* has always been conceived as one of the defining attributes of intelligent agents. While the past years have seen considerable progress regarding theoretical aspects of autonomy, and while autonomy has been identified as an enabler for new computing paradigms such as grid computing, (web-)service-oriented computing or ubiquitous computing, autonomy as a *software property* is still miles away from implementation. Because of the *legal responsibility* of designers or users for the actions of autonomous software, the implementation of autonomy will require rigorous modelling and verification, so as to ensure maximum dependability. We take a first step in this direction by introducing a formal language ASL (Autonomy Specification Language) that allows for a precise specification of the activities to be carried out by a set of agents, the deontic constraints imposed on these activities, and the implications of activity execution on particular constraints (i.e., constraint dynamics). Agent autonomy is implicit in an ASL specification as the degrees of freedom left to the agents for the execution of activities.

## 1 Introduction

Since the inception of distributed artificial intelligence, *autonomy* has always been conceived as one of the defining attributes of intelligent agents. In the past years, particular interest has been paid to the theoretical aspects of autonomy and related concepts (like the control of and cooperation between agents), and considerable progress has been made in formally defining these [10, 5]. In addition to that, the increasing complexity of software in domains like e/m-commerce, telecommunications, logistics, knowledge management, and simulation of social and economic processes on the one hand and the identification of autonomy as an enabler for emerging information processing paradigms such as grid computing, (web-)service-oriented computing or ubiquitous computing on the other have given rise to a more general interest in autonomy as a *software property*. Nevertheless, software systems that tap the full potential of intelligent agents and have autonomy as a *real* property[1] rather than just a catchy label are still miles

[1] This means decision and action choice for working and interacting towards a design objective even under critical and unexpected circumstances and without substantial human support or intervention.

J.P. Müller and F. Zambonelli (Eds.): AOSE 2005, LNCS 3950, pp. 1–15, 2006.

away from implementation. The main reason for this is obvious: while (technically) each piece of software can be given the autonomy to act on its own, it will always be the designers or users who are *responsible* for its actions in a legal sense. Hence, the only way towards the implementation of autonomy is via a *systematic* process of *rigorous modelling and verification*, so as to ensure maximum dependability of systems that are given the permission to act autonomously. Without this dependability, it is unlikely that autonomously acting agents will be broadly used in industrial, commercial and scientific applications.

We respond to this challenge and take a first step by introducing a formal language ASL (Autonomy Specification Language) that allows for a precise specification of the activities to be carried out by a set of agents, the deontic constraints imposed on these activities, and the implications of activity execution on particular constraints (i.e., constraint dynamics). Agent autonomy is implicit in an ASL specification as the degrees of freedom left to the agents for the execution of activities, so that its type and degree can be precisely tailored to the task at hand. ASL further allows for the automatic detection and handling of norm conflicts, such that conflicts can either be resolved at design time or appropriate measures can be taken regarding their runtime settlement. What distinguishes ASL from existing role- and norm-based models of agent interaction is its operational character and its expressiveness and flexibility particularly w.r.t. agent autonomy.

The remainder of this paper is structured as follows. Section 2 introduces ASL and gives a formal definition of its syntax. Throughout this section, the expressiveness and flexibility of ASL is illustrated in the context of an agent-based electronic trading platform. Section 3 identifies different types of conflicts in an autonomy specification and proposes strategies for their identification and resolution. Section 4 then discusses the features of ASL, compares it to related work and points to some shortcomings and future improvements.

## 2 The Autonomy Specification Language ASL

The basic view underlying ASL is that agents are embedded in a social frame that regulates their behaviour. This social frame, henceforth called *role space*, is composed of a set of *roles* which are available to the agents and through which they can try to achieve individual and joint objectives. An agent may own several roles at the same time, and the same role may be owned by several agents. In the context of this paper, roles serve as a means for specifying desired behaviour and for achieving behavioural predictability, but *not* to make sure that agents never exhibit unexpected and undesirable behaviour (which would simply be impossible if autonomy is taken seriously). In particular, roles may not fully specify or constrain the behaviour of potential owners, but leave room for individuality (so that different agents may fill in the same role differently, put emphasis on different aspects, etc.).

Formally, a role in ASL consists of a set of *activities* to which *norms* and *sanctions* are attached. As the owner of a role, an agent is exposed to all the norms and sanctions attached to the role-specific activities. ASL distinguishes between three different types of norms (namely permissions, obligations, and interdictions) and two types of sanctions (reward and punishment). While norms correspond to behavioural expectations held by agents against each other in their capacities as role owners, sanctions denote (potential) consequences of norm-conforming and norm-violating behaviour. Hence, through norms and sanctions, a system designer can explicitly specify the limits within which an agent is supposed to act autonomously, and how these limits are enforced.

### 2.1 Notational Preliminaries

The syntax of ASL will be given as a set of production rules in extended Backus-Naur form (more precisely, these rules resemble a context-free grammar $G$, and this grammar generates the language $L(G)$ of valid ASL specifications). For the sake of readability, *nonterminals* (to be replaced) and ASL-specific **keywords** and `special symbols` (which both are terminal symbols) are written in different fonts.

### 2.2 Basic Language Constructs

**Role Spaces.** The most general abstraction employed by ASL is that of a role space composed of several roles to be played by the individual agents in their attempt to achieve their goals. This is captured by the nonterminal *role-space-spec*[2] and the production rule

*role-space-spec* ::= **role space** *role-space-id* `{` *role-spec*$^+$`}`

where *role-space-id* is an identifier[3] composed of letters "L" and digits "D" and beginning with a letter, i.e.,

*role-space-id* ::= L { L | D }*

*role-space-id* (i.e. any result of its replacement) is referred to as a *role space identifier*. The nonterminal *role-spec*, which allows for the specification of roles as sets of activities, can be replaced according to the rule

*role-spec* ::= **role** *role-id* `{` *activity-spec*$^+$`}`

where *role-id* is a *role identifier* and *activity-spec* is given by the rule

*activity-spec* ::= *basic-activity-spec* | *activating-activity-spec* | *deactivating-activity-spec* | *request-activity-spec*

The four nonterminals on the right hand side of this rule, corresponding to the different kinds of activities in ASL, are treated in section 2.3.

*Example 1.* Consider an agent-based electronic supply chain management system, for which the system designers have identified five roles "European supplier", "US supplier", "European assembly manager","US assembly manager", and "member of the board of directors". In ASL, this role structure can be written as

---

[2] Hence, *role-space-spec* is the starting symbol of the grammar $G$ that generates ASL.

[3] All the different kinds of identifiers used throughout this paper are assumed to be defined in this way, individual identifiers are further assumed to be unique.

```
role space eSUPPLY
{ role EUROsupplier {...} role USsupplier {...}
  role EUROamg {...} role USamg {...} role MBdir {...} }
```

where the "..." remain to be filled with the appropriate activity specifications.

**Variables.** In ASL, variables can be specified explicitly according to the production rule

```
variable-spec ::= variable-id of type variable-type [ variable-range ]
```

where `variable-id` is an identifier and `variable-type` is a data type, i.e.,

```
variable-type ::= { nat | int | real | bool | char | string | identifier }
```

All types but **identifier** are standard primitive types known from various high-level programming languages. The type **identifier**, which encompasses all legal identifiers and has no operations defined on it, serves to enable a designer to effectively refer to specific roles and activities (details on these follow below). Optionally, variable domains can be restricted explicitly by giving possible (ranges of) values after the type in square brackets (e.g. [1..100] or [EUROamg, USamg]).

**Status Statements, Norms, and Sanctions.** In ASL, each role is defined through a set of characteristic activities. Attached to each activity of each role is at least one *status statement* that specifies the norms and sanctions an agent playing the role is exposed to with respect to this particular activity. ASL distinguishes three types of norms – permission (indicated by the keyword **p**), obligation (**o**), and interdiction (**i**) to carry out the activity – and two types of sanctions – reward (**re**) and punishment (**pu**) – that apply in the case of norm conformance and norm deviation, respectively.

As we have already said at the beginning of section 2, it is unrealistic to assume that agents as autonomous entities do always act in accordance with available norms (especially in *open* environments characterised by a changing population of heterogeneous, self-interested agents). Instead, agents may ignore or violate norms, be it intentional or not. ASL takes care of this fact by enabling designers to explicitly specify the consequences of norm-conforming and norm-deviating behaviour in terms of positive and negative sanctions (i.e., reward and punishment). In other words, norms alone do not impose any limitations on possible agent behaviour (since this is impossible due to our definition of autonomy), they rather work indirectly via the agent's internal reasoning about the attached sanctions, making certain behaviours (which may be undesirable from the designer's point of view) undesirable for the agent. Hence, it is the responsibility of the system designer to devise a set of norms that prevent undesirable behaviour and the appropriate sanctions to enforce these norms. In addition to that, norms can be coupled to logical conditions that specify the circumstances under which they are valid and apply.

Alternatively, the three types of norms (in combination with the sanctions attached to them) can be viewed as different ways to specify the boundaries of agent autonomy: while obligations and interdictions state which activities are outside an agent's range of behavioural choice and control, permissions state which activities are within. Putting sanctions aside, an agent may, but need not execute a *permitted* activity – the execution is neither mandatory (as in the case of an obligation) nor forbidden (as in the case of an interdiction). Whether or not an agent executes such an activity solely depends on his own decision about how to pursue his goals.[4]

Returning to the ASL syntax, a designer can distinguish between two different types of status statements (i.e. norm-sanction pairs) attached to an activity:

- *independent* status statements (keyword **ind**) an agent becomes subject to as a direct consequence of entering the role to which the activity belongs; and
- *dependent* status statements (keyword **dep**) an agent as owner of the respective role only becomes subject to if they are explicitly "activated" by another agent (through the execution of special *activating activities*, details on which are given in section 2.3).

Hence, dependent status statements allow for the specification of *adjustable autonomy* [9], and the status statements attached to activating activities resemble a kind of "meta-autonomy" (i.e. autonomy w.r.t. influencing others' autonomy), and so on. Formally, status statements are given by the following rule:

*status-statement-spec* ::= ≤ { **ind** | **dep** *role-id* } ≥ : *norm-spec*
[± *sanction-spec* ]

The *norm specification* is defined as

*norm-spec* ::= **norm** ≤ { **p** | **o** | **i** } ≥ ≤*condition*≥

where `condition` is a standard Boolean expression over the variables of the activity to which the status statement is attached (evaluating to **true** or **false**) and denotes when the norm is actually valid. The *sanction specification* is given by

*sanction-spec* ::= **sanc** ≤ { **re** | **pu** } ≥ ≤*sanction-ref*≥

Details on `sanction-ref` will be given at the end of section 2.3, for now it shall suffice to view `sanction-ref` as a (unique) identifier referring to a particular sanction. The following examples shall illustrate the use of status statements.

*Example 2.* Consider a status statement ≤**ind**≥ : **norm** ≤**p**≥ ≤ **true**≥ attached to an activity Deliver of the role EUROsupplier (a complete specification of this activity will be provided in example 3 in section 2.3). Accordingly, each agent acting as EUROsupplier is permitted (as indicated by **p**) to carry out this activity (i.e., to deliver material) under any circumstances (as `condition` is **true**) and without any sanction coupled to this permission. Being an independent status statement (**ind**), an agent becomes subject

[4] In fact, for truly autonomous agents (which only judge norms by the personal consequences of attached sanctions) the distinction between different types of norms does not increase the expressiveness of ASL, since assigning both a positive and a negative sanction to each activity would suffice to fully specify the range of behavioural choice. This is an interesting similarity to deontic logic, where each of the operators can be defined via the respective other, and we will return to this aspect in the following section in the context of requests.

to this permission automatically when entering the role EUROsupplier. Further assume that the Deliver activity contains ≤**dep** EUROamg≥ : **norm** ≤**o**≥ ≤ material = "steel"≥ ± **sanc** ≤**pu**≥ ≤ChargeFine(500)≥ as a second status statement. As indicated by "**dep** EUROamg", this status statement can be activated by agents acting as European assembly manager (how this can be done is described in the following section). Through this activation, a European supplier (more precisely, an agent owning the role EUROsupplier) becomes obliged (**o**) to fulfil all requests for delivering steel (from now on, and no matter what quantity of steel is requested). Moreover, this status statement says that a violation of this obligation results in a punishment (**pu**) in the form of a $500 fine (as indicated by "ChargeFine(500)").

**Assuming a Closed World.** A well known assumption in AI (and the modelling realm in general) is that of a *closed world*, stating that everything that cannot be shown to be true is assumed to be false. ASL adopts this principle in that every activity not *explicitly* declared as being permitted, obligatory or interdicted (under certain conditions), is *implicitly* assumed to be interdicted (under these conditions).[5] In software engineering terms, this corresponds to the *least privileges* and *complete mediation* design principles for secure software. The former principle states that users and programs should be endowed with as few privileges as possible, and the latter states that only those activities – more specifically, those data accesses – being explicitly allowed should in fact be executable. Obviously, implicit interdiction also requires an implicit sanction to be effective, which we assume to be the "grounding" sanction described in the following section.

## 2.3 Activity Specifications

Around the status statements defined in the previous section, we will now introduce the ASL syntax for four different types of activities, namely *basic*, *activating*, *deactivating* and *request*. The nonterminal symbols corresponding to these different types are `basic-activity-spec`, `activating-activity-spec`, `deactivating-activity-spec`, and `request-activity-spec`, respectively.

**Basic Activities.** All activities that concern the handling of resources and events are referred to as basic activities. Examples for resources to be handled are time, money, or data, and examples for events are the access to a database, the delivery of goods, the execution of a negotiation protocol, or the response to an environmental chance. In ASL, basic activities are specified according to the production rule

*basic-activity-spec* ::= **act** *activity-id*(*variable-id**)
{ *variable-spec** ;
**status range** *status-statement-spec*+ }

where `activity-id` is an identifier. The activity takes a (possibly empty) list of parameters and contains a specification of all these variables and any additional (e.g. global)

[5] It should be noted that while practically there is no difference between implicit and explicit interdictions, the latter can be used *deliberatively* – through the execution of activating activities – to "override" permissions and obligations.

ones referred to by the activity specification. At the core of the activity specification is a nonempty set of status statements, the activity's *status range*.

*Example 3.* Consider the following basic activity specification as part of the role US-supplier:

```
act Deliver (material, quantity)
{ material of type string["steel", "silver", "gold", "platinum"],
  quantity of type nat[1 .. 1000];
  status range
  <ind> : norm <o> <quantity ≥ 100> + sanc <pu> <ChargeFine(500)>
  <dep USamg> : norm <p> <quantity < 100>
  <dep MBdir> : norm <i> <quantity > 50 and material = "silver"> +
                sanc <pu> <WithdrawRole> }
```

According to the independent status statement of this activity, a US supplier must (**o**) fulfil any delivery request with a quantity of at least 100. If this obligation is violated, the responsible US supplier has to pay a fine (more precisely, the agent who violated this norm in his capacity as US supplier). What's implicit in this independent status statement is that delivery of quantities *below* 100 is forbidden, but due to the first dependent status statement a US assembly manager can permit a US supplier to obey such requests (for any kind of material given in the variable specification). The second dependent status statement says that a member of the board of directors (MBdir) can forbid (**i**) a US supplier to fulfil requests for delivering more than 50 units of silver. An agent is no longer allowed to act as US supplier if he violates this interdiction (indicated by "WithdrawRole").

**Activating and Deactivating Activities.** As we have already mentioned, ASL explicitly captures adjustable autonomy (i.e. autonomy that changes over time) and meta-autonomy (i.e. autonomy w.r.t. influencing others' autonomy) by means of so-called activating and deactivating activities, which serve to activate and deactivate dependent status statements and thus dynamically expose role owners to certain norms and sanctions. The ASL syntax of activating activities is given by the rule

```
activating-activity-spec ::= act activity-id
                             activate activity-id of role-id
                             { variable-spec*;
                               status-range-spec;
                               impact status-statement-spec+ }
```

The first `activity-id` is a unique identifier for the activating activity, while the second `activity-id` and the `role-id` identify the activity being affected. The status statements included in `impact-spec` are those statements of that activity that are activated (i.e. the same that occur in the corresponding dependent status statement). Deactivating activities (nonterminal `deactivating-activity-spec`) are specified analogously with **activate** replaced by **deactivate** (the meaning of this should be clear).

Obviously, a sound ASL specification should include one corresponding activating activity for each dependent status statement in order to ensure that each such statement can be activated (and also a deactivating activity if it should be possible to deactivate it afterwards). Compared to that, independent status statements are inherently active and they concern agents immediately upon entering a role. Finally, it should be emphasised that activating and deactivating activities apply at the role rather than the individual agent level (i.e., a status statement can only be activated for *all* agents acting as owners of a particular role).

*Example 4.* Consider the basic activity Deliver of a US supplier as defined in example 3. According to the first dependent status statement of this activity, a US supplier can be permitted by a US assembly manager to fulfil delivery requests under certain circumstances. Consequently, within the role USamg there should be an activating activity corresponding to this "permissive" status statement. Assume that this activating activity is given by the following specification:

```
act PermitDeliver
activate Deliver of USsupplier
{ EcoSituation of type string["poor", "medium", "excellent"] ;
  status range
  ≤ind≥ : norm ≤p≥ ≤true≥
  ≤dep MBdir≥ : norm ≤o≥ ≤EcoSituation = "poor"≥ ± sanc ≤re≥ ≤EarnBonus(500)≥
  impact
  ≤dep USamg≥ : norm ≤p≥ ≤quantity < 100≥ }
```

As desired, the **impact** part includes the first status statement (i.e., "≤**dep** USamg≥ ...") of the Deliver activity of a US supplier, thus clearly identifying both the activity to be affected and the effect of executing the activating activity (i.e., US assembly managers are granted the permission to deliver less than 100 pieces of material). The respective deactivating activity (for example called ForbidDeliver) will only differ by the keyword **activate** replaced by **deactivate** and will have just the opposite effect (in this case revoking the above permission). A pair of corresponding activating and deactivating activities hence facilitates the exertion of full control over the adjustable autonomy inherent in a dependent status statement. The semantics of the status range is the same across the different activity types (basic, activating and deactivating). Hence, according to the independent status statement, a US assembly manager is permitted (**p**) to execute this activating activity (hence to permit US suppliers to fulfil deliver requests with an order volume lower than 100) without any restrictions (**true**). According to the dependent status statement, a US assembly manager can be obliged (**o**) by a member of the board of directors (MBdir) to carry out this activating activity, provided that the economic situation is rated as poor. By following this obligation, a US assembly manager earns a bonus.

**Request Activities.** ASL allows a designer to explicitly specify requests for carrying out activities through so-called *request activities*. Request activities may be viewed as requests for behaving cooperatively by executing the requested activity. This not only allows for modelling autonomy w.r.t. issuing requests, but also enables a precise definition of the notion of "not executing an action $a$" often found in deontic frameworks, namely as "not executing $a$ (immediately) *when requested*". The ASL syntax of request activities is defined quite similar to that of (de)activating activities by the rule

```
request-activity-spec ::= act activity-id
                          request activity-id of role-id
                          { variable-spec*;
                            status-range-spec }
```

with nonterminals as defined above. Again, the first `activity-id` serves to identify the request activity, while the second together with the `role-id` refers to the activity being requested. Observe that the parameters are determined by the activity being requested and need not be specified again. Possible restrictions on the parameters can be expressed by means of the request activity's status range.

*Example 5.* Assume that the following request activity specification forms part of the role USamg:

```
act RequestDeliver
request Deliver of USsupplier
{ material of type string["steel", "silver", "gold", "platinum"],
  quantity of type nat[1 .. 1000] ;
  status range
  <ind> : norm <p> <quantity ≤ 200>
  <dep MBdir> : norm <i> <material = gold> + sanc <pu> <WithdrawRole> }
```

According to this, a US assembly manager (i.e., an agent in his capacity as a US assembly manager) is permitted under certain conditions (as given in the status range) to request US suppliers to deliver certain types of material (namely, steel, silver, gold and platinum). The independent status statement says that a US assembly manager is permitted to order up to 200 units of material. According to the dependent status statement, once activated through a member of the board of directors, a US assembly manager is interdicted to request the delivery of gold.

An important feature w.r.t. the expressiveness and flexibility of ASL is that activities of any type can be subject to both (de)activating and request activities. In particular, this means that ASL allows for the formulation of "crossed" and "self-referential" constructs such as requests for requests, requests for disallowing certain activities (i.e. requests for carrying out activating or deactivating activities) and so on.

## 2.4 Modelling Sanctions and Autonomy Dynamics

So far, we have not given a formal definition of the nonterminal `sanction-ref` introduced on page 5 and have rather referred to sanctions by some abstract identifiers. By means of request activities, we are now able to introduce a natural yet much more expressive model of sanctioning. This can be done by defining a basic activity for every action that is to be executed as the result of a sanction (like paying a fine, for example), which is obligatory for every role it is part of. However, the corresponding request activity (which is required to put this obligation into practise) may not normally be executed, but is triggered *automatically* upon norm violation.[6]

[6] More precisely, this resembles an executive authority that constantly monitors all active norms and is allowed to execute the corresponding request activity – and does so – in case of a norm violation.

For sanctions to be of any use in the presence of really autonomous agents, failure to execute a sanctioning activity (which has become obligatory by the "triggered" request) will again have to be sanctioned, until ultimately some *grounding sanction* is reached (e.g. role withdrawal, as used in some of the above examples).[7] To enable the use of sanctioning activities in a status statement, we finally define

```
sanction-ref ::= activity-id(variable-id*)
```

*Example 6.* Consider the following definition of a basic activity PayFine as part of the role USsupplier. It takes the amount of the fine as a parameter and is grounded in role withdrawal.

```
act PayFine (amount)
{ amount of type int ;
  status range
  <ind> : norm <o> <true> + sanc <pu> <WithdrawRole> }
```

The corresponding request activity (invoked automatically if USsupplier violates certain norms) then forms part of the role specification for the executive authority:

```
act ChargeFine
request PayFine of USsupplier
{ status range
  <ind> : norm <p> <true> }
```

Besides sanctioning, activities that are triggered automatically upon norm conformance or violation can also be used for modelling a wide variety of autonomy dynamics like, for example, alternatives in norms, reciprocal norms, or contrary-to-duty obligations. For example, the obligation to do either $X$ or $Y$ can be modelled by means of deactivating activities that remove the obligation for either of the two as soon the other one is performed (i.e. as a reward). As an example for contrary-to-duties, consider a contract according to which a seller is obliged to deliver some goods, and a buyer is obliged to pay a certain price (not necessarily after the goods have been delivered). However, if the buyer fails to pay for the goods, the seller must no longer deliver them (in addition to the buyer being fined). This situation can be modelled by means of a deactivating activity which impacts the seller's obligation (to deliver) and is triggered as a punishment for violating the obligation to pay. What is particularly interesting about this model of a contract is that the buyer's refusal to pay for the goods explicitly excuses the seller from delivering. The formalisation of these two examples in ASL is left to the interested reader as an exercise.

## 3 Autonomy-Induced Conflicts

Since ASL does not impose any limitations whatsoever on the different status statements in an activity (e.g., regarding their number or kind), the corresponding norms

[7] By this, we implicitly assume that (at least) this grounding sanction can always be enforced. The existence of such a grounding sanction is crucial for retaining control over any system in which autonomy is involved.

may be inconsistent. To this end, we will now define three basic types of autonomy-induced conflicts in terms of such inconsistencies and show how these can be detected and resolved at design time.

It should be noted that in the context of this paper the term *conflict* is used to denote conflicts between norms (as these, and possible other conflicts caused directly by them, are the conflicts that can be treated on the level of an ASL specification). The (low-level, design-time) conflict resolution strategies presented here do not address exactly the same problems as the (high-level, runtime) ones usually investigated in the context of agents, like negotiation, mediation, arbitration, etc. (see, e.g. [8, 13]). They should hence be seen as a supplement (able to completely avoid certain high-level conflicts) rather than an alternative.

### 3.1 Types of Conflicts

In the following, let

```
S1 = <status-type1>: norm <norm-type1> <condition1>...
S2 = <status-type2>: norm <norm-type2> <condition2>...
```

be two status statements that are part of the status range of an activity $\mathcal{A}$. $\mathcal{S}1$ and $\mathcal{S}2$ are then said to constitute a *potential conflict* if and only if

(i) $\mathcal{S}1$ and $\mathcal{S}2$ have one of the following three norm constellations:
- *norm-type1* = **o** and *norm-type2* = **i** ("OI conflict")
- *norm-type1* = **p** and *norm-type2* = **o** ("PO conflict")
- *norm-type1* = **p** and *norm-type2* = **i** ("PI conflict") and

(ii) it can happen that `condition1` and `condition2` evaluate to **true** at the same time (i.e., both $\mathcal{S}1$ and $\mathcal{S}2$ are applicable for a particular request).

A potential conflict of type OI turns into an actual conflict of this type, if both $\mathcal{S}1$ and $\mathcal{S}2$ are activated and a request for executing $\mathcal{A}$ is available for which both $\mathcal{S}1$ and $\mathcal{S}2$ are applicable. As mentioned above, permissions imply decision choice on the part of an agent, so the situation is somewhat different for conflicts of types PO and PI. A potential conflict of type PO turns into an *actual* PO conflict if additionally the agent being requested to execute $\mathcal{A}$ *prefers* to *not* execute $\mathcal{A}$ (i.e. to not fulfil the request, which is in accordance with the permission $\mathcal{S}1$) while at the same time being obliged to ($\mathcal{S}2$). Similarly, a potential conflict of type PI turns into an actual conflict of this type if additionally the requested agent prefers to execute $\mathcal{A}$ (i.e. to fulfil the request in accordance with the permission $\mathcal{S}1$) while at the same time being interdicted to do so ($\mathcal{S}2$).

*Example 7.* First, consider the independent status statement and the second dependent status statement of the Deliver activity specified in example 3 as part of the role USsupplier. Since the conditions of both evaluate to **true** for a request of at least 100 units of silver, they constitute a potential OI conflict. This can also be understood as a conflict between the roles USsupplier (as the independent status statement becomes active automatically through entering this role) and MBdir. An example for a potential PO conflict is given by the two status statements of the activating activity PermitDeliver given in example 4, where both the condition of the independent status statement and that of the dependent statement evaluate to **true** if EcoSituation = poor. This conflict can also be seen as a conflict between the roles USamg (which includes the activity) and MBdir (through which the dependent status statement can be activated). Finally, the two dependent status statements of the Deliver basic activity constitute a potential PI conflict, as both are activated through a request for delivering $x$ units of silver where $51 < x < 100$. This may also be understood as a conflict between the roles USamg and MBdir, through which the two status statements can be activated.

### 3.2 Conflict Detection

As only the status statements of a single activity may lead to conflicts in the above sense, their detection at design time reduces to a pairwise comparison of status statements and can be fully automatised by means of the following, rather simplistic, algorithm:

```
for each role R ∈ role-space-spec {
  for each activity A ∈ R {
   for each S1 ∈ status range of A {
    for each S2 ∈ status range of A \ {S1} {
     if (norm-type1 and norm-type2 are of type OI, PO or PI) {
      test whether there is a variable assignment that satisfies
      both condition1 and condition2 } } } }
```

For conditions encoded in propositional logic (or first order logic with finite domains), the innermost tests are decidable, and at most $n \cdot m^2$ of the tests are required, where $n$ is the total number of activities for all roles and $m$ is an upper bound for the number of status statements included in the status range of a particular activity. However, a single test may take time exponential in the number of variables shared by `condition1` and `condition2`.

### 3.3 Conflict Resolution

Given that all potential conflicts in an ASL specification can be identified, we will now present three specific strategies for the resolution of such conflicts. All of them are based on specifying at design time which of two (or more) conflicting norms will actually be enforced.

- *Norm ordering*: define an order (a reflexive, antisymmetric, transitive relation) $\prec_N$ on the three norms **o**, **i** and **p**, determining which of two norms overrules the other in case of a conflict. This ordering can be *partial* (e.g., **i** $\prec_N$ **o** and **p** $\prec_N$ **o**) or *total* (e.g., **i** $\prec_N$ **o** $\prec_N$ **p**).
- *Role ordering*: define a (total or partial) order $\prec_R$ on roles, determining which of two roles involved in a conflict dominates the other. This strategy is often found in human organisations (where the decisions of one role may be overruled by a superior), and it makes sense because, as we have seen above, a conflict between two status statements can always be attributed to the roles to which the status statements belong or by which they have been activated.
- *Status statement ordering*: impose an order $\prec_S$ on conflicting status statements. Again, this order can be *total* (in this case meaning that all pairs of *conflicting* status statements are ordered) or *partial*.

These strategies differ significantly w.r.t. their granularity. For example, norm ordering is rather unspecific, but fair in the sense that it is uniform across all roles. On the other hand, status statement ordering allows for responding to conflicts in a direct and highly specific manner, but at the risk of resulting in a very heterogeneous collection of relationships between norms. For instance, consider four status statements $\mathcal{S}1$ to $\mathcal{S}4$ with $\mathtt{norm\text{-}type1} = \mathtt{norm\text{-}type4} \neq \mathtt{norm\text{-}type2} = \mathtt{norm\text{-}type3}$, where $\mathcal{S}1$ is in conflict with $\mathcal{S}2$ and $\mathcal{S}3$ is in conflict with $\mathcal{S}4$. Irrespective of the individual norm types (but also in a possibly counterintuitive way), these statements can be ordered according to $\mathcal{S}1 \prec_S \mathcal{S}2$ and $\mathcal{S}3 \prec_S \mathcal{S}4$. Role ordering lies somewhere in between the other two strategies, but has the additional appeal of being the most "natural" approach.

Most importantly, both total norm ordering and total status statement ordering are guaranteed to resolve *all* OI/PO/PI conflicts (while role ordering obviously doesn't help to resolve conflicts between one and the same role). The same effect can be achieved by appropriately combining different partial orderings. Such a combination is appealing as it allows for balancing the specificities of different conflict resolution strategies, but has to be done carefully because of potential "meta-conflicts" between the strategies. For example, norm ordering and status statement ordering may put certain status statements into a different order. Such meta-conflicts can be resolved at design time by imposing an order (i.e., a meta-strategy) on the strategies (or strategy types) themselves.

*Example 8.* Again consider the two dependent status statements included in the status range of the basic activity Deliver defined in example 3. As described above, these statements constitute a potential PI conflict, which can be resolved by imposing an order on permissions and interdictions (i.e., **p** $\prec_N$ **i** or **i** $\prec_N$ **p**). Now assume that the first dependent status statement (i.e., "≤**dep** USamg≥ : **norm** ≤**p**≥ ...") should "override" the second one (i.e., "≤**dep** MBdir≥ : **norm** ≤**i**≥ ..."), while in all other cases the decisions of a member of the board of directors should overrule that of a US assembly manager. This can be realised by imposing the desired order on the two status statements (i.e., "≤**dep** USamg≥ ..." $\prec_S$ "≤**dep** MBdir≥ ...") and on the roles (i.e., MBdir $\prec_R$ USamg) and by combining these two orderings according to the meta-strategy $S \prec R$.

## 4 Discussion

After this extensive treatment of the ASL syntax, we will now summarise the essential features of ASL, compare it to related work and point to some shortcomings that call for further research.

**Features of** ASL**.** From the engineering point of view, ASL offers two main benefits. First, it is a highly expressive language that enables designers to specify agent autonomy at a very precise level. Consequences of both norm-conforming and norm-deviating behaviour can be captured by means of positive and negative sanctions. Instead of making any assumptions about norm conformance or deviation, this exerts control on agents via their internal reasoning without limiting their autonomy. In a way, ASL is *neutral* w.r.t. autonomy (i.e. neither biased for nor against it). The fact that no assumptions whatsoever (e.g. mentalistic or based on social commitments) are made about the type or internal structure of agents is also reflected in the fact that ASL focuses on the role rather than the individual agent level. Context sensitivity of activities and norms (and thus adjustable autonomy) can be captured by means of activating and deactivating activities, which may either be executed at will by other agents or follow implicitly in case of conformance with or deviation from certain norms. Request activities can be used to explicitly model cooperation and coordination between agents. Finally, nested activity constructs of arbitrary complexity can be formalised in a natural way, such as requests for requests or requests for activating activities. A second key feature of ASL is that it allows for the detection and resolution of autonomy-induced conflicts already at design time. To this end, different types of conflicts and different strategies for their resolution have been identified. While this does not render high-level conflict resolution techniques usually investigated in the context of agents, like negotiation, mediation or arbitration (see, e.g. [8, 13]) unnecessary, it makes the most of what can already be done a design time. To have at least a partial alternative to the high-level strategies is important, because the former are not always applicable in real-world contexts (e.g., due to limited communication bandwidth, knowledge, or time available to identify potential compromises and put them into practice).

**Related Work.** There are several existing approaches for modelling the interaction of autonomous agents, mainly in the area of electronic institutions and organisations. [3] introduces an abstract, normative, role-based model for interactions between autonomous agents within an organisation. This model uses a deontic temporal logic to formalise contracts about agents' capabilities and obligations. [12] presents a framework for the normative specification of electronic organisations of autonomous agents at different levels of abstraction. [11] uses a special deontic and action logic, with includes "acting in a role" as first-order concept, to devise and reason about role-based models of groups of autonomous agents. While both ASL and the above approaches (as well as several others, e.g. [2, 4, 6, 14, 15]) use deontic concepts to specify (the boundaries of) autonomous behaviour, there are three main differences. Firstly, ASL has been built top-down for maximum expressiveness and flexibility, especially w.r.t. agent autonomy. Secondly, it lends itself very well to an operational or procedural interpretation, which is useful when an abstract specification is to be transformed into a concrete (i.e. implementable) agent system. Thirdly, ASL includes a notion of autonomy-induced conflict, and allows for handling such conflicts and hence reducing the inherent contingency of autonomous systems already at design time. There also exists a close relationship between ASL and policy specification languages, in particular the Ponder language [1]. Ponder is a declarative, strongly-typed, and object-oriented language for the specification of security policies and for policy-based management of computer networks and distributed systems [7]. It is fully implemented and supported by a number of tools.

**Future Work.** In this respect, part of our future research will be concerned with a more detailed investigation of the fundamental relationship between agent autonomy and security policies in general and the languages ASL and Ponder in particular. Unlike Ponder, ASL as defined in this paper does not include the usual (object-oriented) constructs for role modelling (inheritance, composition, etc.) and assignment to individual agents. While this does not limit the expressiveness of ASL, it would be rather cumbersome to have certain activities (like the "sanctioning" activity PayFine) that are part of a large number of roles.

On the conceptual side, we see two main shortcomings of ASL in its current form. First, it would be desirable to introduce *explicit* time and hence allow for the specification of deadlines as temporal constraints on norms (i.e. the time interval between a request, the execution of the corresponding activity and the initiation of a possible sanction) or other temporal aspects of autonomy (e.g. norms that are valid only at a certain time). Second, giving a formal (e.g. possible worlds) semantics to ASL will provide a proper theoretical grounding and ultimately pave the way for model checking the autonomy-related properties of a system. Our current research addresses these issues to further improve the expressiveness of ASL and support the engineering of autonomy as a property of dependable software systems.

## References


1. N. Damianou, N. Dulay, E. Lupu, and M. Sloman. The ponder policy specification language. In *Proceedings of the 2nd International Workshop on Policies for Distributed Systems and Networks*, volume 1995 of *Lecture Notes in Computer Science*, Bristol, UK, 2001. Springer.
2. F. Dignum. Autonomous agents with norms. *Artificial Intelligence and Law*, 7:69–79, 1999.
3. V. Dignum. *A model for organizational interaction: based on agents, founded in logic*. PhD thesis, Utrecht University, The Netherlands, 2004.
4. M. Esteva. *Eletronic institutions: from specification to development*. PhD thesis, IIIA, Spain, 2003.
5. H. Hexmoor, C. Castelfranchi, and R. Falcone. *Agent autonomy*, volume 7 of *Multiagent Systems, Artificial Societies, and Simulated Organizations (MASA)*. Kluwer Academic Publishers, 2003.
6. F. Lopez y Lopez, M. Luck, and M. d'Inverno. Constraining autonomy through norms. In *Proceedings of the First International Joint Conference on Autonomous Agents and Multiagent Systems (AAMAS)*, 2002.
7. E. Lupu and M. Sloman. Towards a role based framework for distributed systems management. *Journal of Network and Systems Management*, 5(1):5–30, 1997.
8. H.-J. Müller and R. Dieng, editors. *Computational conflicts. Conflict modeling for distributed intelligent systems*. Springer, Berlin, 2000.
9. D. Musliner and B. Pell. Agents with adjustable autonomy. Papers from the AAAI spring symposium. Technical Report SS-99-06, AAAI Press, Menlo Park, CA, 1999.
10. M. Nickles, M. Rovatsos, and G. Weiß, editors. *Agents and computational autonomy. Potential, risks, and solutions*, volume 2969 (Hot Topics) of *Lecture Notes in Artificial Intelligence*, Berlin, Germany, 2004. Springer.
11. O. Pacheco and J. Carmo. A role based model for the normative specification of organized collective agency and agents interaction. *Journal of Autonomous Agents and Multi-Agent Systems (JAAMAS)*, 6(2):125–184, 2003.
12. J. Salceda. *The role of norms and electronic institutions in multi-agent systems applied to complex domains*. PhD thesis, Technical University of Catalonia, Spain, 2003.
13. C. Tessier, L. Chaudron, and H.-J. Müller, editors. *Conflicting agents. Conflict management in multiagent systems*, volume 1 of *Multiagent Systems, Artificial Societies, and Simulated Organizations (MASA)*. Kluwer Academic Publishers, 2000.
14. H. Verhagen. *Norm Autonomous Agents*. PhD thesis, Department of System and Computer Sciences, The Royal Institute of Technology and Stockholm University, 2000.
15. G. Weiß, M. Rovatsos, M. Nickles, and C. Meinl. Capturing agent autonomy in roles and XML. In *Proceedings of the Second International Joint Conference on Autonomous Agents and Multiagent Systems (AAMAS)*, pages 105–112, 2003.

# Hermes: Designing Goal-Oriented Agent Interactions

Christopher Cheong and Michael Winikoff

RMIT University, Melbourne, Australia
{chris, winikoff}@cs.rmit.edu.au

**Abstract.** Interactions between agents are traditionally specified as interaction protocols using notations such as Petri nets, AUML, or finite state machines. These protocols are a poor fit with autonomous proactive agents since protocols are message-centric and do not support goals. Additionally, interaction protocols prescribe how interactions are carried out by agents, thus limiting the flexibility of the interactions. This also limits robustness, by reducing the available options for recovering from failure. In this paper we propose a goal-oriented approach to interaction. Since we aim at a useful and practical approach that can be used by practising software engineers, a design methodology is an important part of our solution. We present the Hermes approach which includes a methodology for designing goal-based interactions, failure handling mechanisms, and a process for mapping design artefacts to an executable implementation.

## 1 Introduction

It has been remarked that there is no such thing as a single agent system. The ability of agents to interact with other agents is essential, and it is desirable for agent interactions to be flexible and robust. Agent interactions are traditionally specified in terms of interaction protocols, expressed in notations such as Agent-UML [1], Petri nets [2], or finite state machines. However, these approaches are not well-suited to agents that are autonomous and proactive. Interaction protocols are at a low level of abstraction and are message-centric in nature since they are defined in terms of legal message sequences.

This results in a number of drawbacks for the agent paradigm. The primary disadvantages are that the protocols are mechanistic and restrict the autonomy of intelligent agents. Since agents are autonomous and able to independently pursue goals and recover from failures, their interactions should exploit, rather than limit, these characteristics. Further disadvantages are that the flexibility and robustness of the interactions are limited (as the degree of flexibility and robustness depend on the number of legal message sequences); where flexibility refers to multiple ways to successfully achieve an interaction and the ability to take *shortcuts* (i.e. by-passing already completed parts of the interaction), and robustness is the ability to recover from and persevere through failures in the interaction.

We propose the concept of *goal-oriented interaction* which is better suited to the agent paradigm's goal-oriented nature. Goal-oriented interactions are defined in terms of the goals of the interaction (*interaction goals*) and temporal constraints. The interacting agents determine how interaction goals are achieved and are restricted by the temporal constraints placed on the interaction goals (IGs). Interactions between agents

J.P. Müller and F. Zambonelli (Eds.): AOSE 2005, LNCS 3950, pp. 16–27, 2006.

occur because the agents involved have certain goals to achieve, and the interactions are a means of achieving the agents' goals.

In traditional protocol designs, the interaction designer explicitly defines a number of legal messages sequences in terms of messages and combining forms such as sequencing, alternatives, and loops. The Hermes design is different in that the interaction designer does not explicitly define legal message sequences. Instead, the interaction is described in terms of interaction goals, available actions, and constraints. The agents then determine what legal message sequences (according to the constraints defined by the interaction designer) are used for the interactions. As such, the message sequences *emerge* from the interaction. This results in a greater degree of flexibility and robustness since there are more legal sequences available than what an interaction designer could have explicit defined.

We aim to devise a *practical* approach that can be used to develop flexible and robust interactions in agent systems which specifically includes a design methodology and execution mechanisms. Our approach is not particularly targeted towards open systems, however, we have developed the work such that it is useable in open systems. We thus introduce *Hermes*[1], which is a domain independent methodology providing a systematic approach for creating goal-oriented interactions and thus moves away from message-centric protocols. Hermes covers the design (section 2), failure handling (section 3) and implementation (section 4) aspects of the agent interaction development process.

## 2 Goal-Oriented Interaction Design

In this section, we explain the Hermes design process. To illustrate our work, we use an e-commerce protocol based on the NetBill [3] protocol in which a Customer purchases goods online from a Merchant. The NetBill protocol was chosen since a number of other approaches to flexible interactions have used it [4, 5, 6], and by using the same example it becomes easier to compare our approach to existing approaches.

Figure 1 provides an overview of the Hermes design process. The process is shown as an incremental mini-waterfall model in which each step is derived from the previous step. However, as is typical of design, the process is applied in an iterative fashion where developing the design may suggest changes to previously developed aspects. For example, identifying the actions (step 3) may suggest additional interaction goals (step 2).

The Hermes design process encompasses not only designing the interaction, but also designing the internals of the agents that participate in the interaction. In order to end up with a complete design that can be implemented we must consider both the inter-agent aspects, as well as internal (intra-agent) aspects.

The first step in the methodology involves the identification of roles and interaction goals. The roles are defined in terms of the participants of the interactions and the interaction goals can be seen as high level goals that need to be achieved for the interaction to be successful. When identifying interaction goals, it is best to think broadly and

[1] In Greek mythology, Hermes was an Olympian god who acted as the herald of the gods and served as their messenger (`http://www.pantheon.org`).

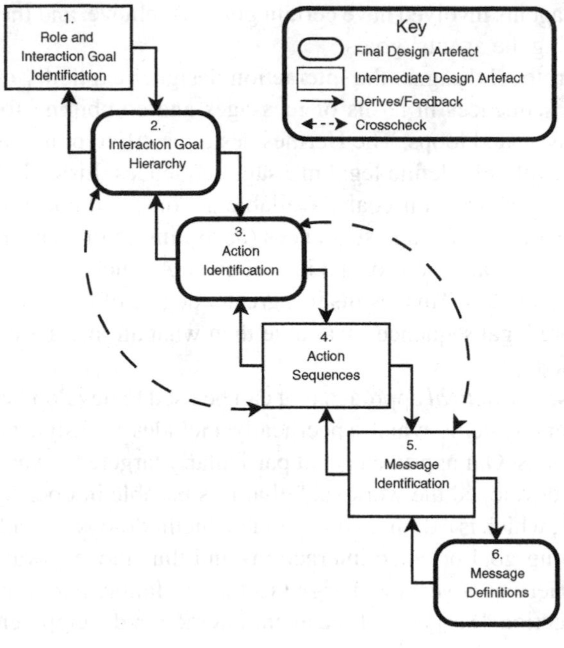


**Fig. 1.** Hermes Methodology Overview Diagram

capture high level interaction goals. Note that interaction goals are goals of the *interaction*, not of a particular agent.

The second step is the refinement and organisation of the interaction goals identified in the previous step. Where possible, the interaction goals identified are broken down into smaller sub-IGs and are organised in a hierarchy as in Figure 2. The hierarchy should only have a single IG at its apex, which captures the overall goal of the entire interaction.

For example, in our e-commerce protocol, the overall goal of the interaction is for the Customer and Merchant to trade cash and goods, thus the top interaction goal is *Trade*.

The *Trade* IG can be further broken down into two more concrete IGs, *Agree* and *Exchange*. Those two IGs can then be broken down even further. Figure 2 shows the interaction goal hierarchy for our protocol, in which the circles represent the interaction goals and the plain lines denote decomposition (i.e. sub-goal relationships). For example, the links between *Trade* and *Agree*, and those between *Trade* and *Exchange* denote that the *Trade* interaction goal is composed of *Agree* and *Exchange*. For the *Trade* IG to be successfully completed, its sub-IGs, *Agree* and *Exchange*, must also be successfully completed. The interaction goal hierarchy is effectively a goal-tree, similar to those used in agent-oriented methodologies such as MaSE [7] or Prometheus [8]. In developing the notations of Hermes we intentionally did not adopt the UML as a starting point. We believe that by doing this we avoided developing notations that were biased by the object-centred viewpoint of the UML.

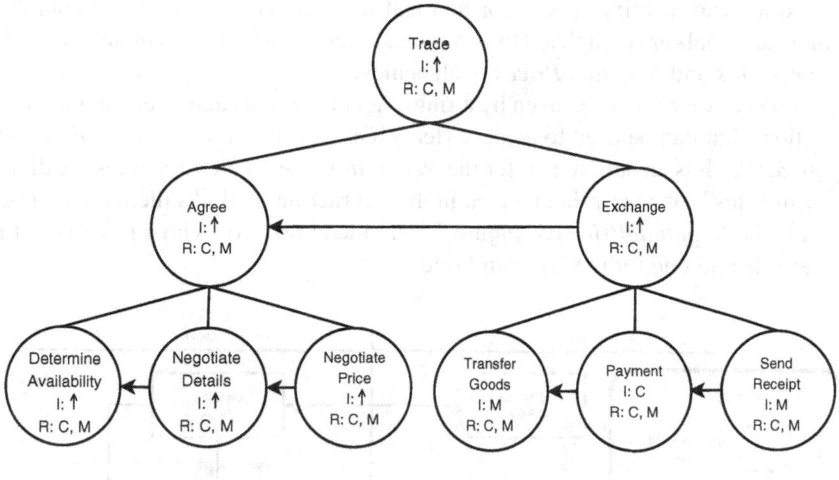


**Fig. 2.** Interaction Goal (IG) Hierarchy Diagram

Once the IGs have been decomposed into smaller and more concrete interaction goals, temporal dependencies (lines with arrowheads on Figure 2) are added. The temporal dependencies allow the interaction designer to place *constraints* on the sequence of the interaction. For example, the line with the arrowhead between *Agree* and *Exchange* implies that the *Agree* interaction goal must be (successfully) completed before the *Exchange* interaction goal can start. The particular design shown in Figure 2 is strongly constrained, however, alternative designs could, for instance, negotiate the details and the price simultaneously.

As the interaction goals are identified and as the interaction goal hierarchy is being laid out, the *roles* involved in the interaction are assigned to interaction goals. In this particular example, it is quite obvious that there are two roles, *Customer* and *Merchant*, and that both roles are involved in every goal of the interaction. In Figure 2, the roles involved are shown in the circles as *R: C, M*, denoting that a particular interaction goal involves the *Customer* and *Merchant* roles.

It is also necessary to identify an *initiator* for every goal of the interaction. The initiator represents the role which initiates and is initially responsible for a particular goal of the interaction. Identifying an initiator is necessary in order to ensure that when an interaction goal is reached, at least one agent has the initiative and will begin interacting in order to achieve the IG. Valid initiators are specified as one of the roles involved in a particular IG (e.g. *C* or *M*) or as ↑ if it is an *inherited* role, i.e. the parent interaction goal's initiator. In Figure 2, the interaction initiator, whether it is the *Merchant*, or *Customer* role, is always responsible for determining the availability of the goods. By contrast, the *Merchant* role is always responsible for the *TransferGoods* and *SendReceipt* IGs, no matter who the interaction initiator is.

The interaction goal hierarchy provides an overview of what goals need to be achieved to complete the interaction. The next step is to determine what actions can be used to achieve a particular (leaf) interaction goal, and what constraints hold between these actions. It is here that we begin to consider the internal design of the agents. Note that there is no need to identify actions for non-leaf-level goals, since they are completed when their sub-goals are completed (e.g. *Agree* is achieved when *DetermineAvailability*, *NegotiateDetails* and *NegotiatePrice* are all achieved).

An *action* is a discrete step, taken by a single agent, towards achieving an interaction goal. Actions that can be used to achieve (leaf) IGs are captured in *Action Maps*, such as Figure 3, which is an action map for the *NegotiatePrice* IG. Action maps are divided into "swim lanes"; one per role involved in the interaction goal. As there are two roles involved in the *NegotiatePrice* IG, Figure 3 is divided into two swim lanes, one for the *Customer* role and one for the *Merchant* role.

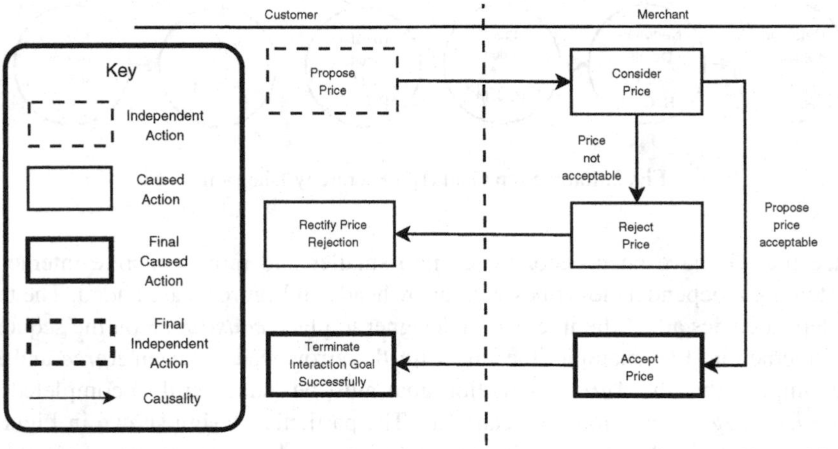


**Fig. 3.** Action Map

The key in Figure 3 illustrates four different action types, each of which has a different meaning and use.

An *Independent Action* is one that can start independently from other actions, i.e. it is not necessarily caused by another action, but it *may* be caused by another action. *Independent Actions* are typically used as entry points into interaction goals and as such, each action map should contain at least one *Independent Action*.

A *Caused Action* is one which cannot start independently and *must* be triggered by another action.

A *Final Caused Action* is a *Caused Action* which terminates the interaction goal for a particular role.

A *Final Independent Action* is an *Independent Action* which terminates the interaction goal for a particular role. *Final Independent Actions* are typically used for roles that only have one action which both starts and terminates an interaction goal.

Performing a final action (either *Final Independent Action* or *Final Caused Action*), does not necessarily mean the interaction goal is successfully achieved, only that it is completed. For example, the interaction designer may wish to end the *NegotiatePrice* IG with failure when a price offer is rejected by the Merchant (but this is not the case in Figure 3).

The causality arrows in figure 3, which can be inter-agent and intra-agent, are used to specify temporal restrictions between the actions. Later in the design process, messages are introduced to allow us to realise these constraints. For example, when the *Customer* executes the *ProposePrice* action, this will cause the *Merchant* to perform the *ConsiderPrice* action, which will trigger another action and so on until the interaction goal is completed.

Where an action has causality links to more than one action the causality arrows are intended to depict alternative possibilities. For example, in the case of the *ConsiderPrice* action on Figure 3, it either triggers an *AcceptPrice* action or a *RejectPrice* action, but not both. Which action is triggered will depend on certain conditions or states. For such situations, labelling the causality arrows with the conditions or states is useful in clarifying the causality path on the action map.

The next step in the design process is for the designer to develop *Action sequence* diagrams by following specific traces from the action maps. Unlike the action maps, which show all possible execution sequences, each action sequence diagram shows *one possible* sequence of actions that can be carried out to achieve the interaction. Figure 4 is an example of a partial action sequence diagram which shows how the *NegotiateDetails* and *NegotiatePrice* goals could be achieved. Actions by particular roles are indicated with the name of the action in a box on the agent's lifeline. Which actions belong to which interaction goal is shown by shading, with the name of the IG at the top-left side of the shaded region.

The purpose of the action sequence diagrams is to check that the actions identified in the action maps are sufficient to allow for a complete and successful interaction to take place, and to ensure that specific interactions that are desired can be generated by the

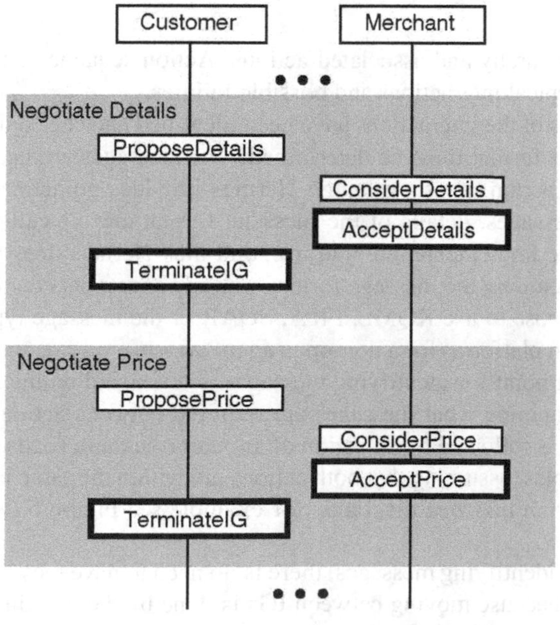


**Fig. 4.** (Partial) Action Sequence Diagram

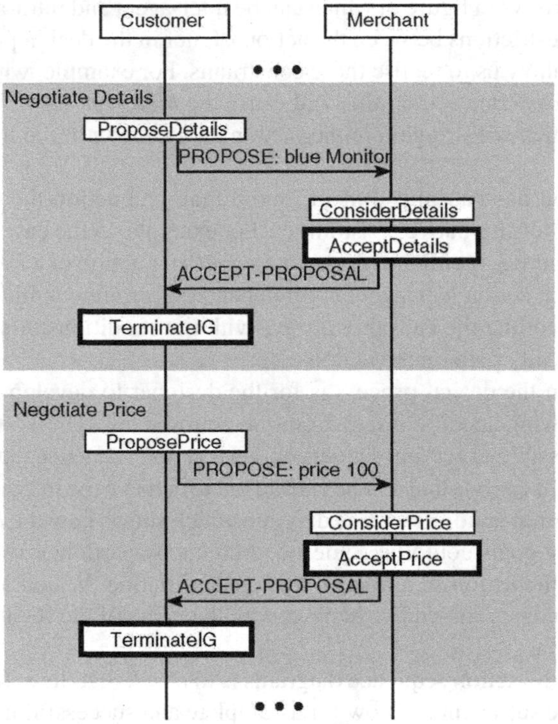


**Fig. 5.** (Partial) Action Message Diagram

interaction goal hierarchy and associated actions. Action sequence diagrams can also be used to show typical interactions and possible failures.

Once the actions of the interactions have been identified and checked, the inter-agent messages and their format must be determined. The messages are used to realise the constraints of the action maps. Although Hermes provides guidelines to assist with identifying the messages, details of the message format are typically specific to the application and the implementation platform, and thus Hermes does not provide any guidelines for developing the message format, nor any constraints on the message format: one could choose to use KQML, FIPA, SOAP, or the message types provided by the implementation platform (for a non-open agent system).

A good starting point for identifying messages is to expand on the action sequence diagrams by determining what messages are required between actions. Whenever an action by one role is followed by an action of another role there needs to be a message between the two roles (assuming that both actions are within the same interaction goal). This results in *action message* diagrams, for example see Figure 5, which is derived from Figure 4.

Note that when identifying messages, there is no need to have messages between the interaction goals, because moving between IGs is done by the coordination plans (see section 4).

## 3 Failure Handling

Successfully handling failure is an important part of enabling agent interactions to be flexible and robust. There are two types of failures in the Hermes methodology: *action failure* and *interaction goal failure*. An action failure is where an action does not achieve its interaction goal. For example, offering a price may fail to achieve the goal of agreeing on a price if the proposed price is rejected. An interaction goal failure is where an interaction goal cannot be achieved. For example, if the price proposed is rejected but a better offer cannot be made then the goal of agreeing on a price cannot be achieved.

An action failure can be recovered from by trying further actions ("*action retry*"). For example, given the actions in Figure 3, suppose that the Customer performs *ProposePrice* and the Merchant rejects the price (i.e. performs the *RejectPrice* action after considering the price). This results in the Customer using the *RectifyPriceRejection* action, which can be used to *retry*, for example by re-performing *ProposePrice* with a different price.

Alternatively, an action failure can cause the interaction goal to fail. In this case, either the interaction as a whole can be *terminated*, or the interaction can be *rolled back* to a previous IG (discussed below). If an action failure is to be handled by failing the interaction goal being pursued, then the appropriate action (e.g. *RectifyPriceRejection*) needs to request a termination of the current IG, or a rollback to a previous IG, specifying an earlier interaction goal as the rollback target.

Rollback is a failure recovery mechanism based on the idea that if previous interaction goals are re-achieved in a different manner, the failed interaction goal may be successfully achieved. Consider an example in which the Customer and Merchant have completed the *NegotiateDetails* interaction goal and have agreed on a product and its details (refer to Figure 2). They proceed to the *NegotiatePrice* IG but cannot agree on a price. One solution is to terminate the interaction, however, a better alternative is for the Customer and Merchant to move back to the *NegotiateDetails* IG, re-negotiate the details of the product and then proceed into the *NegotiatePrice* IG again with different product details.

When and where an interaction can be terminated is domain and application specific, and therefore it is up to the designer of the interaction to determine this. Similarly, when and to where rollback is permitted is domain and application specific, and is determined by the designer. The designer thus needs to indicate for each interaction goal whether termination is permissible from that IG, whether rollback is permissible, and if so, to which interaction goals it should be allowed to roll back to. For example, the *NegotiatePrice* IG allows termination, and allows rollback to the *DetermineAvailability* and *NegotiateDetails* IGs.

## 4 Implementing Goal-Oriented Interactions

We implement goal-oriented interactions by mapping the design artefacts to collections of plans, to be used by an agent platform which supports goal-plan agents (e.g. JACK[2],

[2] `http://www.agent-software.com/`

Jadex[3], JAM[4], and Jason[5]). In this section we briefly sketch how the design produced by following the Hermes process is mapped to collections of plans. For more details on this process, refer to [9].

There are three types of plans: *Interface*, *Coordination*, and *Achievement* plans. Coordination plans are used for coordinating the agents through the interaction. They contain coordination rules as defined by the temporal links and sub-goal relationships on the IG-hierarchy diagram. Achievement plans are used to take steps towards achieving an *interaction goal* (e.g. a *ProposeDetails* Achievement plan is a step towards achieving the *NegotiateDetails* IG). Interface plans (which are not part of the Hermean design process) are used to convert inter-agent messages into events and goal events for internal agent processing. For example, when a Merchant receives a *NegotiateDetails* message from a Customer. The message is handled by the Merchant's *HandleProposeMessage* Interface plan which converts the message to a *proposeDetails* goal event and dispatches it.

Figure 6 depicts an overview of the different plan types required for goal-oriented interactions and shows how they are inter-connected. The beliefset between the different plan types is used to coordinate the agents through the different interaction goals.

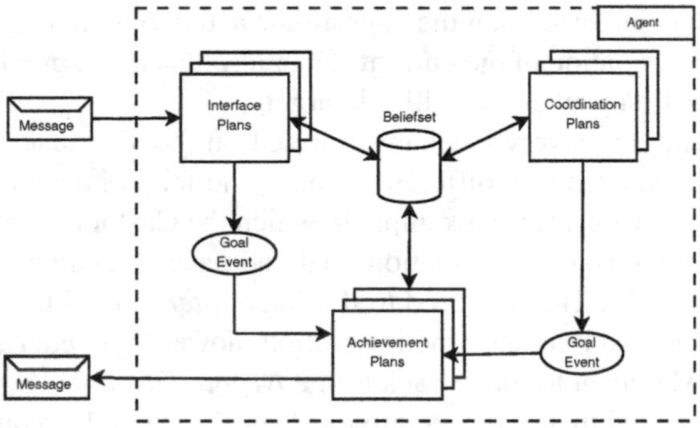


**Fig. 6.** Implementation Overview

## 5 Results

The design for the NetBill interaction that we have presented has been implemented by following the mapping of the previous section, and this implementation is able to produce a range of interactions, including the following sample execution trace in which a Merchant sells blue and yellow monitors at the minimum prices of $110 and $100 respectively, and a Customer seeks to purchase a monitor at a maximum price of $100 with the following colour preferences: red, blue, yellow, and green. It is obvious that a successful interaction will result in the Merchant selling a yellow monitor to the

[3] `http://vsis-www.informatik.uni-hamburg.de/projects/jadex/`
[4] `http://www.marcush.net/IRS/irs_downloads.html`
[5] `http://jason.sourceforge.net/`

Customer at $100. In this example, we demonstrate how this is achieved and explain the advantages of using goal-oriented interactions and the Hermes methodology.

The first interaction goal to achieve is straight-forward (refer to Figure 2). The Customer checks the availability of monitors with the Merchant. If monitors are available, the interaction proceeds, otherwise it terminates. In this example, we assume that monitors are available.

To achieve the next interaction goal, *NegotiateDetails*, the Customer proposes a red monitor to the Merchant. However, as the Merchant only sells blue and yellow monitors, it sends a rejection message. Upon receiving the rejection message, the Customer uses the *action retry* failure recovery mechanism and proposes its second colour preference, blue.

As the Merchant sells blue monitors, it sends an accept message and the interaction proceeds to the *NegotiatePrice* IG. The Customer and Merchant then haggle for a while, however, as the Merchant's minimum price for blue monitors ($110) is higher than the Customer's maximum price ($100) an agreement cannot be reached, and the Merchant sends a reject message. At this point, the current IG fails and the interaction cannot proceed successfully unless the colour of the monitor can be altered. Thus, the Customer uses the *rollback* failure recovery mechanism and proposes a rollback to the *NegotiateDetails* IG. The Merchant rolls back to the proposed IG, sends an accept message to the Customer, and the Customer also rolls back to the *NegotiateDetails* IG.

As the Customer knows that red and blue monitors have resulted in failure, it proposes its next preference, yellow. The Merchant accepts the details and the *NegotiateDetails* goal is achieved. Haggling then re-commences, but this time the Customer is able to propose a price ($100) which the Merchant accepts. The interaction then continues with the *Exchange* IG.

## 6 Discussion

We have presented Hermes, a goal-oriented agent interaction methodology that includes a design process, failure recovery mechanisms and a mapping from design artefacts to an executable implementation. The goal-oriented approach to agent interactions adds a greater degree of flexibility and robustness to interactions than message-centric protocols. This is largely due to the emergent message sequences of goal-oriented interactions.

The flexibility and robustness of the interaction are further increased by adding failure recovery mechanisms, which essentially increase the number of legal message sequences by allowing agents to retry particular actions (i.e. action retry) and (in certain circumstances) to return to previous points in the interaction and re-perform parts of the interaction to attain more desirable results (i.e. rollback). Therefore, our example can be made even more flexible and robust by adding more actions and rollbacks, e.g. more actions to achieve the *TransferGoods* and *Payment* IGs, and rollbacks from the *TransferGoods* and *Payment* IGs.

There are also other approaches which achieve similar results by moving away from message-centric protocols. These include approaches based on *social commitments* [6, 5, 10], Kumar *et al.*'s *landmark-based* approach [11], and Hutchison and Winikoff's *goal-plan* approach [4].

Approaches based on social commitments such as Yolum and Singh's commitment machines [6, 5] or the work of Flores and Kremer [10] capture the meanings of agents' actions in terms of their effects on social commitments. A social commitment is made from one agent to another and represents a condition which an agent will endeavour to bring about for another agent[6]. Commitments are attained and manipulated through inter-agent communicative acts. Therefore, in the course of interacting, agents create and manipulate commitments. Although both approaches allow for complex interactions which would be difficult to implement with message-centric protocols, their design aspects are not well defined. It is not obvious how to determine what commitments are required for a given interaction.

In Kumar *et al.*'s work [11], it is argued that the states of affairs brought about by a communicative act is more important than the communicative act itself. As such, the focus of the work is on the states of affairs, which are represented as landmarks. Thus, an interaction involves navigating through landmarks to reach a desired final state of affairs. Their work is theoretical in nature, and requires significant expertise in modal and temporal logics. Although an implementation ("STAPLE") has been mentioned, no details have been published beyond two posters [12, 13].

Hutchison and Winikoff's approach [4], involves modelling protocols as goals and plans. This involves determining the goals of the protocol and defining plans which are able to achieve the goals. Their work can be seen as a predecessor to our work: it gives neither a detailed design process, nor a mapping from design to implementation.

The Hermes design approach is incomplete in that it only covers interaction: other aspects of design such as determining what agent types should exist, are not addressed. As such, we have integrated Hermes with Prometheus [14], a complete agent-oriented methodology.

Since some of the Hermean design diagrams appear to be similar to UML (e.g. Hermean action maps and UML activity diagrams), we will investigate to what extent Hermes can use the UML. Finally, as we aim for Hermes to be practical, tool support is an important area for future work.

Hermes' design methodology and notation will also require further refinement as we undertake research into adapting Hermes to function with a wider range of interactions, including those which involve many agents and many instances of a given role (such as auctions, where there are $N$ bidders).

Currently, the implementation sketched in section 4 assumes that the agents are implemented using a goal-plan platform. One area for further work is to look at ways of supporting a wider range of agent platforms.

Other, longer term, areas for future work include looking at the verification of goal-oriented interactions, and an experimental evaluation of the approach.

## Acknowledgements

We would like to acknowledge the support of Agent Oriented Software Pty. Ltd. and of the Australian Research Council (ARC) under grant LP0453486.

[6] Flores and Kremer define commitments as being to perform actions, rather than to bring about conditions.

## References


1. Huget, M.P., Odell, J.: Representing agent interaction protocols with agent UML. In: Proceedings of the Fifth International Workshop on Agent Oriented Software Engineering (AOSE). (2004)
2. Reisig, W.: Petri Nets: An Introduction. EATCS Monographs on Theoretical Computer Science. Springer-Verlag (1985) ISBN 0-387-13723-8.
3. Sirbu, M., Tygar, J.D.: NetBill: An Internet Commerce System Optimized for Network-Delivered Services. IEEE Personal Communications **2** (1995) 34 – 39
4. Hutchison, J., Winikoff, M.: Flexibility and Robustness in Agent Interaction Protocols. In: Workshop on Challenges in Open Agent Systems at the First International Joint Conference on Autonomous Agents and Multi-Agents Systems. (2002)
5. Yolum, P., Singh, M.P.: Reasoning about commitments in the event calculus: An approach for specifying and executing protocols. Annals of Mathematics and Artificial Intelligence (AMAI), Special Issue on Computational Logic in Multi-Agent Systems **42** (2004) 227–253
6. Yolum, P., Singh, M.P.: Flexible protocol specification and execution: Applying event calculus planning using commitments. In: Proceedings of the 1st Joint Conference on Autonomous Agents and MultiAgent Systems (AAMAS). (2002) 527–534
7. DeLoach, S.A., Wood, M.F., Sparkman, C.H.: Multiagent systems engineering. International Journal of Software Engineering and Knowledge Engineering **11** (2001) 231–258
8. Padgham, L., Winikoff, M.: Developing Intelligent Agent Systems: A Practical Guide. John Wiley and Sons (2004) ISBN 0-470-86120-7.
9. Cheong, C., Winikoff, M.: Hermes: Implementing goal-oriented agent interactions. In: Proceedings of the Third international Workshop on Programming Multi-Agent Systems (ProMAS). (2005)
10. Flores, R.A., Kremer, R.C.: A principled modular approach to construct flexible conversation protocols. In Tawfik, A., Goodwin, S., eds.: Advances in Artificial Intelligence, Springer-Verlag, LNCS 3060 (2004) 1–15
11. Kumar, S., Huber, M.J., Cohen, P.R.: Representing and executing protocols as joint actions. In: Proceedings of the First International Joint Conference on Autonomous Agents and Multi-Agent Systems, Bologna, Italy, ACM Press (2002) 543 – 550
12. Kumar, S., Cohen, P.R., Huber, M.J.: Direct execution of team specifications in STAPLE. In: Proceedings of the First International Joint Conference on Autonomous Agents & Multi-Agent Systems (AAMAS 2002), ACM Press (2002) 567–568
13. Kumar, S., Cohen, P.R.: STAPLE: An agent programming language based on the joint intention theory. In: Proceedings of the Third International Joint Conference on Autonomous Agents & Multi-Agent Systems (AAMAS 2004), ACM Press (2004) 1390–1391
14. Cheong, C., Winikoff, M.: Improving flexibility and robustness in agent interactions: Extending Prometheus with Hermes. In Garcia, A., Choren, R., Lucena, C., Romanovsky, A., Holvoet, T., Giorgini, P., eds.: Software Engineering for Multi-Agent Systems IV. Lecture Notes in Computer Science. Springer-Verlag (2005)

# Modeling Social Aspects of Multi-Agent Systems: The AML Approach

Radovan Cervenka, Ivan Trencansky, and Monique Calisti

Whitestein Technologies, Panenska 28, 811 03 Bratislava, Slovakia
Tel.: +421 (2) 5443-5502; Fax: +421 (2) 5443-5512
{rce, itr, mca}@whitestein.com
http://www.whitestein.com

**Abstract.** This paper presents modeling concepts and mechanisms of the *Agent Modeling Language* (*AML*) to model social aspects of multi-agent systems. The modeling of structural, behavioral as well as attitudinal aspects of multi-agent systems from the social perspective is discussed and demonstrated on examples.

## 1 Introduction

*Multi-agent systems* (*MAS*) are generally perceived as systems comprised of a number of autonomous agents situated in a common environment. Agents in such systems are rarely isolated. More often they are required to interact with each other so that the desired functionality and properties of the systems could emerge. These features of MAS are not always derivable or representable solely on the basis of properties and capabilities of their individual component agents, but also arise from agents' mutual relationships, interactions, coordination mechanisms, social attitudes (e.g. common or individual beliefs, goals, intentions, desires, commitments), etc., which are commonly referred to as social aspects of multi-agent systems. Social ability of agents is thus one of their most fundamental properties and therefore of central concern for the most of the MAS modeling approaches.

From a social perspective, the following aspects are commonly considered in MAS models:

– *Social structure* concerning mainly with the (1) identification of societies (groups, organizations, institutions, etc.) which can evolve within the system, (2) specification of their properties, (3) identification of comprised roles, social entities that can participate in such societies, roles they can play, (4) specification of the society structure (in terms of social relationships), etc.
– *Social behavior* covering such phenomena as (1) social dynamics, i.e. temporal relationships and causality of social events (i.e. changes of the society state) such as the formation/abolition of societies, the entrance/withdrawal of an entity to/from a society, acquisition/disposal/change of a role played by an entity, modification of properties of a society or its members, etc., (2) social interactions, i.e. how individuals and/or societies interact with others

J.P. Müller and F. Zambonelli (Eds.): AOSE 2005, LNCS 3950, pp. 28–39, 2006.

in order to exchange information, coordinate their activities, etc., (3) social activities, i.e. activities of single social entities or aggregate/emergent activities of societies which influence or are influenced by the state or behavior of other members of the society or the society itself, and (4) norms, i.e. rules or standards of behavior shared by members of a society.
- *Social attitudes* addressing the individual and/or common tendencies (usually expressed in terms of motivations, needs, wishes, intentions, goals, beliefs, commitments, etc.) to anything of a social value.

The purpose of this paper is to present the AML approach to modeling the above-mentioned social aspects of MAS. The focus, however, due to limitation in paper length, is on the structural aspects and role modeling. Details of modeling behavior (used for modeling social behavior) and mental attitudes (used for modeling social attitudes) will be described in forthcoming papers.

The rest of the paper is structured as follows: Section 2 presents a short summary of other approaches to modeling social aspects of MAS. Section 3 provides a brief introduction to AML, Section 4 discusses modeling of social structures, Section 5 modeling of social behavior, and Section 6 modeling of social mental aspects in AML. The conclusions and future work directions are drawn in Section 7.

## 2 Related Work

Most of the currently available agent-oriented modeling languages and methodologies consider social modeling as one of the crucial activities. The proposed approaches, however, differ in the scope and supported modeling concepts.

Several approaches (e.g. Gaia [1, 2], MaSE [3]) model MAS societies in terms of organizations (or groups) composed of a collection of roles related to one another and participating in patterns of interactions with other roles. The agents are then specified in terms of a set of roles they play. These approaches explicitly assume that the inter-agent relationships and the abilities of agents do not change at run-time, and that all the agents are explicitly designed to cooperatively achieve common goals.

The later version of Gaia [2] extends the former one in order to better suit to open MAS by introducing two new abstractions: (1) organizational rules (explicit identification of relationships and constraints between roles and protocols) and (2) organizational structures (explicit specification of organizations in terms of their topology and control regime).

The notions of groups (agentified and non-agentified), roles, agents and agent role assignments are the basic building blocks for defining agent societies in *AUML* (see [4, 5, 6]). The concept of agent role assignment in AUML is not considered to be static, but can change over time. For modeling changes in role playing, AUML makes use of dynamic classification of agents according to the roles which assignments to agents can change over time. For modeling social interactions AUML provides an extended version of UML interactions (for details see [6]).

*AALAADIN* [7] also defines a meta-model of multi-agent systems based on the three main concepts of agents, groups, and roles. The groups in AALAADIN can be dynamically created, and agents can dynamically enter or leave groups. To model dynamics of organizations Organizational Sequence Diagrams (a variant of UML Sequence Diagrams) are introduced.

To model social aspects of MAS, the TAO methodology (accompanied with MAS-ML modeling language) [8] also uses concepts like agents, object and agent roles, organizations, interactions, beliefs, goals, plans and actions in the common way. In addition to these the support for modeling the social dynamics is also provided. In particular, TAO supports modeling of a dynamic organization and agent instance creation, processes concerned with agents entering/leaving organizations, and processes of commitments to (disposal of) played roles.

*AOR* [9] differentiates between different types of manifestation of behavior within a society of agents: particularly communicative and non-communicative action events, commitments/claims (coupled with the corresponding types of action events), and non-action events. Commitment and claim processing includes their: creation, cancellation, waiving, delegation, assigning, and fulfilling.

However, none of the aforementioned modeling approaches covers the social aspects, as identified in Sect. 1, completely. Our aim, thus, was to develop a modeling language which overcomes deficiencies of existing languages and provides a rich set of constructs to model all the three social perspectives, i.e. social structure (Sect. 4), social behavior (Sect. 5), and social attitudes (Sect. 6).

## 3 AML

The *Agent Modeling Language* (*AML*) [10, 11] is a visual modeling language for specifying, modeling and documenting systems that incorporate concepts drawn from the MAS theory. It is specified as a *conservative extension of UML 2.0*[1] [13]–called *AML Metamodel and Notation*–which augments UML with several modeling concepts appropriate for capturing typical MAS concepts. Above this, two UML profiles, in particular *UML 1.* Profile for AML* (based on UML 1.*) and *UML 2.0 Profile for AML* (based on UML 2.0), are provided. These profiles allow straightforward implementation of AML into existing UML 1.* and UML 2.0-based CASE tools respectively.

AML provides a consistent set of modeling constructs designed to capture the various aspects of multi-agent systems, i.e. ontologies, MAS entities, social aspects, behavior abstraction and decomposition, communicative interactions and interaction protocols, services, observations and effecting interactions, mental aspects used for modeling mental attitudes of autonomous entities, MAS deployment, and agent mobility. Details about how AML modeling elements can be used to model particular social aspects are described in following sections.

[1] A conservative extension of UML is a strict extension of UML which retains the standard UML semantics in unaltered form [12].

# 4 Modeling Social Structure

For modeling structural aspects of agent societies, to some extent, modeling elements of UML can be used. However, to allow building of more concise and comprehensive models of MAS societies, AML offers several modeling elements designated to explicitly represent various (MAS) society abstractions. In particular these are: social entities, entity roles, social relationships, play associations and role properties.

## 4.1 Social Entities

*Entities* represent objects that can exist in the system independently of other objects. AML defines the following entities: agents, resources, environments, and organization units. Entities are usually modeled at the level of types (specialized UML classes), but can also be modeled at the instance level by UML instance specifications classified according to their corresponding types. All entities can make use of modeling mechanisms inherited from UML class, i.e. they can own features, participate in varied relationship types, be internally structured into parts, own behaviors, etc. In addition to these, AML allows to specify also possibility to own capabilities, perform speech act based interactions, provide and use of services, own perceptors and effectors, play roles, be characterized in terms of mental attitudes, etc.

*Social entities* are entities possessing social abilities. By *social ability* we understand the ability to (1) participate in societies and social relationships, (2) manifest social behavior, and (3) have social attitudes. Two of the above mentioned entities, agents and organization units, are also social entities.

*Agent type* is a specialized UML class used to model the type of *agents*, i.e. self contained entities that are capable of interactions, observations and autonomous behavior within their environment.

*Organization unit type* is a specialized environment type[2] used to model the type of an *organization unit*. From an external perspective, organization units represent coherent autonomous entities, the features and behavior of which are both (1) emergent properties and behavior of all their constituents, their mutual relationships, observations and interactions, and (2) the features and behavior of organization units themselves. From an internal perspective, organization units are types of environment that specify the social arrangements of entities in terms of structures, interactions, roles, constraints, norms, etc.

Organization units are thus used to model societies (groups, organizations, institutions, etc.). They are not considered to be static, i.e. their properties, structure, behavior, social attitudes, comprised roles, participating entities and their features, etc. can change over time (for details see Sect. 5).

Fig. 1 (a) shows an example of a class diagram depicting a generic organization structure of a software development project. The project teams (ProjectBoard,

[2] *Environment type* is an element used to model a specific aspect of a system's inner environment, i.e. the logical or physical surroundings of entities which provide conditions under which the entities exist and function.

TechnicalTeam, AnalysisTeam, etc.) are modeled by means of organization unit types, their social relationships by means of social associations (Sect. 4.2), and a project role (ProjectManager) by means of the entity role type (Sect. 4.3).

Using the specified types, the internal structure of the organization unit type SoftwareDevelopmentProject is modeled in Fig. 1 (b). It defines the parts which represent comprised entity role (pm) and lower-level organization units (pb, ana, imp, and tst). Connectors between them declare instances of the social associations specified at the class level, and therefore use the same adornments as the corresponding associations.

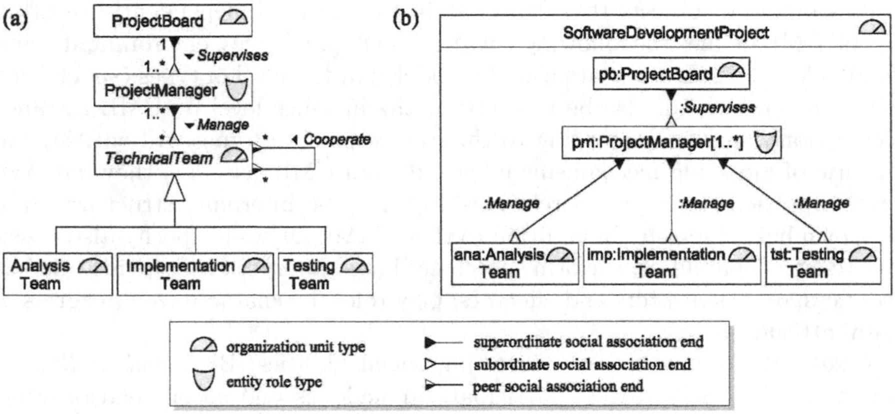


**Fig. 1.** Example of class-level organization structure model

## 4.2 Social Relationships

*Social relationship* is a particular type of connection existing between social entities related to or having to deal with each other. Apart from other general-purpose UML relationships applicable in social models (generalization, aggregation, association, etc.), AML defines a special type of property, called the *social property*, used to model social relationships. It can be used either in the form of an owned *social attribute* or as the end of a *social association*. Social property, in addition to UML property, allows to specify the relationship's social role kind. AML supports two predefined kinds of social relationships, peer-to-peer and superordinate-to-subordinate, and the analogous social role kinds: peer, superordinate, and subordinate (for details see [10]). The set of supported social role kinds can be extended as required (e.g. to model producer-consumer, competitive, or cooperative relationships).

Fig. 1 (a) shows superordinate-to-subordinate social associations between ProjectBoard (superordinate—shown as a filled triangle placed at the association end) and ProjectManager (subordinate—shown as a hollow triangle placed at the association end), and ProjectManager (superordinate) and TechnicalTeam (subordinate). Particular technical teams are related by the peer-to-peer relationships which is represented by the social association Cooperate attached to the TechnicalTeam organization unit type (peer social property kind is shown as a half-filled triangle placed at the end of association). Connectors representing instances of the previously defined social associations are depicted in Fig. 1 (b).

### 4.3 Entity Roles

In AML, *social roles* (i.e. abstractions of features, behavior, attitudes, participation in interactions, and services required or provided to other roles or social entities in a particular social situation) are modeled by entity role types. Entity roles types thus can be used to specify (1) social structures, (2) positions[3], and also (3) required structural, behavioral and attitudinal features of their constituents.

Technically, entity role types are specialized UML classes which can own capabilities, perform speech act based interactions, provide and use services, own perceptors and effectors, be characterized in terms of mental attitudes, etc. Each entity role type should be realized by a specific implementation possessed by a social entity type which can play it. An instance of the entity role type is called *entity role*[4]. It represents the execution of behaviors, usage of features and/or participation in interactions as defined by the particular entity role type. A given entity role exists only while a behavioral entity instance plays it.

The AML approach provides the possibility to model social roles at both the class level (where the required types of features and behavior are defined) and the instance level (where the concrete property values and behavior realization of a particular role playing can be specified) explicitly.

### 4.4 Entity Role Playing

The ability of a social entity to play an entity role is modeled by special structural feature called *role property*.

Role property is a specialized UML property used to specify that an instance of its owner (an entity type) can play one or several entity roles of the entity role type specified as the property's type. An instance of a role property's owner is called the *entity role player* (or simply *player*). An instance of the role property's type represents the played entity role. The role property can be used either in the form of a *role attribute* or as the member end of a *play association*.

One entity can at each time play several entity roles. These entity roles can be of the same as well as of different types. The multiplicity defined for a role property constraints the number of entity roles of given type, the particular entity can play concurrently. Additional constraints which govern playing of entity roles can be specified by UML constraints.

---

[3] A *position* is a set of roles typically played by one agent [14]. Positions are in AML explicitly modeled by means of composed entity roles types.

[4] AML uses the term "entity role" to differentiate agent-related roles from the roles defined by the UML 2.0, i.e. roles used for collaborations, parts, and associations.

The AML approach to mode role playing allows:

- Specification of the *possibility* to play particular entity roles by entities expressed at the class level, and the *actual playing* of entity roles by instances expressed at the instance level.
- Separation of entity's own features and behaviors from the features and behaviors required for playing an entity role in a particular situation.
- Separation of a specification of the features, behavior, and attitudes required (or expected) from a potential player of that entity role, from their actual realization by actual players.
- Specification of the behavior related to role playing, e.g. role playing dynamics, life cycle of roles, reasoning about roles, etc. (for more details see Sect. 5).

Fig. 2 shows an example of specifying entity role types (abstract ProjectMember and all its concrete subclasses), their attributes, and social associations. The possibility to play instances of concrete entity role types by agents of the type Person, represented by the play associations is also depicted.

Fig. 3 shows the instantiation of the previously defined types in the model of a system's snapshot, where the agent Alan, of type Person, plays two entity roles (testerAlan and analystAlan), and agent John, also of type Person, as the project manager (entity role pmJohn) is Alan's boss. This example also demonstrates the ability of AML to explicitly specify slots and social links of entity roles played under certain circumstances (specified for analystAlan).

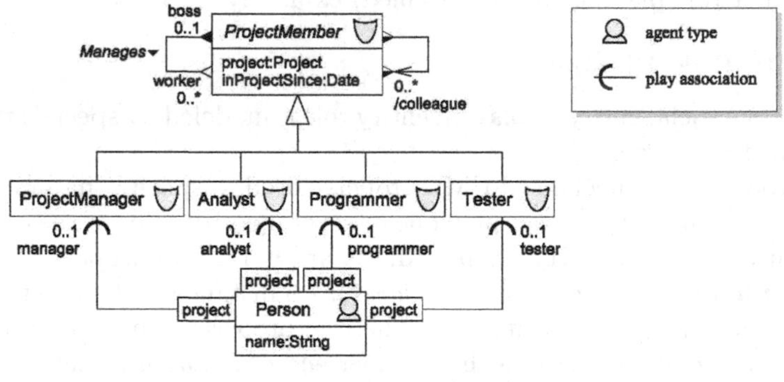


**Fig. 2.** Example of entity roles types and play associations

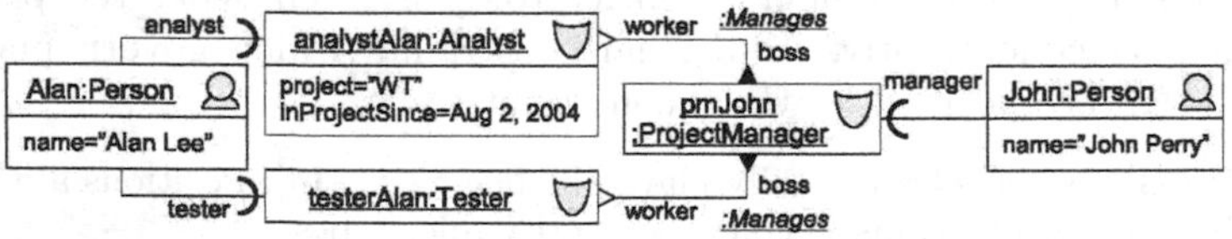


**Fig. 3.** Example of the entity role instantiation and playing

# 5 Modeling Social Behavior

Social behavior is the behavior of a social entity (behavior of a single social entity, or emergent behavior of a society) which influences or is influenced by the state (social features, attitudes, etc.) or behavior of other social entities (members of the society or the society itself). Social behavior thus covers social dynamics, social interactions, and social activities.

This section briefly describes how AML extensions to UML behavioral models can be used to model social behavior.

## 5.1 Social Dynamics

The central modeling mechanism for modeling social dynamics are state machines as the most appropriate mechanism for modeling state transitions in reaction to events. Incorporation of AML specific actions into the UML state machines allows explicit modeling of: the formation/abolition of societies, the entrance/withdrawal of an entity to/from a society, acquisition/disposal/change of a role by an entity, etc.

## 5.2 Social Interactions

To model social interactions, AML defines specialized modeling constructs for modeling speech act based interactions, observations and effecting interactions.

The extensions toward modeling social interactions are twofold: generic and communicative interaction specific. Generic extensions to UML interactions are provided to in order to model interactions between groups of entities (using *multi-message* and *multi-lifeline*), dynamic change of object's attributes (to express changes in internal structure of organization units, social relationships, or played entity roles, etc.) induced by interactions (using *attribute change*), modeling of messages and signals not explicitly associated with an invocation of corresponding methods and receptions (using *decoupled message*). Communicative interaction specific extensions comprise: modeling of speech-acts (using *communicative acts*), speech act based interactions (by *communicative interactions,* which are specialized UML interactions), and patterns of interactions (by means of *interaction protocols*).

AML furthermore defines several constructs for modeling observations (i.e. the ability of entities to observe features of other entities) and effecting interactions (i.e. the ability of entities to manipulate, or modify the state of, other entities). Observations are modeled as the ability of an entity to perceive the state of (or to receive a signal from) an observed entity by means of *perceptors. Perceptor types* are used to specify (by means of *perceiving acts*) the observations an owner of a perceptor of that type can make. The specification of which entities can observe others, is modeled by a *perceives* dependency. Different aspects of effecting interactions are modeled analogously, by means of *effectors, effector types*, *effecting acts*, and *effects* dependencies.

Fig. 4 shows an example of the communicative interaction in which the attribute change element is used to model change of entity roles played by agents.

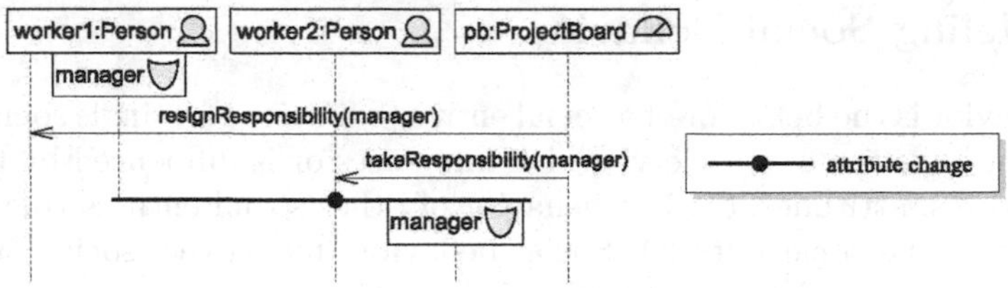


**Fig. 4.** Example of a social interaction with entity role changes

The diagram realize the scenario of replacing a project manager by another person, as described by the scenario shown in Fig. 5. An agent worker1 is a manager (modeled by its role property manager). After receiving a message resignResponsibility from the project board (pb) it stops playing the role of project manager. At the same time another person, worker2, takes the responsibility, as the result of previously received message takeResponsibility sent by the project board, and starts to play the role of the project manager (modeled by the manager property of worker2).

### 5.3 Social Activities

For modeling social activities UML activities can be used. However, to allow development of more concise and comprehensive models, AML offers several additional modeling concepts and mechanisms.

To allow modeling of modification of social features (i.e. social relationships, roles played, social attitudes), all of them are modeled as structural features of entities. This allows to make use of some UML actions of manipulation with structural features, to model modification of social structures, reasoning about played entity roles, access and reason about social attitudes, execute social behavior, etc.

Furthermore, AML defines specific actions to: create/play and dispose entity roles, send and receive messages of social communicative interactions, percept and effect other entities, commit to and decommit from goals, etc.

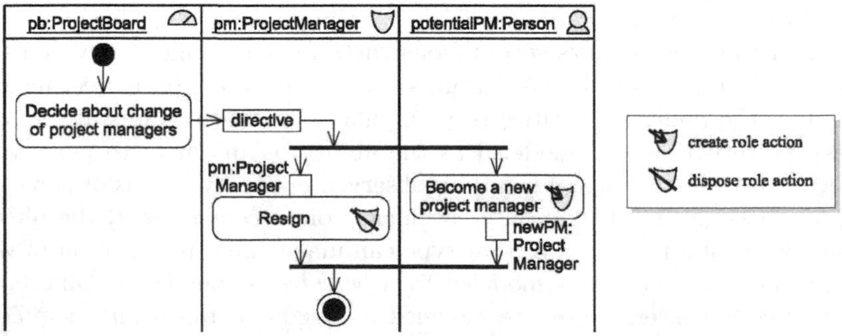


**Fig. 5.** Example of activity comprising the social actions inducing changes of entity roles

Fig. 5 shows an example of the activity describing the scenario of replacement the project manager by another person. The project board (organization unit pb) decides about the replacement, and informs the current project manager (entity role pm) together with a new potential project manager (agent potentialPM) about the decision. The current project manager stops playing its role of the project manager (expressed by the dispose role action Resign) and the new project manager starts to play its new entity role (specified by the create role action Become a new project manager creates a new entity role newPM).

## 6 Modeling Social Attitudes

For modeling types of social attitudes AML offers constructs of mental modeling, particularly: *beliefs*, *goals*, *plans*, and *mental relationships* (used to represent logical relationships between mental states such as means-ends, decomposition, correlation, contribution, etc.). Social attitudes of entities are modeled by means of special type of UML property called *mental property*. It can be used either in the form of an owned *mental attribute* or as the end of a *mental association*.

In general, two kinds of social attitudes can be recognized:

1. social attitudes shared by several entities within a society, e.g. common beliefs and goals, plans which include collaboration of several entities, etc., and
2. social attitudes of individual entities to anything of a social value, e.g. commitment to perform a social action, beliefs in some facts about other entities.

Social mental models often contain explicitly modeled relationships between mental states of different socialized entities. For instance cooperative entities share their goals, trusted entities share their beliefs, superordinate entities dictate their goals or form goals of subordinate entities, competitive entities have goals in contradiction, etc. These situations can be explicitly expressed by mental relationships.

Fig. 6 depicts a model excerpt showing social mental model of cooperating organization unit types AnalysisTeam and ImplementationTeam. They share common goal SatisfyQualityCriteria and belief that "the produced/consumed analysis

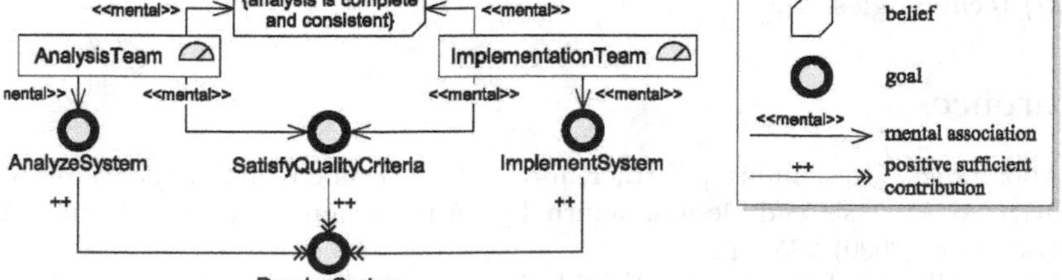


**Fig. 6.** Example of individual and common goals and beliefs

is complete and consistent". Apart from the common mental attitudes, the teams have also specific purposes modeled as decidable goals, particularly the AnalysisTeam has the AnalyzeSystem and the ImplementaionTeam has the ImplementSystem. Positive necessary contribution to the overall project's goal to develop the system (DevelopSystem) is also shown.

## 7 Conclusions and Further Work

Within the currently available agent-oriented modeling languages, AML provides the most comprehensive set of mechanisms for modeling social aspects in MAS. It covers the broadest range of all the three social perspectives, i.e. social structure (Sect. 4), social behavior (Sect. 5), and social attitudes (Sect. 6).

This has been achieved (1) by the incorporation and unification of the most significant concepts from the broadest possible set of existing multi-agent theories, abstract MAS models, modeling and specification languages, methodologies, agent platforms and multi-agent driven applications, and (2) by the extension of the above with new modeling concepts to account for aspects of multi-agent systems thus far covered insufficiently, inappropriately or not at all.

Furthermore, AML assembles all these concepts into a unified, consistent and easily extensible framework specified by the AML meta-model (covering abstract syntax and semantics of the language) and notation (covering the concrete syntax), and is specified as a conservative extension of UML 2.0.

AML has already been successfully applied as a language for modeling requirements, analysis and design of applications in several research and commercial software development projects. The applications were built in various domains, e.g. planning of surgical operations, simulation of societies, and distributed network management systems. These projects tested AML under real-world conditions and proved that it is a useful tool for modeling complex, concurrent, distributed and intelligent systems.

Even if the current version of AML provides well-defined, sufficiently comprehensive and stable generic mechanisms for modeling social aspects, by exploiting the UML extensibility mechanisms and flexible architecture of AML specification, some language improvements and extensions are foreseen. It is also planned to create technology-specific modeling frameworks (re-usable model libraries) and AML extensions which will customize and extend the generic AML modeling constructs to enable modeling of specific architectural concepts of particular (MAS) technologies.

## References

1. Wooldridge, M., Jennings, N.R., Kinny, D.: The Gaia Methodology for Agent-Oriented Analysis and Design. Journal of Autonomous Agents and Multi-Agent Systems **3** (2000) 285–312
2. Zambonelli, F., Jennings, N., Wooldridge, M.: Developing Multiagent Systems: The Gaia Methodology. ACM Trans. on Software Engineering and Methodology **12** (2003) 317–370

3. DeLoach, S., Wood, M., Sparkman, C.H.: Multiagent Systems Engineering. International Journal of Software Engineering and Knowledge Engineering **11** (2001) 231–258
4. Odell, J., Parunak, H., Fleischer, M.: The Role of Roles in Designing Effective Agent Organizations. In Garcia, A., Lucena, C., Zambonelli, F., Omicini, A., Castro, J., eds.: Software Engineering for Large-Scale Multi-Agent Systems, Lecture Notes on Computer Science volume 2603, Berlin, Springer (2003) 27–28
5. Odell, J., Parunak, H., Brueckner, S., Fleischer, M.: Temporal Aspects of Dynamic Role Assignment. In Giorgini, P., Muller, G., Odell, J., eds.: Agent-Oriented Software Engineering (AOSE) IV. LNCS 2935, Berlin, Springer-Verlag (2004)
6. Huget, M.: Agent UML Notation for Multiagent System Design. IEEE Internet Computing **8** (2004) 63–71
7. Ferber, J., Gutknecht, O.: A meta-model for the analysis and design of organizations in multi-agent systems. In: 3rd Int. Conference on Multi-Agent Systems (ICMAS'98), IEEE Computer Society (1998) 128–135
8. Silva, V., Lucena, C.: From a Conceptual Framework for Agents and Objects to a Multi-Agent System Modeling Language. In: Autonomous Agents and Multi-Agent Systems. Volume 9. Springer Science+Business Media B.V. (2004) 145–189
9. Wagner, G.: The Agent-Object-Relationship Meta-Model: Towards a Unified Conceptual View of State and Behavior. Information Systems **28** (2003) 475–504
10. Cervenka, R., Trencansky, I.: Agent Modeling Language: Language Specification. Version 0.9. Technical report, Whitestein Technologies (2004) URL: http://www.whitestein.com/pages/solutions/meth.html.
11. Cervenka, R., Trencansky, I., Calisti, M., Greenwood, D.: AML: Agent Modeling Language. Toward Industry-Grade Agent-Based Modeling. In Odell, J., Giorgini, P., Muller, J., eds.: Agent-Oriented Software Engineering V: 5th International Workshop, AOSE 2004, Springer-Verlag (2005) 31
12. Turski, W., Maibaum, T.: The Specification of Computer Programs. Addison-Wesley (1987)
13. OMG: Unified Modeling Language: Superstructure. Version 2.0. ptc/03-08-02 (2003)
14. Alencar, E., Castro, J., Cysneiros, G., Mylopoulos, J.: From Early Requirements Modeled by the i* Technique to Later Requirements Modeled in Precise UML. In: Anais do III Workshop em Engenharia de Requisitos, Rio de Janeiro, Brazil (2000) 92–109

# Requirements Elicitation for Agent-Based Applications

Rubén Fuentes, Jorge J. Gómez-Sanz, and Juan Pavón

Universidad Complutense Madrid, Dep. Sistemas Informáticos y Programación*,
28040 Madrid, Spain
{ruben, jjgomez, jpavon}@sip.ucm.es
http://grasia.fdi.ucm.es

**Abstract.** Requirements Elicitation for a software system is a key stage in a successful development. At the same time, it is one of the most challenging, because requirements have to consider the mutual influences between the envisioned system and the human context where it will work. These influences cover aspects such as organization, motivation, evolution, and cognition, taking place in a specific setting. The agent paradigm facilitates the analysis of these features because of its intentional and social nature. Nevertheless, determining the information that should be obtained and the way it should be modelled is not a trivial task. Developers are experts in software systems but they are not always familiarized with the concrete domain of those systems. The Requirements Elicitation Guide, a technique based on the Activity Theory from Social Sciences, can be applied to support developers in these issues. This guide empowers the development team with the experience of Social Sciences in these issues. This paper introduces the guide and shows its application in a case study about a web application.

**Keywords:** Multi-Agent Systems Development, Activity Theory, Activity Checklist, Requirements Elicitation.

## 1 Introduction

The requirements of a software system are concerned with the high-level goals that the system has to accomplish, their operationalization through the specification of services and constraints, and the assignment of those responsibilities to actors such as humans, devices, or software [12]. The analysis of these elements involves the study of the human context in which the system will act [15]. Besides, this study is not an isolated initial stage of development, since most of modern software processes are iterative and incremental. That is why Requirements Elicitation (RE) demands new tools for the understanding of the human context and its combination with the information about the system, along the different iterations in the development cycle. This implies a new perspective with respect to traditional methods of Software Engineering [7, 15].

---

* This work has been funded by the Spanish Council for Science and Technology under grant TIC2002-04516-C03-03.

J.P. Müller and F. Zambonelli (Eds.): AOSE 2005, LNCS 3950, pp. 40 – 53, 2006.

In the case of agent-oriented methodologies, the paradigm facilitates this integration with its conceptual framework. The same abstractions about societies of intentional actors that interact to solve problems can be applied to model both the system and its human environment in a uniform way [13, 6]. Successful examples of this approach are KAOS [2], i* [19], and Tropos [17]. Nevertheless, obtaining the information about these requirements is still a hard work, as it involves the study of intentional and organizational patterns about agents and the environment, which do not belong to the common expertise of software developers. The weaknesses of previous methodologies mainly lie in the processes and guides they use for this study in RE. For instance, both i* and Tropos use diagrams to capture the requirements of the system. Besides, Tropos includes formal techniques to support this task. However, the problem is that they rely on developers' skills to determine what the relevant features of the system and its context are. KAOS further provides a meta-model that conducts the gathering, although this meta-model barely considers the social environment. Our aim is to overcome these limitations with guidelines and processes about the environment for RE in agent-oriented methodologies.

Social Sciences [7] can provide theoretical, conceptual, and methodological support to collect these requirements, and to ease the understanding of those aspects related with people and their organizations. Our approach adopts the *Activity Checklist* (AC) [10] as the basis for requirements elicitation. The AC is an analytical tool of the *Activity Theory* (AT) [18, 14], which has been developed in the fields of Sociology and Psychology. The use of AT and its techniques with agent-oriented methodologies is feasible because they share a common intentional and social perspective of their objects of study. The AC has been already applied in the field of Human-Computer Interaction (HCI) where it is used to analyze the impact of new technologies in human activities [8, 9]. This tool reminds practitioners the information that should be considered when analyzing these interactions. Its hints take the form of questions in natural language.

Despite of its advantages, the AC has to be adapted for its use in RE of agent-based applications. AT researchers conceived the AC for its use in social studies and it is centred on a very specific domain, HCI. In order to apply the AC in multi-agent systems (MAS) development, we need to undertake some changes about the focus and the level of detail in the information, or different formalisms to work with MAS specifications. The result is the Requirements Elicitation Guide (REG), which was firstly introduced in [5]. This guide is a tool to analyze the key intentional and social features of a MAS and its context, as the original AC makes with HCI. Here, the REG extends the AC to tackle with the specific problems of RE for MAS.

The REG contains *questions* that arise from those in the AC. They represent the information that AT considers important to elicit about activities. The answers that customers and developers provide to REG *questions* are the requirements of the software system. Neither customers nor developers are experts in AT and they do not usually share a common background. Therefore, to facilitate the task of discussing and obtaining the information, the REG offers customized views of the information to each group. On one side, there are specific versions of the REG for given target domains, where customers are experts (this is further explained in section 4). On the other side, developers obtain descriptions of requirements in terms of their own agent-oriented methodologies, in which they are experts (this is discussed in section 5). This multiple representation is possible thanks to the use of AT as a lingua franca for requirements. The *questions* have possible answers that are described as structural patterns with a UML based notation for AT concepts. These UML diagrams act as frames with slots that are filled up with users' requirements. After that, an automated translation process adds those requirements to the original specifications of the MAS in the language of the particular agent-oriented methodology (see [4] for a detailed description of the translation). The translation uses mappings between AT and agent concepts. Besides RE and translation, answers to *questions* are the input for other AT based process, like the checking of social properties in the MAS [3].

The rest of the paper presents more details about the points of this introduction. Section 2 makes a brief overview of AT and the AC. Section 3 presents the REG and the structure for *questions*. Section 4 describes the process to develop versions of the REG for specific application domains. Section 5 shows how to use the REG with an agent-oriented methodology and section 6 illustrates this use for a case study about an e-bookstore. Finally, section 7 discusses the advantages and limitations of the approach from the results of our experimentation.

## 2 Activity Theory and the Activity Checklist

*Activity Theory* (AT) [18] is a philosophical, conceptual, and analytical framework to study human practices. Its fundamental unit of analysis is the *activity*, which reflects a process. The *activity* only has true meaning in its context, which is social and environmental, and along a temporal dimension. From the AT point of view, both the individual and the environment are interlinked and mutually influence each other.

The context of the *activity* is called the *activity system* [11]. It includes concepts to describe both the individual and social levels of the *activity*. The individual level is focused on the *subject*. The *subject* is the active element that carries out the *activity* in order to satisfy some needs, his *objectives*. The *objectives* are satisfied by the *outcome* of the *activity*. This *outcome* is the result of transforming the *object* of the *activity* using *tools*. The social level is built around the concept of *community*. An *activity* can involve several *subjects* and each of them can play several roles and have multiple motives. The *community* is composed by those *subjects* who share the same *object*. *Rules* determine the norms coming from the society that apply to individuals. The *division of labour* establishes how the *community* is organized to transform the *object*.

These concepts are illustrated with the case study of section 6 about a bookstore in a university (see Fig. 6 and Fig. 7). Bookstore employees, students, and teachers are the *subjects* of this problem and constitute a *community*. For instance, students try to buy their books at the best prices, what is one of their *objectives*. To achieve this goal they carry out different *activities*, like comparing offers of different bookstores. In these *activities*, they use *tools* as their knowledge about sources of information, newspapers, or Internet. The roles of *subjects* in the *activity* are established by the *division of labour* while the way of interacting in the society depends on the *rules*. The *outcome* of this *activity* is a choice about where to buy.

The *Activity Checklist* (AC) [10] is built around these AT concepts and principles to elicit the knowledge that allows describing an *activity system*. It shows the contextual design space that represents the main features of the *activity* and its environment as specified by AT. This aim is accomplished through a hierarchical structure organized in *areas*, *aspects*, and *questions*. The *areas* are related with the generic spheres of concern about an *activity*. Each *area* has a description of its intended meaning and includes different views of a social activity, the *aspects*. *Aspects* describe parts of the environment as seen by users. *Questions* gather the information about their related *aspects*. With the answers to the *questions*, researchers can elicit users' knowledge based on the theoretical basis of AT. This knowledge can be then translated to concrete properties of the system under study. Instances of *areas*, *aspects*, and *questions* of the AC are shown in Table 1.

**Table 1.** Examples of *areas*, *aspects*, and *questions* from the *Activity Checklist*

| Areas | Aspects | Sample questions |
|---|---|---|
| Means/ ends | Alternative ways to attain target goals through lower-level goals. | Is there any functionality of the system that is not actually used? If yes, which actions were intended to be supported with this functionality? How do users perform these actions? |
| Environment | Role of existing technology in producing the outcomes of target actions. | Is target technology integrated with other tools and materials? |
| Learning/ cognition/ articulation | Self-monitoring and reflection through externalization. | Is externally distributed knowledge easily accessible when necessary? |
| | Possibilities for simulating target actions before their actual implementation. | Does the system provide representations of user's activities that can help in goal setting and self-evaluation? |
| Development | Anticipated changes of target actions after new technology is implemented. | Are users' attitudes toward the system becoming more or less positive? |
| | | Are there negative or positive side-effects associated with the use of the system? |

As Table 1 shows, the AC is written in natural language and with many terms from Social Sciences. In addition, it does not provide hints about the way of asking the *questions* to common customers or representing users' answers with AT concepts. Thus, its use by non-experts in AT is rather difficult. For this reason we have developed the Requirements Elicitation Guide (REG), which is characterized by being application domain specific and using agent-related concepts, what improves its usability in the development of agent-based applications.

## 3 The Requirements Elicitation Guide

The Requirements Elicitation Guide (REG) preserves the hierarchical structure of the AC that includes *areas*, *aspects*, and *questions*. However, to overcome the difficulties to apply the AC that were described in the previous section, the REG adopts a new structure to represent *questions*. This structure has to accomplish several purposes:

- *Departure point for discussion about requirements*. The *questions* point out features of the system or its context to which the development team should pay attention.

- *Propose generic answers*. A *question* has a related set of *answers* that represent possible requirements elicited by that *question*.
- *Source of information about requirements for the development process*. The *answers* have to ease the recording of the knowledge they gather. This information should be available in a suitable format for automated processing to enable the use of software tools that avoid users' overload.

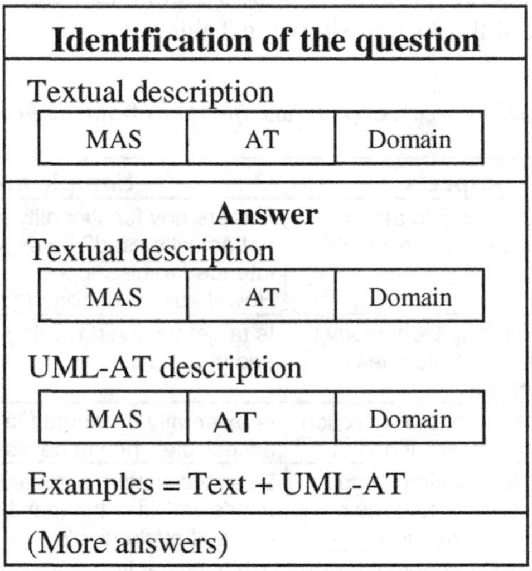


**Fig. 1.** Structure for *questions* of the Requirements Elicitation Guide

The main components of the structure of *questions* appear in Fig. 1:

- *Identification* of the question in the REG. It is an identifier of the form *Question i.j.k.* where *i* is the *area*, *j* is the *aspect*, and *k* is the *question* in the *aspect*.
- *Textual description*. It explains the information about the MAS that the *question* tries to elicit, why it should be gathered, and how it can affect other requirements.
- *Answers*. The *question* has related some possible generic *answers* to it and instantiated examples of those *answers* in previous projects.

The structure contains different views for both the *question* and its *answers* according to their intended audience. There are descriptions for AT experts (i.e. *AT*), MAS developers (i.e. *MAS*), and customers (i.e. *Domain*). *AT* views are mainly used for building the REG. They explain the motivation of considering the *question* or *answer* for the REG from the point of view of social sciences. *MAS* and *Domain* views are used in the development of the REG to describe the knowledge of their corresponding experts and in the RE of a given project.

The *answers* are a key element to collect the requirements related with the *question*. They complement the descriptions of the *questions* with further explanations about what information to elicit. Therefore, an *answer* has a textual form and a UML-AT description to gather the information.

UML-AT [3] is an extension of UML to describe MAS with AT concepts. It is specified as an UML profile [16] that defines the concepts and relationships already described in section 2. It considers as well additional elements to improve the expressiveness of the resulting language, such as contribution relationships between concepts (this is inspired by i* [19]). The full specification of UML-AT can be found at *http://grasia.fdi.ucm.es/at/uml-at*.

The UML-AT diagrams satisfy several goals for RE. First, they disambiguate the textual explanation of *answers* with descriptions in a software design language. Second, they give hints to developers about how requirements, that is, the real answers to *questions*, can be represented in the design language. Third, it is a suitable representation to record information obtained in the elicitation.

The UML-AT diagrams have slots for the name, type, and value of their elements and properties. These slots can contain fixed elements, which are inside double quotes, or variables. When a *question* is solved, one of its *answers* is fulfilled (maybe partially). Some variables in that *answer* are substituted with specific information. The instantiated UML-AT form represents new information for requirements in a design language. As these slots are shared between the UML-AT representation for domain experts and that for developers, they allow the exchange of information. Customers use them to provide the requirements for the remaining development process and developers to give feedback to customers about those requirements.

| **Question 1.2.3** |
|---|
| Textual description<br>MAS = Adding the new functionality to the system will cause some negative effect over the goals of actors in the environment?<br>AT = Is there any inconvenient for the organization or groups in it about building the new component?<br>Domain = If the software carries out the proposed task, will the interest of some people in the organization be harmed? |
| **Answer**<br>Textual description<br>MAS = The new *Task* pursues the *Goal of the Task*. The context of the system includes the *Organization*, which pursues, among others, the *Goal of the Organization*. The satisfaction of the *Goal of the Task* will imply the presence of evidences that reduces the possibilities of satisfaction of the *Goal of the Organization*.<br>AT = The *Component* is intended to satisfy the *Goal of the Component*. This *objective* is contradictory with the *Goal of the Group*, which represents a need of the *community Group*.<br>Domain = The new *Task* tries to satisfy a *goal* detected in your organization *Goal of the Task*. However, it is possible that this *goal* can affect negatively to some members or groups in your organization. That is to say that those groups have their own objectives, like *Goal of the Group*, that cannot be satisfied (or be difficultly) at the same time the *Goal of the Task*. |

**Fig. 2.** Example of *question* of the Requirements Elicitation Guide in its basic version. Textual description of question and an answer.

**Answer**

UML-AT description

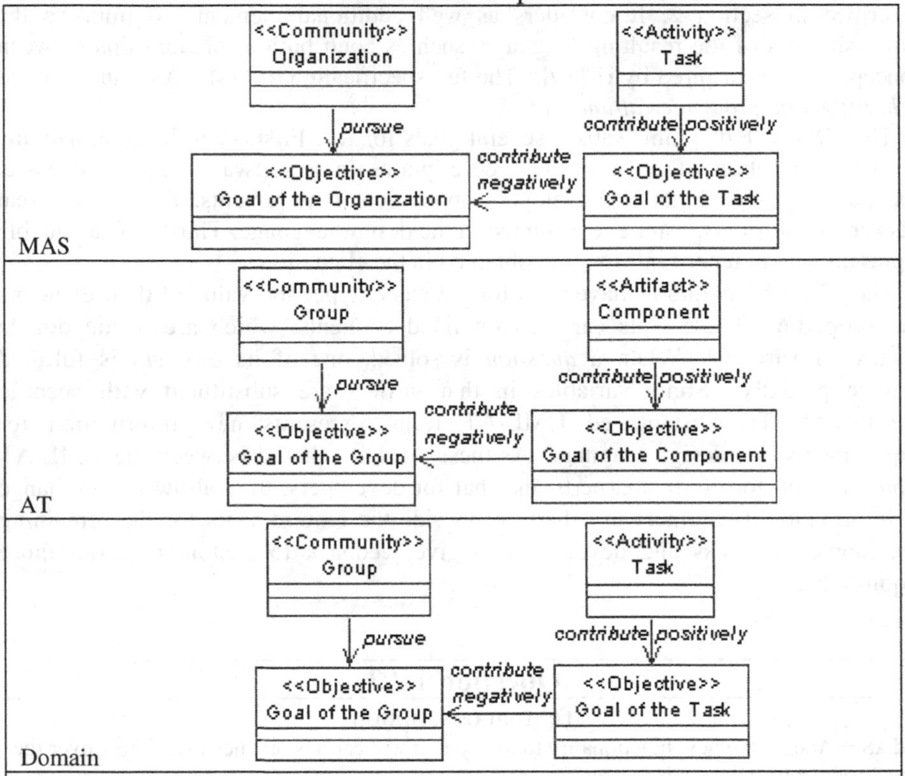


Bindings for diagrams

Organization = Group, Goal of the Organization = Goal of the Group,
Task = Component, Goal of the Task = Goal of the Component

Examples

Like the diagram in **Fig. 8** and its explanation.

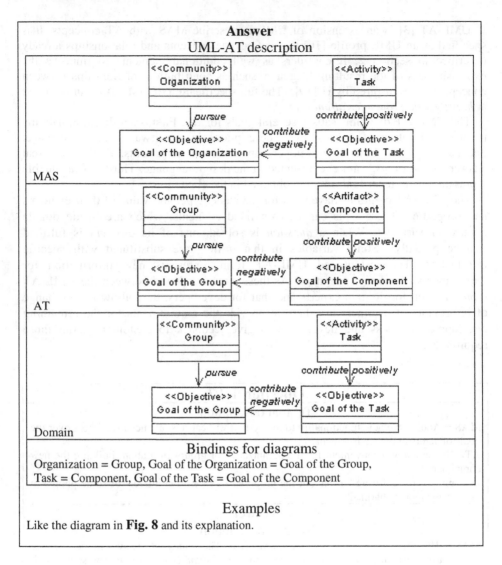

**Fig. 3.** Example of *question* of the Requirements Elicitation Guide in its basic version. UML-AT description of an answer and examples.

Fig. 2 and Fig. 3 show a summarized example of a *question* from the basic version of the REG. The example just includes the introductions for the *question*, one of its *answers*, and its views; it omits the longer explanations of these elements. Because the basic version of the REG is for general MAS, the domain and MAS views are quite similar. These *questions* are applied in section 0 of this paper and in [5]. A full REG is described at *http://grasia.fdi.ucm.es/at/reg*.

# 4 Creation of the REG for Specific Application Domains

Once that there is a structure for the REG, developers use the process of Fig. 4 to create concrete REGs. Its product is a set of *areas*, *aspects*, and *questions* represented with the structure of Fig. 1 for the requirements elicitation of agent oriented applications in a specific domain.

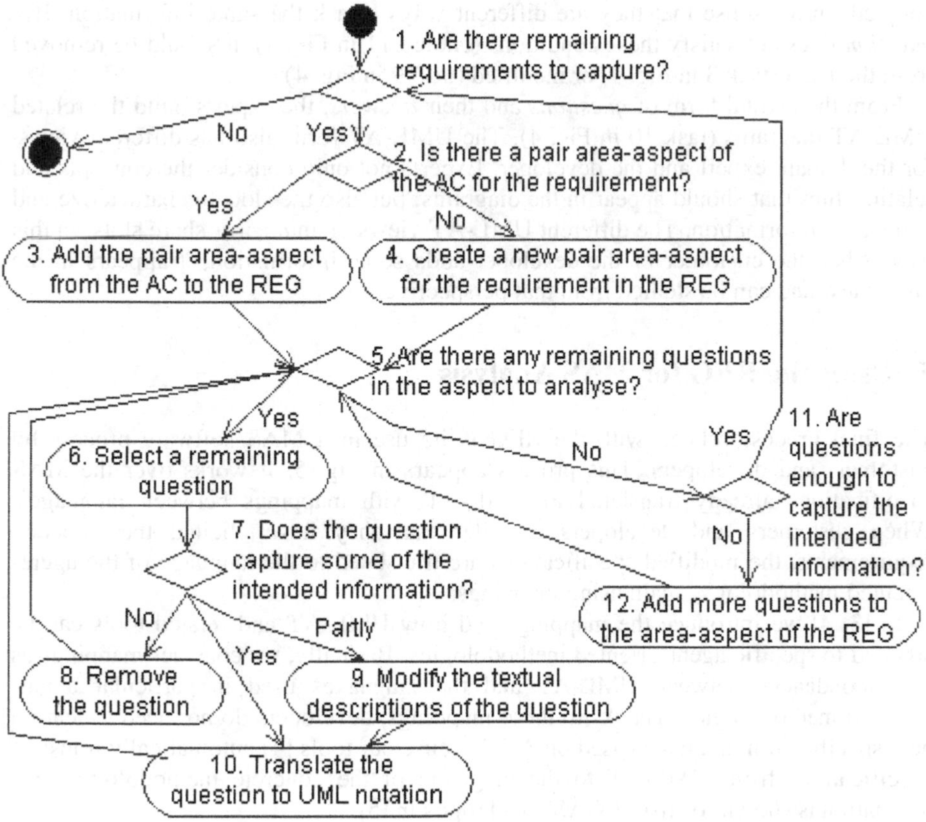


**Fig. 4.** Process to develop a domain specific Requirements Elicitation Guide

The team that develops the REG for a given domain carries out iterations for different requirements (choice numbered as 1 in Fig. 4). These requirements can be proposed by any actor in the process and they represent information that, according to his field of experience, should be gathered. If the team agrees that the proposed requirement is important information for the system, they have to determine what *area* and *aspect* are adequate for the requirement (choice 2 in Fig. 4). In the case of *areas*, the team just chooses the best-suited for the information under study, while in the case of *aspects* they can select an existing one from the AC (task 4 in Fig. 4) or the REG, or create another in the REG (task 3 in Fig. 4).

For the selected pair *area-aspect*, the team provides a set of *questions* that will be able to elicit the new requirement. In the case that the *aspect* already exists in the AC, the AC *questions* are imported into the REG. Initially, these AC *questions* only have their textual description from the AT point of view (task 12 in Fig. 4). If it is a completely new *aspect*, the experts have to write sketches of *questions* that point out to information related with the requirement (task 12 in Fig. 4). Anyway, for every *question*, experts discuss and propose the textual form of their views and *answers*. Those forms have to be understandable and meaningful in their field and be highly-coupled, in the sense that they are different ways to ask the same information. If a *question* does not satisfy these conditions (choice 11 in Fig. 4), it should be removed from the REG (task 8 in Fig. 4) or modified (task 9 in Fig. 4).

From the textual form of *questions* and their *answers*, the experts build the related UML-AT diagrams (task 10 in Fig. 4). The UML-AT form also has different views, for the domain expert and the developer. Experts not only consider the concepts and relationships that should appear in the diagrams, but also the slots to characterize and collect the information. The different UML-AT views of an *answer* share slots. In this way, when the customer or the developer adds some information, it appears in the other view and can be studied from that perspective.

## 5 Using the REG for MAS Analysis

The final process related with the REG is its use in a MAS software process by customers and developers. This process appears in Fig. 5. It works over the MAS specifications already translated to UML-AT with mappings between languages. When customers and developers consider that they have elicited the intended requirements, the modified specifications are translated to the language of the agent-oriented methodology, again using mappings.

In [3, 4] we introduce the mappings and how UML-AT and related tools can be adapted to specific agent-oriented methodologies. Basically, we consider mappings as correspondences between UML-AT and the languages used in particular agent-oriented methodologies. Thanks to these mappings, developers do not need to learn a new specification language based on AT, because our tools [4] automatically translate specifications from UML-AT to the language of the concrete methodology. This translation is shown for INGENIAS and Tropos in [5].

The RE process itself begins with the selection of the *question* to answer (sub-task 2 in task 3). The REG helps the team in this selection with its hierarchical structure. According to the searched information, customers and developers navigate the REG from the more generic information to the most specific, that is, from *areas* to *aspects* and from these to *questions*. After that, there is a discussion about the *question*. The explanations (sub-task 3 in task 3) show the meaning of the *question* and the *answers* and assist to understand the kind of proper information for those requirements. Besides, there are examples from other projects in the domain about answers for the *question* (sub-task 4 in task 3). When the team agrees the answer, they fill up the slots in the UML-AT form of one of the *answers* (sub-task 6 in task 3). The overall discussion is contextualized with existing specifications (sub-task 5 in task 3). So, for

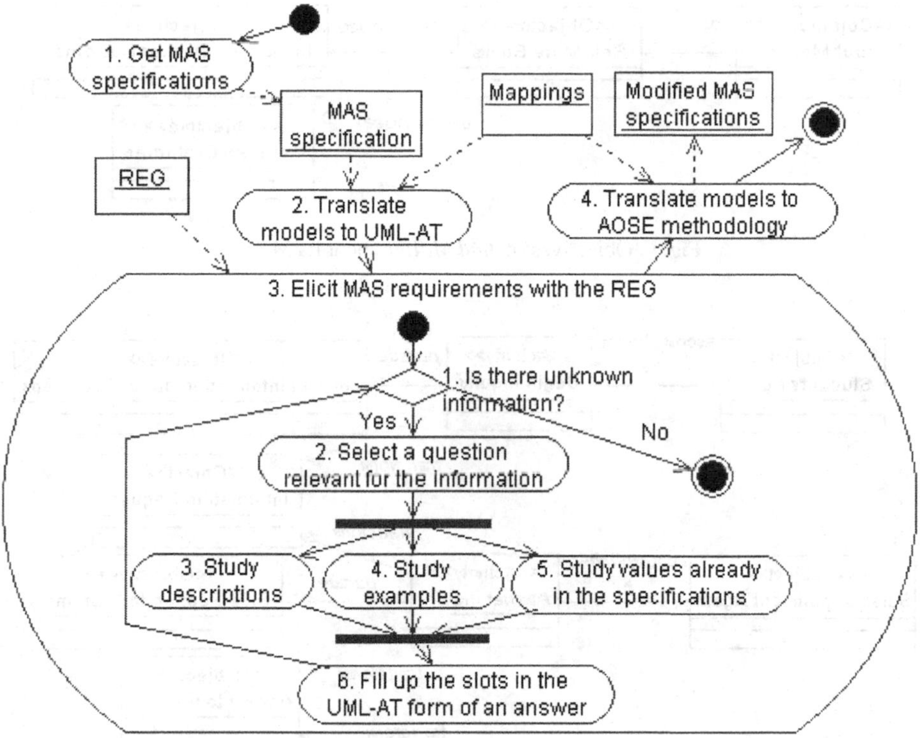


**Fig. 5.** Use of the Requirements Elicitation Guide in a project

instance, customers can know what groups, restrictions, or devices are already in the specifications and use them for the slots of the current *question*.

## 6 An Example of Application for an e-Bookstore

To show the use of the REG for MAS in a specific domain, we have selected a case study based on *Juul Møller Bokhandel A/S* [1]. *Juul Møller* is a bookstore company that works with the Norwegian School of Management (NSM). The students of the NSM are its main customers. As a consequence of the uprising of bookstores based on e-commerce, *Juul Møller* wants to evolve its business model too. Its objective is to define a MAS for bookselling in Internet where its company, the NSM, teachers, and students work together and share interests.

The current example begins with part of the MAS specifications already available[1]. They can be seen in Fig. 6 and Fig. 7 and are focused on the functionality that the MAS of *Juul Møller* gives to students when they want to compare its services with those of other bookstores in Internet. These tasks allow the students to know the availability of books or to compare prices.

[1] The full specifications of the case study with INGENIAS are available at *http://grasia.fdi.ucm.es/ingenias*. Their translation to UML-AT is omitted for brevity.

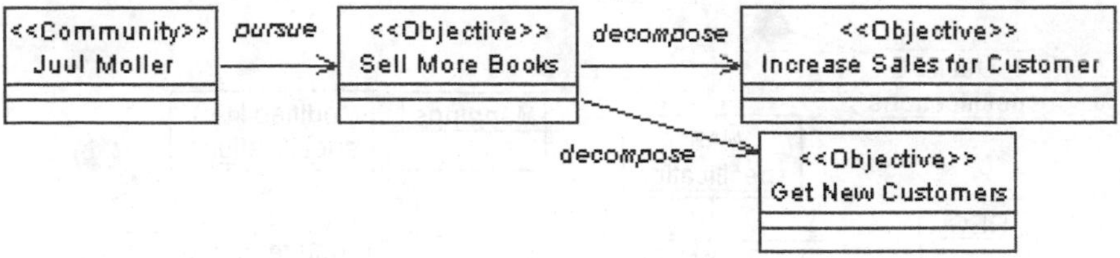


**Fig. 6.** Objectives of *Juul Møller* about its MAS

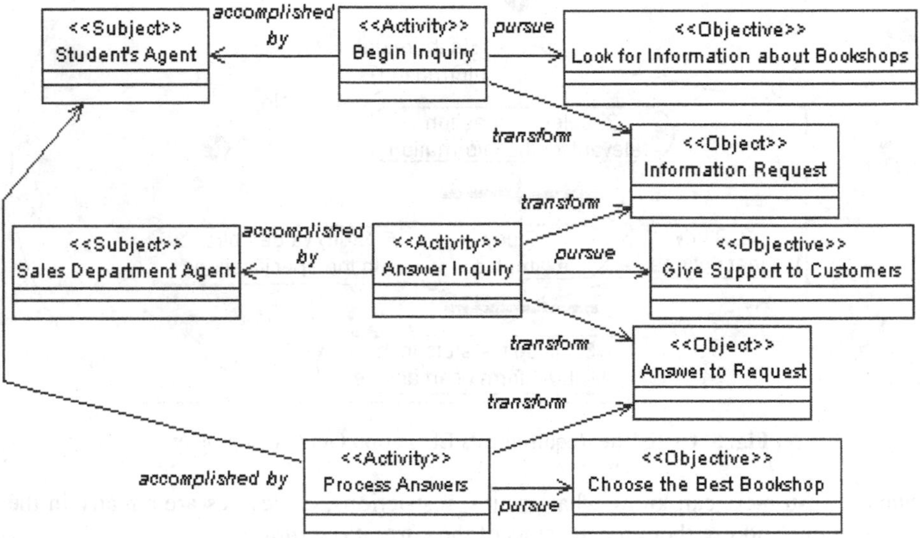


**Fig. 7.** Workflows of inquiries about prices of other bookstores

Fig. 4 illustrates that the main objective of the company *Juul Møller* is *Sell More Books*. This goal can be achieved by satisfying the goals *Get New Customers* or *Increase Sales for Customer*.

Fig. 7 shows one of the workflows of the MAS. In order to get that students frequently visit its website, the MAS of *Juul Møller* provide several services. Among them, there is the possibility of comparing the prices of *Juul Møller* with those of popular bookstores in Internet (such as *Amazon.com* or *Blackwell's*). The *subjects* "*... Agent*" are the agents in the MAS that act on behalf of the students and of the Sales Department in the *Juul Møller* bookstore. The *Student's Agent* carries out the *Begin Enquiry activity* to provide the *Information Request object* about the books to be compared. The *Sales Department Agent* processes the *object* and generates the *Answer to Request*. Finally, the *Student's Agent* receives and processes this *object* to obtain the comparison.

The development team, which includes representatives from the *Juul Møller* bookstore, experts in e-commerce, and MAS developers, wants to know if these activities have influence over other objectives in the problem. Here, the team can use different *aspects* from the REG like "Criteria for success or failure of achieving goals", "Tools and materials shared between several users", or "Potential conflicts between objectives". In this case, they choose other *aspect*, "Goals of the new component", and the *question* "Is there any inconvenient for the organization or groups in it about building the new component?". This belongs to the textual form of the *question* in the *AT* view. Fig. 8 shows the answer when the *question* is posed with the goal *Give Support to Customers* as opposed to the objectives of *Juul Møller*.

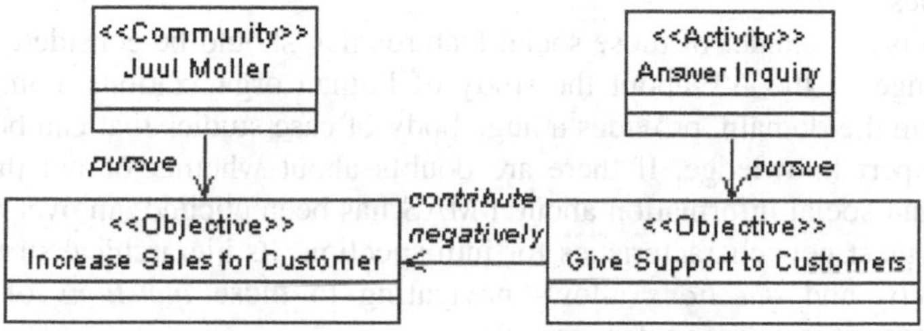


**Fig. 8.** *Question* about the drawbacks of comparing prices with other bookstores. On the left original UML-AT form of the *answer*; on the right, fulfilled answer using equivalences [5].

Fig. 8 shows that some employees of *Juul Møller* are worried about the activities to increase the students' visits. If their company is frequently worse in the comparatives, they will lose buyers. With this situation, it is evident that either the specifications are incomplete or this support that harms sales should be removed from the system.

A possible starting point to solve the problem arising from Fig. 8 is to know who in *Juul Møller* proposes this service. There is an *aspect* "Actors in the new system" where we find the *question* "Who is interested in this service being provided to customers?". Besides the *Sales Department Agent* that appears in Fig. 7, the answer to the new *question* tells the team that the *Advertising Department Agent* is also interested in that task. As agents are intentional entities, if this agent wants the task being executed is because it satisfies one of its objectives. To collect this information the team uses the *aspect* "Objectives to create the new component" that includes the *question* "Why does the actor/organization want to provide the service? Which are their objectives?". The customers' answer in this case is that they hope that the activity helps them to the *Make Advertising objective*, what will increase sales.

Advertisements in the MAS have some limitations. The previous study of users' behaviour considers that the website of *Juul Møller* should have a differentiated character from those of its competitors. Direct advertising (e.g. *banners* and *popups*) in websites annoys users. Thus, it will be better to make advertisements based on users' preferences. The relationship of these objectives with the previous one of *Make Advertising* was gathered with the *question* "Do this action indirectly contribute to other objectives?". The answers allow including in the specifications the relationships of positive contribution between the objectives *Increase Sales for Customer* and *Make Advertising* and between this and *Know Customers' Preferences*. With the new information, Fig. 7 changes to add a new objective *Know Customers' Preferences* to the activity *Answer Inquiry*.

## 7 Conclusions

This paper shows the Requirements Elicitation Guide (REG) as a tool based on AT to gather requirements about the social environment of MAS. Its main advantages are: to have a memo of the intentional and social aspects that should be considered about system requirements, specially from an agent-oriented perspective; to provide guidelines that help on deciding where to continue with the elicitation when obvious requirements have been obtained; to have a tool applicable with most agent-oriented methodologies.

The REG is a reminder of those social features that should be considered in MAS. The knowledge of the AT about the study of human organizations, complemented with that from the domain, provides a huge body of case studies that can be used as a source of expert knowledge. If there are doubts about whether or not the relevant intentional and social information about a MAS has been elicited, an overview of the REG can suggest new characteristics for introspection. Its hierarchical structure with *areas*, *aspects*, and *questions* allows navigating to those *questions* of the REG relevant for the information under scrutiny.

The REG does not intend to build a new methodology for MAS development. It is a set of tools for support in existing methodologies. This elicitation process analyzes and specifies requirements with concepts close to those of MAS. The representation of *questions* with UML-AT allows translating the information about requirements to agent-oriented languages with correspondences among vocabularies. Its main limitation comes from the specification of the UML-AT representation of *questions*. This task is where the AT concepts have to be identified over the textual form of the *answers* to the *question*, and this textual form is ambiguous in essence. That is, this task heavily relies on the own interpretation of the people who do it.

Finally, note that the application of the REG does not pretend to elicit every possible requirement of a MAS in every setting. It is a generic guide in the process of elicitation that needs customization for concrete domains, and can be complemented with other techniques of Requirements Engineering.

## References

1. Andersen, E.: *Juul Møller Bokhandel A/S*. Case Study at http://www.espen.com/. 2001.
2. Dardenne, A, van Lamsweerde, A., Fickas, S.: *Goal-directed Requirements Acquisition*. Science of Computer Programming, 20, pp. 3-50. 1993.
3. Fuentes, R., Gómez-Sanz, J.J., Pavón, J.: *Activity Theory for the Analysis and Design of Multi-Agent Systems*. In Proceedings of the 4th International Workshop on Agent Oriented Software Engineering (AOSE 2003), Melbourne, Australia, July 2003. Lecture Notes in Computer Science, 2935, pp. 110–122. Springer Verlag, 2003.
4. Fuentes, R., Gómez-Sanz, J.J., Pavón, J.: *Social Analysis of Multi-Agent Systems with Activity Theory*. In Proceedings of CAEPIA 2003, San Sebastian, Spain, November 2003. Lecture Notes in Artificial Intelligence, 3040, pp. 526-535. Springer Verlag, 2004.
5. Fuentes-Fernández, R.: *Activity Theory for the Development of Multi-agent Systems*. (in Spanish: *Teoría de Actividad para el Desarrollo de Sistemas Multi-Agente*). Ph. D. thesis, Dep. of Sistemas Informáticos y Programación, Univ. Complutense Madrid, Spain. 2004.

6. Gómez-Sanz, J., Pavón, J.: *Methodologies for Developing Multi-Agent Systems.* Journal of Universal Computer Science, 10 (4), pp. 359-374. 2004.
7. Goguen, J. A., Linde, C.: *Techniques for requirements elicitation.* In Proceedings of the 1st IEEE International Symposium on Requirements Engineering (RE'93), San Diego, USA, January 1993, pp. 152-164. IEEE Computer Society Press, 1993.
8. Gould, E., Verenikina, I., Hasan H.: *Activity Theory as a Basis for the Design of Web Based System of Inquiry for World War 1 Data.* In Proceedings of the 23rd IRIS Conference, Lingatan, Sweden, August 2000, pp. 761-770. 2000.
9. Hedestig, U., Kaptelinin, V.: *Re-contextualization of teaching and learning in videoconference-based environments: An empirical study.* In Proceedings of CSCL 2002, Computer Support for Collaborative Learning: Foundations for a CSCL Community.
10. Kaptelinin, V., Nardi, B. A., Macaulay, C.: *The Activity Checklist: A tool for representing the "space" of context.* Interactions, 6 (4), pp. 27-39. 1999.
11. Kuutti, K.: *Activity Theory as a potential framework for Human-computer interaction research.* In B.A. Nardi, (ed.), context and consciousness: Activity Theory and Human-Computer Interaction. Cambridge, MA, USA: MIT press. 1996.
12. van Lamsweerde, A., Willemet, L.: *Inferring Declarative Requirements Specifications from Operational Scenarios.* IEEE Transactions on Software Engineering, Special Issue on Scenario Management, December 1998.
13. van Lamsweerde, A.: *Requirements Engineering in the Year 00: A Research Perspective.* In Proceedings of the 22nd International Conference on Software Engineering (ICSE-2000), Limerick, Ireland, June 2000. ACM Press.
14. Leontiev, A. N.: *Activity, Consciousness, and Personality.* Englewood Cliffs, NJ, USA: Prentice-Hall. 1978.
15. Nuseibeh, B., Easterbrook, S.: *Requirements Engineering: A Roadmap.* In Proceedings of the 22nd International Conference on Software Engineering (ICSE-2000), Limerick, Ireland, June 2000.
16. OMG: *Unified Modeling Language Specification. Version 1.5.* 2003 http://www.omg.org
17. Perini, A., Bresciani, P., Giunchiglia, F., Giorgini, P., Mylopoulos, J.: *A Knowledge Level Software Engineering Methodology for Agent Oriented Programming.* In Proceedings of the 5th International Conference on Autonomous Agents, Montreal, Canada, May 2001.
18. Vygotsky, L. S.: *Mind and Society.* Cambridge MA, USA: Harvard University. 1978.
19. Yu, E.: *Strategic Modelling for Enterprise Integration.* In Proceedings of the 14th World Congress of the International Federation of Automatic Control (IFAC'99), Beijing, China, July 1999.

# Formalisation and Analysis of the Temporal Dynamics of Conditioning

Tibor Bosse[1], Catholijn M. Jonker[2], Sander A. Los[3], Leendert van der Torre[4,5], and Jan Treur[1]

[1] Vrije Universiteit Amsterdam, Department of Artificial Intelligence, De Boelelaan 1081a, NL-1081 HV Amsterdam, The Netherlands
{tbosse, treur}@cs.vu.nl
http://www.cs.vu.nl/~{tbosse, treur}

[2] Radboud Universiteit Nijmegen, Nijmegen Institute for Cognition and Information, Montessorilaan 3, 6525 HR Nijmegen, The Netherlands
C.Jonker@nici.ru.nl
http://www.nici.ru.nl/~catholj

[3] Vrije Universiteit Amsterdam, Department of Cognitive Psychology, Van der Boechorststraat 1, 1081 BT Amsterdam, The Netherlands
sa.los@psy.vu.nl
http://www.cs.vu.nl/~cogsci/cogpsy/sander

[4] Centrum voor Wiskunde en Informatica, Kruislaan 413, 1098 NL Amsterdam, The Netherlands
torre@cwi.nl
http://homepages.cwi.nl/~torre

[5] Delft University of Technology, Mekelweg 4, 2628 CD Delft, The Netherlands

**Abstract.** In order to create adaptive Agent Systems with abilities matching those of their biological counterparts, a natural approach is to incorporate classical conditioning mechanisms into such systems. However, existing models for classical conditioning are usually based on differential equations. Since the design of Agent Systems is traditionally based on qualitative conceptual languages, these differential equations are often not directly appropriate to serve as an input for Agent System design. To deal with this problem, this paper explores a formal description and analysis of a conditioning process based on logical specification and analysis methods of dynamic properties of conditioning. Specific types of dynamic properties are global properties, describing properties of the process as a whole, or local properties, describing properties of basic steps in a conditioning process. If the latter type of properties are specified in an executable format, they provide a temporal declarative specification of a simulation model. Global properties can be checked automatically for simulated or other traces. Using these methods the properties of conditioning processes informally expressed by Los and Heuvel [8] have been formalised and verified against a specification of local properties based on Machado [9]'s mathematical model.

J.P. Müller and F. Zambonelli (Eds.): AOSE 2005, LNCS 3950, pp. 54 – 68, 2006.

## 1 Introduction

Intelligent Agents often operate in dynamic and uncertain environments. Therefore, an important challenge for Agent-Oriented Software Engineering is to incorporate learning mechanisms into Agent Systems. A basic learning mechanism that can be found in many organisms is *classical conditioning*. Thus, in order to create Intelligent Agents Systems with abilities matching those of their biological counterparts, a natural approach is to build classical conditioning into such systems, e.g., [1].

However, in the literature classical conditioning is usually described and analysed informally. If formalisation is used, this is often based on mathematical models using differential equations, e.g., Dynamic Systems Theory [11]. In contrast, Agent-Based Systems traditionally make use of logical, conceptual languages, such as Golog [12] or 3APL [4]. Most of these languages are good for expressing qualitative relations, but less suitable to work with complex differential equations. Therefore, using mathematical models as a direct input for the design of Agent Systems is not trivial.

To bridge the gap between the quantitative nature of existing conditioning models and the conceptual, logical type of languages typically used to design Agent Systems, this paper introduces a logical approach for the analysis and formalisation of conditioning processes that combines qualitative and quantitative concepts, cf. [6]. Using this approach, the dynamics of conditioning are analysed both at a local and at a global level. First a local perspective model for temporal conditioning in a high-level executable format is presented, based on the idea of *local dynamic properties*. This executable model can be compared to (and was inspired by) Machado [9]'s differential equation model. Some simulation traces are shown. Next, as part of a non-local perspective analysis, a number of relevant *global dynamic properties* of the conditioning process are identified and formalised. These dynamic properties were obtained by formalising the informally expressed properties to characterise temporal conditioning processes, as put forward by Los and Heuvel [8]. It has been automatically verified that (under reasonable conditions) these global dynamic properties are satisfied by the simulation traces. Thus, it is validated that the local dynamic properties can be used as requirements for the design of adaptive agents. This finding offers possibilities to extend existing methodologies for Agent-Oriented Software Engineering by including learning mechanisms as observed in nature.

In Section 2, first some basic concepts of classical conditioning are introduced. Based on these concepts, Section 3 briefly describes Machado [9]'s mathematical model for conditioning. Next, Section 4 introduces our logical approach to modelling dynamic process, and Section 5 applies this approach to Machado's model. Some resulting simulation trace that were generated on the basis of the logical model are shown in Section 6. In Section 7, a number of relevant global dynamic properties are described (cf. [8]), that are expected to hold for conditioning processes. In Section 8 these global properties are automatically checked against the simulation model. Section 9 concludes the paper with a discussion.

## 2 Basic Concepts of Conditioning

Research into conditioning is aimed at revealing the principles that govern associative learning. To this end, several experimental procedures have been developed. In classical conditioning, an organism is presented with an initially neutral conditioned stimulus (e.g., a bell) followed by an unconditioned stimulus (e.g., meat powder) that elicits an innate or learned unconditioned response in the organism (e.g., saliva production for a dog). After acquisition, the organism elicits an adaptive conditioned response (also saliva production in the example) when the conditioned stimulus is presented alone. In operant conditioning, the production of a certain operant response that is part to the volitional repertoire of an organism (e.g., bar pressing for a rat) is strengthened after repeated reinforcement (e.g., food presentation) contingent on the operant response.

In their review, Gallistel and Gibbon [5] argued that these different forms of conditioning have a common foundation in the adaptive timing of the conditioned (or operant) response to the appearance of the unconditioned stimulus (or reinforcement). This feature is most apparent in an experimental procedure called trace conditioning, in which a blank interval (or 'trace') of a certain duration separates the conditioned and unconditioned stimulus (in classical conditioning) or subsequent reinforcement phases (in operant conditioning). In either case, the conditioned (or operant) response obtains its maximal strength, here called *peak level*, at a moment in time, called *peak time*, that closely corresponds to the moment the unconditioned stimulus (or reinforcement) occurs.

For present purposes, we adopt the terminology of an experimental procedure that is often used to study adaptive timing and the possible role of conditioning in humans. In this procedure, a trial starts with the presentation of a *warning stimulus* (S1; comparable to a conditioned stimulus). After a blank interval, called the *foreperiod* (FP), an *imperative stimulus* (S2, comparable to an unconditioned stimulus) is presented to which the participant responds as fast as possible. The *reaction time* (RT) to S2 is used as an estimate of the conditioned state of preparation at the moment S2 is presented.

In this type of research, FP is usually varied at several discrete levels. That is, S2 can be presented at several moments since the offset of S1, which are called *critical moments*. The moment that is used for the presentation of S2 on any given trial is called the *imperative moment* of that trial. In a *pure block*, the same FP is used across all trials of that block. That is, in a pure block there is one critical moment that corresponds to the imperative moment on each trial. In a *mixed block*, all levels of FP occur randomly across trials. That is, a mixed block has several critical moments, but on any specific trial, only one of the moments is the imperative moment.

## 3 Modelling by Differential Equations

Machado [9] presented a basic model of the dynamics of a conditioning process. The structure of this model, with an adjusted terminology as used by [7], is shown in Figure 1. The model posits a layer of *timing nodes* (Machado calls these *behavioral states*) and a single *preparation node* (called *operant response* by Machado). Each timing node is connected both to the next timing node and to the preparation node. The connection between each timing node and the preparation node (called *associative link* both by Machado and within the current paper) has an adjustable weight associated to it. Upon the presentation of a warning stimulus, a cascade of activation propagates through the timing nodes according to a regular pattern. Owing to this regularity, the timing nodes can be likened to an internal clock or pacemaker. At any moment, each timing node contributes to the activation of the preparation node in accordance with its activation and its corresponding weight. The activation of the preparation node reflects the subject's preparatory state, and is as such related to reaction time for any given imperative moment.

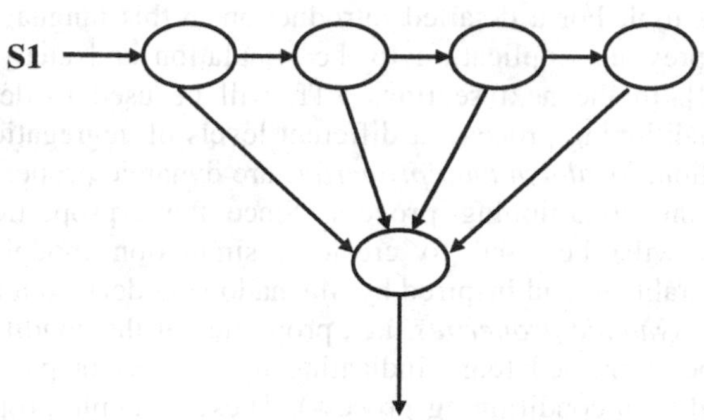

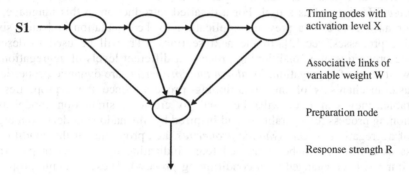

**Fig. 1.** Structure of Machado's conditioning model (adjusted from [9])

The weights reflect the state of conditioning, and are adjusted by learning rules, of which the main principles are as follows. First, *during* the foreperiod extinction takes place, which involves the decrease of weights in real time in proportion to the activation of their corresponding timing nodes. Second, *after* the presentation of the imperative stimulus a process of reinforcement takes over, which involves an increase of the weights in accordance with the current activation of their timing nodes, to preserve the importance of the imperative moment. In [9] the more detailed dynamics of the process are given by a mathematical model (based on linear differential equations), representing the (local) temporal relationships between the variables involved. For example, $d/dt\ X(t,n) = \lambda X(t,n-1) - \lambda X(t,n)$ expresses how the activation level of the n-th timing node $X(t+dt,n)$ at time point $t+dt$ relates to this level $X(t,n)$ at time point t and the activation level $X(t,n-1)$ of the (n-1)-th timing node at time point t.

# 4 Modelling by Dynamic Properties

As discussed above, mathematical models based on differential equations can be used to model local temporal relationships within conditioning processes. However, conditioning processes can also be characterised by temporal relationships of a less local form. As an example, taken from [8], a dynamic property can be formulated expressing the monotonicity property that 'the response level increases before the critical moment is reached and decreases after this moment'. This is a more global property, relating response levels at any two points in time before the critical moment (or after the critical moment). Therefore it is useful to explore formalisation techniques, as an alternative to differential equations, to express not only for local properties, but also for non-local properties. A second limitation of differential equations is that they are based on quantitative (calculational) relationships, whereas also non-quantitative aspects may play a role (for example, the monotonicity property mentioned above). This suggests that it may be useful to explore alternative formalisation techniques for dynamic properties of conditioning processes that allow one to express both quantitative and non-quantitative aspects.

As already mentioned in the Introduction, the approach presented in this paper indeed uses alternative formalisation languages to express dynamic properties of conditioning processes, both for local and global properties and both for quantitative and non-quantitative aspects. To this end the *Temporal Trace Language* TTL is used as a tool. For a detailed introduction to this language, see [6]. For an example of a previous application to the simulation and analysis of cognitive processes, see [2]. In the next sections TTL will be used to describe dynamic properties of a conditioning process at different levels of aggregation. At the lowest level of aggregation, *local dynamic properties* are dynamic properties of the basic mechanisms of the conditioning process. Since these properties are executable, they can (and will) be used to create a simulation model of a conditioning process (comparable to and inspired by Machado's model). At a higher level of aggregation, *global dynamic properties*, i.e., properties of the conditioning process as a whole, will be expressed (e.g., indicating how a certain pattern of behaviour has been changed by a conditioning process). These dynamic properties were obtained by formalising the informally expressed properties to characterise temporal conditioning processes, as put forward by Los and Heuvel [8]. In addition, it will be shown that the global properties are satisfied by the traces generated on the basis of the local properties.

# 5 Local Dynamic Properties

A selection of the local properties (LPs) we defined in order to describe the basic mechanisms of the conditioning process is presented below. A local property generally has the format $\alpha \twoheadrightarrow \beta$, indicating that $\alpha$ leads to $\beta$, after a certain (specified) delay. The concepts used within the dynamic properties (called *state properties*) are described in Table 1.

As Machado [9]'s model was used as a source of inspiration, for some of the properties presented below the comparable differential equation within Machado's model is given as well. However, since Machado's mathematical approach differs at several points from the logical approach presented in this paper, there is not always a straightforward 1:1 mapping between both formalisations. For instance, state property X(n,u) within our TTL formalisation has a slightly different meaning than the corresponding term X(t,n) in Machado's differential equations. In the former, n stands for the timing node, u stands for the activation level, and X(n,u) stands for the fact that timing node n has activation level u. In the latter, t stands for a time point, n for the timing node, and X(t,n) as a whole for the activation level.

**Table 1.** State Properties

| | |
|---|---|
| X(n,u) | Timing node n has activation level u. In the current simulation, n ranges over the discrete domain [0,5]. Thus, our model consists of six timing nodes. The activation level u can take any continuous value in the domain [0,1]. |
| W(n,v) | Associative link n has weight v. Again, n ranges over the discrete domain [0,5]. The weight v can take any continuous value in the domain [0,1]. |
| R(r) | The preparation node has response strength r (a continuous value in the domain [0,1]). |
| S1(s) | Warning stimulus S1 occurs with strength s. Within our example, s only takes the values 0.0 and 1.0. However, the model could be extended by allowing any continuous value in-between. |
| S2(s) | Imperative stimulus S2 occurs with strength s. |
| Xcopy(n,u) | Timing node n had activation level u at the moment of the occurrence of the last imperative stimulus (S2). See dynamic property LP4 and LP6. |
| instage(ext) | The process is in a stage of extinction. This stage lasts from the occurrence of S1 until the occurrence of S2. |
| instage(reinf) | The process is in a stage of reinforcement. This stage starts with the occurrence of S2, and lasts during a predefined reinforcement period (e.g. 150 msec). |
| instage(pers) | The process is in a stage of persistence. This stage starts right after the reinforcement stage, and lasts until the next occurrence of S1. |

Using the concepts described in Table 1, the following local properties have been specified to describe the basic mechanisms of the conditioning process:

**LP1 Initialisation**
The first local property LP1 expresses the initialisation of the values for the timing nodes and the associative links. Formalisation (for n ranging over [0,5]):

start ↠ X(n, 0) ∧ W(n, 0)

**LP2 Activation of initial timing nodes**
Local property LP2 expresses the activation (and adaptation) of the $0^{th}$ timing node. Immediately after the occurrence of the warning stimulus (S1), this state has full strength. After that, its value decreases until the next warning stimulus. Together with LP3, this property causes the spread of activation across the timing nodes. Here, $\lambda > 0$ is a rate parameter that controls the speed of this spread of activation, and step is a constant indicating the smallest time step in the simulation. For the simulation experiments presented in the next section, $\lambda$ was set to 10 and step was set to 0.05.

X(0, u) ∧ S1(s) ↠ X(0, u*(1-λ*step)+s)

Comparable differential equation in Machado [9]'s model:

$d/dt\ X(t,0) = -\lambda X(t,0)$.

**LP3 Adaptation of timing nodes**
LP3 expresses the adaptation of the $n^{th}$ timing node (for n ranging over [1,5]), based on its own previous state and the previous state of the $n\text{-}1^{th}$ timing node. Together with LP2, this property causes the spread of activation across the timing nodes. Here, $\lambda$ is a rate parameter that controls the speed of this spread of activation (see LP2).

X(n, u1) ∧ X(n-1, u0) ↠ X(n, u1+λ*(u0-u1)*step)

Comparable differential equation in Machado [9]'s model:

$d/dt\ X(t,n) = \lambda X(t,n-1) - \lambda X(t,n)$.

**LP4 Storage of timing nodes at moment of reinforcer**

LP4 is needed to store the value of the $n^{th}$ timing node at the moment of the occurrence of the imperative stimulus (S2). These values are used later on by property LP6.

X(n, u) ∧ S2(1.0) →→ Xcopy(n, u)

**LP5 Extinction of associative links**

LP5 expresses the adaptation of the associative links during extinction, based on their own previous state and the previous state of the corresponding timing node. Here, α is a learning rate parameter. For the simulation experiments presented in the next section, the value 2 was chosen for α, inspired by [7]. This rather high value for α causes the model to adjust quickly to changing temporal regimes.

instage(ext) ∧ X(n, u) ∧ W(n, v) →→ W(n, v*(1-α*u*step))

Comparable differential equation in Machado [9]'s model:

$d/dt\ W(t,n) = -\alpha X(t,n)W(t,n)$

**LP6 Reinforcement of associative links**

LP6 expresses the adaptation of the associative links during reinforcement, based on their own previous state and the previous state of Xcopy. Here, β is a learning rate parameter. For the simulation experiments presented in the next section, the value 2 was chosen for β, inspired by [7].

instage(reinf) ∧ Xcopy(n, u) ∧ W(n, v) →→ W(n, v*(1-β*u*step) + β*u*step)

Comparable differential equation in Machado [9]'s model:

$d/dt\ W(t,n) = \beta X(T,n)[K-W(t,n)].$

**LP7 Persistence of associative links**

LP7 expresses the persistence of the associative links at the moments that there is neither extinction not reinforcement.

instage(pers) ∧ W(n, v) →→ W(n, v)

**LP8 Response function**

LP8 calculates the response by adding the discriminative function of all states (i.e., their associative links * the degree of activation of the corresponding state).

W(1, v1) ∧ W(2, v2) ∧ W(3, v3) ∧ W(4, v4) ∧ W(5, v5) ∧ X(1, u1) ∧ X(2, u2) ∧ X(3, u3) ∧ X(4, u4) ∧ X(5, u5) →→ R(v1*u1 + v2*u2 + v3*u3 + v4*u4 + v5*u5)

**LP9 Initialisation of stage pers**

LP9 expresses that the initial stage of the process is pers.

start →→ instage(pers)

**LP10 Transition to stage ext**

LP10 expresses that the process switches to stage ext when a warning stimulus occurs.

S1(1.0) →→ instage(ext)

**LP11 Persistence of stage ext**

LP11 expresses that the process persists in stage ext as long as no imperative stimulus occurs.

instage(ext) ∧ S2(0.0) →→ instage(ext)

**LP12 Transition to stage reinf and pers**

LP12 expresses that the process first switches to stage reinf for a while, and then to stage pers when an imperative stimulus occurs. Notice that LP12a and LP12b must have different timing parameters to make sure both stages do not occur simultaneously.

S2(1.0) ↠ instage(reinf) (LP12a)
S2(1.0) ↠ instage(pers) (LP12b)

**LP13 Persistence of stage pers**

LP13 expresses that the process persists in stage pers as long as no warning stimulus occurs.

instage(pers) ∧ S1(0.0) ↠ instage(pers)

Note that the translation from differential equations to local properties in TTL is relatively easy to make. Assuming some experience with both kinds of modelling, a set of differential equations as given above can be translated within a couple of hours.

## 6 Simulation Examples

A software environment has been developed that generates simulation traces of the conditioning process, based on an input consisting of dynamic properties in formal format. A large number (about 20) of such traces have been generated, with different parameters for foreperiod (50, 100, 150, 200, 300, and 500 msec) and block type (pure blocks and mixed blocks), selected on the basis of [7]. An example of such a trace can be seen in Figure 2. Here, time is on the horizontal axis. Each time unit corresponds to 50 msec. The relevant concepts (S1, instage(ext), instage(pers) and R) are on the vertical axis. This trace is based on all local properties presented above. For almost all properties, the timing parameters (0,0,1,1) were used. Exceptions are the properties LP4, LP12a and LP12b. For these properties, the timing parameters were respectively (0,0,1,3), (0,0,1,3) and (3,3,1,1), where 3 corresponds to the reinforcement duration (i.e., 150 msec).

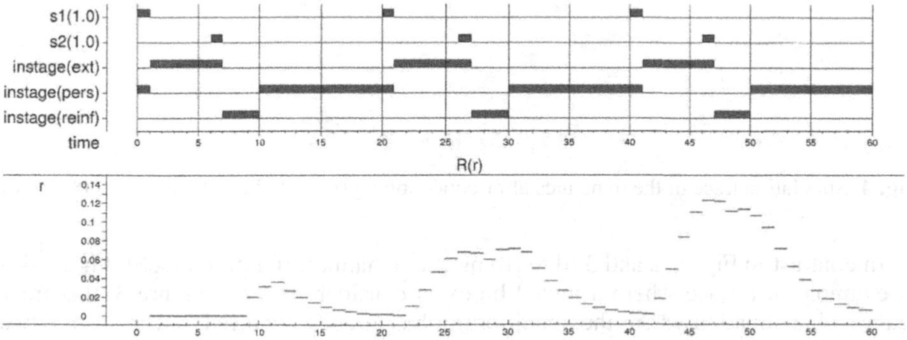


**Fig. 2.** Simulation trace of the dynamics during conditioning (pure block, FP=300 msec)

Figure 2 describes the dynamics *during* (not after) a conditioning process. To be specific, this trace describes the dynamics of a person that is subject to conditioning in a pure block with a foreperiod of 6 time units (i.e., 300 msec). As can be seen in the trace, the level of response-related activation increases on each trial. Initially, the subject is not prepared at all: at the moment of the imperative stimulus (S2), the level of response is 0. However, already after two trials a peak in response level has developed that coincides exactly with the imperative moment.

Figure 3 describes the dynamics of the same pure block (with foreperiod of 300 msec) *after* the conditioning has taken place. At this moment, the internal model has evolved in such a way that the subject is maximally prepared (response strength r > 0.4) at the critical moment (i.e., after 300 msec), even without the actual occurrence of an imperative stimulus S2.

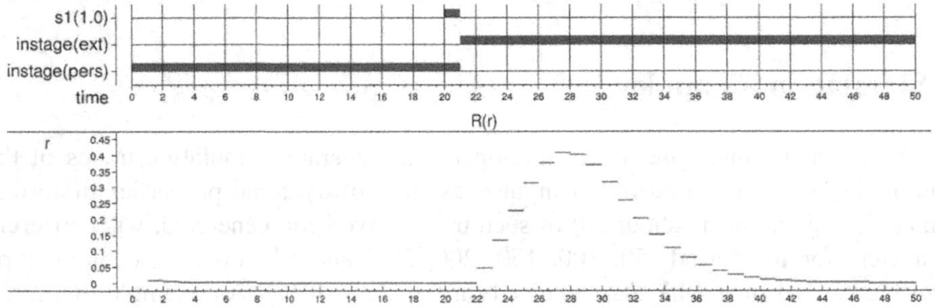


**Fig. 3.** Simulation trace of the dynamics after conditioning (pure block, FP=300 msec)

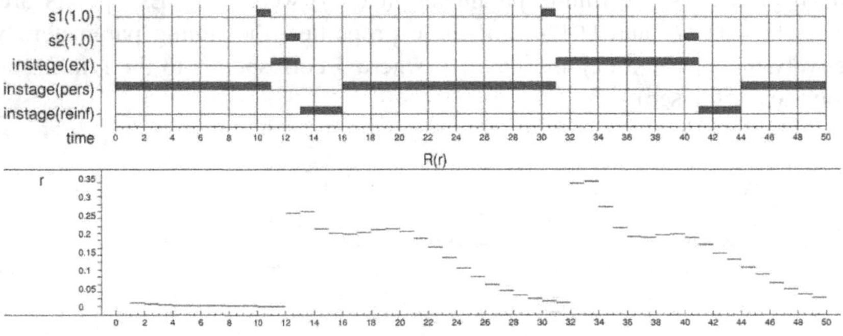


**Fig. 4.** Simulation trace of the dynamics after conditioning (mixed block, FP=100 & 500 msec)

In contrast to Figure 2 and 3 (describing the dynamics of a pure block), Figure 4 is an example of a trace where a mixed block is considered. As in Figure 3, this trace deals with a situation where the conditioning has already occurred, but this time, two types of foreperiod (FP=100 and FP=500 msec) have randomly been presented during the preceding trials. As a consequence, the curves that plot the response level have two peaks: one for each critical moment. The current trace shows two trials: one in which the imperative moment corresponds to the first critical moment, and one in which it corresponds to the second critical moment.

As mentioned above, a number of similar experiments have been performed, with different parameters for foreperiod and block type. The results were consistent with the data produced by Machado.

# 7 Analysis of Global Dynamic Properties

In [8], the following properties of the overall conditioning process are put forward:

'Corresponding to each critical moment there is a state of conditioning, the adjustment of which is governed by learning rules of trace conditioning (specified subsequently).'

(1) 'The state of conditioning implicates an increase and decay of response-related activation as a critical moment is bypassed in time.'

(2) 'the conditioned response takes more time to build up and decay and its corresponding asymptotic value is lower when its corresponding critical moment is more remote from the warning signal.'

(3) 'on any trial, the strength of the conditioned response corresponding to a critical moment is reinforced (i.e., increased toward its asymptote) if and only if that critical moment coincides with the imperative moment.'

(4) 'on any trial the strength of the conditioned response is extinguished (i.e., driven away from its asymptote) if and only if its corresponding critical moment occurs before the imperative moment, whereas it is left unaffected if its corresponding critical moment occurs later than the imperative moment.' [8], p. 372.

These properties have a rather informal and non-mathematical nature. Below it is shown how they can be formalised gradually. Each property is presented first in a semi-formal notation, following by the formal (TTL) notation.

**GP1 has_global_hill_prep(γ,t1,t2,s1,a,u)**

The first global property GP1 is a formalisation of informal property (1) presented above. In semi-formal form, it describes the following:

'In trace γ, if at t1 a stimulus s1 starts, then the preparation level for action a will increase from t1 until t2 and decrease from t2 until t1 + u, under the assumption that no stimulus occurs too soon (within u time) after t1.'

In formal (TTL) notation this property looks as follows:

∀t', t", s', p', p", x, x'
stimulus_starts_at(γ, t1, s1, x) &
¬ stimulus_starts_within(γ, t1, t1+u, s', x') &
has_preparation_level_at(γ, t', p', a) &
has_preparation_level_at(γ, t", p", a)
⇒ [t1 ≤ t' < t" ≤ t2 & t" ≤ t1 + u ⇒ p' < p" ] &
[t2 ≤ t' < t" ≤ t1 + u ⇒ p' > p" ]

**GP2 pending_peak_versus_critical_moment(γ1,γ2,t1,t2,c1,c2)**

Global property GP2 is a formalisation of informal property (2). Its semi-formal description is as follows:

'If for trace γ2 at time t2 peak time c2 is more remote than peak time c1 for γ1 at time t1, then at t2 in γ2 the pending peak level is lower than the pending peak level at t1 in γ1.'

The formalisation is as follows:

$\forall$s1, a, p1, p2
has_pending_peak_level(γ1, t1, c1, p1, s1, a) &
has_pending_peak_level(γ2, t2, c2, p2, s1, a)
$\Rightarrow$ [ c1 < c2 $\Rightarrow$ p1 > p2 ]

**GP3 dynamics_of_pending_preparation(γ,t1,t2,c,v,p,p',s1,s2,a, d,ε)**
GP3 is a formalisation of both informal property (3) and (4) together. Its semi-formal description is as follows:

'If t1 < t2
and at t1 the pending preparation level for time t1+v, action a, and stimuli s1 and s2 is p,
and at t2+d the pending preparation level for time t2+d+v, action a, and stimuli s1 and s2 is p',
and in trace γ at time t1 a stimulus s1 starts,
and in trace γ at time t2 a stimulus s2 starts,
and in trace γ the maximum peak level for a is pmax,
and in trace γ the minimum preparation level for a is pmin,
then:
t2 ∈ [ t1+c-ε, t1+c+ε ] iff p' > p (reinforcement, given p<pmax)
t2 > t1+c+ε iff p' < p (extinction, given that p > pmin)
t2 < t1+c-ε iff p' = p (persistence)'

Here, parameter d refers to the time needed to process the events (d > 0), and c refers to a critical moment. The formalisation is as follows:

dynamics_of_pending_preparation(γ, t1, t2, c, v, p, p', s1, s2, a, d, ε) $\Leftrightarrow$
reinforcement(γ, t1, t2, c, v, p, p', s1, s2, a, d, ε) &
extinction(γ, t1, t2, c, v, p, p', s1, s2, a, d, ε) &
persistence(γ, t1, t2, c, v, p, p', s1, s2, a, d, ε)

reinforcement(γ, t1, t2, c, v, p, p', s1, s2, a, d, ε) $\Leftrightarrow$
$\forall$x1, x2, pmin, pmax
two_stimuli_occur(γ, t1, t2, c, v, p, p', s1, s2, a, d)
$\Rightarrow$ [ p < pmax $\Rightarrow$ [ t2 ∈ [ t1 + c - ε, t1 + c + ε ] $\Leftrightarrow$ p' > p ]]

extinction(γ, t1, t2, c, v, p, p', s1, s2, a, d, ε) $\Leftrightarrow$
$\forall$ x1, x2, pmin, pmax
two_stimuli_occur(γ, t1, t2, c, v, p, p', s1, s2, a, d)
$\Rightarrow$ [ p > pmin $\Rightarrow$ [ t2 > t1 + c + ε $\Leftrightarrow$ p' < p ]]

persistence(γ, t1, t2, c, v, p, p', s1, s2, a, d, ε) $\Leftrightarrow$
$\forall$ x1, x2, pmin, pmax
two_stimuli_occur(γ, t1, t2, c, v, p, p', s1, s2, a, d)
$\Rightarrow$ [ t2 < t1 + c - ε $\Leftrightarrow$ p' = p ]

two_stimuli_occur(γ, t1, t2, c, v, p, p', s1, s2, a, d) $\Leftrightarrow$
t1 < t2 & has_pending_preparation_level(γ, t1, t1+v, p, s1, s2, a) &
has_pending_preparation_level(γ, t2+d, t2+d+v, p', s1, s2, a) &
stimulus_starts_at(γ, t1, s1, x1) &
stimulus_starts_at(γ, t2, s2, x2) &
target_action_for(a, s2) &
is_a_critical_moment(c) &
maximum_peak_level(γ, pmax, a) &
minimum_preparation_level(γ, pmin, a)

## 8 Checking Global Properties on Traces

In addition to the software described in the Simulation section, other software has been developed that takes traces and formally specified properties as input and checks whether a property holds for a trace. Using automatic checks of this kind, the four formalised properties based on [8] have been checked against traces describing the dynamics *after* conditioning (like the ones depicted in Figure 3 and 4). This section discusses the results of these checks.

**GP1 has_global_hill_prep(γ,t1,t2,s1,a,u)**

This property turned out to hold for the generated traces, as long as reasonable values are chosen for the parameters. In particular, the parameters should meet the following conditions:

- t1 = a time point when s1 occurs
- t2 = t1 + duration of s1 + length of FP
- u = iti (the intertrial interval during the preceding conditioning process)

For example, the following property holds: has_global_hill_prep(γ1, 20, 27, s1, a, 20), where γ1 is the trace provided in Figure 3. Thus, for this trace the following holds: if at time point 20 a stimulus s1 starts, then the preparation level for action a increases from 20 until 27 and decreases from 27 until 40, under the assumption that no stimulus occurs between 20 and 40.

**GP2 pending_peak_versus_critical_moment(γ1,γ2,t1,t2,c1,c2)**

Checking property GP2 involves comparing two traces. Basically, it states that in traces where the foreperiod is longer, the level of response is lower. In order to check GP2, several traces have been generated that are similar to the trace in Figure 3, but each with a different foreperiod. For all combinations of traces, the property turned out to hold. To take an example, the following property holds: pending_peak_versus_critical_moment(γ1, γ2, 20, 20, 6, 7), where γ1 is the trace provided in Figure 3, and γ2 is a similar trace with FP=7. This means that, if for trace γ2 at time 20 peak time 7 is more remote than peak time 6 for γ1 at time 20, then at 20 in γ2 the pending peak level is lower than the pending peak level at 20 in γ1.

**GP3 dynamics_of_pending_preparation(γ,t1,t2,c,v,p,p',s1,s2,a, d,ε)**

Property GP3 combines property (3) and (4) as mentioned in the previous section. Basically, the property consists of three separate statements that relate the strength of the conditioned response (p) to the critical moment (t1+c) and the imperative moment (t2), by stating that:

| | |
|---|---|
| GP3A. | p increases iff t2 = t1+c |
| GP3B. | p decreases iff t2 > t1+c |
| GP3C. | p remains the same iff t2 < t1+c |

An example of this property with reasonable parameter values is: dynamics_of_pending_preparation(γ, 10, 12, 10, 10, p, p', s1, s2, a, 18, 0), where γ is the trace depicted in Figure 4. However, this property turned out not to hold. A close examination of Figure 4 will reveal the cause of this failure. This trace describes a mixed block with two types of foreperiod (FP=2 and FP=10). At time point 10, a warning stimulus (S1) occurs. At this time point, the pending preparation level for the latest critical moment (time point 20) has a certain value. And since this critical moment occurs after the occurrence of S2 (the imperative moment: time point 12), the pending preparation level for the latest critical moment should remain the same, according to property GP3C above. However, in the trace in question this is not the case (see Figure 4: in the second curve the second peak is slightly lower than in the first curve). Hence, it may be concluded that property GP3C (sub-property persistence presented earlier) does not hold for the chosen parameters. Fortunately, an explanation of this finding can be found in a later section of [8], where the authors revise their original model as follows:

> 'According to the original model, extinction and reinforcement affect each state of conditioning in an all-or-none way, thereby excluding a coupling between states of conditioning corresponding to adjacent critical moments. According to the revised model, extinction and reinforcement affect the states of conditioning more gradually across the time scale, resulting in a coupling between adjacent states.' [8], p. 383.

The revision of the model also implies a revision of property GP3. To be more specific, sub-property persistence can be changed into the following:

$t2 < t1 + c - \varepsilon$ iff $p' \in [p - \delta, p + \delta]$

Here, $\delta$ is a tolerance factor allowing a small deviation from the strength of the original response. After adapting GP3 accordingly, the property turned out to hold.

## 9 Discussion

To bridge the gap between the quantitative nature of existing conditioning models and the conceptual, logical type of languages typically used to design Agent Systems, in this paper a logical approach was introduced for the analysis and formalisation of conditioning processes that combines qualitative and quantitative concepts. Using this approach, the dynamics of conditioning have been analysed both at a local and at a global level.

From a local perspective, a model for temporal conditioning in a high-level executable format was presented, based on the idea of local dynamic properties. This model can be compared to (and was inspired by) Machado [9]'s differential equation model, and has been used to generate a number of simulation traces.

Next, as part of a non-local perspective analysis, a number of relevant *global dynamic properties* of the conditioning process have been identified and formalised. It has been confirmed, by means of formal verification, that the assumptions of the informal conditioning model proposed by Los and Heuvel [8] are global properties of the formal model developed by Machado [9], given certain restrictions of the parameter values, and given slight adaptations of the persistence rule given by GP3C. This is an important finding, because the global properties have proved to be highly useful in accounting for key findings in human timing, see [7], [8]. Thus, it was validated that the local dynamic properties can be used as requirements for the design of adaptive agents. As a result, existing methodologies for Agent-Oriented Software Engineering can be extended by including learning mechanisms as observed in nature. Currently, most research on reinforcement learning in Multi-Agent Systems concentrates only on the correctness of a response, not on its timing. By considering temporal aspects, the research presented in this paper is novel.

One crucial finding the global properties can deal with effectively is the occurrence of sequential effects of FP. These effects entail that on any given trial, RT is longer when the FP of that trial is shorter than the FP of the preceding trial relative to when it is as long as or longer than the FP of the preceding trial. Stated differently, RT is longer when the imperative moment was bypassed during the FP on the preceding trial than when it was not bypassed during FP on the preceding trial, see, e.g., [8], [10]. This finding is well accounted for by the learning rules formulated as GP3. According to GP3B, the state of conditioning (p) associated with a critical moment is subject to extinction when a critical moment is bypassed during FP (i.e., $t_2 > t_1 + c$), which is neither the case for the imperative moment, where according to GP3A reinforcement occurs (i.e., $t_2 > t_1 + c$), nor for critical moment beyond the imperative moment, where the state of conditioning persists according to GP3C (i.e., $t_2 < t_1 + c$). Note that the adjustment of GP3C suggested by the present check of global properties does not compromise the effectiveness of these learning rules, because the tolerance factor $\delta$ is small relative to the extinction described by GP3B.

In fact, the addition of the tolerance area $\delta$ to GP3C, might prove to be helpful in accounting for a more subtle effect in the extant literature. This concerns the finding that the FP-RT functions obtained in pure and mixed blocks cross over at the latest critical moment. Specifically, in pure blocks, the FP-RT function has been found to be upward sloping, given a minimal FP of about 250 – 300 msec. By contrast, in mixed blocks, the RT is slowest at the shortest critical moment (due to the influence of sequential effects described in the previous paragraph) and decreases as a negatively accelerating function of FP. At the latest critical moment the pure and mixed FP-RT functions come together, presumably because this moment is never bypassed during FP on the preceding trial, allowing the state of conditioning to approach its asymptotic value in either case. Sometimes, though, a cross-over of the two FP-RT functions is reported, which has been shown to be particularly pronounced in certain clinical populations, such as people diagnosed with schizophrenia (see [13] for a review). This finding may be related to the failure to confirm GP3C without the allowance of a tolerance area $\delta$. Thus, it could be that, for certain parameter settings, the state of conditioning corresponding to the latest critical moment approaches its asymptotic value more closely when a shorter FP occurred on the preceding trial (which is often the case in mixed blocks) than when the same FP occurred on the preceding trial (as is always the case in pure blocks).

Concerning related work, in [3] another formal model is described of the dynamics of conditioning processes, using a similar modelling approach. However, whilst the current paper focuses on human conditioning, the work presented in [3] focuses specifically on the conditioning mechanisms of the sea hare *Aplysia*, of which the neural mechanisms are much simpler and therefore better understood. As a consequence, that model describes the conditioning process at a neural level, whereas the model presented in the current paper is at a functional level. Another difference is that the current paper concentrates more on the temporal aspects of the conditioning.

Since the results of our simulation model were found to be consistent with the model of [9], our model was implicitly compared with empirical work. However, in future work, it will be compared explicitly with empirical data. Since the checking software can take traces of different format as input, it will be possible to verify the global properties shown in Section 7 against experimental human conditioning traces.

## Acknowledgements

This paper was improved thanks to some valuable comments of anonymous referees.

## References

1. Balkenius, C. and Morén, J. (1999). Dynamics of a classical conditioning model. *Autonomous Robots, 7*, 41-56.
2. Bosse, T., Delfos, M.F., Jonker, C.M., and Treur, J. (2003). Analysis of Adaptive Dynamical Systems for Eating Regulation Disorders. *Proc. of the 25th Annual Conf. of the Cognitive Science Society, CogSci'03*. Mahwah, NJ: Lawrence Erlbaum Associates, Inc.
3. Bosse, T., Jonker, C.M., and Treur, J. (2005). Simulation of Conditioning Mechanisms in Agents. In: Balsa, J., Moniz, L., and Reis, L.P. (eds.), *Proceedings of the Third Workshop on Multi-Agent Systems: Theory and Applications, MASTA'05*.
4. Dastani, M., Dignum, F., and Meyer, J-J.Ch. (2003). *3APL: A Programming Language for Cognitive Agents*. ERCIM News, European Research Consortium for Informatics and Mathematics, Special issue on Cognitive Systems, No. 53.
5. Gallistel, C.R. and Gibbon, J. (2000). Time, rate, and conditioning. *Psychological Review*, vol. 107, pp. 289-344.
6. Jonker, C.M. and Treur, J. (2002). Compositional Verification of Multi-Agent Systems: a Formal Analysis of Pro-activeness and Reactiveness. *International Journal of Cooperative Information Systems*, vol. 11, pp. 51-92.
7. Los, S.A., Knol, D.L., and Boers, R.M. (2001). The Foreperiod Effect Revisited: Conditioning as a Basis for Nonspecific Preparation. *Acta Psychologica*, 106, pp. 121-145.
8. Los, S.A. and van den Heuvel, C.E. (2001). Intentional and Unintentional Contributions to Nonspecific Preparation During Reaction Time Foreperiods. *Journal of Experimental Psychology: Human Perception and Performance*, vol. 27, pp. 370-386.
9. Machado, A. (1997). Learning the temporal Dynamics of Behaviour. *Psychological Review*, vol. 104, pp. 241-265.
10. Niemi, P. and Naatanen, R. (1981). Foreperiod and Simple Reaction Time. *Psychological Bulletin*, vol 89, pp. 133-162.
11. Port, R.F. and van Gelder, T.J. (1995). *Mind as Motion: Explorations in the Dynamics of Cognition*. MIT Press, Cambridge, Mass.
12. Reiter, R. (2001). *Knowledge in Action: Logical Foundations for Specifying and Implementing Dynamical Systems.* MIT Press.
13. Rist, F. and Cohen, R. (1991). Sequential effects in the reaction times of schizophrenics: crossover and modality shift effects. In E.R. Steinhauer, J.H. Gruzelier, & J. Zubin, *Handbook of schizophrenia*, vol. 5: Neuropsychology, psychophysiology and information processing (pp. 241-271). Amsterdam: Elsevier.

# Incorporating Commitment Protocols into Tropos

Ashok U. Mallya and Munindar P. Singh

Department of Computer Science, North Carolina State University,
Raleigh, NC 27695-7535, USA
{aumallya, singh}@ncsu.edu

**Abstract.** This paper synthesizes two trends in the engineering of agent-based systems. One, modern agent-oriented methodologies deal with the key aspects of software development including requirements acquisition, architecture, and design, but can benefit from a stronger treatment of flexible interactions. Two, commitment protocols declaratively capture interactions among business partners, thus facilitating flexible behavior and a sophisticated notion of compliance. However, they lack support for engineering concerns such as inducing the desired roles and selecting the right protocols. This paper combines these two directions. For concreteness, we choose the Tropos methodology, which is strong in its requirements analysis, but our results can be ported to other agent-oriented methodologies.

Our approach is as follows. First, using Tropos, analyze requirements based on dependencies between actors. Second, select top-level protocols based on the actors' hard goals, while respecting the logical boundaries of their interactions. Third, select refined protocols based on the actors' soft goals. Consequently, Tropos provides a rigorous basis for modeling and composing protocols whereas the protocols help produce perspicuous designs that respect the participants' autonomy. We evaluate our approach using a large existing case.

## 1 Introduction

Tropos is an agent-based software methodology that uses the notions of goals, plans to achieve goals, and dependencies among the goals and plans of agents [2]. The dependencies help capture the relationships between the various stakeholders in the system being engineered. Following $i^*$ [7], Tropos gives prominence to identifying stakeholders and their goals early.

Commitment protocols model interactions among autonomous agents in terms of their content rather than in terms of low-level message exchanges [6]. Commitment protocols form building blocks for (and correspond to vertical slices of) flexible business processes, each protocol ideally addressing a logically well-encapsulated interaction for a specified purpose. For example, the purchase and shipping protocols would have logically distinct purposes and involve distinct roles. Specific agents would play suitable roles in different protocols to obtain a business process.

While both of the above approaches have strengths, they also have some limitations where a synthesized approach would help. Tropos models dependencies among stakeholders well and accommodates their evolution as the goals and plans of the stakeholders are refined. The requirements serve as reminders and guards throughout the development process. However, Tropos does not capture agent interaction requirements in the early stages. Protocols are not identified until the penultimate (detailed design)

J.P. Müller and F. Zambonelli (Eds.): AOSE 2005, LNCS 3950, pp. 69–80, 2006.

stage whereas dependencies are defined early. Protocols evolve as the design progresses. Tropos can benefit from an interaction model that allows interactions to be refined with each successive stage of software development. On the other hand, the theory of commitment protocols does not address how interaction protocols and the contexts of their application can be identified in a multiagent system. Tropos can provide cues for identifying protocols because it identifies actors, their goals, their plans to achieve goals and dependencies.

CONTRIBUTIONS. Our work contributes to both Tropos and the theory of commitment protocols. Through protocols, our approach gives interactions the same status as goals in Tropos. Interactions among independent parties can be captured early and successively refined based on a theory of protocol subsumption. Because of its identification of stakeholders and their goals, dependencies, and plans, Tropos provides a valuable approach in which to identify and refine commitment protocols. We illustrate our approach via an example of a large software system that was developed using Tropos.

ORGANIZATION. The rest of this paper is organized as follows. Section 2 introduces Tropos and our running example. Section 3 describes commitments, protocols, and allied concepts. Section 4 lists important properties of dependencies, which are used to develop the guidelines of our methodology for incorporating commitment protocols into Tropos in Section 5. Section 6 compares our contributions to the literature and outlines some directions for enhancement.

## 2 Background: Tropos by Example

Tropos uses the following key concepts:

- ACTOR: An actor models an entity that has goals or plays a part in the software being developed. Actors are similar to agents or roles, in traditional terminology.
- RESOURCE: A physical entity or a piece of information.
- GOAL: A goal corresponds to an actor's desire. *Hardgoals* are measurable, whereas *softgoals* are subjective.
- PLAN: A plan is an abstract description of steps to be taken to achieve a goal.
- DEPENDENCY: An actor (*depender*) can depend on another (*dependee*) for acquiring a resource, satisfying a goal, or executing a plan. The resource, goal, or plan is the *dependum*. The *reason* for a dependency is a plan, goal, softgoal, or resource (belonging to the depender) for which the depender depends on the dependee.

Tropos uses three methods, all from an actor's perspective, for refining goals and identifying plans to achieve them.

- *Means-end analysis* identifies plans, resources, or goals (*means*) to satisfy a specified goal or plan (*end*). When a plan is the end, the means can be another plan or a resource, but not a goal.
- *AND-OR decomposition* breaks up plans into subplans. AND requires all subplans; OR requires one. Likewise for goals and subgoals.
- *Contribution analysis* identifies the positive and negative impact that a plan, a goal, or a resource may have on the achievement of a goal.

Table 1 summarizes the stages of Tropos and how they use the concepts of actor, goal, plan, dependency, and capability.

**Table 1.** Tasks performed in modeling actors, dependencies, goals, plans, and capabilities in different stages of Tropos. Within each stage, the different modeling techniques are not ordered.

| | 1. Early Requirements | 2. Late Requirements | 3. Architectural Design | 4. Detailed Design |
|---|---|---|---|---|
| Actor Modeling | Identify "top-level" actors actors or stakeholders in domain. | Introduce system as an actor called system-actor. | Decompose system-actor into subactors. Identify all dependencies. | Define agents to model capabilities of system-actor and its subactors. |
| Goal Modeling | Refine goals using means-end analysis, AND-OR decomposition, and contribution analysis. Find new dependencies. | | | |
| Plan Modeling | Refine plans using the three plan analysis methods analogous to goal analysis. | | | |
| Dependency Modeling | Identify dependencies between stakeholders using goal modeling. | Model dependencies between system-actor and other actors. | Model dependencies between subactors of the system-actor to identify capabilities. | |
| Capability Modeling | | | Identify capabilities of subactors required to handle dependencies with all others. | |

**The eCulture Example**

Tropos was used to develop the *eCulture System* for the Trentino provincial government (called *PAT*) [2]. This system provides information about cultural services such as museums to citizens and tourists.

EARLY REQUIREMENTS. Figure 1 identifies four stakeholders (top-level actors) in the *eCulture System*: Citizen, PAT, Visitor, and Museum, along with their goals and dependencies. The above actors have the goals get cultural info, increase Internet use, enjoy visit, and provide cultural services, respectively, the last two being softgoals. Citizen depends on PAT, taxes well spent being the reason for the dependency.

Next, the model of Figure 1 is refined via goal and plan analyses. During goal analysis, each goal is either *expanded* into subgoals using AND-OR decomposition, *delegated* to a new or existing actor, or *accepted* by an actor as its own. Tropos performs goal and plan modeling for different actors using label propagation to check that all the root goals, i.e., goals that the modeling began with, are accepted by some actor. Figure 2 shows the partial result of such a goal and plan analysis. The get cultural info hardgoal, which is a root goal for the actor Citizen, is OR-decomposed into two subgoals—visit cultural institutions and visit cultural web systems. Under means-end analysis, the latter subgoal yields the plan visit eCulture as a means. This plan is AND-decomposed into two subplans, namely, use eCulture and access Internet. The

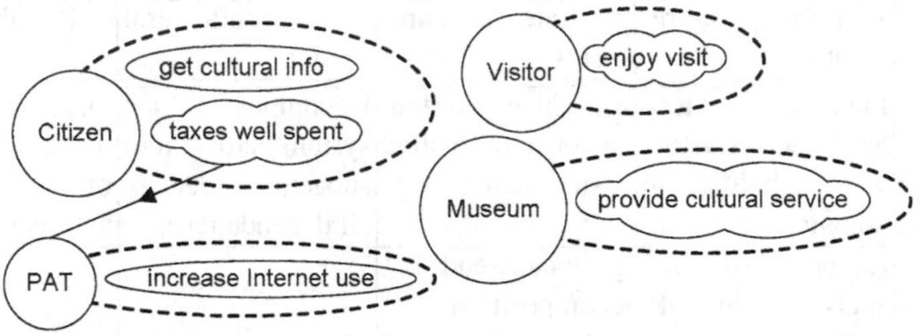


**Fig. 1.** Actors identified in early requirements. Actors are circles, their scopes demarcated by dotted ovals. Hardgoals are solid ovals; softgoals are clouds. Dependencies are lines with arrowheads at their center, going from the depender (or from the reason) to the dependee (or to the dependum).

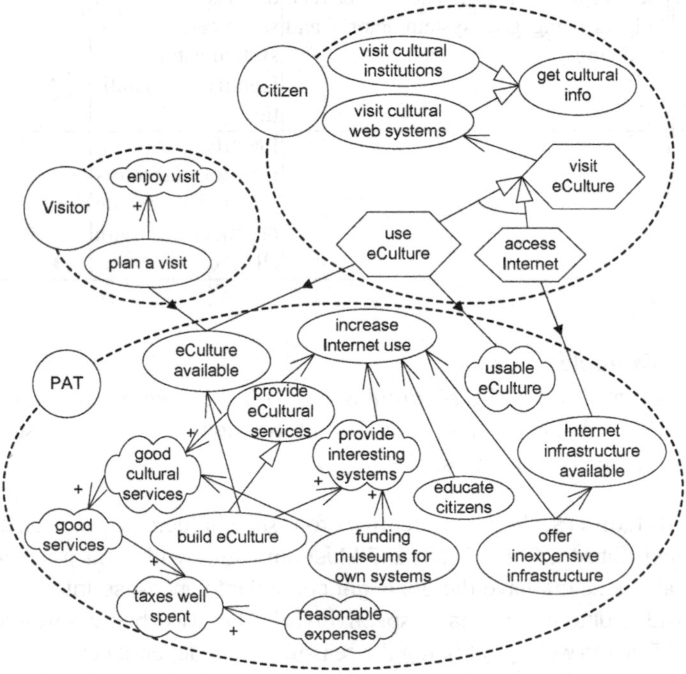


**Fig. 2.** Actor model after early requirements. Plans are hexagons; AND decompositions are arrows with empty triangles as arrowheads, with an arc spanning over all the arrows; OR decompositions are similar, but without the spanning arc. Contributions are a + or a − next to an arrowhead; means-end relationships are similar, but without the + or the −.

softgoal taxes well-spent—the reason for Citizen's dependency on PAT—is delegated to PAT, which accepts it.

LATE REQUIREMENTS. During late requirements, the software system is introduced as an actor, called the *system-actor*. Dependencies between existing actors (stakeholders) and the system-actor are identified, and goal and plan analyses are performed. Figure 3 shows part of the actor model for PAT, Citizen, Museum, and the system-actor eCulture. This figure also shows a part of the goal model for eCulture. For example, PAT depends on eCulture for the softgoal usable eCulture and for the hardgoal provide eCultural services, among others. Goal analysis performed on these goals from the point of view of eCulture results in both goals being adopted by eCulture and decomposed as shown in the goal diagram (within the dotted oval) in Figure 3.

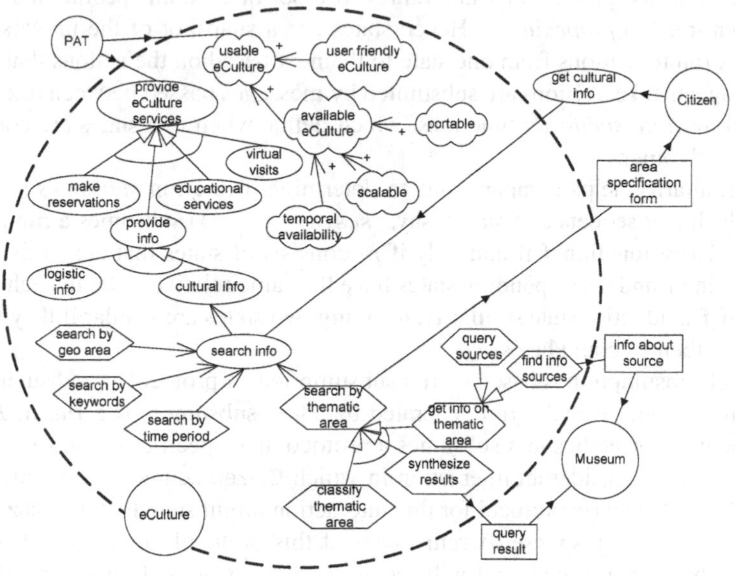


**Fig. 3.** Partial actor and goal models showing dependencies of PAT, Citizen, and Museum on the system-actor eCulture. Resources are rectangles.

ARCHITECTURAL DESIGN. During architectural design, eCulture is decomposed into several subactors, including an actor Info Broker introduced to satisfy the goal provide info. Goal and plan analyses are performed after identifying the dependencies between the new subactors and the other actors.

## 3 Background: Commitments and Protocols

A *commitment* is a directed obligation from one agent to another, within a social context. A commitment $\mathsf{C}(x, y, G, p)$ denotes that the agent $x$ (*debtor*) is responsible to the agent $y$ (*creditor*) for bringing about the *condition* $p$ within a social context $G$. The condition is expressed in a suitable formal language. *Conditional* commitments, denoted by $\mathsf{CC}(x, y, G, p, q)$, mean that $x$ is committed to $y$ to bring about $p$ if $q$ holds. Conventionally, six commitment operations are defined. A commitment can be *created, canceled,* or *discharged.* The creditor of a commitment can be *released* by the debtor. Further, the creditor can *cancel* the commitment, usually based on a suitable compensation for the cancellation.

Commitment protocols are driven by the creation and transformation of commitments between their participants rather than by a rigid sequence of steps. Thus commitment protocols are akin to goal-based interactions. Here, we summarize an existing framework in which a subsumption hierarchy is defined over protocols such that a refined protocol is subsumed by the protocol it refines.

A protocol allows a set of computations or *runs*. Each run is a sequence of *states*. Each state is an assignment of truth values to a set of domain-specific and generic, commitment-related *propositions*. Hence states are a snapshot of the universe of the protocol. A run transitions from one state to the next based on the actions that the participating agents take. Actions are substituted by messages passed between roles. States are related by *state-similarity* functions, which define when two states are considered similar to each other.

State-similarity helps compare runs to determine if one run *subsumes* another. A run $r_1$ (which is a sequence of states, say, $\langle s_0 s_1 s_2 \ldots s_{|r_1|} \rangle$) subsumes a run $r_2$ under a state-similarity function $f$ if and only if $r_2$ consists of states that are similar (under $f$) to states in $r_1$ and corresponding states have the same relative order in each run. For example, if $f$ is identity-state similarity, meaning two states are similar if they have the same labels, then $r_2$ could be $\langle s_1 s_2 \rangle$.

Protocol subsumption is based on run subsumption. A protocol $P_1$ subsumes a protocol $P_2$ if and only if every run generated by $P_2$ is subsumed by a run in $P_1$. That is, a protocol that specifies less subsumes a protocol that specifies its runs in more detail. For example, consider an interaction in which Citizen acquires some information from eCulture. A generic protocol for this interaction might state that the Citizen sends a query and awaits a response. A refinement of this protocol might state that Citizen must login, be authenticated, and will receive a response based on its credentials as identified by eCulture. Both protocols enable the same top-level interaction, i.e., transferring information from eCulture to Citizen. A system designer can use either protocol, possibly based on the context in which the system is deployed. Commitments help us reason about similarities and differences among protocols, and provide, through definitions state-similarity functions, a basis for judging subsumption among protocols. These concepts are discussed in greater detail elsewhere [5].

## 4 Dependencies in Tropos

We propose the use of commitment protocols in Tropos with actors as agents, and dependencies between actors as the bases of application of these protocols. This section describes intuitions about dependencies in Tropos that are used when developing and applying protocols.

In Tropos, a plan is a sequence of steps that an actor may take in order to achieve a certain goal, and a goal is a state which the actor wants to bring about. Plans are *means* to achieve goals. Plans are *executed*, goals are *achieved*, and resources are *made available*. Nine types of dependencies can exist between actors in Tropos, since dependums on the dependee's side and reasons on the depender's side can be either a plan, a hardgoal, or a resource. These dependency types are shown in Figure 4, leading to the following observation about the operational behavior of the dependencies.

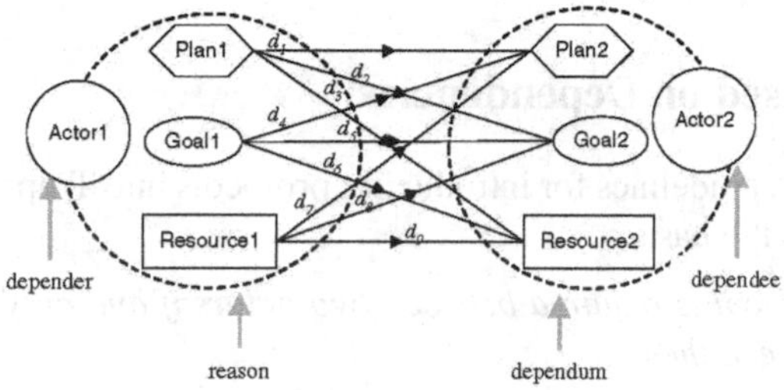


**Fig. 4.** Types of dependencies in Tropos

**Observation 1.** *The reason of a dependency cannot be executed to completion, achieved, or made available till its dependum is executed (at least partially), achieved, or made available.* ∎

This is based on the assumption that all dependencies are required for their reason to succeed. For instance, a plan cannot be executed to completion if the goal that it depends on is not achieved. Dependencies can be fulfilled multiple times. For example, the dependency on the resource query result between the eCulture and the Museum is fulfilled every time eCulture makes a query result available to the museum.

**Observation 2.** *A dependency's reason is an actor's local view of an interaction protocol.* ∎

For example, the access Internet plan of Citizen is the citizen's view of the interaction it has with PAT on the dependum Internet infrastructure available. If a dependency is one of several dependencies realized by a single protocol, then that dependency is only part of the actor's view of that protocol.

**Observation 3.** *Outgoing dependencies can be propagated up the hierarchy in AND-decomposition trees.* ∎

Generally, outgoing dependencies from all non-root nodes of an AND tree can be propagated to the root. In essence, a tree can be captured with just its root node as the reason for all its outgoing dependencies. Consider PAT's plan search by thematic area and its AND decomposition tree, as in Figure 3. This plan is the reason for the dependency on the resource query result, because synthesize results, a non-root node in the AND tree, depends on query result. The outgoing dependency has therefore been propagated up the tree.

With means-end trees and OR-decomposition trees, since only one of the non-root nodes need to be achieved, executed, or made available, the dependencies cannot always be propagated to the root. Consider PAT's plan find info sources in Figure 3. This plan is part of the OR tree with the plan get info on thematic area as its root. find info sources has a dependency on Museum for info about source. This dependency cannot be propagated up to the root plan get info on thematic area because there is an alternative way—query sources—of executing the root plan without involving any dependency.

Designers propagate dependencies down the hierarchy as part of Tropos, when goals and plans are refined.

## 5 Protocols Based on Dependencies

This section provides guidelines for introducing protocols into Tropos using dependencies among actors as the basis.

**Guideline 1.** *A protocol is required between two actors if and only if at least one dependency exists between them.* ▪

A single protocol might *realize* all associated dependencies between actors. This protocol would be coherent only if the dependencies were somehow related. For example, both the dependencies between eCulture and Citizen shown in Figure 2 can be realized by a single protocol since the dependencies are part of a coherent interaction in which Citizen queries and receives information from eCulture. System designers can thus state the relationships between dependencies in terms of interactions between actors.

Conversely, consider actors that have multiple, unrelated dependencies realized by a single protocol. Such a protocol would not be the best design because it combines independent interactions. OWL-P is a framework for describing, composing, and enacting protocols [3]. The composition makes use of a designer-specified *profile*, which includes axioms specifying correspondences between roles, messages, and data in the protocols being combined. As an example, consider Figure 5, which is a part of Figure 3. Let the dependency between eCulture and Citizen on get cultural info be realized by an *information transfer* protocol with two roles: *information provider* and *information consumer*. Let the dependency on area specification form be realized by a *form filling* protocol with two roles: *form creator* and *form filler*. These two protocols can be combined by specifying in the composition profile that Citizen plays the roles information consumer and form filler, and eCulture plays the roles information provider and form creator. The composition profile would also specify that the form data be filled before the cultural information is provided. Under such a scheme, a protocol that realizes unrelated dependencies between two actors would not have any composition axioms other than the ones required to bind roles between the protocols. That is, protocols group related dependencies, defining interactions in coherent units rather than as unrelated dependencies.

**Guideline 2.** *Protocols cannot realize dependencies that have softgoals as dependums or reasons.* ▪

Whereas softgoals can be used by designers to refine protocols, they cannot be realized using protocols since the achievement of softgoals is not objectively verifiable.

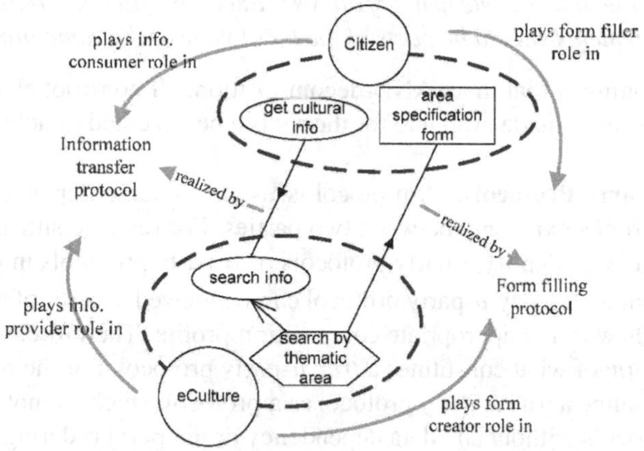


**Fig. 5.** Realizing dependencies using one protocol each. Actors play multiple roles.

**Identifying Related Dependencies.** Relationships between dependencies can be identified only by the system designer, based on expert knowledge about the stakeholders and actors. However, additional information about potential relationships between dependencies can be obtained from the structure of the AND-OR decomposition and the means-end analysis. Detecting sets of related dependencies corresponds to identifying and demarcating the scope of a protocol. Identifying relationships between dependencies also indicates how a protocol should be designed. Here, we describe the guidelines for identifying related dependencies and how they correspond to protocols.

**Guideline 3.** *If the means for an end are reasons for dependencies, those means should either be parts of local views of different runs of the same protocol or parts of local views of different protocols that achieve the same interaction. This guideline applies to OR decompositions as well.* ▪

The means for an end are possible ways to achieve or execute the end. If a plan or a goal has many means, any one of them is a way for executing the plan or achieving the goal. If means are reasons for dependencies, then they are an actor's view of a protocol. Therefore, multiple means for a common end provide different views of an actor's involvement in an interaction whose essence is the same: to achieve the end. As an example, consider PAT's goal search info, as shown in Figure 3. This goal can be achieved by 4 means, search by geo area, search by time period, search by keywords, and search by thematic area. All these means are different plans for PAT's view of an information-searching interaction with Citizen. Hence, all these means can be designed as local views of different runs of an information-searching protocol or as local views of runs of different protocols to search for information.

When a plan or a goal is OR decomposed, executing any one of the child plans or satisfying any one of the child goals is sufficient to execute or satisfy the parent plan or goal respectively. The same reasoning as applied to means-ends applies to OR decompositions as well. The child plans or goals are equivalent to each other in what they provide to the actor.

**Guideline 4.** *If the non-root elements of an AND decomposition are reasons for dependencies, those elements should be parts of the local view of the same protocol.* ▪

Again, the reasoning is that in an AND-decomposition, all non-root elements must be executed, achieved, or made available for the root to be executed or achieved.

**Identifying 3-Party Protocols.** A protocol is used to realize dependencies, and dependencies in Tropos exist only between two parties. For realistic situations, however, we need to be able to identify 3-party protocols or $n$-party protocols in general, where $n > 2$. We first note that any $n$-party protocol can be viewed as a set of at most $\frac{n(n-1)}{2}$ 2-party protocols with the appropriate composition profile. Therefore, we need an operational definition of what constitutes a *true* $n$-party protocol. For the purposes of this discussion, we define a true $n$-party protocol as a protocol which cannot be broken into constituent protocols without any data dependency or temporal ordering among them.

**Guideline 5.** *If the AND decomposition tree has dependencies, either incoming or outgoing, with two different actors, a 3-party protocol exists between them.* ▪

This guideline is based partly on Observations 1 and 2. Consider the dependencies shown in Figure 6 for example. Actor $A_0$ has an AND tree, shown partially to ignore unnecessary detail. The root of this tree is plan $p_1$, which has been AND decomposed. Actor $A_1$ depends on plan $p_1$ via the dependency $d_1$. Further, there exist a non-root node $p_2$ which depends on actor $A_2$ via the dependency $d_2$. From Observation 1, we know that $p_1$ will not be executed to completion until $p_2$ is. Also, from Observation 2, we know that $p_1$ and $p_2$ are local views of some interaction protocol. Therefore, we infer that the protocol that realizes $d_1$ depends on the protocol that realizes $d_2$. Therefore, based on our operational definition of a true $n$-party protocol, the model shown in Figure 6 warrants the use of a 3-party protocol. As a more realistic example, albeit a variation of the above, consider the plan search by thematic area belonging to PAT in Figure 3. This plan depends on Citizen, and has an AND descendant synthesize results, which depends on Museum. Therefore, this plan cannot be executed to completion without the help of both Citizen and Museum. Therefore, a 3-party protocol can be used here.

**Guideline 6.** *If a resource belonging to one actor is the dependum for a dependency with a second actor and a reason for a dependency with a third actor, a 3-party protocol exists between the the actors.* ▪

For example, PAT depends on Citizen for the resource area specification form, as shown in Figure 3. If Citizen depended on some actor other than PAT for this resource, then a

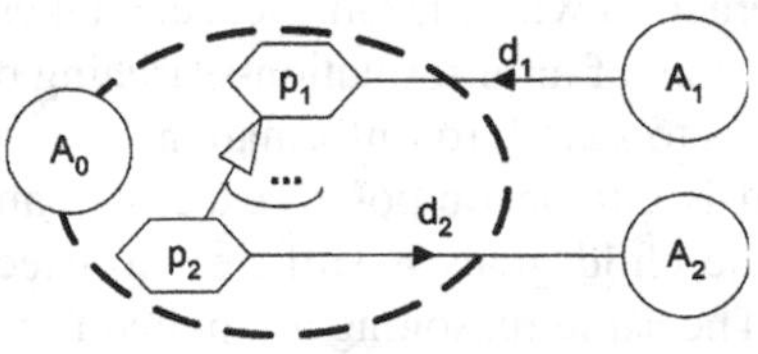


**Fig. 6.** Identifying 3-party protocols based on plan dependencies among 3 actors

3-party protocol would be required because of the data-dependency between the protocols realizing these dependencies.

**Refining Protocols.** We have shown how protocols can be applied in Tropos models. An advantage of using commitment protocols in Tropos is that protocols can be refined with successive stages of software development. We proposed a protocol-design methodology based on hardgoals and the plans that achieve them. Refinement of these protocols should be based on the softgoals of the participants. In this regard, softgoals are analogous to the private policies of a protocol-participant. We intend to develop this line of research in future work.

## 6 Discussion

This paper demonstrated how protocols can be introduced into an agent-based software engineering methodology, Tropos. Tropos benefits from our approach, because (1) protocols capture the dynamic, or runtime behavior of the software system being developed before the implementation stage in addition to the static dependencies between actors; (2) protocols decouple the meaning of an interaction by treating them as entities in their own right, which can be tailored to suit the needs of their participants and local policies at runtime; (3) Treating protocols as coherent units captures realistic interactions among autonomous entities. This is an advantage over a client-server model in which protocols are part of the logic embedded in the server.

Likewise, we contribute to commitment protocols by describing guidelines for designing them from requirements. Specifically, dependencies, means-end models, and AND-OR decomposition models in Tropos provide points of reference for using protocols between actors. Tropos provides the scope, i.e., boundaries, for the protocols.

**Related Literature.** Our work relates to software engineering and multiagent systems. Yu & Mylopolous explain the importance of identifying dependencies among autonomous entities in organizational settings, e.g., for business processes [8]. They describe how dependencies based on resources and goals can be used to re-engineer business processes, since dependencies help answer "what-if?" and "why?" questions about changes in business processes. Whereas Yu & Mylopolous describe how to introduce a dependency model into an existing business processes, we describe how protocols, which can be used to construct business processes, can be developed based on the requirements.

Giorgini *et al.* present a rigorous analysis of goal decomposition in Tropos [4]. They develop algorithms to identify contributions among goals and possible conflicts among goals. This work would help our research in identifying valid refinements of protocols based on goals.

Gaia, KAOS, MaSE, and SADDE are a few other important agent-oriented methodologies [1]. Tropos differs from these in including an early requirements stage. Besides the early requirements gathering stage, Gaia differs from Tropos in that Gaia describes roles in the software system being developed and identifies processes that they are involved in as well as safety and liveness conditions for the processes [9]. Gaia incorporates protocols under the *interactions model* and can be used with commitment protocols. However, the lack of a reasoning scheme based on early requirements—to answer "why?" questions—limits the flexibility of Gaia's protocols.

The work presented here is new. Whereas we have chosen Tropos for incorporating a notion of interactions into the various stages of software design, we aim to study how other agent-oriented engineering methodologies (which may not include a notion of dependencies) can incorporate commitment protocols as a design abstraction.

## Acknowledgment

We thank Amit Chopra, Nirmit Desai, and the anonymous reviewers for valuable comments. This research was supported partly by the National Science Foundation under its Digital Society and Technology Program in the Intelligent Information Systems Division under grant DST-0139037 and partly by the DARPA Information Exploitation Office under contract F30603-00-C-0178.

## References

1. Federico Bergenti, Marie-Pierre Gleizes, and Franco Zambonelli, editors. *Methodologies and Software Engineering for Agent Systems: The Agent-Oriented Software Engineering Handbook.* Kluwer Academic, 2004.
2. Paolo Bresciani, Anna Perini, Paolo Giorgini, Fausto Guinchiglia, and John Mylopolous. Tropos: An agent-oriented software development methodology. *Journal of Autonomous Agents and Multi-Agent Systems*, 8(3):203–236, May 2004.
3. Nirmit Desai, Ashok U. Mallya, Amit K. Chopra, and Munindar P. Singh. Interaction protocols as design abstractions for business processes. *IEEE Transactions on Software Engineering*, 31(12):1015–1027, 2005.
4. Paolo Giorgini, John Mylopolous, and Roberto Sebastiani. Goal-oriented requirements analysis and reasoning in the tropos methodology. *Engineering Application of Atrificial Intelligence Journal*, 18(2), 2005. To Appear.
5. Ashok U. Mallya and Munindar P. Singh. An algebra for commitment protocols. *Journal of Autonomous Agent and Multiagent Systems*, 2006.
6. Munindar P. Singh, Amit K. Chopra, Nirmit V. Desai, and Ashok U. Mallya. Protocols for processes: programming in the large for open systems (extended abstract). In *OOPSLA '04: Companion to the 19th annual ACM SIGPLAN Conference on Object-Oriented Programming Systems, Languages, and Applications*, pages 120–123, New York, NY, USA, 2004. ACM Press.
7. Eric Yu. *Modeling Strategic Relationships for Process Reengineering*. PhD thesis, University of Toronto, 1995.
8. Eric S. K. Yu and John Mylopoulos. An actor dependency model of organizational work: with application to business process reengineering. In *COOCS '93: Proceedings of the conference on Organizational computing systems*, pages 258–268. ACM Press, 1993.
9. Franco Zambonelli, Nicholas R. Jennings, and Michael Wooldridge. Developing multiagent systems: The Gaia methodology. *ACM Transactions on Software Engineering Methodology*, 12(3):317–370, 2003.

# Zooming Multi-Agent Systems

Ambra Molesini[1], Andrea Omicini[2], Alessandro Ricci[2], and Enrico Denti[1]

[1] DEIS, Alma Mater Studiorum—Università di Bologna,
viale Risorgimento 2, 40136 Bologna, Italy
ambra.molesini@unibo.it, enrico.denti@unibo.it

[2] DEIS, Alma Mater Studiorum—Università di Bologna a Cesena,
via Venezia 52, 47023 Cesena, Italy
andrea.omicini@unibo.it, a.ricci@unibo.it

**Abstract.** Complex systems call for a hierarchical description. Analogously, the engineering of non-trivial MASs (multiagent systems) requires principles and mechanisms for a multi-layered description, which could be used by MAS designers to provide different levels of abstraction over MASs.

In this paper, we first advocate the need for *zooming mechanisms*, promoting a coherent and consistent multi-layered view of agent systems. After surveying the best-known AOSE methodologies, we focus on the scaling mechanisms of the OPM process-oriented methodology. Then, by adopting SODA as our reference, we show how an AOSE methodology can be enhanced with simple yet expressive zooming mechanisms. Finally, we present a simple case study where the enhanced agent-oriented methodology (SODA+zoom) is exploited and put to the test.

## 1 Zooming as a Principle in the Design of MASs

As advocated in [1], MASs (multiagent systems), once developed up to their full potential, can be generally seen as representing a class of complex artificial systems, wide and meaningful enough to legitimate, in principle, the application to MASs of the general principles and laws governing complex systems. While *modelling* complex systems and understanding their behaviour and dynamics is the most relevant concern in many areas, such as economics, biology, or social sciences, the complexity of *construction* is of paramount interest when dealing with software systems—MASs in particular. Drawing results from heterogeneous scientific areas, and bringing them to the MAS field, is then particularly meaningful and promising when principles and ideas that are known to *model* and describe complex systems in general are taken and shown to be applicable and useful to *build* MASs—in other terms, become ideas and principles for agent-oriented engineering processes and methodologies.

### 1.1 Hierarchies in Complex Systems

According of the theory of hierarchies [2], all biological systems are amenable to be represented as organised on different layers, ranging from genes and cells

J.P. Müller and F. Zambonelli (Eds.): AOSE 2005, LNCS 3950, pp. 81–93, 2006.

up to organisms, species and clades. Each level is essential to the general understanding of the system's wholeness, and is autonomous with its own laws, patterns and behaviour. At the same time, no level can be understood in isolation independently of all the other levels, and the system as a whole can be understood only through the understanding and representation of all its levels.

When generally ascribed to complex system, this sort of "hierarchy principle" might also be seen as a defining one: that is, a complex system is a system requiring layers—independent but strongly correlated ones—in order to fully understand and reproduce its dynamics and behaviour. When brought to MASs, in particular, this first suggests that MAS models, abstractions, patterns and technologies can be suitably categorised and compared using a layered description, as shown in [1]. More simply and directly, when applied to the engineering of MASs, the hierarchy principle suggests that agent-oriented processes and methods should support some forms of MAS layering, allowing engineers to design and develop MAS along different levels of abstractions—a number of independent, but strictly related, MAS layers.

Accordingly, one should expect that existing methodologies actually do support abstractions and processes for MAS layering. Quite interestingly, however, current AOSE methodologies offer very little (if any) support for hierarchical representation of MASs. So, in the following subsection we first survey the main AOSE methodologies to look for some support for layered representation of MAS, then we advocate the need of a simple layering mechanism (called here *zooming*) to be applied to any meaningful agent abstraction at any stage of the MAS engineering process.

## 1.2 Zooming in AOSE Methodologies

Many methodologies exist in the literature aimed at the engineering of artificial systems in terms of MASs. Some example are Gaia [3], MaSE [4], Tropos [5], MESSAGE [6], Prometheus [7]. Although none of those methodologies provides MAS engineers with an explicit layering mechanism, some of them exhibit some implicit mechanisms that make it possible in some sense to analyse the system at different levels of detail.

At the best of our knowledge, the most cited AOSE methodology, Gaia, does not introduce any mechanism providing for MAS layering. In MaSE, instead, two models allow MASs to be represented at different levels of abstraction: the *creating-agent-classes* model should provide a high-level vision of the MAS agents and of their main conversations; instead, the *assembling-agent-classes* model "zooms" on the inner agent structure, and provides for a number of predefined components, which may also have sub-architectures (with further subcomponents) of their own.

Tropos promotes a form of refinement across different stages of the MAS analysis process, such as when the *actor* and *dependency* models built in the *early requirements* phase are extended during the *late requirements* phase by adding the system-to-be as another actor, along with its inter-dependencies with social actors. Also MESSAGE use a refinement model in the analysis phase: the level 0 model gives an overall view of the system, its environment, and its global functionality; next level 1 defines thc structure and the behaviour of entities such as organisation, agents, tasks, goals, domain entities; further levels (2, 3, ...) might be defined for pointing out specific aspects of the system dealing with functional requirements, as well as non-functional requirements such as performance, distribution, fault tolerance, security. In Prometheus, a progressive refinement process is used which starts by describing agents internals in terms of capabilities. The internal structure of each capability is then given, optionally using or introducing further capabilities, which are refined in turn until all capabilities have been defined: capabilities nesting is allowed, thus allowing for arbitrarily many layers, in order to achieve an understandable complexity at each level.

The above forms of layering, however, are quite limited. First of all, they enforce only a top-down, mono-directional form of zooming—so, refinement allowed, abstraction not allowed. Then, they have ony a pre-fixed scope and structure, which limit in principle their flexibility and possibly their ability to fit the many different MAS application scenarios. Mechanisms for zooming are then not explicit, and no ontological support is currently provided by any of the available AOSE methodologies to the best of our knowledge.

### 1.3 Zooming in OPM

It is quite curious to observe that a non-AOSE approach such as OPM (Object Process Methodology [8]) directly supports zooming in several forms—even though the word *zooming* is used there with a more specific meaning.

**OPM in Short.** OPM is an integrated approach to the study and development of systems in general, and software systems in particular. Its basic premise is that objects and processes are two types of equally important classes of things, which together describe the function, structure and behaviour of systems in a single framework in virtually any domain. OPM unifies the system lifecycle stages—specification, design and implementation—within one frame of reference, using a single diagramming tool—Object-Process Diagrams (OPDs)—and a corresponding subset of English, called Object-Process Language (OPL). Unlike the object-oriented approach, behaviour in OPM is not necessarily encapsulated within a particular class construct. Using stand-alone processes, one can model a behaviour that involves several object classes and is integrated into the system structure. Processes can be connected to the involved object classes through procedural links, which are divided, according to their functionality, into three groups: enabling links, transformation links, and control links.

At the core of our interest here, as far as layer mechanisms are concerned, OPM adopts *detail decomposition*: rather then decomposing a system according to its various aspects (as in UML [9]), decomposition is based on the system level of abstraction. OPM built-in *scaling* (refinement/abstraction) mechanisms—unfolding/folding, in-/out-zooming, expressing/suppressing—greatly help manage system complexity. Unfolding/folding is applied by default to objects for detailing/hiding their structural components (parts, specialisations, features, or instances). In-/out-zooming is applied by default to processes for detailing/hiding their sub-process components and details of the process execution. Expression/suppression provides for showing/hiding the states of an object class.

Despite the different names, all the OPM scaling mechanisms (which we often collectively denote as zooming in this paper) allow engineers to work middle-out: MAS engineers can choose to start at any arbitrary abstraction level, and then achieve both the most detailed level and the most abstract level, along with the entire spectrum of intermediate levels between these two extremes.

**OPM/MAS Even in Shorter.** So, no surprise that OPM was extended in order to support concepts from the agent field. OPM/MAS [10] takes MAS building-blocks from the Gaia methodology. The set of MAS building blocks is divided into two groups: the first contains static, declarative building blocks, while the second group contains building blocks with behavioural, dynamic nature. The building blocks in the first group—which includes organisation, society, platform, rule, role, user, protocol,belief, desire, fact, goal, intention, and service—are modelled as OPM objects; the building blocks in the second group—which includes agent, task, and messaging—are modelled using the process concept.

OPM/MAS is indeed the first actual effort to introduce the zooming mechanism into a methodology for modelling multi-agent systems. However, apart from the obvious problems raising from the uneven mixture of the so-different OPM and Gaia approaches, OPM zooming mechanisms appear too generic for Gaia-derived agent abstractions, which were not conceived with zooming in mind. For instance, in-zooming an agent according to OPM rules would generally lead to another object, in general, or to another agent, more plausibly: no way that an activity represented at a given abstraction level as an agent could become a society of agents at the next, more refined level.

That is why in this paper we try the other way round: so, we do not start from a non-agent methodology with good zooming mechanisms, and then "agentify" it—the OPM/MAS approach. Instead, we take a simple, bare-bone AOSE methodology (that is, SODA), and introduce mechanisms for layering and zooming, expressive and general enough to be applicable to any key abstraction—such as roles, agents, societies, interaction rules.

Accordingly, in the next section we first introduce the basic concept of SODA. Then, we introduce zooming in SODA, by discussing its general model and main features. Last section is devoted to illustrating a simple case study, where SODA and the new zooming mechanisms are put to the test.

## 2 Zooming SODA

In this section we discuss a possible approach to the introduction of a zooming mechanism in SODA (Societies in Open and Distributed Agent spaces), an agent-oriented methodology for the analysis and design of agent-based systems [11].

### 2.1 SODA in Short

SODA is a methodology for the analysis and design of agent-based systems. As an explicit choice, SODA concentrates on inter-agent issues, like the engineering of societies and infrastructures for multi-agent system. Since this conceptually covers all the interaction within an agent system, the design phase deeply relies on the notion of *coordination model* [12]. In particular, coordination models and languages are taken as the source of the abstractions and mechanisms for the engineering of agent societies: social rules are designed as coordination laws and embedded into coordination media, and the social infrastructure is built upon the coordination system.

**Analysis.** The SODA analysis phase is based on three models—the *role model*, the *resource model*, and the *interaction model*. Since analysing a system in SODA amounts to defining some concepts and their relationships, an effective way to express such models is via suitable relational tables. In particular:

- in the **role model**, first the application goals are modelled in terms of the (*individual* and *social*) *tasks* to be achieved: each individual task is then associated to a *role*, while each social task is associated to a *group*. So, the role model can be represented by defining a *Role Table* (Table 1) and a *Group Table* (Table 2), respectively. In addition, since SODA associates *interaction protocols* to roles and *interaction rules* to groups, one extra column is added to such tables, to represent these associations. At a finer-grain level of detail, however, each group, too, is associated to a set of roles—the *social* roles: correspondingly, further Role Tables can be introduced to express these relationships—one (social) Role Table for each group. As a result, Role Tables are exploited to express both the individual roles (one table) and the social roles (as many tables as the groups are). Of course, the interaction protocols associated to roles and the interaction rules associated to groups are further detailed in the interaction model (Tables 4 and 5 below).
- in the **resource model**, the application environment is modelled in terms of available services, associated to abstract *resources*. These are further associated to a *policy*, intended as a set of access permissions associated to a role or group. Table 3 expresses this relationship, also listing the

**Table 1.** Role Table

| Role | Task | Interaction protocol |
|---|---|---|
| *role name* | *task name* | *list of protocols* |

**Table 2.** Group Table

| Group | Social Task | Interaction rules |
|---|---|---|
| *group name* | *social task name* | *list of rules* |

**Table 3.** Resource Table

| Resource | Services | Policy | Interaction Protocols |
|---|---|---|---|
| *resource name* | *services name* | *list of access permission* | *list of protocol* |

interaction protocols associated to each resource (again, details about interaction protocols and rules are provided in the interaction model—Tables 4 and 5).

– the **interaction model** is aimed at modelling the interaction among roles, groups and resources: each interaction protocol is individually denoted, then defined in terms of the information required / provided by roles and resources (Table 4). Analogously, interaction rules govern interaction within groups (Table 5).

**Table 4.** Interaction Protocols Table

| Interaction protocol | Information required | Information provided |
|---|---|---|
| *name of protocol* | | |

**Table 5.** Interaction Rules Table

| Interaction rule | Rule description |
|---|---|
| *name of rule* | *description* |

**Design.** The SODA design phase is based on three strictly related models, which derive from the models defined in the analysis phase; in particular, the analysis role model maps on the design *agent model* and *society model*, while the analysis resource model maps on the design *environment model*. The analysis interaction model, in its turn, generates the interaction protocols and coordination rules referenced by the design models. So, more precisely:

– in the **agent model**, individual and social roles are mapped upon *agent* classes: each agent class is then characterised by the task, the interaction protocols associated to its role, and the resources that need be accessed, with the corresponding set of permissions (Table 6). Again, the interaction protocols referenced here are the same defined in the Table 4 of the analysis phase.

– in the **society model**, groups are mapped onto agent societies (Table 7), each organised around a *coordination medium*—the abstraction provided by coordination model for coordination purposes—along with the corresponding coordination rules; these are the design counterpart of the analysis interaction rules defined in Table 5. Again, for each society, the required resources should also be specified.

**Table 6.** Agent Table

| Agent | Role | Interaction protocol | Resources | Permissions |
|---|---|---|---|---|
| *agent name* | *role name* | *list of protocols* | *list of resources* | *list of permissions* |

**Table 7.** Society Table

| Society | Group | Coordination medium | Resources | Coordination rule |
|---|---|---|---|---|
| *society name* | *group name* | *medium* | *resources* | *list of rules* |

- in the **environment model**, the resources identified in the analysis phase (together with the corresponding policies) are mapped onto *infrastructure* classes at the design phase, and are associated to *topological abstractions.*

We skip further details that are not relevant for this paper: interested readers can refer to [11].

### 2.2 SODA+zoom

Following the principles sketched in Section 1, we introduce here a simple layering principle, called *zooming*, to the models defined in the analysis stage, in particular with the specific aim of scaling with the complexity of tasks description. Along this line, also the models defined at the design stage become layered, given their direct relation with the layers in the analysis phase.

Layering is a general principle for complex systems: correspondingly, zooming should be applicable as widely as possible. So, apart from zooming tasks, SODA+zoom makes it possible to zoom roles, resources, interaction protocols and interaction rules. For the same reason, zooming should affect all the different phases of the engineering process. So, as just mentioned above, "zoomable" abstractions in the analysis phase are matched by design abstractions that can be zoomed as well—for instance, zooming a role in the analysis phase leads to zooming the corresponding agent in design phase, and vice versa. For the sake of simplicity, however, in the rest of this paper, we mostly focus on the applications of zooming to tasks and roles / agents, deferring the investigation on the implications of the zooming mechanism in terms of the other SODA abstractions to our next papers.

Each layer contains a description of the models (role, resource, interaction) at a given level of abstraction, here represented using the previous tables. Each layer is labelled with a number: as a convention, the uppermost layer is layer 0—which represents the most abstract view of the MAS. So, zooming a model at layer L results in a model at either layer L+1 (in-zooming) or L-1 (out-zooming).

The first idea of the zooming principle may come from the basic intuition that what can be described as a (non-trivial) individual task IT assigned to a role R at the layer L, can also be zoomed into a social task ST assigned to a group Gr at the layer L+1—possibly the simplest and most intuitive example of in-zooming in SODA+zoom. In the tabular description, this means that an entry of a Role Table at layer L can be exploded into an entry of the Group Table at layer L+1, plus all the information concerning the new group—that is, a Role Table describing the social roles of the new group, an Interaction Protocol Table describing the interaction protocols of the social roles, and an Interaction Rule Table describing the interaction rules of the group. The new group at the layer L+1 possibly leads to the introduction of a new Resource Table, with resources that are "visible" only at this level of abstraction, and are then not perceived by roles / groups of the upper layers.

Dually, as in-zooming allows for more and more detailed views over the systems, out-zooming provides engineers with a mechanism for abstraction. For example, a social task ST assigned to a group Gr at layer L could be abstracted (out-zoomed) into an individual task IT assigned to an individual role R at (more abstract) layer L-1, thus concealing the social roles of Gr. In this way, we allow engineers to provide a more concise description of MASs, where the unnecessary details that could hinder system understanding are abstracted away, and only the main entities and their mutual relationships are actually accounted for. Also, the availability of symmetric and uniform in-/out-zooming mechanisms promote middle-out approaches to the engineering of MASs.

In order to track the relationships between two subsequent layers, a *Zooming Table* is used. One column of the table contains the name of the abstraction at layer L, while the other column reports the name of the corresponding zoomed abstraction(s) at the subsequent layer L+1 (in-zooming) or L-1 (out-zooming). For instance, when in-zooming a role R at layer L to a group Gr at layer L+1, the first column will be labelled by L and contain the name R of the role in-zoomed, whereas the second column will be labelled by L+1 and contain the name of the corresponding group Gr. As natural, the same Zooming Table can be used to represent the dual process of out-zooming group Gr to role R from layer L+1 to layer L.

It is worth noting that the zooming mechanism includes a sort of *consistency rule* such that if R is the role at layer L zoomed to group Gr at layer L+1, then *(i)* the set IN(R) of the information required characterising the interaction protocol of R must be a subset of the union of all the sets describing the information required by the social roles SR of the group Gr; *(ii)* the set OUT(R) of the information provided characterising the interaction protocol of R must be a subset of the union of all the sets describing the information provided by the social roles SR of the group Gr.

The zooming mechanism provided for the model at the analysis stage has a direct consequence on the models and diagrams identified at the design stage. For each layer defined at the analysis stage, in fact, there is a corresponding layer at the design stage, matching the models described in SODA. As a result, for instance, if agent class C in the design phase maps a role R at the layer L in the analysis phase, and R is in-zoomed into the group Gr at the layer L+1, then society S mapping group Gr should also result by in-zooming C in the design phase—and vice versa for out-zooming.

## 3 The Case Study

In order to exemplify SODA+zoom, we briefly discuss a case study, concerning the management of an Internet web site of a university course through the use of a MAS. For the sake of simplicity, we here focus on the analysis stage. System requirements include the support for:

- authenticated login;
- publication of teaching material and exercises;
- download of teaching material and exercises;
- automatic exercise correction, intended as a check on *(i)* the format of the submitted material, *(ii)* the material originality, *(iii)* the actual correction, *(iv)* the test and *(v)* final assessment.

The analysis of the MAS is described in two layers.

At Layer 0 (Fig. 1) the role model is described by a Role Table with four individual roles, a Group Table concerning the *exercise* Group, and a Role Table describing the social roles of the *exercise* Group. The Resource Table (not shown for the lack of space) contains two distinct resources, Login Manager and Data Manager, the former providing login and registration services, the latter storage service for exercises and student material. The interaction model is described by the Interaction Protocols Table of the individual and social roles, and by the Interaction Rules Table for the *exercise* Group.

Then, Layer 1 (Fig. 2) specifies the description of the structures obtained by zooming the *corrector* role into a new group called *correctorGroup*, which introduces some new social roles (described in the Role Table). The Interaction Protocols Table details the protocols of the newly-introduced social roles, and the Interaction Rules Table contains the rules of the *correctorGroup* group. In this case, the Zooming Table that connects the two layers has simply one entry:

| Layer 0 | Layer 1 |
|---|---|
| role: *corrector* | group: *correctorGroup* |

The two layers at the analysis stage are mapped onto two layers at the design stage (not shown here for the lack of space). The effect of zooming applied in the analysis concerns the introduction of a Society Table with a CorrectorSociety entry at Layer 1 (which maps the *correctorGroup* at Layer 0 in the analysis stage), zooming the CorrectorAgent entry in the Agent Table defined at Layer 0 (which maps the Corrector role on the analysis side).

## 4 Conclusion and Future Work

In this paper we argued that any methodology aimed at engineering complex artificial systems should provide engineers with some layering principles, such as zooming mechanisms, allowing for expressive and consistent multi-layer descriptions of systems. Taking inspiration from the scaling mechanisms of OPM, we

Layer 0: Role Table

| Role | Task | Interaction protocol |
|---|---|---|
| *authenticate user* | login | authenticate protocol |
| *register* | insert student | insert protocol |
| *writer* | write material | write protocol |
| *reader* | read material | read protocol |

Layer 0: Group Table

| Group | Social task | Social Roles | Interaction rule |
|---|---|---|---|
| *exercise* | exercise management | *compiler*, *exerReader*, *developer*, *corrector* | download rule, upload rule, update profile rule |

Layer 0: Social Role Table (*exercise* group)

| Social role | Task | Interaction protocol |
|---|---|---|
| *compiler* | write the text of new exercise | compiler protocol |
| *exerReader* | download new exercise | exer-reader protocol |
| *developer* | upload the developed exercise | developer protocol |
| *controller* | control the state of the exercise | controller protocol |
| *corrector* | correct and assess the exercise | corrector protocol |

Layer 0: Interaction Protocols Table

| Interaction protocol | Information required | Information provided |
|---|---|---|
| authenticate protocol | access permissions | username and password |
| insert protocol | username and password | student's profile |
| write protocol | | text of material |
| read protocol | specific material | |
| compiler protocol | | text of new exercise |
| exer-reader protocol | specific exercise | |
| developer protocol | | developed exercise |
| controller protocol | state of the exercise | |
| corrector protocol | exercise | assessment of exercise |
| ... | ... | ... |

Layer 0: Interaction Rules Table

| Interaction rule | Rule description |
|---|---|
| download rule | download enabled only if at least one exercise is present |
| upload rule | it should not be possible to deliver an exercise twice |
| update profile rule | a student's profile may be updated only when the exercise is in state "assessmentOK" |

**Fig. 1.** Tables at the Layer 0, in top-down order: the Role Table containing individual roles, the Group Table with the *exercise* Group, the Role Table with the social roles of the *exercise* Group, the Interaction Protocols Table (here describing roles only) and the Interaction Rules Table

Layer 1: Group Table

| Group | Social task | Interaction rule |
|---|---|---|
| *correctorGroup* | correct and evaluate the exercise | format rule, originality rule correct rule tester rule evaluated rule |

Layer 1: Social Role Table (*correctorGroup* group)

| Social role | Task | Interaction Protocol |
|---|---|---|
| *formatChecker* | check the format of delivered exercise | format protocol |
| *originalityChecker* | check that the students did not copy the exercise | originality protocol |
| *correctChecker* | correcting the delivered exercise | correct protocol |
| *tester* | testing the delivered exercise | tester protocol |
| *evaluator* | exercise assessment | evaluated protocol |

Layer 1: Interaction Protocols Table

| Interaction protocol | Information required | Information provided |
|---|---|---|
| format protocol | delivered exercise | "formatOk" or nothing |
| originality protocol | delivered exercise and "formatOk" | "originalityOk" or nothing |
| correct protocol | delivered exercise and "originalityOk" | "correctOk" or nothing |
| tester protocol | delivered exercise and "correctionOk" | "testOk" or nothing |
| evaluated protocol | delivered exercise and "testOk" | "assessmentOk" or nothing |

Layer 1: Interaction Rules Table

| Interaction rule | Rule description |
|---|---|
| format rule | format check possible only if at least one exercise was delivered |
| originality rule | originality check possible only if an exercise is in state "formatOk" |
| correct rule | correction possible if at least an exercise is in state "originalityOk" |
| tester rule | test possible only if at least one exercise is in state "correctOk" |
| evaluated rule | assessment possible only if at least one exercise is in state "testOk" |

**Fig. 2.** Tables at Layer 1, in top-down order: the Group Table with the *correctorGroup* corresponding to the *corrector* role in Layer 0, the Role Table with the social roles of the *correctorGroup*, the Interaction Protocols Table with the protocols of the social roles, and the Interaction Rules Table with the rules of the *correctorGroup*

showed how an AOSE methodology like SODA can be enhanced with a simple yet expressive zooming mechanism, and put it to the test by discussing a case study.

In the literature, other object-oriented methodologies are defined that support some sort of layering: among these, the Booch method [13], EROOS [14] and OSA [15]. Both Booch method and EROOS define iterative processes: phases are often repeated, each time focusing on a more detailed level of abstraction. While commonalities and differences with OPM were already stressed in Subsection 1.3, OSA is somehow similar to SODA+zoom in the uniform, bidirectional application of its zooming mechanism, as "... High-Level Object Classes have exploded and imploded views. An exploded view shows what a High-Level Object Class contains, while the imploded view hides its contents ...". However, how OSA mechanism could provide for recursion (to allow for an unlimited number of abstraction layers), and how it could be generalised to be applicable to anything else than Object Classes is frankly unclear from the available literature. Two other approaches that may present some similarities with SODA+zoom are CRC cards [16] and Use cases [9]. CRC cards may look similar in that their representation recalls SODA's table-based representation, and for the attribution of tasks and responsibilities to roles. Use cases focus on user interaction with the system, while SODA aim to capturing interaction in its most general acceptation.

Apart from testing our extended methodology in the large, future work will be mostly devoted to understanding the full implications of zooming in terms of the fundamental agent-oriented abstractions. In particular, we plan to focus on artefacts for MAS, and try to understand how features like linkability and distribution can promote the use of zooming in the engineering of a MAS environment.

## References


1. Omicini, A., Zambonelli, F.: MAS as complex systems: A view on the role of declarative approaches. In Leite, J.A., Omicini, A., Sterling, L., Torroni, P., eds.: Declarative Agent Languages and Technologies. Volume 2990 of LNAI. Springer-Verlag (2004) 1–17 1st International Workshop (DALT 2003), Melbourne, Australia, 15 July 2003. Revised Selected and Invited Papers.
2. Grene, M.J.: Hierarchies in biology. American Scientist **75** (1987) 504–510
3. Wooldridge, M., Jennings, N.R., Kinny, D.: The GAIA methodology for agent-oriented analysis and design. Autonomous Agents and Multi-Agent Systems **3** (2000) 285–312
4. Wood, M.F., DeLoach, S.A.: An overview of the Multiagent Systems Engineering methodology. In Ciancarini, P., Wooldridge, M.J., eds.: Agent-Oriented Software Engineering. LNCS, Springer (2001) 207–221 1st International Workshop (AOSE 2000), Limerick, Ireland, 10 giugno 2000. Revised Papers.
5. Bresciani, P., Giorgini, P., Giunchiglia, F., Mylopoulos, J., Perini, A.: Tropos: An agent-oriented software development methodology. Autonomous Agents and Multi-Agent Systems **8** (2004) 203–236
6. Caire, G., Coulier, W., Garijo, F.J., Gomez, J., Pavòn, J., Leal, F., Chainho, P., Kearney, P.E., Stark, J., Evans, R., Massonet, P.: Agent oriented analysis using Message/UML. In Wooldridge, M.J., Weiss, G., Ciancarini, P., eds.: Agent-Oriented Software Engineering II. Volume 2222 of LNCS., Springer (2002) 119–135 2nd International Workshop (AOSE 2001), Montreal, Canada, 29 May 2001. Revised Papers and Invited Contributions.
7. Padgham, L., Winikof, M.: Prometheus: A methodology for developing intelligent agents. In Giunchiglia, F., Odell, J., Weiss, G., eds.: Agent-Oriented Software Engineering III. Volume 2585 of LNCS. Springer (2003) 174–185 3rd International Workshop (AOSE 2002), Bologna, Italy, 15 luglio 2002. Revised Papers and Invited Contributions.
8. Dori, D.: Object-Process Methodology: A Holostic System Paradigm. Springer (2002)

9. UML: Home page. (`http://www.uml.org/`)
10. Sturm, A., Dori, D., Shehory, O.: Single-model method for specifying multi-agent systems. In Sandholm, T., Yokoo, M., eds.: 2nd International Joint Conference on Autonomous Agents and Multiagent Systems (AAMAS 2003), New York, NY, USA, ACM Press (2003) 121–128
11. Omicini, A.: SODA: Societies and infrastructures in the analysis and design of agent-based systems. [17] 185–193
12. Ciancarini, P., Omicini, A., Zambonelli, F.: Multiagent system engineering: The coordination viewpoint. In Jennings, N.R., Lespérance, Y., eds.: Intelligent Agents VI. Agent Theories, Architectures, and Languages. Volume 1757 of LNAI. Springer (2000) 250–259 6th International Workshop (ATAL'99), Orlando, FL, USA, 15–17 July 1999. Proceedings.
13. Hamilton, J.A., Pooch, U.W.: A survey of object-oriented methodologies. In Engle, Jr., C.B., ed.: TRI-Ada '95: Ada's role in global markets: solutions for a changing complex world, New York, NY, USA, ACM Press (1995) 226–234
14. EROOS: Home page. (`http://www.cs.kuleuven.ac.be/cwis/research/som/EROOS/`)
15. OSA: Home page. (`http://osm7.cs.byu.edu/OSA/tutorial.html`)
16. Beck, K., Cunningham, W.: A laboratory for teaching object-oriented thinking. SIGPLAN Notices **24** (1989) 1–6 Special Issue: Proceedings of the 1989 ACM Conference on Object-Oriented Programming Systems, Languages and Applications (OOPSLA'89), New Orleans, LA, USA, 1–6 October 1989.
17. Ciancarini, P., Wooldridge, M.J., eds.: Agent-Oriented Software Engineering. Volume 1957 of LNCS. Springer (2001)

# Improving AOSE with an Enriched Modelling Framework

Richard Hill, Simon Polovina, and Martin D. Beer

Web & Multi-Agents Research Group,
Faculty of Arts, Computing, Engineering & Sciences,
Sheffield Hallam University,
Sheffield, United Kingdom
{r.hill, s.polovina, m.beer}@shu.ac.uk

**Abstract.** We describe an approach to the development of a complex social care system that defines specific steps along the path to MAS implementation. In particular we explore the use of conceptual knowledge modelling techniques by means of conceptual graphs and a transactions-based architecture for model verification during requirements gathering, together with a translation to AUML for design specification, and propose a rigorous framework to enrich and extend existing AOSE methodologies. The resulting output from Transaction Agent Modelling (TrAM) can then be developed further using the agent development toolkit of choice.

## 1 Introduction

Multi-Agent Systems (MAS) are proving a popular approach for the representation of complex computer systems. The many emerging approaches and tools for Agent Oriented Software Engineering (AOSE) assist the generation of MAS models, enabling the translation of specifications to program code, but there still remains a gap between abstract initial requirements and MAS design specification. Abstract models are assembled and are iterated into a series of design models using the Unified Modelling Language (UML) or more recently, Agent-oriented UML (AUML) [1].

To prevent significant disparities between program code and the more abstract models, AOSE methodologies such as Gaia [22], Prometheus [14], Zeus [13] and MaSE [6] have emerged and attempt to provide a unifying development framework. Except for Tropos [4] however, little work has been published that encompasses the whole cycle from initial requirements capture through to implementation of MAS. Tropos attempts to facilitate the modelling of systems at the knowledge level and highlights the difficulties encountered by MAS developers, especially since notations such as UML force the conversion of knowledge concepts into program code representations [4]. As a methodology Tropos seeks to capture and specify 'soft' and 'hard' goals during an 'Early Requirements' capture stage, in order that the Belief-Desire-Intention (BDI) architectural model [10] of agent implementation can be subsequently supported. Whilst

J.P. Müller and F. Zambonelli (Eds.): AOSE 2005, LNCS 3950, pp. 94–108, 2006.

model-checking is provided through the vehicle of Formal Tropos [8], this is an optional component and is not implicit within the MAS realisation process.

Extensions to the UML meta model such as AUML [1], have simplified the design and specification of agent characteristics such as interaction protocols, yet the process of gathering and specifying initial requirements is often limited to the discipline and experience of the MAS designer, using established notations such as UML's use case diagrams [21].

This paper therefore describes an improved MAS design framework that places a greater emphasis upon the initial requirements capture stage by supplementing the modelling process with Conceptual Graph notation [19]. Section 2 describes the proposed process before an exemplar case study in the Community Healthcare domain is explained in Section 3. A MAS model is built and checked to explicate the process in detail, illustrating the significance of the results.

## 2 Representing the Model

Our experience with AUML has led us to conclude that whilst this notation permits models to be created at differing levels of abstraction, it is still possible to produce models of a MAS that are mutually exclusive, requiring significant design experience to refine the detailed model to a point where it achieves the original goals. Some of the higher-order issues are often not explored sufficiently, leading to a system design replicating inefficiencies that existed in the original system. Whilst AUML offers use-case analysis as a high-level requirements gathering notation, we propose that a notation be used to supplement the process that permits the capture of qualitative topics, in order that the essential issues within 'the big picture' are retained and explored.

### 2.1 Conceptual Graphs

Conceptual graphs (CGs) [20] are a means by which otherwise intricate logic can be expressed in a more human readable form, whilst remaining rigorous in their formalism and suitable for exchange between computer systems. They are represented in both text (Linear Form) and graphical format (Display Form), the latter assisting human comprehension during requirements gathering and systems analysis. Using Display Form (DF), concepts and relations are represented by rectangles and ellipses respectively. Relations are linked to concepts by arrows (arcs). The consideration of concepts facilitates the lucid representation of qualitative problem domains [17].

### 2.2 Model Verification

UML provides robustness diagrams as a means of supporting the process of model checking, by allowing system analysts to examine the collaborations within a model before progressing to sequence models. However, it is possible to derive sequence models directly from use cases as there is no verification discipline enforced within the notation. We chose to represent the requirements capture process at a much more abstract level, by considering a means by which a model could incorporate verification. This would assist the whole process by:

- Enforcing a rigour upon the requirements capture stage, to elicit agents, roles and ontological terms from a conceptual perspective.
- Providing a model check much earlier in the process, supporting the design and deployment of robust MASs.

In a MAS trading environment, the goal-directed behaviour of an agent dictates that success occurs when both parties have gained from their participation in a transaction. In essence, the transaction describes a condition where both parties have exchanged resources, resulting in a 'balance'. Using the 'Event Accounting' model [9], Polovina [15] describes a robust means of modelling transactions.

All transactions comprise two Economic Events, denoted by *a and *b. The transaction is complete when both Economic Events balance, which indicates that *a always opposes *b, representing 'debits' and 'credits'. Additionally there are two related Economic Resources, *c and *d, each having independent source and destination agents.

Figure 1 illustrates how CGs have been used to represent the transaction model [15], using the Event Accounting model as a basis [9].

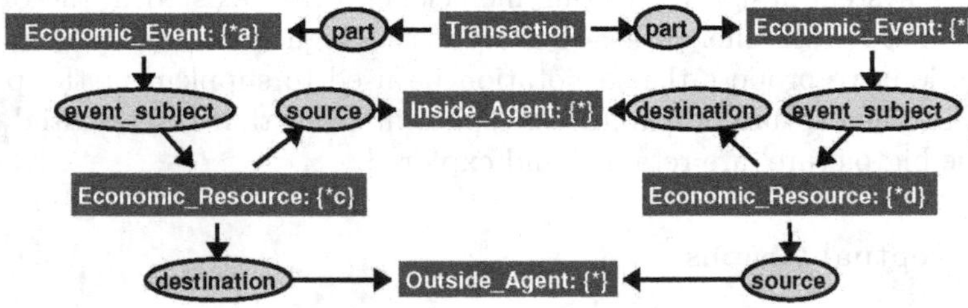


**Fig. 1.** Transaction model

After the initial requirements have been captured and modelled, further analysis is conducted using AUML to generate the required programming specifications. Therefore agent system specifications that incorporate an established, robust transaction model can be developed.

CGs and the transaction model address the difficulties identified in Section 1 in the following ways:

1. The transactions approach makes model verification implicit as any missing nodes (concepts or relations) render the model out of balance and thus unable to satisfy both sides of the transaction.
2. The richness of conceptual graphs permits qualitative issues to be challenged and documented, before refining further by drilling down for more detail.

Qualitative reasoning is an important agent capability and the use of conceptual graphs addresses this at the earliest opportunity within the design life-cycle.
3. Roles are identified using the transaction model via the 'inside' and 'outside' agents.
4. Ontological terms are derived from the transaction model during the process of capturing requirements. Again, the inherent balance check of the model ensures that terms are agreed upon before the model is complete. This process ensures that debates about slot names are conducted sooner rather than later, having the immediate benefit of specifying more of the system detail before translation to AUML.
5. CGs are similar to AUML in that there are some obvious mappings from concepts to agents. Our experiences with AUML illustrated that actors translated to agents, though further analysis work suggested that the actors could be decomposed into several agents.

A combination of the requirement for a transactions-based model, and a need to represent a deployment domain that is inherently complex, has led to the development of a MAS design framework that embodies the notion of robustness, whilst also representing the real-world scenario more faithfully, negating the need to compromise the implementation unduly.

### 2.3 Transaction Agent Modelling (TrAM)

A successful requirements capture process should incorporate the following:

- A means of modelling the concepts in an abstract way, that facilitates the consideration of qualitative issues.
- An ability to reveal more system requirements to supplement the obvious actor-to-agent mappings.
- An explicit means of model-checking before detailed analysis and design specification.
- Improved support for capturing domain terms, with less reliance upon domain experts.

This approach enforces a rigour upon the requirements capture stage that is currently lacking from a range of AOSE design methodologies such as Gaia [22] and Prometheus [14]. The process is described in [11], [12], [16], [18] and is as follows:

1. *Use Case Analysis* - Requirements are gathered initially and represented as use case models.
2. *Model Concepts* - The high level concepts are modelled and used to describe the overall scenario.
3. *Transform with Transaction Model and Generate Ontology of Types* - The high level model is transformed with the Transaction Model (TM)[19], which ensures that a balance-check rigour is imposed upon the model, plus a rudimentary hierarchy of ontological terms is generated.
4. *Model Specific Scenarios* - Specific instances of the system are modelled.

5. *Inference with Queries and Validate* - The model is tested by inferencing queries to elicit rules for the ontology and refine representation.
6. *Translate to Design Specification* - The model is transformed into a design-level specification such as AUML.

Use of the framework is now illustrated with the aid of a case study in the community healthcare domain.

## 3 A Community Healthcare Case Study

To further illustrate this approach, we shall describe the modelling of a multi-agent system for community healthcare management. Home based community care delivery is an example of a complicated, multi-agency social care system that is plagued with inefficiencies and logistical problems [2], [3]. Social care systems typically comprise a large number of autonomous functions and services, each interacting and communicating with a variety of protocols. Unfortunately the difficulties of representing such a system limit any improvements to an individual's quality of life, which is contrary to what the system is attempting to achieve. The first stage is to examine the use cases within the system.

### 3.1 Use Case Analysis

The scenario is represented at the highest level with a Conceptual Graph model derived from the use cases. Figure 2 illustrates the healthcare scenario modelled as a Conceptual Graph (CG).

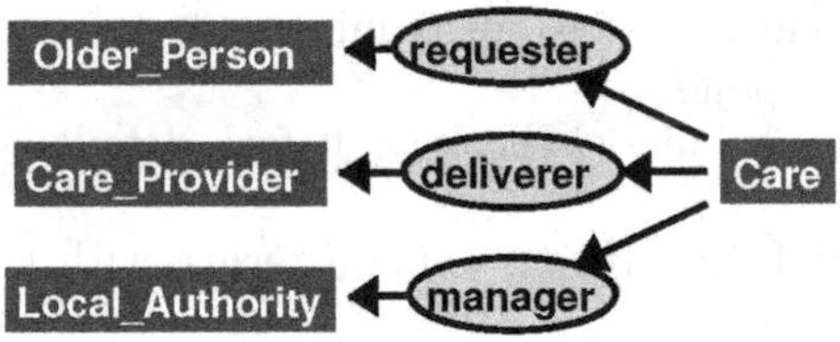


**Fig. 2.** Conceptual Graph model of healthcare scenario from use Cases

- *Older Person* - An infirm, older person that chooses to continue to live in their own home and request care support from the Local Authority.
- *Local Authority* - A localised representative body of the UK Government that manages and administrates the delivery of healthcare services.
- *Care Provider* - A private organisation that delivers care services into the Older Persons' home environment on behalf of the Local Authority.

### 3.2 Model Concepts

A illustrated in Figure 2, the healthcare scenario concepts are modelled with Conceptual Graphs (CG) [12], [16].

### 3.3 Transform with Transaction Model and Generate Ontology of Types

As described in previous work [11], [12], [16], [18] the Transaction Model (TM) is a useful means of introducing model-checking to the requirements gathering process [19]: pp 110-111. This capture of requirements at the outset ensures that the model-checking is not 'bolted-on' as an afterthought, as the models are incomplete until both sides of a transaction 'balance'. This has been shown to lucidly represent qualitative transactions such as 'quality of care received' [16]. The specialisation of the generic TM CG of Figure 1 onto the community healthcare scenario is illustrated by the CG in Figure 3. This specialisation serves two fundamental objectives:

1. The concepts identified within the care scenario are represented as a transaction thus 'economic events' and 'economic resources' are balanced;
2. Each concept is classified in terms of type, therefore a hierarchy of types, which is an important element of an ontology, is derived.

It is not clear from the outset (Figure 2) which party pays the bill for the care, or who was the 'source' of the money. The UK Welfare System has three particular scenarios:

1. The Local Authority pays for the care in full.
2. The Older Person pays for the care in full.
3. The Local Authority and the Older Person make 'part payments' that amount to 100% of the care cost.

In order to satisfy the TM we therefore derive 'Purchase_Agent' as the supertype of 'Local_Authority' and 'Older_Person'. Determining terms for the ontology is an important step during the agent realisation process. Whilst it is feasible to depend upon existing processes for the most part, the most significant contribution of this stage is the implicit 'balance check' that immediately raises the developer's awareness of the need for appropriate terminology. Figure 4 illustrates the type hierarchy deduced from Figure 3.

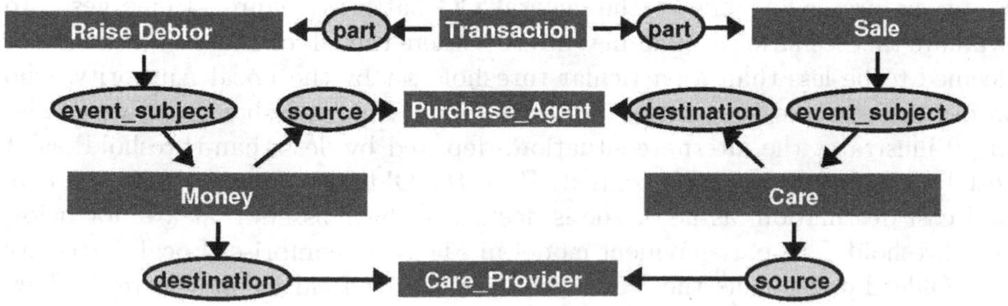


**Fig. 3.** Healthcare scenario after application of TM

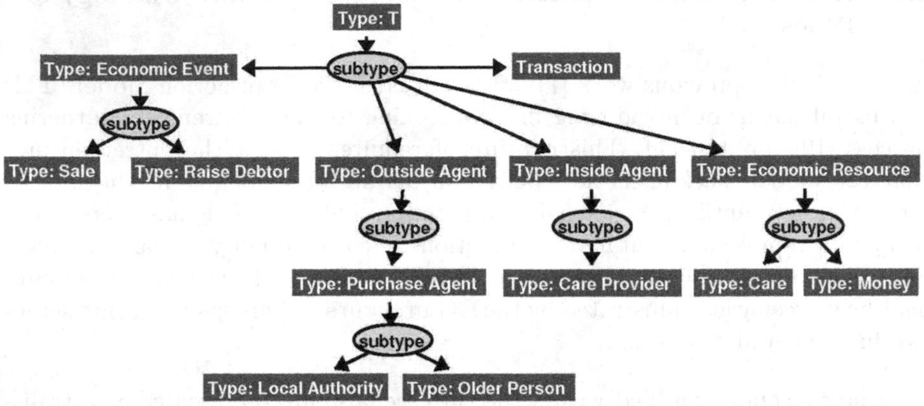


**Fig. 4.** Type hierarchy after transformation with TM

### 3.4 Model Specific Scenarios

Once the generic model has been created, it is tested with some general rules. We first explore the specific scenario whereby an Older Person has been assessed and is deemed to be eligible to receive care at zero cost. In this particular case (highlighted in Figure 5), we see that the 'source' of the money to pay for the care is the Local Authority 'Sheffield City Council (SCC)', who also manage the provision of the care. The care package is not delivered by the Local Authority however; this is sold to them by private organisations, hence the need for a 'Care Provider', in our case, 'Meals on Wheels'. Since the Local Authority incurs the cost of the care package, that is its destination. Note that each concept in this figure now has a unique reference, denoting a specific instance. Conversely, the scenario exists where the Older Person is deemed to have sufficient monetary assets not to warrant a free package of care (Figure 6), where it can also be seen that the care package is still managed by the Local Authority.

### 3.5 Inference with Queries and Validate

From the preceeding figures the general CG pattern (Figure 7) emerges. To evaluate this scenario we examine the case where the Older Person's 'Assets' are deemed to be less than a particular threshold set by the Local Authority, who would therefore be the destination of the care. Figure 8 shows this case. Figure 9 illustrates the alternate situation, depicted by 'less-than-threshold' asset test being set in a negative context. Here the Older Person would be the care and cost destination, as he or she is deemed to have assets that are not below the threshold. The part-payment model in Figure 10 comprises Local_Authority and Older_Person, plus the Purchase_Agent derived earlier in Figure 9. However, Figure 10 does not allow joint parties to be the Purchase_Agent. Therefore we re-iterate the model further to support Figure 11. Here the Local_Authority

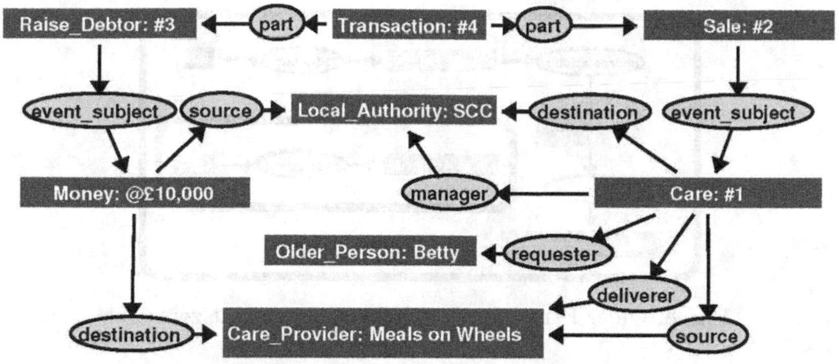


**Fig. 5.** Local Authority (LA) pays for healthcare (Assets low)

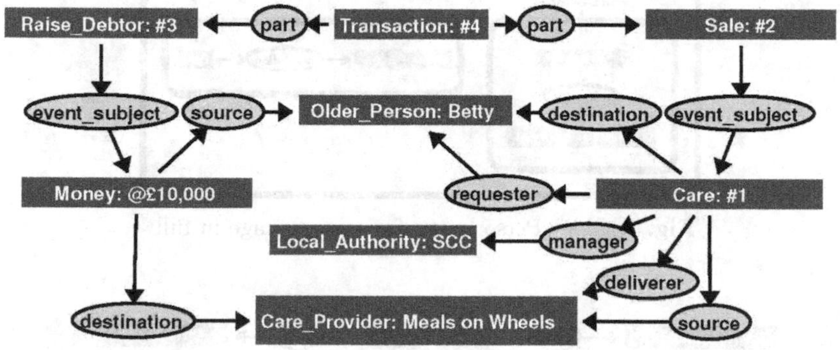


**Fig. 6.** Older Person (OP) pays for healthcare (Assets NOT low)

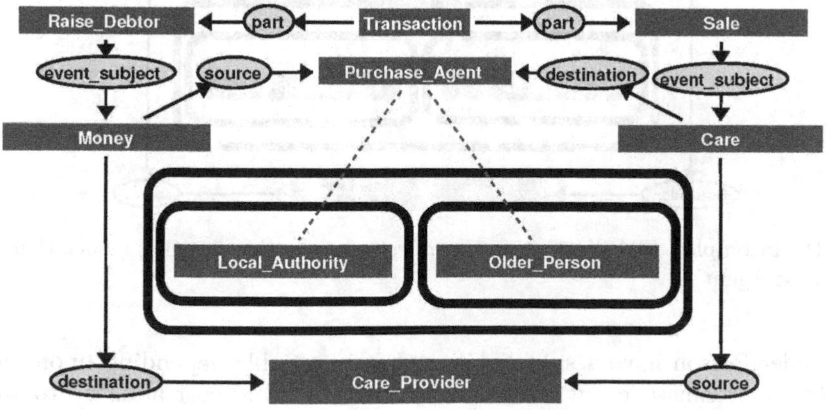


**Fig. 7.** Emergent general CG pattern for this TM

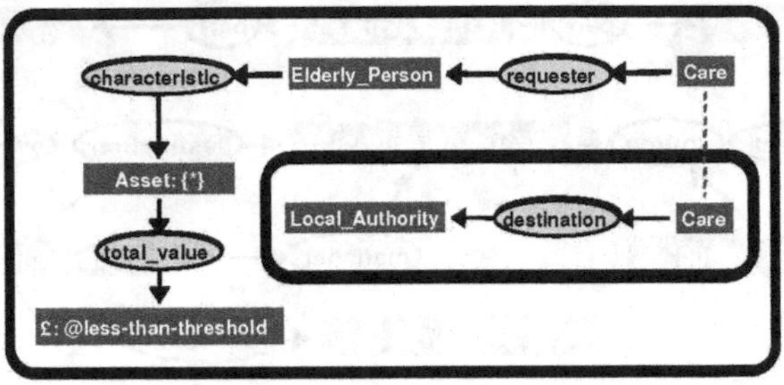


**Fig. 8.** Older Person receives package of care at zero cost

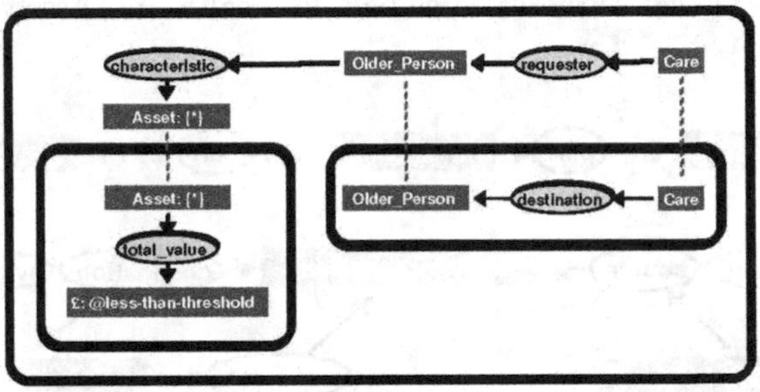


**Fig. 9.** Older Person pays for care package in full

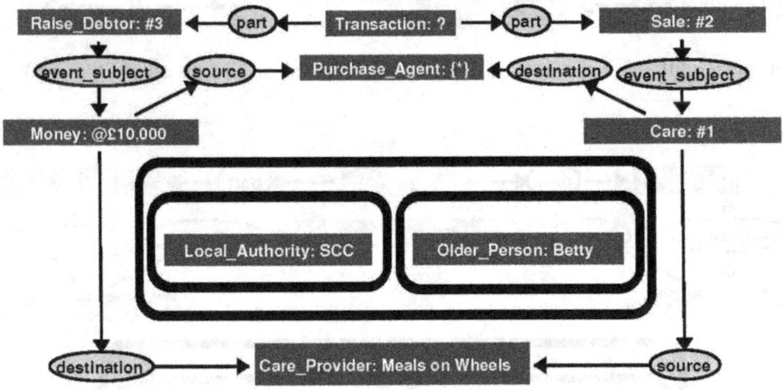


**Fig. 10.** Incomplete TM illustrating two purchasing parties awaiting association with 'Purchase Agent'

and Older_Person have a split liability that is variable depending upon an individual's circumstances whilst ensuring that the total cost adds up to 100%. The Older_Person and Local_Authority agents are no longer sub-types of the Purchase_Agent as originally illustrated, but are instead associated via 'liability' relations. Referring back to the hierarchy of types defined in Figure 4, we can now

**Fig. 11.** Part-payment situation with shared liabilities

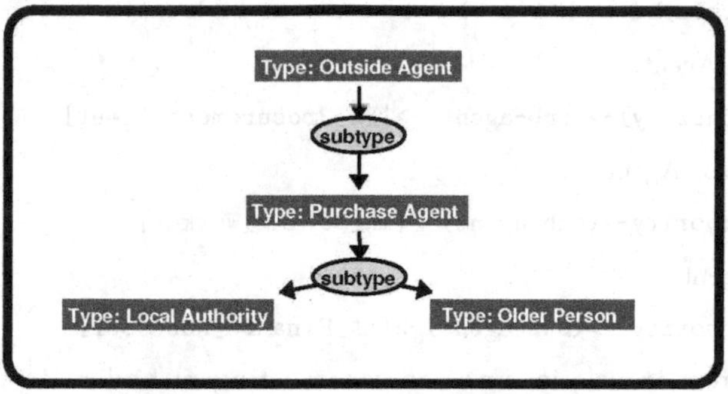


**Fig. 12.** Ontological component that is no longer valid

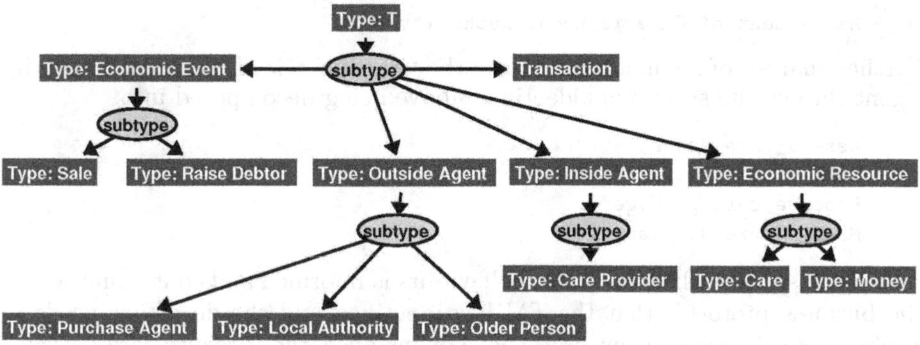


**Fig. 13.** New Ontology

create a rule to supplant the ontology for the model. Figure 12 thus depicts an ontological component that is no longer valid, hence set in a negative context (or Peirce cut [19]). Given the refinements discovered, the community care ontology is updated in Figure 13 and the TM in Figure 14 to show the liability relationship. The co-referent links are now valid thus the model can now be completed, enabling all three of the payment scenarios to be accommodated in one model.

### 3.6 Translate to Design Specification

Once the CG representations have been verified against the TM, it is then possible to perform a translation to a design specification. The 'inside' and 'outside' agents in the TM serve to provide direct mappings as follows:

- Inside Agent: Purchase_Agent, with liabilities jointly satisfied by Local_Authority (SCC) and Older_Person ('Betty')
- Outside Agent: Care_Provider ('Meals_on_Wheels')

Further iterations and graph joins (omitted for brevity) would illustrate the following additional agents (where LA represents Local Authority):

- Care Request Agent:

  `[Older_Person]`

- Purchasing Agent:

  `[Local_Authority]->(sub-agent)->[LA_Procurement_Agent]`

- Care Assessor Agent:

  `[Local_Authority->(sub-agent)->[LA_Social_Worker]`

- Finance Agent:

  `[Local_Authority]->(sub-agent)->[LA_Finance_Assessor]`

From these direct translations we can construct agent bodies, to which specific sub-tasks can be assigned. Each of the behaviours is informed by the relations specified within the TM. For instance, referring back to Figure 2 the key abstract definition is that:

```
Management of Care is Local Authority.
```

Further analysis of the models results in the 'manage' role of the Local Authority Agent through its sub-agents identified above being decomposed into:

```
Assess_care_needs;
Confirm_financial_eligibility;
Procure_care_package;
Manage_care_delivery.
```

The process of revealing the agent behaviours is informed and contextualised by the business protocols that the TM has identified and the developer needs to apply across the many agent protocols. For instance, the 'Procure_care_package' behaviour can be represented by the FIPA Iterated Contract Net protocol [7], thus devolving the task of obtaining the cheapest care package available to that protocol to which a given task may be best suited. This approach thus creates a situation whereby the method of requirements capture concentrates on what the MAS must deliver from the outset to implementation, assisting the developer in determining the extent to which the solution is influenced by the business model. Further refinement of the model with other methodologies is not precluded however, as the core transactional behaviours have now been established, verified and available for inclusion as needed.

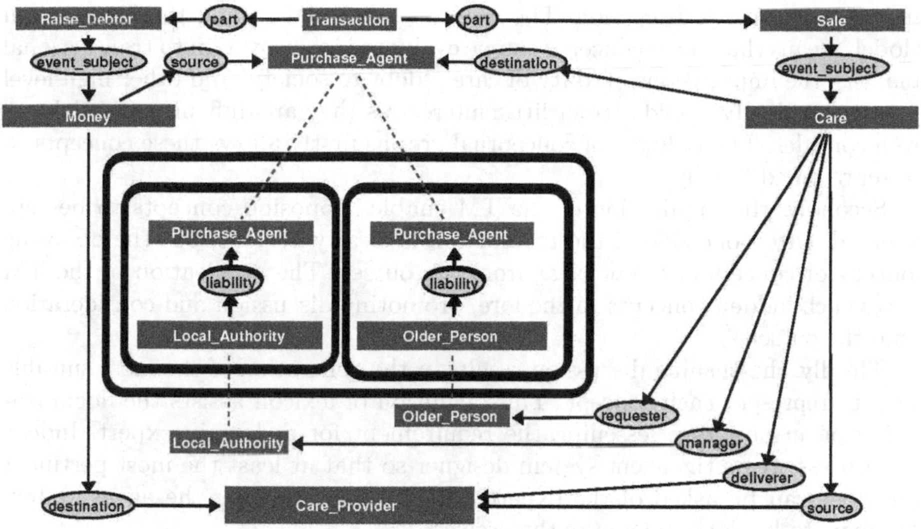


**Fig. 14.** Refined model to accommodate part-payment scenario

## 4 Conclusions

Our approach has enabled the early elicitation of domain knowledge, and subsequent ontology specification, whilst incorporating a robust transaction model from the beginning. This has allowed representations of agent-managed transactions to be assembled at a much faster rate, especially since we have greater confidence that the underlying design is based upon a solid framework. The key features of this approach are as follows:

1. CGs represent the problem in a more abstract way, and provide a foundation for modelling the knowledge exchange within a system. The abstraction is such that high-level, qualitative issues such as 'quality of health care received' are addressed, so it is feasible that the system is questioned from the point of view of concepts, rather than relying on an individual's prior experience.
2. CGs are similar to AUML in that there are some obvious mappings from concepts to agents, however there are also subtleties that CGs appear to reveal more consistently. The important point to note here is that the models are derived after considering issues at a much higher abstraction, thus resulting in a somewhat different view at micro-level.
3. The inherent balance check of the model ensures that ontological terms are agreed upon before the model is complete.
4. The transactions approach makes model verification implicit as any missing nodes (concepts or relations) renders the model out of balance and thus unable to satisfy both sides of the transaction.

The TrAM approach enriches the 'early requirements' stage of AOSE. Producing conceptual graph models enables higher-order issues to be captured, scrutinised and considered in an abstract way. This compliments any use case analysis, and promotes early discussion. The use of a particular graph, the Transaction Model, means that these concepts can be evaluated in a way akin to transactional analysis; the implications of 'duty of care', 'debt to society' and other high level concepts typically would attract little interest as they are difficult to model and even consider. The richness of conceptual graphs firstly allows these concepts to be represented lucidly.

Secondly, the application of the TM enables opposing concepts to be represented. Often one side of the transaction is clearly evident, but the opposing concept or concepts are not clear from the outset. The application of the TM forces such hidden concepts to the fore, promoting discussion and consideration from the outset.

Thirdly, the ensuing discussion results in the generation of the most suitable term to represent each concept. This definition of lexicon assists the documentation of an ontology, lessening the requirement for a domain expert. Indeed the process steers the agent system designer so that at least the most pertinent questions can be asked of the expert, rather than requiring the agent system designers to be domain experts themselves.

Finally, the ability to logically prove the conceptual graphs, combined with inferencing allows the models to be tested and validated much earlier in the agent system design process. Current methodologies such as Tropos and Prometheus go some way to address the issue of gathering requirements earlier, but the method of attributing 'hard' and 'soft' goals is still abitrary, requiring a degree of domain expertise. TrAM addresses this by allowing more abstract models to be constructed initially; detail can always be added by further iterations, together with the application of a TM pattern that forces analysis of opposing components of the transaction. In summary we have described a framework for modelling MASs that incorporates model checking to support the development of robust systems. The use of CGs and the notion of transactions enriches the requirements capture stage and serves as a precursor to existing AOSE methodologies that require a design representation such as AUML as an input. We feel that this would be a suitable 'bolt-on' discipline for the myriad of agent-oriented software engineering methodologies that lack the necessary detail for successful MAS requirements capture.

## 5 Further Work

We have now established a route from abstract requirements gathering through to design specification that incorporates two significant events:

1. The high-level model is represented as CGs and then verified using a prcoess of de-iteration and double negation upon the transactional model.
2. The resulting model is then translated into an AUML design specification.

Both of these processes have been conducted manually so far, and we are now exploring the automation of inferencing for the model verification stage, and translation from Conceptual Graph Interchange Format (CGIF) into AUML.

## Acknowledgements

This project is in receipt of an AgentCities Deployment Grant from the European Union AgentCities.rtd Project (IST-2000-28385).

## References

1. Bauer, B., Müller, J. P., and Odell, J., (2000), 'Agent UML: A Formalism for Specifying Multi-agent Software Systems', in Agent-Oriented Software Engineering, vol. 1957, Ciancarini, P. and Wooldridge, M. J., Eds. Springer-Verlag, 2000, pp. 91-104.
2. Beer, M. D., Bench-Capon, T. J. M. and Sixsmith, A., (1999) 'Some Issues in Managing Dialogues between Information Agents', In Proceedings of Database and Expert Systems Applications '99, Lecture Notes in Computer Science 1677, Springer, Berlin, 1999, pp. 521-530.
3. Beer, M. D, Huang, W., and Sixsmith, A. (2002), 'Using Agents to Build a Practical Implementation of the INCA (Intelligent Community Alarm) System', in L. C. Jain, Z. Chen, & N. Ichalkaranje, 'Intelligent Agents & their Applications', Springer, pp320-345.
4. Bresciani, P., Giorgini, P., Giunchiglia, F., Mylopoulos, J., and Perini, A., (2004) 'TROPOS: An Agent-Oriented Software Development Methodology', Journal of Autonomous Agents and Multi-Agent Systems, vol. 8, pp. 203-236, 2004.
5. Dau F., Lecture Notes in Computer Science 2892: 'The Logic System of Concept Graphs with Negation: And Its Relationship to Predicate Logic', Heidelberg: Springer-Verlag, 2003
6. DeLoach, S., (1999) 'Multi-Agent Systems Engineering: A Methodology and Language for Designing Agent Systems', citeseer.ist.psu.edu/deloach99multiagent.html
7. Foundation for Intelligent Physical Agents, 'FIPA Iterated Contract Net Interaction Protocol Specification'. Accessed: 2005, 11/21. 2000. http://www.fipa.org/specs/fipa00030/PC00030D.html
8. Fuxman, A., Kazhamiakin, R., Pistore, M., and Roveri, M., (2003) 'Formal Tropos: language and semantics (Version 1.0)'. Accessed: 2005, 4th November. 2003. http://www.dit.unitn.it/ ft/papers/ftsem03.pdf
9. Geerts, G., and McCarthy, W., 'Database Accounting Systems', in Information Technology Perspectives in Accounting: and Integrated Approach, Eds. B. Williams and B. J. Sproul, Chapman and Hall Publishers, 1991, pp. 159-183.
10. Georgeff, M. P., Pell, B., Pollack, M. E., Tambe, M., and Wooldridge, M., (1999) 'The Belief-Desire-Intention Model of Agency', in ATAL '98: Proceedings of the 5th International Workshop on Intelligent Agents V, Agent Theories, Architectures, and Languages, 1999, pp. 1-10.
11. Hill, R., Polovina, S., Beer, M. D., (2004) 'Towards a Deployment Framework for Agent-Managed Community Healthcare Transactions', The Second Workshop on Agents Applied in Health Care, 23-24 Aug 2004, Proceedings of the 16th European Conference on Artificial Intelligence (ECAI 2004), Valencia, Spain, IOS Press, 13-21.
12. Hill, R., Polovina, S., Beer, M. D., (2005) 'From concepts to agents: towards a framework for multi-agent system modelling', AAMAS '05: Proceedings of the fourth international joint conference on Autonomous agents and multiagent systems, AAMAS '05, Utrecht, The Netherlands, ACM Press, pp1155-1156.
13. Nwana, H., Ndumu, D., Lee, L., and Collis, J., (1999) 'ZEUS: A Tool-Kit for Building Distributed Multi-Agent Systems', *Applied Artifical Intelligence Journal*, vol. 13, no. 1 pp129-186.

14. Padgham, L., Winikoff, M., (2002) 'Prometheus: A Methodology for Developing Intelligent Agents', In: Proceedings of the Third International Workshop on Agent-Oriented Software Engineering, at AAMAS 2002.
15. Polovina, S., 'The Suitability of Conceptual Graphs in Strategic Management Accountancy (PhD Thesis)', 1993, Available at http://www.polovina.me.uk/phd
16. Polovina, S., Hill, R., Crowther, P., Beer, M. D., (2004) 'Multi-Agent Community Design in the Real, Transactional World: A Community Care Exemplar', Conceptual Structures at Work: Contributions to ICCS 2004 (12th International Conference on Conceptual Structures), Pfeiffer, H., Wolff, K. E., Delugach, H. S., (Eds.), Shaker Verlag (ISBN 3-8322-2950-7, ISSN 0945-0807), 69-82.
17. Polovina, S. and Heaton, J., (1992), 'An Introduction to Conceptual Graphs', AI Expert, 7(5), May, 36-43.
18. Polovina, S., Hill, R., (2005), 'Enhancing the Initial Requirements Capture of Multi-Agent Systems through Conceptual Graphs', Proceedings of 13th International Conference on Conceptual Structures (ICCS '05): Conceptual Structures: Common Semantics for Sharing Knowledge, July 18-22, 2005, Kassel, Germany, Springer, 439-452.
19. Sowa, J. F., 'Knowledge Representation: Logical, Philosophical and Computational Foundations', Brooks-Cole, 2000.
20. Sowa, J. F., 'Conceptual Structures: Information Processing in Mind and Machine', Addison-Wesley, 1984.
21. OMG, 'Unified Modeling Language Resource Page', vol. 2004, http://www.uml.org/
22. Wooldridge, M., Jennings, N., Kinny, D.(2000), 'The Gaia Methodology for Agent-Oriented Analysis and Design', In: Autonomous Agents and Multi-Agent Systems 3, pp. 285-312.

# Dealing with Adaptive Multi-agent Organizations in the Gaia Methodology

Luca Cernuzzi[1,2] and Franco Zambonelli[1]

[1] Università di Modena e Reggio Emilia, DISMI,
Via Allegri 13, Reggio Emilia, Italia
{franco.zambonelli, cernuzzi.luca}@unimore.it
[2] Universidad Católica "Nuestra Señora de la Asunción",
DEI Campus Universitario, Asunción, Paraguay

**Abstract.** Changes and adaptations are always necessary after the deployment of a multiagent system (MAS), as well as of any other type of software systems. Some of these changes may be simply perfective and have local impact only. However, adaptive changes to meet changed situations in the operational environment of the MAS may have global impact on the overall design. In this paper, we analyze the issue of continuous design change/adaptation in a MAS organization, and the specific problem of how to properly model/design a MAS so as to make it ready to adaptation. Following, the paper focuses on the Gaia methodology and analyzes – also with the help of an illustrative example – its suitability in supporting and facilitating adaptive changes in MASs organizations, and its advantages and limitations with this regard over a number of different agent-oriented methodologies.

**Keywords:** Agent Oriented Methodologies, Design for Change, Adaptive Organizations, Methodologies Evaluation.

## 1 Introduction and Motivation

A great deal of efforts in the Agent-oriented Software Engineering (AOSE) area focuses on the definition of methodologies to guide the process of engineering complex software systems based on the multiagent systems (MAS) paradigm [6], [20]. AOSE methodologies, as they have been proposed so far, mainly try to suggest a clean and disciplined approach to analyze, design and develop MASs, using specific methods and techniques.

However, very few of the AOSE methodologies proposed so far explicitly take into account the maintenance phase of the MAS, that is, all those engineering work that has to be performed on the MAS after its deployment. In general, maintenance of a software system is required for several reasons. Corrective maintenance aims at fixing those errors that unavoidably will show up after the deployment of the system itself, independently on how extensively it was tested. Perfective maintenance is required to improve the functionalities and the performances of the system, and also to better fulfill the original requirements. Adaptive maintenance aims at tuning the software systems accordingly to changes in either the requirements or in the environment

J.P. Müller and F. Zambonelli (Eds.): AOSE 2005, LNCS 3950, pp. 109 – 123, 2006.

(operational or social) in which the system operates. While corrective and perfective maintenance typically have local impact only (i.e., in the case of MASs, on the internal structure of agents and on the structure of some communication protocols), adaptive maintenance may have global impact on the overall design of systems (i.e., on the overall architecture/organization of MASs).

Information systems studies outline that the phase of maintenance costs almost the 60% [1], [10] of the entire cost of systems over their lifecycle. Although there are no specific studies of this kind already available for MASs, it is reasonable to assume that MASs too will experience a similar trend, and possibly even more exacerbated as far as adaptive maintenance is concerned. While agents and MASs are often claimed as a promising approach to deal with the dynamism of modern scenarios, i.e., to deal with dynamic and open interactions and to interact in a dynamic environment, current AOSE methodologies typically promote the definition of static architecture design for the overall organization of a MAS (i.e., for the roles to be played by the agents of a system and for the relations among these roles), and are not conceived to be ready for changes in the MAS organization after its deployment.

From now to the moment in which we will be able to design and deploy – in a trustworthy and reliable way – fully autonomous and self-adaptive software systems, capable of re-organizing themselves to answer to changed conditions without any human intervention, we will probably have to wait several years. In the meantime, we may nevertheless need to better understand which the right directions to achieve this are, and we must provide engineers with suitable conceptual and practical tools to facilitate the adaptive maintenance of MASs. In other words, an AOSE methodology should not only facilitate the effective development of a MAS answering to specific requirements, but should also accompany designers through the entire software lifecycle and should facilitate developers work whenever adaptive software maintenance requires structural changes in the overall organization of a MAS.

In this paper, we focus on the design for change issue and on the issue of continuous design change/adaptation. We analyze, also with the help of a simple yet representative application example, how a MAS may require frequent and unexpected re-structuring of its global organization to adapt to changed situations. In particular, the aim of the analysis is also to outline the characteristics that an AOSE methodologies should exhibit to support the modeling and the development of adaptive MASs. The presence of such characteristics can notably reduce maintenance costs and, in the future, can facilitate the integration of self-adaptive features in MASs.

To ground the discussion, a specific attention is posed on the Gaia methodology [19], which exhibits some of the specific characteristics that make it somewhat more suitable than other methodologies to deal with adaptive changes. In particular, we show that Gaia facilitates engineers to face the likely changes that will appear in a MAS after its deployment, limiting the efforts required to re-model the evolving systems.

The following of this paper is organized as follows. Section 2 explores the need for adaptive MAS organization. Section 3 discusses the aspects of the Gaia methodology that can promote a design for change perspective. Section 4 compares with other AOSE methodologies. Section 5 concludes.

## 2 On the Need for Adaptive MAS

MASs, as well as the great majority of modern software systems, are likely to be subject to a large number of adaptive changes during their life-cycle, some of which may affect the very structure of the system.

In traditional software engineering discipline, special efforts have been devoted to the *design for change* issue, trying to anticipate the likely changes and adaptations that are frequently required to almost all software products after their deployments. However, those efforts have normally pointed out the anticipation of predictable changes that do not mainly influence the global design of the system under construction. Thus, it is yet an open issue how to undertake continuous design change/adaptation during the whole lifecycle of a system that may imply re-structuring its global organization. And such an issue is expected to be particularly critical for MASs, which are often conceived to operate in very dynamic operational environments.

Following in this section, we present the conference management system example (paradigmatic of a larger class of applications), illustrating how unexpected changes in the real-world organization forces important changes in the MAS organization, and discusses the requirements for an AOSE methodology to support adaptive MASs and the design-for-change perspective.

### 2.1 The Conference Management System Example

Let us consider an agent-based system for supporting the process of producing the technical program for an international conference. We assume the readers of this paper are mostly knowledgeable with this, but let us summarize in any case the key characteristics of this process.

The process may be subdivided into three phases:

- The *submission phase*: the program committee chair (PC Chair) and the organizer distribute the call for papers. The authors submit their papers. The papers are classified (according to specific criteria), a submission number is assigned to each paper and the authors are notified about that.
- The *review phase*: the PC Chair distributes the papers among the PC Members which are in charge of providing reviews for those papers. The PC Chair collects back reviews, decides upon the acceptance/rejection of papers, and eventually notifies authors of the decision. Considering all the accepted papers, the PC Chair prepares the conference program.
- The *publishing phase*: the authors of the accepted papers have to produce a revised version of their papers. The publisher has to collect these final versions and compose the proceedings.

The process clearly involves three loosely interacting phases, each involving different actors, and naturally leads to conceiving one MAS for supporting the activities of each phases. There, personal agents will be naturally associated to the actors involved in the process (authors, PC Chair, PC Members, reviewers) to support their work. It is also natural that the roles played by each agent reflect the ones played by the associated actor in the conference organization. This may require agents to interact both directly with each other (according to patterns that will reflect the patterns of interactions in the real-world organizations), and indirectly (via exchanges of papers and review forms).

This said, the process of designing a MAS to support the organization of a conference may at appear very simple and intuitive, as critical design choices (the types and roles of agents involved, the structure of the organizations and of inter-agent interactions) naturally derive from the structure of the real-world organization.

## 2.2 Unexpected Changes: A Real-World Example

What the above discussion of the conference management example misses in identifying is that, for a conference, the overall structure of the real-world organization may dramatically vary from year to year. First, since the organizers involved change from year to year, some changes in the organization may be directly induced by them based on personal attitudes and opinions. Second, factor such as the hotness of the conference topics and the effectiveness of the conference advertising may dramatically affect the number of submitted papers. Thus, the need of changing the structure of the management process may be forced by the need of keeping it manageable. This is particularly true for the reviewing phase, which involves a large number of actors, with different duties and variously interacting with each other.

To mention a real-world example, we can consider the biyearly ISAS/SCI conference series (ISAS Multiconference on Systemics Cybernetics and Informatics). ISAS/SCI started as a single mono-track conference in 1995 with 55 presented papers (the number of submitted papers being directly proportional to this). Then, the conference grew up very fast, to become a huge multi-conference and, in 2001, to reach a number of 1859 presented papers. As it can be seen from Table 1, such a pronounced growth has not occurred on a large time, and a dramatic growing is exhibited for any two consecutive editions. Personal acquaintances of the first author have confirmed that, although a continuous growth was indeed expected, no one in the organization would have expected such a dramatic trend of growth.

**Table 1.** The Size of the ISAS/SCI Conference

| YEAR | NUMBER OF PRESENTED PAPERS |
|---|---|
| 1995 | 55 |
| 1997 | 248 |
| 1999 | 754 |
| 2001 | 1859 |

Accordingly, to meet the increasing number of papers to deal with in the review process (as light as this can be, there is indeed some reviewing for papers in the conference), the ISAS/SCI conference had always to underwent serious and unexpected re-thinking of its organization. In 1995 it relied solely on a PC Chair and a limited group of PC Members for the review process, whose outcome were a single proceedings volume. In contrast, in 2001, there were a General PC Chair, Vice-Chairs for a large number of special-tracks (mini-conferences), each with their own PC, and hosting within a number of special-sessions, and were been published a total of 9 proceedings volumes.

In addition to the above ones, adopted by ISAS/SCI, a number of additional organizational structures can be though (and are often applied) for different conferences' sizes and characteristics. The PC Chair can partition papers among PC members which have in turn to recruit the necessary number of reviewers for their papers, or each PC member can be in charge of collecting a single review for papers. Reviewers can be asked to bid for papers, in a sort of "paper market" or can be dictated which papers to review. All of which can be organized into multi-level hierarchies on need.

What we think is most interesting in the example of conference management, is that information about what the size of the conference will be (and thus about what the most proper organizational structure to adopt is) is generally available only a few days before the review process has to begin, that is when submitted papers gets incoming. This clearly forces a dramatically fast re-structuring in the organization (unless one wants to stick to an unsuitable organizational structure) and, in the case the process is supported by a MAS, requires an extremely fast adaptation of the MAS structure. These problems, to different extents, occur in all those software systems devoted to support processes in an increasingly dynamic economy.

### 2.3 Requirements for Adaptive MAS and Design-for-Change

In very general terms, adaptation is the result of a bi-directional relationship between a system (e.g., a MAS organization) and the environment in which it situates (e.g., the real-world organization and its operational environment): modifications in the real-world organization or in the operational environment may imply modifications in the topological structure of MAS organization and in the control regime of its interactions.

Different studies exist that analyze the organizational aspects of MASs and their possible structures [7], some of which paying specific attention to adaptive MASs structures [13], [9]. However, a few of these studies constructively propose software engineering solutions to deal with continuously adapting MASs organizations.

Recently, several research efforts are being devoted to promote self-organization in complex software systems and, specifically, self-adaptive capabilities for multiagent systems [21]. These studies explore the possibility for complex MASs to either exploit adaptive self-organization phenomena or to promote self-inspect and self-reorganization in order to preserve specific functional and non-functional characteristics despite contingencies in the operational environment. A number of algorithms and tools are becoming available, but the time for deployment of self-adaptive software systems and MASs is far to come.

In any case, it is worth outlining that, even if effective mechanisms of self-adaptation were available, the problem of having a MAS properly capture not only internal needs of efficiency but also external needs of the stakeholders (e.g., the conference organizers in our example) is open. How can one MAS inspect and get feedbacks from the real-world organization to which it belongs to adapt accordingly? While waiting for self-adaptive MASs to come, an AOSE methodology should definitely promote a design-for-change perspective, enabling designer and developers to rapidly re-work the structure of a MAS to have it suit novel needs.

To promote such a design-for-change perspective we need *modularity* and *separation of concerns*. In particular, when dealing with both the design and development of a MAS, one should clearly separate those aspects of the system that are intrinsic to the definition of the problem itself from those that, instead, derives from contingent choices based on the actual characteristics of the operational environment and/or the real-world organization. For example, in the conference management example, this means separating those functionalities and inter-dependencies intrinsic in a process of reviewing (e.g. functionalities of PC Chair and of reviewers, and protocols for sending back review forms) from those that instead derives form a specific contingent choice (e.g., separating the role of PC Member from that of reviewer, and relying on paper bidding for assigning reviews). In that way, whenever unexpected changes occur, designers and developers are facilitated in identifying where to focus to restructure the MAS as needed without impacting on the whole system.

## 3 Modeling Adaptive MASs with Gaia

As far as we know, none of the currently available AOSE methodologies for MASs development explicitly accounts for a design-for-change perspective. Nevertheless, some of them already exhibit specific aspects which can at least promote a design for change. One of these, focus of this section, is the Gaia methodology [19].

### 3.1 Gaia in a Nutshell

Gaia focuses on the use of organizational abstractions to drive the analysis and design of MASs. Gaia models both the macro (social) aspect and the micro (agent internals) aspect of a MAS, and devotes a specific effort to model the organizational structure and the organizational rules that govern the global behavior of the agents in the organization. What makes Gaia somewhat suitable for a design-for-change perspective is its clear separation between the analysis and the architectural design phases.

The goal of the analysis phase in Gaia, covering the requirements in term of functions and activities, is to firstly identify which loosely couple sub-organizations possibly compose the whole systems and then, for each of these, produce four basic abstract models: *(i)* the environmental model, to capture the characteristics of the MAS operational environment; *(ii)* a preliminary roles model, to capture the key task-oriented activities to be played in the MAS; *(iii)* a preliminary interactions model, to capture basic inter-dependencies between roles; and *(iv)* a set of organizational rules, expressing global constraints/directives that must underlie the MAS functioning.

The above analysis models are used as input to the architectural design phase. In particular, the architectural design phase is in charge of defining the most proper organizational structure for the MAS, i.e., the topology of interactions in the MAS and the control regime of these interactions, which most effectively enables to fulfill the MAS goals. The definition of the organizational structure has to account for a variety of factors, including the need of somewhat reflecting the structure of the real-world organization in the MAS structure, the characteristics of the environment and of the patterns of access to it, the need of simplifying the enactment of the organizational rules, the need to respect any identified non-functional requirement, as well as the obvious need to keep the design as simple as possible. Once the most appropriate organizational structure is defined, the roles and interactions models identified in the analysis phase (which were preliminary, in that they were not situated in any actual organizational structure) can be finalized, to account for all newly identified interactions and possibly for newly identified roles.

Past the architectural design phase, the detailed design involves identifying: *(i)* an agent model, i.e., the set of agent classes in the MAS, implementing the identified roles, and the specific instances of these classes; and *(ii)* a services model, expressing services and interaction protocols to be provided within agent classes. The result of the design phase is assumed to be something that could be implemented in a technology neutral way.

### 3.2 Factors Facilitating Adaptivity in Gaia

As from the short description above, Gaia prescribes to clearly separate the analysis phase, in which the basic characteristics of the system-to-be are captured and organized, from the architectural design phase, where all the results of the analysis are put at work to identify the most suitable organizational structure. The above clear separation, together with the specific structuring of the analysis phase and of its models, are important factors to facilitate adaptive changes, according to what specified in Subsection 2.3.

The result of the analysis phase in Gaia is very modular, clearly separating basic characteristics/functionalities of the systems, (i.e., the preliminary roles and interactions models) from characteristics of the operational environment (i.e., the environmental model) and from any additional constraints that the MAS will have to respect (i.e., the organizational rules). This implies that whenever contingencies calls for a re-thinking of some of the MAS specifications, the clear separation of concerns of the Gaia analysis models is likely to avoid global re-thinking of the whole analysis and, depending on the types of contingencies, promote a local tuning of a limited set of models. For instance, some functional changes in "how" a sub-task is expected to be achieved will impact on the preliminary role model only; some changes in the global constraints the MAS has to respect implies changes in the organizational rules only.

The prescription to delay the identification of the organizational structure to the architectural design phase is also of paramount importance. In fact, more than the outcome of the analysis, it is the choice of a specific organizational structure that is more likely to be affected by contingencies. Besides properly structuring the functional requirements of the analysis phase, the choice of a specific organizational structure has to take into account and is affected by a number of non-functional requirements and by various characteristics of the operational environment and of the real-world organization. Thus, whenever contingencies call for adaptive changes in the MAS, it is very likely that these contingencies will call for a new organizational structure, which in Gaia can be selected without globally affecting the design.

In fact, the analysis outcome of Gaia is a set of preliminary roles and interactions models that exhibit no dependencies on a specific organizational structure. In the architectural design phase, after having chosen a specific organizational structure, the roles and interaction models can be finalized. Consequently, it is possible in the final roles and interaction models to clearly identify those roles and interactions which are intrinsic of the systems (i.e., those already identified from the analysis) from those that, instead, derives from the adoption of a specific organizational structure. Accordingly, whenever contingencies call for a new organizational structure, the designer is clearly facilitated in determining what parts of the system requires some sort of re-design and what parts, instead, can be left unchanged.

Thus, even if Gaia does not yet define any specific guidelines for adaptive maintenance, its structuring of the development process somewhat facilitates adaptive changes, and also enables an effective re-use of previous experiences and models. In fact, an expert designer can easily apply known organizational structures – possibly being supported by the availability of catalogues of organizational patterns – in the context of a particular system, so as to more easily chose and specify a specific organizational structure for a MAS-to-be, and – if this is the case – so as to easily re-shape the organizational structure of an existing system that requires some adaptation.

### 3.3 The Conference Management System in Gaia

To better ground the discussion and exemplify, we now try to put these concepts at work in the conference management system example. So, we orderly describe the various phase of the process of analysis and design of such system in Gaia,

*Possible Sub-organizations*
As already stated, in the conference management example, three loosely coupled sub-organizations can be clearly identified, independently of the conference size. The first is the organization responsible for the submission process, the second is the organization responsible for the review process, and the third is the organization responsible for the publication of the proceedings. There are agents/roles (with specific competences) that participate in some organizations and not in others, while others like the PC Chair are likely to participate in all sub-organizations. Therefore, these three processes can dealt with by analyzing them as three separated MASs. For space reasons, hereinafter we focus on the review process only, and discuss the impact of the conference size on the actual design and on design changes.

*Environmental Model*
In the review process application, the environmental model simply reduces to a virtual computational environment of PDF papers (possibly enriched with XML semantic descriptions) and txt review forms. Agents can use some kind of shared database to manage the submitted papers, the reviewers information and the reviewers forms.

*Preliminary Roles Model*
The analysis phase can clearly identify the tasks and the structure of the roles, independently of any contingent choice for the organizational structure, but based on the functional specifications only. Therefore, in the organization of the review process there exists a few clearly identifiable functional roles: the role in charge of selecting reviewers and assigning papers to them (ReviewCatcher), the role of filling review forms for assigned papers (Reviewer), the role in charge of collecting and ranking the reviews (ReviewCollector) and the role of finalizing the technical program (DoProgram). An example of role schema for the ReviewCatcher role is presented in Figure 1.

Clearly, depending on the actual organizational structures chosen to fit the conference size, different actors (e.g., the PC Chair, the PC Members or External Reviewers) may be called to play such roles.

| **Role Schema:** `ReviewCatcher` |
|---|
| **Description:**<br>This role is in charge of selecting reviewers and distributing papers among them. |
| **Protocol and Activities:**<br>`CheckPaperTopic`, `CheckRefereeExpertise`,<br>`CheckRefereeConstraints`, `AssignPaperReferee`,<br>`ReceiveRefereeRefuse`, `UpdateDBSubmission`, `UpdateDBReferee` |
| **Permissions:**<br>Reads *paper_submitted* // in order to check the topic and authors<br>*referee-data* // in order to check the expertise and constraint (i.e. the referee is one of the authors, or belong to the same organization<br>Changes *DB Submission* // assigning a referee to the paper<br>*DB Referee* // assigning the paper to the referee incrementing the number of assigned papers |
| **Responsibilities:**<br>*Liveness*:<br>`ReviewCatcher = (CheckPaperTopic.CheckRefereeExpertise.`<br>`CheckRefereeConstraints.AssignPaperReferee.`<br>`[ReceiveRefereeRefuse] \| UpdateDBSubmission.`<br>`UpdateDBReferee)`$^n$<br>*Safety*:<br>• AssignPaperReferee =>*Referee* $\neq$ *authors* ^ *Referee_organization* $\neq$ *authors_ organizations*<br>• $\forall$ paper: *number_of_referees* = 3 |

**Fig. 1.** The *ReviewCatcher* functional role schema

*Preliminary Protocols Model*

As for the preliminary roles model, some preliminary interaction protocols may be identified to apply whatever the conference size (e.g., a protocol involving ReviewCatcher roles and Reviewers roles for assigning papers to review). However, until the organizational structure is defined, some of the protocols may remain dangling (i.e., without clearly identified roles involved) or fully unidentified.

*Organizational Rules*

Organizational rules in the conference management systems may dictate constraints on who can review what papers (i.e., to one to review his/her own papers), and on how the review process should proceed (i.e., by having at least three reviews by three different reviewer for each paper). Some examples of organizational rules related to the review process have been presented in [19]. Again, such rules typically express constraints that are mostly independent from any specific internal definition of roles and that abstract from any specific organizational structure, i.e., the above rules must apply both for a small and for a large conference.

*Choice of the Organizational Structure*
Here comes the deal. The organizational structure is the aspect of the system that is more likely to be affected by the conference size (as already discussed in Subsection 2.2).

Let us firstly assume that the conference organizers expect a limited number of submissions, and then decide to organize the review process around a simple hierarchy (see Figure 2).

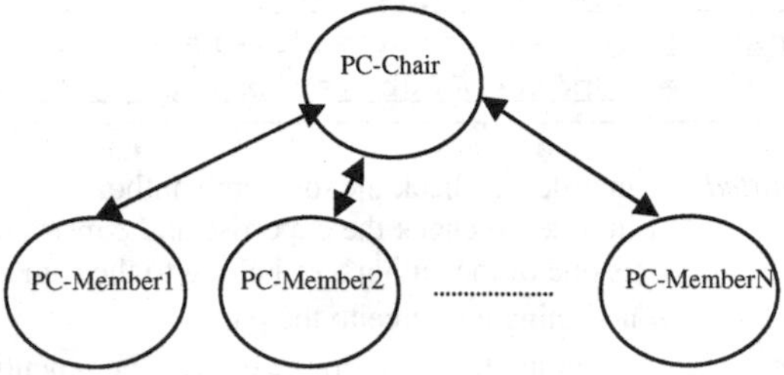


**Fig. 2.** The *paper review organization* structure for a small conference

The PC Chair plays the ReviewCatcher role and distributes the papers among the PC Members, which simply acts playing the role of Reviewers. The PC-Members, eventually send back reviews to the PC Chair, which thus plays also the ReviewCollector role. Based on this, the preliminary roles identified in the analysis already suffice, and they can be simply organized (via properly completing the interactions model) into a hierarchy.

*Completion of Preliminary Roles and Protocols Models*
Once identified the organizational structure, the roles and protocol models can be finalized, by binding dangling references.

*Adoption of a Different Organizational Structure*
Now let us assume that the number of submissions is much higher than expected. At this point, the conference organizers may decide to adopt a different structure, i.e., a multilevel hierarchy, implying some change also in the underlying MAS supporting the process.

The multilevel hierarchy could be organized as follows. The PC Chair will have to play a new – previously not identified – role of ReviewPartitioner (see Figure 3), to partition papers "by areas" and distribute each partition to specifically appointed Vice Chairs, each in charge of handling papers in his/her area of competence. These Vice Chairs than have to act as ReviewCatcher for their assigned partitions, recruiting PC Members as Reviewers. Vice Chairs also play as ReviewCollector for their partition, and the same do the PC Chair for the whole set of reviews.

Now, what should a designer do if forced to switch from the "small conference" design to the "large conference" design? Well, due to the modularity of Gaia models and the clear separation from analysis and architectural design phase, the designer can easily re-use all previously identified models of the analysis, re-applying them in the sub-hierarchics of Vice Chairs and PC Members, and introducing the new role of "ReviewPartitioner" to define the upper level of the hierarchy.

| |
|---|
| **Role Schema:** `ReviewPartitioner` |
| **Description:**<br>This role is in charge of distributing papers among Vice-Chairs according to the area of competence. |
| **Protocol and Activities:**<br>`CheckPaperTopic`, `CheckViceChairArea`, `AssignPaperViceChair`, `UpdateDBSubmission` |
| **Permissions:**<br>Reads *paper_submitted* // in order to check the topic and authors<br>*Vice-Chair-data* // in order to check the area<br>Changes *DB Submission* // assigning the paper to a Vice-Chair area |
| **Responsibilities:**<br>*Liveness*:<br>`ReviewPartitioner = (CheckPaperTopic.CheckViceChairArea.AssignPaperViceChair.UpdateDBSubmission)`$^{\omega}$<br>*Safety*:<br>• ∀ paper assigned to a ViceChairArea |

**Fig. 3.** The new *ReviewPartitioner* role schema

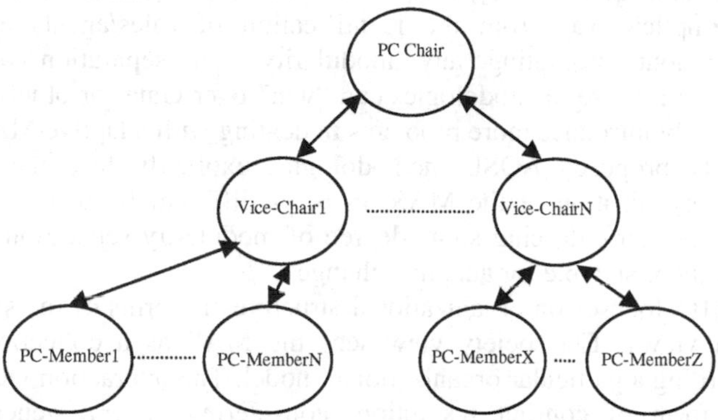


**Fig. 4.** The *paper review organization* structure for a large conference

*Detailed Design*

Clearly, the detailed design of agents and services is not particularly affected by the specific organizational structure, as far as the "intrinsic" roles and interactions are concerned (Figure 5 shows the Agent model related to the reviewing process for a multilevel hierarchy organization). As far as the additional roles and interactions introduced because of a specific organizational structure are involved (e.g., the

ReviewPartitioner role), these are very likely to be roles and interactions that recur over and over in the design of MAS organizations, thus making it possibly for designers to re-use from past experience of from catalogue of MAS organizational patters.

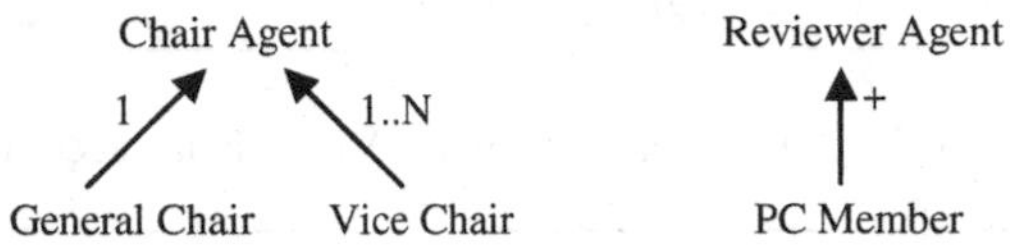


**Fig. 5.** The *Agent model* for a large conference

## 4 Other AOSE Methodologies

The issue of continuous design change/adaptation in MASs organizations has been the subject of several studies [9], [13]. For instance, the approach proposed in [14] is concerned with the agents generation at run-time in response to changes in requirements or in the environment. However, the specific problem of how to properly analyze, design, and develop a MAS so as to make it ready to adaptation is definitely under-studied.

Unlike Gaia, several other AOSE methodologies proposed in the literature simply miss in identifying a clear separation of the intrinsic aspects of a MAS (as identified in Gaia analysis) from the architectural aspects (i.e., the organizational structure in Gaia). For instance, methodologies such as Roadmap [15], Prometheus [17], MaSE [8], AOR [18], and DESIRE [2], simply consider the organizational structure to derive in an implicit way from the identification of roles/agents and of their interactions, without promoting any modularity and separation of concerns. Accordingly, even if these methodologies can "win" over Gaia for other aspects (cfr. [4]), they inherently introduce more problems in dealing with adaptive MAS.

More recently proposed AOSE methodologies explicitly face the problem of structuring the organization of the MAS, in ways different from that of Gaia, but nevertheless somewhat enforcing some degree of modularity separation of concerns that make them more suitable for adaptive change.

MASSIVE [16] focuses on organizational structures in terms of the society views and interaction views. The society view sees the MAS as a collection of agents structured according a particular organizational model. The interaction view is seen as a generalized form of conflict resolution, considering several generic form of interaction not limited to the traditional form of communication. The explicit definition of these views goes in the suggested directions of making the organizational aspects explicit, and can facilitate adaptive organizational changes.

To capture the organizational perspective, Tropos [3], [12] includes actors diagrams for describing the network of social dependency relationships among actors (modeling an agent, a role or a set of roles), and rationale diagrams for analyzing and trying to fulfill the specified goals of the actors. Also in the architectural design phase, more systems actors are introduced and goals and tasks assigned to the systems are deeper specified in term of sub-goals and sub-tasks. As already stated, this clear focus of Tropos on the definition of the organizational structure is a key requirement for promoting adaptive organizational changes.

Ingenias [12] proposes an approach which is nearest to that of Gaia in considering the organizational perspective. Moreover, it has the advantage of doing so according to a refinement approach. In the analysis-inception phase, organization models are produced to sketch how the MAS looks like (the MAS architecture). This result is refined in the analysis-elaboration phase to identify common goals of the agents and relevant tasks to be performed by each agents. In the design-elaboration phase workflows among the different agents are added to improve the organization model, and finally, in the design-construction phase social relationships of dependency (that clarify organization behavior) are defined. Again, we consider the Ingenias approach somewhat suitable in a design-for-change perspective.

The Agent Modeling Language - AML approach devotes special attention to the social/organizational aspects [5] introducing different diagrams to capture the social structure, the social behavior and the social attitudes. However, AML more than a complete methodology is a modeling language: one of its main contributions is its powerful notation being specified as a conservative extension of UML 2.0.

It is also important to highlight that most the methodologies (including Gaia) are concerned with the analysis and design processes only [4]; few are trying to cover the development and deployment of the system; less yet are concerned with the maintenance stage of the system. Thus, even when a methodology is more suitable for a design-for-change perspective, a specific attention to the maintenance process and the definition of proper guidelines for change and adaptation are lacking, which is a great limitation for modern methodologies.

As a final point, it is also worth outlining that the dynamism of modern scenarios and need of nearly continuous adaptive changes makes the traditional "waterfall" software process model, upon which most methodologies (including Gaia) explicitly or implicitly rely, very unsuitable [4]. Evolutionary process models and, more specifically, agile extreme process models may better facilitate engineers in the adaptive design maintenance of a MAS system. However, current agile and extreme software process models focus on small- to medium-size projects, and are not yet ready to tackle the complexity of developing large-scale adaptive MAS.

## 5 Conclusions and Future Work

In this paper, we have discussed the issue of continuous design change/adaptation that may affect a MAS during its lifetime. We used the conference management system as a representative example of adaptive MAS, to show how changes may require re-structuring the global organization of a MAS. Then, also with the help of the case study example, we have discusses how Gaia (i.e., the way in which Gaia models and organizes the identification of the organizational structure and of the rules governing the general behavior of the MAS) can to some extent facilitate engineers in tackling the likely changes that will appear in a MAS after its deployment. A comparison with other AOSE methodologies shows that other methodologies other than Gaia exhibit similar characteristics and are quite supportive of a design-for-change perspective.

Our current research work is focused on proposing more specific guidelines and conceptual tools to support engineers with in the adaptive maintenance of a MAS system, as well as, for the same purposes, in integrating in Gaia a more iterative and agile software process [4]. An additional issue that we consider very important to study relates to adaptation at the implementation level, i.e., how does changes in the design reflect in the implementation and what different problems may arise at this level that we have still not identified? The final long-term goal of these is to eventually reach a point in which we will be able to develop and deploy MASs that are able to autonomously self-adapt their behavior and to re-structure their internal organization in response to contingencies.

## References

1. Boehm, B.: Software Engineering Economics, Prentice-Hall, Englewood Cliffs (NJ) (1981)
2. Brazier, F., Jonker, C., and Treur, J.: Principles of Component-Based Design of Intelligent Agents. Data and Knowledge Engineering, vol. 41, No. 2, (2002) 1-28
3. Bresciani, P., Perini, A., Giorgini, P., Giunchiglia, F., and Mylopoulos, J.: A Knowledge Level Software Engineering Methodology for Agent Oriented Programming. In: Proceedings of the 5th International Conference on Autonomous Agents. ACM Press, Montreal (Canada), (2001) 648-655
4. Cernuzzi, L., Cossentino, M., Zambonelli, F.: Process Models for Agent-based Development, Journal of Engineering Applications of Artificial Intelligence, Vol. 18, No.2, (2005) 205-222.
5. Cervenka, R., Trencansky, I. and Calisti, M.: Modeling Social Aspects of Multi-Agent Systems: the AML Approach. In this volume.
6. Ciancarini, P. And Wooldridge, M.: Agent-Oriented Software Engineering. Proceedings of the 1st International Workshop on Agent-Oriented Software Engineering, Springer Verlag, LNCS, Vol. 1957, (2001) 1-24
7. Colman, A. and Han, J.: Organizational abstractions for adaptive systems, Technical Report No: SUTIT-TR2004.03/SUT.CeCSES-TR003, School of Information Technology, Swinburne University of Technology, June (2004)
8. DeLoach, S., Wood, M. and Sparkman, C.: Multiagent Systems Engineering. International Journal of Software Engineering and Knowledge Engineering, vol. 11, No. 3, (2001) 231-258
9. Dignum, V., Sonenberg, L., and Dignum, F.: Dynamic Reorganization of Agent Societies, In Vouros, G. (Ed.), *Proceedings of Workshop on Coordination in Emergent Agent Societies* CEAS at ECAI 2004, Valencia, Spain, 22-27 September (2004)
10. Ghezzi, C., Jazayeri, M., and Mandrioli, D.: Fundamentals of Software Engineering. Prentice Hall International, Upper Saddle River, NJ (USA) (1991)
11. Giunchiglia, F., Mylopoulos, J. and Perini A.: The Tropos Software Development Methodology: Processes, Models and Diagrams. Proceedings of Agent-Oriented Software Engineering (AOSE-2002), July 2002, Bologna (Italy), (2002) 63-74
12. Gómez-Sanz, J. and Pavón, J., 2003. Agent Oriented Software Engineering with INGENIAS. Proceedings of the 3rd Central and Eastern Europe Conference on Multiagent Systems, Springer Verlag, LNCS 2691, pp. 394-403
13. Horling, B. and Lesser, V.: A Survey of Multi-Agent Organizational Paradigms. The Knowledge Engineering Review. 2005, to appear.

14. Jayaputera, G., Zaslavsky, A. and Loke, S.: Approach to Dynamically Generated User-Specified MAS. In this volume.
15. Juan, T., Pearce, A. and Sterling, L.: ROADMAP: Extending the Gaia Methodology for Complex Open Systems. Proceeding of the First International Conference on Autonomous Agents and Multi-Agent Systems - AAMAS '02, July 15-19, 2002, Bologna (Italy), (2002) 3-10
16. Lind, J., 2001. Iterative Software Engineering for Multiagent Systems, the MASSIVE Method. Springer Verlag, New York, Secaucus, NJ, USA
17. Padgham, L. and Winikoff, M.: Prometheus: A Methodology for Developing Intelligent Agents. Proceedings of the First International Conference on Autonomous Agents and Multi-Agent Systems - AAMAS '02, Third International Workshop on Agent-Oriented Software Engineering AOSE-2002, July 15, 2002, Bologna (Italy), (2002) 135-146
18. Wagner, G.: The Agent-Object-Relationship Metamodel: Towards a Unified View of State and Behavior. Information Systems, Vol. 28, No. 5, July, 2003, Elsevier, (2003) 475-504
19. Zambonelli, F., Wooldridge, M. and Jennings, N. R.: Developing Multiagent Systems: The Gaia Methodology. ACM Transaction on Software Engineering and Methodology, vol. 12, No. 3, (2003) 417-470
20. Zambonelli, F. and Omicini, A.: Challenges and Research Directions in Agent-Oriented Software Engineering. Journal of Autonomous Agents and Multiagent Systems, vol. 9, No. 3, Kluwer Academic Publishers, (2004) 253-283
21. Zambonelli, F. et al.: Spray Computers: Explorations in Self-organization. Journal of Pervasive and Mobile Computing, vol. 1, No. 1, (2004) 1-20

# Implementing Validated Agents Behaviours with Automata Based on Goal Decomposition Trees

Gaële Simon and Marianne Flouret

LIH, Université du Havre, 76058 Le Havre Cedex, France
Gaële.Simon@univ-lehavre.fr, Marianne.Flouret@univ-lehavre.fr

**Abstract.** In order to provide an effective tool allowing to implement validated agents behaviours, this paper first presents a Goal Decomposition Tree (GDT), a model to specify behaviours both in procedural and declarative ways. A GDT allows the designer to verify the specified behaviour. This model is then used to generate a behaviour automaton using automata composition patterns associated to operators used in the tree. This process allows to obtain a finite expression representing all valid behaviours of agents of a MAS.

## 1 Introduction

The work presented in this paper takes place in a global approach whose goal is to define a complete process to implement a validated MAS starting from a problem specification. Indeed, our approach consists in the following steps:

- an agentification method [8] that helps to determine the set of agents which must be used to solve a given problem;
- an agent design model, called Goal Decomposition Tree (GDT), to help to specify a verifiable agent behaviour;
- a proof system [8, 12] to prove that the agent model specifies a behaviour which satisfies the main goal of the agent;
- an implementation model (SPACE, [13]), based on automata, that can be automatically generated from the verified agent model.

Then this paper only presents one of these steps, that is the building of agents behaviour automata (from trees previously obtained).

As for MaSE methodology [6], our approach can be seen as a "formal transformation system". Indeed, in [4], such a system is defined as providing "automated support to system development, giving the designer much more confidence that the resulting system will operate correctly, despite its complexity". More precisely, "Since each transformation preserves correctness from one model to the next, the developer has much more confidence that no inconsistencies or errors occured during the design process". This is one of the main goals of our approach. An important advantage of this kind of approach is that "Transformation systems also provide traceability from the system requirements through the development process to the final executable code"([4]).

J.P. Müller and F. Zambonelli (Eds.): AOSE 2005, LNCS 3950, pp. 124–138, 2006.

In order to be able to implement and validate an agent, its behaviour must be clearly specified. In our proposition, this specification is based on a Goal Decomposition Tree (GDT). This tree helps to describe how an agent can manage its goals in order to satisfy its main goal. A GDT is a specification of a complex temporal logic formula describing how the agent can be satisfied. The main contribution of this model is to provide enough tools to make its proof possible. An important aspect of a GDT is that it is also intended to be used to directly generate the behaviour of the agent to which it is associated. Indeed, as explained in [14], "the biggest role of goals in agents is thus not the ability to reason about them but their motivational power of generating behaviour". Moreover, "A certain plan or behaviour is generated *because* of a goal". It is exactly what a GDT allows to express.

An other and complementary way to represent the intrinsic agents behaviours is the use of automata. Finite state automata are not only used in language theory but also in various areas, such as systems and networks, or image compression [5]. Agent behaviours have yet been represented by automata or structures similar to automata. In [7], Ferber presents such structures, but in our approach the language properties linked to automata are used, that is not allowed for example by ATN. Moreover we also use operations on automata. Indeed, one of the advantages of this formalism is the rational result it gives and then the finite expression of an agent behaviour which corresponds to all its possible successive operations. GDT and automata are two formalizations to represent these behaviours and automata can be seen as interpreters of GDTs. Lötzsch et al. used similar structures in [11] but their state machines do not correspond to our automata as they do not code behaviours at the same level. Moreover they do not provive all valide behaviours unlike GDT. The building of our agents behaviour automata can be compared with tasks diagrams created for each agent in MaSE conception step. But, in our model, an agent is represented by only one automaton when , in MaSE, there is an automaton for each component of an agent. This implies that, in our model, agent communications and actions are formalized with the same automaton. Indeed, communications (or "conversations") can be seen as actions. Our automata are goal oriented as they are built from GDTs, unlike MaSE in which components are linked to tasks. In previous works, solutions to translate temporal formula into automata in order to verify such formula by model-checking have been proposed [15]. As a GDT is the expression of a complex temporal logic formula, these works may be compared with our proposal. However, in these works, two hypotheses, are considered : the world can be modelized by a finite-state automaton and formula specify behaviours of closed systems, with no interaction with an environment. None of this both hypotheses can be considered as true in our case.

Here, we present a direct translation from a GDT into an automaton. The main advantage of this process is to obtain a validated implementation of the agent behaviour. Moreover, as the automaton can be generated automatically, the designer can only focus on the behaviour design. As a consequence, it avoids the introduction of new errors at the implementation step. In [9], Kaelbling has proposed the GAPPS system, this formalism allows programmers to describe how to achieve goals, but if it proves that the goals to achieve are well scheduled, our model tries to show that the scheduled achievement of goals leads to their parent goal achievement.

A way to generate (in fact to represent) automata and their combinations is the use of matrices that we will present below.

During the execution of the MAS, automata also allow to keep up with the behaviours of the associated agents at any time, and to know their past behaviour. In fact, we directly have a trace of the tests and actions performed by the agents.

The next section deals with the building of a GDT defining the behaviour of an agent. The last part presents the generation of the behaviour automaton of an agent using its GDT. We illustrate our work with a part of a prey-predator case study (completely developped in [8]).

## 2 Decomposing Goals into Subgoals

### 2.1 Introduction

The main advantage of a GDT is to provide a declarative description of goals. Several works have already pointed out the advantage to have a declarative description of goals [17], [14]. Many multiagent models or systems are essentially focused on procedural aspects of goals which is important in order to obtain an executable agent. But the declarative aspect of goals is also very important. Indeed, as it is said in [17], "by omitting the declarative aspect of goals, the ability to reason about goals is lost. Without knowing what a goal is trying to achieve, one can not check wether the goal has been achieved, check wether the goal is impossible". In [14], the authors say that declarative goals "provide for the possibility to decouple plan execution and goal achievement". A GDT is a partial answer to these requirements : as it will be shown in next sections, a GDT allows to describe both procedural and declarative aspects of goals management.

Nodes of a GDT correspond to goals the agent has to solve. As in [17], goals are considered as states of the world the agent has to reach. Several kinds of goals have been defined using three different criteria. This typology of goals is usefull both for the verification of the consistency of the tree and to guide the definition of the behaviour automaton. Inside the tree, a goal is decomposed into subgoals using decomposition operators. In our vision, subgoals correspond to sufficient conditions for the satisfaction of the parent goal. The method TAEMS [16] does not use goals buts tasks. However subtasks used in TAEMS can be directly compared to subgoals used in our work.

A decomposition operator encapsulates a set of mechanisms corresponding to a typical goals management behaviour ([14], [17]). Each operator is specified by different kinds of semantics:

- a goal decomposition semantics describing how a goal can be decomposed into subgoals with this operator;

- a semantics describing how to deduce the "type" of the parent goal knowing the types of its subgoals;
- a semantics allowing to associate an *automata composition pattern* to each operator. These patterns are used incrementally to obtain the complete automaton describing the agent behaviour. This semantics is described in Section 3;
- a semantics allowing to associate a local proof schema and a context propagation schema to each operator. These two kinds of schemas are used to prove the agent behaviour (ie. to prove that its goals management behaviour allows to satisfy its main goal). This semantics is not described in this paper.

The Section 2.2 defines the notion of goal as it is used in this work and describes the typology of goals which has been defined. The Section 2.3 describes the set of operators allowing to decompose a goal into subgoals inside the GDT. For each operator, the two first semantics described before are given. Last but not least, the Section 2.4 shows how a GDT can be built using the tools described in the two previous sections.

## 2.2 Goals and Typology of Goals

In the context of a Goal Decomposition Tree, a goal is defined by a name and a satisfaction condition. Satisfaction conditions allow to specify goals formally with respect to the declarative requirements for goals described in the previous section. A goal is considered to be solved if its satisfaction condition is logically true. Satisfaction conditions are expressed using a temporal logic formalism which is a subset of TLA [10]. Satisfaction conditions use variables which are supposed to be properties maintained by the agent. Thus, specifying goals of an agent helps also to define the set of properties of the agent and also variables defining the view of the agent on its environment.

A typology of goals has been defined in order to distinguish more precisely different ways to manage goals decomposition. In the context of a GDT, each goal can be characterized by three criteria which can be combined independently. These criteria are:

- **the location of the goal in the tree:** A goal associated to a leaf node is called *elementary goal*. Other goals are called *intermediate goals*. Elementary goals are not only defined by a name and a satisfaction condition but also by a set of actions. The execution of these actions are supposed to solve the goal ie to make its satisfaction condition true. They correspond to the procedural aspect of goals described in the previous section. Intermediate goals are specified by a name, a satisfaction condition and also a Local Decomposition Tree (LDT). A LDT contains a root node corresponding to the intermediate goal and a decomposition operator which creates as many branches (and subgoals) as needed by the operator. It describes how the intermediate goal can be decomposed into subgoals. The number and the order of subgoals to be solved to satisfy the parent goal depends on the chosen operator (see next section for more details).

- **the satisfiability mode:** *Necessarily Satisfiable Goals (NS)* are goals such that, once all what must be done to solve the goal has been executed, the satisfaction condition of the goal is always true. *Not Necessarily Satisfiable goals (NNS)* are complementary to the previous ones. It is the more prevalent case. For this kind of goal, one can not be sure that the goal will be solved after its actions or its decomposition (and the subgoals associated to this decomposition) have been executed or satisfied. This kind allows to take into account that some actions or some decompositions can only be used in certain execution contexts.
- **the laziness of the goal:** For *Lazy goals (L)*, their associated actions or LDT is considered if and only if their satisfaction condition is false before. On the contrary, for *Not Lazy goals (NL)*, the associated set of actions or LDT is always executed.

Each criterion has two possible values which implies that eight effective kinds of goals can be used in the tree. The Figure 1 summarizes the graphical notations which have been introduced for these criteria.

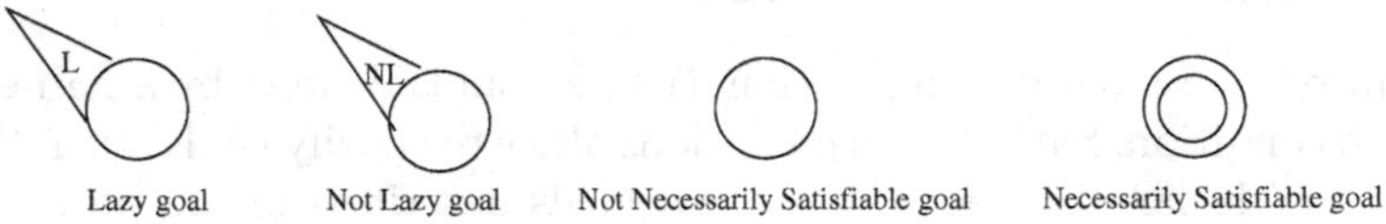


**Fig. 1.** NS,NNS, lazy and not lazy goals

### 2.3 Decomposition Operators

In this section, available decomposition operators are described. For each operator, the two first semantics are given that is to say the decomposition semantics and the goals types composition semantics. The goals types composition semantics is based only on the satisfiability criterion of goals. The decomposition semantics of each operator describes how many goals must be solved and in which order to be able to satisfy the parent goal. It is important to notice that the satisfaction of this decomposition *implies* the satisfaction of the parent goal.

Eight operators have been proposed:

- **AND:** it corresponds to the "logical" *and* operator.
- **OR:** it corresponds to the "logical" *or* operator.
- **SEQAND:** it is a sequential version of AND.
- **SEQOR:** it is a sequential version of SEQOR.
- **SYNCSEQAND:** it is a synchronised version of SEQAND (ie. the solving process of the two subgoals can not be interrupted by an other agent).
- **SYNQSEQOR:** it is a synchronised version of SEQOR.
- **CASE:** it allows to decompose a goal into subgoals according to conditions defined by logical expressions. These logical expressions use the same

variables as satisfaction conditions. The decomposition semantics of this operator states that the disjunction of the logical expressions corresponding to the conditions must be true when the parent goal is decomposed. The principle is that if a condition is true, the corresponding subgoal must be solved.
- **ITER:** it allows to express a progress notion during the solving process of a goal.

Only SEQAND and ITER operators are described below.

**SEQAND Operator.** This operator corresponds to a "sequential AND" operator. Indeed, the main difference with the AND operator is that the two subgoals must be solved in the order specified by the operator. As far as the composition semantics is concerned, the subgoals can be either NS or NNS. The parent goal is NS only if its two subgoals are NS, it is NNS otherwise.

**ITER Operator.** This operator is an unary one. The main difference between this operator and the others is that its behaviour depends on the satisfaction condition of the parent goal. The decomposition semantics of this operator states that the satisfaction condition of the subgoal must be true several times in order the satisfaction condition of the parent goal to become true. This operator is very important because it allows to take into account a progress notion inside a goal solving process. In other words, each time the subgoal is satisfied, the satisfaction of the parent goal must be closer. However, sometimes it is possible that the subgoal can not be satisfied (because the context of the agent has changed for example). In this case, the satisfaction degree of the parent goal stays at the same level and the subgoal must be solved again. The important characteristic of this operator is that the satisfaction level of the parent goal can not regress after a satisfaction step of the subgoal, even if this step has failed. The goals types composition semantics specifies that the subgoal can be either necessarily satisfiable either not. However, the parent goal is always necessarily satisfiable. Indeed, the behaviour of the operator implies that the solving process of the subgoal stops when the satisfaction condition of the parent goal is true which implies that this one is necessarily satisfiable.

## 2.4 The GDT Design Process

A Goal Decomposition Tree (GDT) specifies how each goal can be solved by an agent. More precisely, the root node of the tree is associated to the main goal of the agent, i.e. the one which is assigned to the agent during the agentification step ([13], [18]). If this goal is solved by the agent, the agent is considered to be satisfied from the multiagent system point of view. The tree describes how this goal can be decomposed in order to be solved using a solution which must be the most adapted to the agent context as possible. Each leaf of the tree corresponds to an elementary goal. The other nodes are associated to intermediate goals which are decomposed using decomposition operators presented in the previous section. Notice that the overall tree can be seen as a collection of local plans allowing to solve each goal. A local plan corresponds to a Local Decomposition Tree associated to a subgoal. The main difference with plans used in [1] is that, in a GDT, they are organised hierarchically.

The building process of the GDT consists in 4 steps. In a first step, a tree must be built by the designer, starting from the main goal of the agent using a top-down process. This first step allows to introduce subgoals with their satisfaction condition, elementary goals with their associated actions and also decomposition operators. The designer must also decide for each goal if it is lazy or not. In the second step of the GDT design process, the designer must decide for each elementary goal if it is necessarily satisfiable or not. In a third step, the type of each intermediate goal, as far as satisfiability is concerned, is computed using the goals types composition semantics of each used decomposition operator. Unlike the first step, this step is a down-top process. During this process, inconsistencies or potential simplifications can be detected. In that case, the first step must be executed again in order to modify the tree.

Once the three first steps have been achieved, a proof of the tree can be built in a fourth step. The process used to achieve this proof is described in details in [12], [8]. Again, this step can lead to detect inconsistencies in the tree based on proof failures.

In a last step, the validated tree is used to build the behaviour automaton of the agent which can then be implemented. This process is described in Section 3. As explained before, the building of the tree leads also to the definition of properties, variables and actions of the agent which are essential parts of an agent model. As a consequence, the GDT and the associated design process can be seen as a design tool for a validated agent model in the context of a MAS design.

This model has been successfully applied to describe the behaviour of a predator agent in a prey/predator MAS [8] which allowed to prove this behaviour. The Figure 2 shows a part of this GDT which describes the behaviour of the predator in order to reach a target cell chosen before. This target cell is supposed to be reachable in one move by the predator. But this cell is not necessarily free. Thats' why the predator must eventually wait for this cell to be free. So, the goal F is satisfied if the predator has effectively reached this target cell. The goal I is satisfied if the predator has moved at a location which is nearer to the target cell than its previous location. The goal J is satisfied if the target cell is free (ie there is not any agent on this cell). The action associated to this goal is to attack the agent located on the target cell. As this goal is a lazy one, this action is performed only if there is an agent on the target cell. The goal K is satisfied if the predator is on the target cell. The action associated to this goal is a move of the predator on the target cell that's why this goal is necessarily satisfiable. This goal can be satisfied only if the goal J has been satisfied before. As a synchronized operator has been used to link J and K, it is ensured that the target cell is free when the goal K is solved.

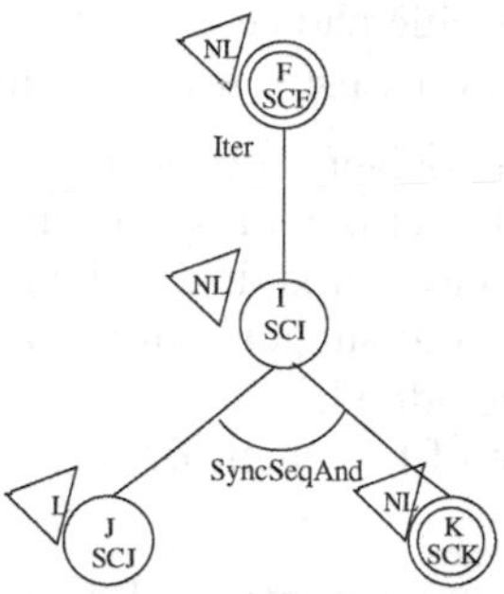


**Fig. 2.** Predator subtree

# 3 Implementing Agents Behaviour with Automata

In our approach, the agents behaviour implementation is based on string to string automata (transducers) [3]. The next section shows that goals and decomposition operators can be represented by string patterns.

## 3.1 Behaviour Automaton

As presented in Section 2.1, a semantics in terms of automata patterns is associated to each decomposition operator. Basic automata are also associated to elementary goals, with specific properties according to their type. As far as intermediate goals are concerned, as they are decomposed into subgoals by decomposition operators, their corresponding automata are obtained by an automata combination, depending on the chosen operator and of automata previously built for subgoals. This combination is specified by an automata composition pattern. In fact, the building of the string automaton of an agent behaviour is obtained by successive such operations. Notice that automata give here a "behaviour schema" for agents but do not claim to define all elements of agents behaviour, like interactions between agents or waiting for messages (but they can appear as actions). Matrices, as presented below, can also be used to represent automata compositions making more direct the building of the final automaton. Before we present the elementary automata and their combination rules, let us recall the definition of a *string to string automaton.* A string to string automaton is defined by a 6-tuple $(\Sigma, Z, Q, I, F, \delta)$ such that: $\Sigma$ is a finite input alphabet, $Z$ is a finite output alphabet, $Q$ is the finite set of states, $I \subseteq Q$ is the set of initial states, $F \subseteq Q$ is the set of final states, $\delta : Q \times \Sigma \rightarrow Q \times Z$ is the application associated to transitions. *Rational expressions* are obtained from the elements of $\Sigma$ or $Z$ by a finite number of combinations of rational laws as $(\cup, \cdot, *)$. The finite expression of an agent behaviour [2] is in fact such a rational expression, with the following equivalence as we work in a logical context: $\cup$ corresponds to the logical Or, $\cdot$ corresponds to our SeqAnd operator and $*$ represents the Iter operator. The adaptation of string to string automata, to allow to describe the behaviour of an agent $a$, follows from a specific choice concerning the meaning of each state and the labels associated to the transitions. They are defined as follows:

$\Sigma$ is the finite set of logical satisfaction conditions $sc$, and their negation, of $a$;
$Z$ is the finite set of possible actions of $a$(associated to elementary goals, described in Section 2.2); no action is denoted 1),
$Q$ represents the set of goals and subgoals of the agent, and two states $'+'$ and $'-'$ (success or failure) are added;
$I$ $= \{i\}$ is the starting state of the agent $a$;
$F$ $= \{+, -\}$.

We can also use a linear representation of automata: matrices. Such a representation of dimension $n$ (the number of states) is a triplet $(\lambda, \mu, \gamma)$ where $\lambda \in \{0,1\}^{1\times n}$ (for each state, 1 if it is an initial one, 0 otherwise) is a row vector coding initial states, $\gamma \in \{0,1\}^{n\times 1}$ a column vector coding the output (by 1 if a state is an output, 0 otherwise) and $\mu : \Sigma^* \rightarrow Z^{n\times n}$ a morphism of monoids coding the transition actions between states for each condition of $\Sigma$, with the matrix $\mu(sc)$. In fact, 0 is added to $Z$ as absorbing action (neutralizing) for matrices products. For our representations, there is only one initial state, and possible output are the $\{+, -\}$ states. Practically, for this representation, we just have to add a numbering for all states. In the sequel we will consider the initial state as the first one in our representation, and the "last" ones will be $\{-\}$ and $\{+\}$. A *path* of an automaton is a sequence of states $p_0, \cdots, p_n$ such that $\forall 1 \leq j \leq n$ there exists $a_j \in \Sigma$,$z \in Z$, $(p_j, z) \in \delta(p_{j-1}, a_j)$. A *successfull path* of an automaton is a path from an initial state $p_0 \in I$ to a final one $p_n \in F$ with $\{p_j\}_{0\leq j\leq n} \in Q^{n+1}, n \geq 1$ and $\{a_j\}_{1\leq j\leq n} \in \Sigma^n$ such that $\delta(p_j, a_{j+1})$ for $0 \leq j \leq n$ exists. The language of the automaton is the labels set of successfull paths (it corresponds to possible behaviours). With the matrix representation, a successful path is $w \in \Sigma^*$ for which $\lambda\mu(w)\gamma \neq 0$.

Here, the language which is considered is a set of logical combinations of formulae of $\Sigma$. Moreover, each successfull path ending by the state $+$ corresponds to a traversal path of the Goal Decomposition Tree of the agent $a$. A *valid behaviour* corresponds to a successfull path in the automaton ending by $+$ which we call a *valid path.* The actions of $Z$ are considered to be associated to the states of the automata, but it is equivalent to a representation with actions over edges, next to logical conditions. Notice that, implicitly, in each state a test action is executed to know wich logical condition is true in order to choose the corresponding edge. Two finite results are obtained from this structure: firstly, the whole set of possible combinations of logical conditions to satisfy the main goal of the agent, and secondly - by reading in the states - the sequence of actions performed by $a$, that is to say valid behaviours. In fact the automaton view gives a rational formalization of the behaviour described by the Goal Decomposition Tree.

### 3.2 Automata Composition Patterns

The behaviour automaton of an agent is built by combinations of elementary automata using automata composition patterns associated to decomposition operators. The elementary automata corresponding to elementary goals (leaves of

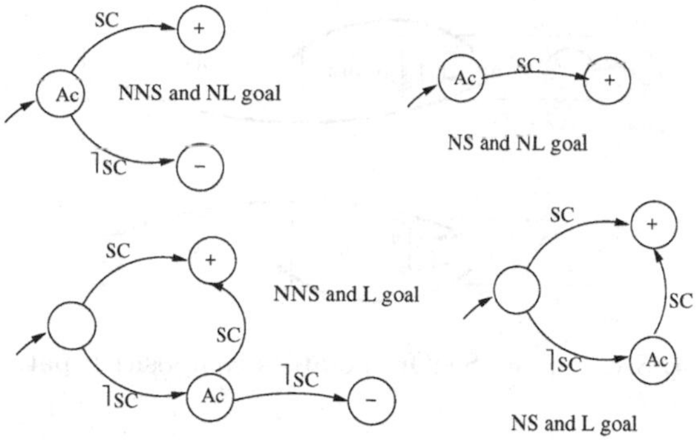


**Fig. 3.** Automata for all kinds of elementary goals

the tree) are defined below. Let $a$ an agent and $N$ an elementary node of its GDT associated to a subgoal $G$. According to the goals typology defined in Section 2.2, four elementary cases have to be distinguished: lazy (L) or not (NL), and necessarily (NS) or not (NNS) satisfiable goals. The Figure 3 shows the elementary automata associated to each case. We denote $A_c$ the set of actions associated to the goal. We can notice that the automaton of a necessarily satisfiable goal has only the state + as final state. Elementary linear representations are associated to each case. For example, a lazy and not necessarily satisfiable goal will be represented by

$$\lambda = (1,0,0,0) \quad \gamma^t = (0,0,0,1) \quad \mu(sc) = \begin{bmatrix} 0\,0\,0\,1 \\ 0\,0\,0\,1 \\ 0\,0\,0\,0 \\ 0\,0\,0\,0 \end{bmatrix} \quad \mu(\neg sc) = \begin{bmatrix} 0 & A_c & 0 & 0 \\ 0 & 0 & 1 & 0 \\ 0 & 0 & 0 & 0 \\ 0 & 0 & 0 & 0 \end{bmatrix}$$

Starting from these automata, we now have to consider their composition which depends on the operators used in the GDT. Let $B_1$ and $B_2$ be the automata of two subtrees. We give in Figures 4, 5, and 7 the composition patterns associated to each operator. A composition pattern specifies how to combine automata associated to subgoals or subtrees in order to produce the automaton of the parent goal. The initial state of the resulting automaton is, as usual, represented by a simple circle with a small arrow which does not come from any other state, and reaching it. Automata of $B_1$ and $B_2$ (elementary or not) are represented with their initial, + and − states. When, by combination, an initial state is not initial anymore, it is drawn with a dotted circle. Dotted arrows starting from an initial state represent new edges reaching states which were already reached by edges coming from the dotted states (old initial states) and with the same labels. Bold arrows represent all edges in the initial automata coming from or reaching a state. When combined, the construction deletes the crossed edges, new ones are added, with the same labels (in fact, the edges are moved). Drawing states + and − in a square means that they are deleted in the resulting automaton.

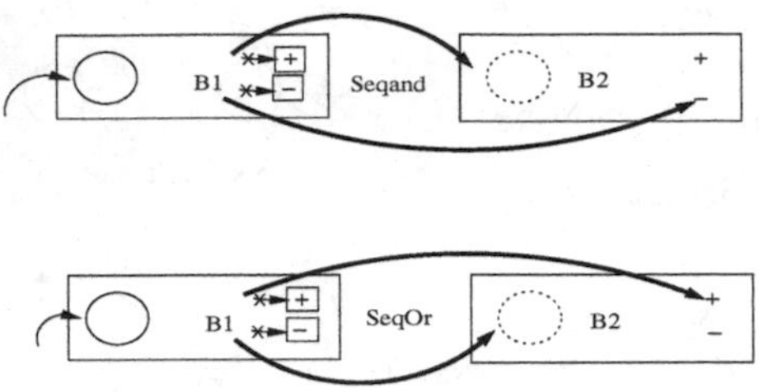


**Fig. 4.** SeqAnd and SeqOr operators composition patterns

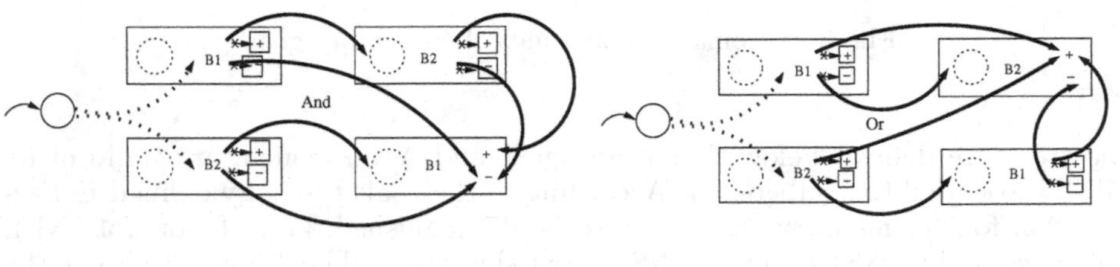


**Fig. 5.** And and Or operators composition patterns

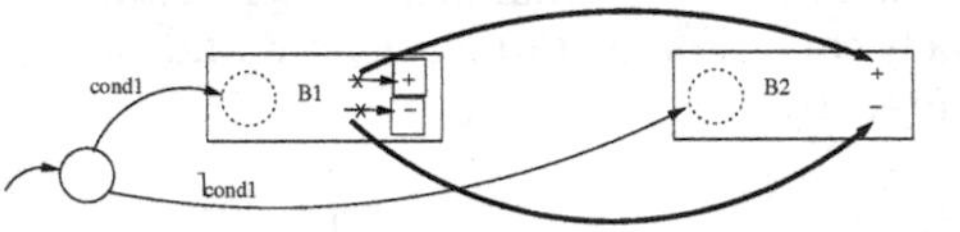


**Fig. 6.** Case operator composition pattern

For all patterns, it is important to precise that each automaton to combine must have exactly one state + and one state −, this last state is added (with no arrow) if it did not exist (in fact if it had been deleted by a previous combination).

All unreachable states (when all edges reaching them have been deleted) are removed in the resulting automaton in order to have only one state + and at most one state −. In the following figures describing composition patterns, the parent node $A$ is a non lazy goal, $B_1$ and $B_2$ are the subgoals. A choice policy (at random,...) must be defined for the first test of the *And* and *Or* operators. We have to notice that patterns of SyncSeqAnd and SyncSeqOr operators are obviously respectively the same as those of the SeqAnd and SeqOr ones.

For the Iter operator, we consider in the Figure 7 that $A$ is the parent goal of $B_1$ and $SC_A$ is its satisfaction condition. The dashed edge represents a unique and new transition. For the automaton of the Case operator (Figure 6) it is supposed that, in the GDT, $C$ is the parent goal, $B_1$ and $B_2$ are the two subgoals, and $cond_1$ is a *Case* condition.

When the parent goal corresponds to a lazy one, these patterns have to be modified by the addition of one state and two edges, as described in Figure 8,

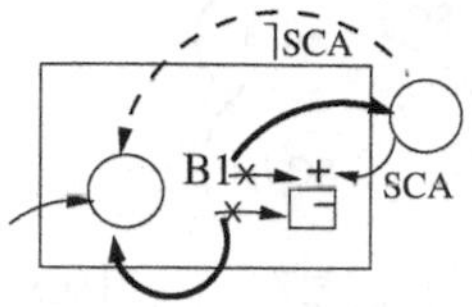


**Fig. 7.** Iter operator composition pattern

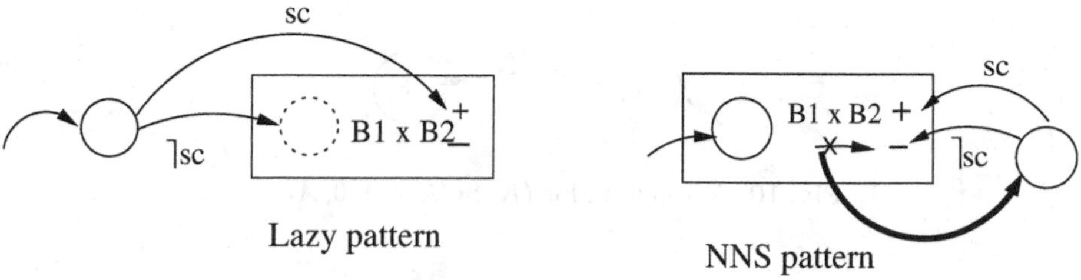


**Fig. 8.** Lazy parent goal and Not necessarily satisfiable parent goal

whatever the operator $x$ used in the figure is. When a parent goal is not necessarily satisfiable, the pattern obtained for this goal must be modified as presented in Figure 8.

We denote $Id_i^{n,0}$ the identity matrix of dimension $n$ where the $i^{th}$ column is null, $Id_i^{n,1}$ the unity matrix in which all rows have been nulled excepted the $i^{th}$, and $T_{i,j}^{n\times m}$ the permutation matrix of $n$ rows, $m$ columns, which permutes columns $i$ and $j$. For the Seqand operation between two subgoals represented by $(\lambda_1, \mu_1, \gamma_1)$ of dimension $n$ and $(\lambda_2, \mu_2, \gamma_2)$ of dimension $m$, the resulting linear composition is defined by $(\lambda, \mu, \gamma)$ of dimension $n + m$ such that

$$\lambda = (1, 0^{1\times(n+m-1)}) \qquad \gamma^t = (0^{(n+m-1)\times 1}, 1)$$

and for each condition $sc$,

$$\mu(sc) = \begin{bmatrix} \mu_1(sc) Id_n^{n,0} Id_{n-1}^{n,0} & \mu_1(sc)(Id_n^{n,1} + Id_{n-1}^{n,1}) T_{1,n}^{n\times m} \\ 0^{m\times n} & \mu_2(sc) \end{bmatrix}$$

Let notice that the order the lazy and not necessarily satisfiable patterns have to be applied does not matter.

### 3.3 Case Study

Here we give a complete example showing how these patterns are used to obtain the behaviour automaton from a subtree of the GDT we have built for the prey-predator system [8] and presented in Figure 2. It shows that the labels of the valid paths of the complete automaton and the logical expression specified by the decomposition tree are equivalent. Figures 9, and 10 represents the automata for goals $J$ and $K$.

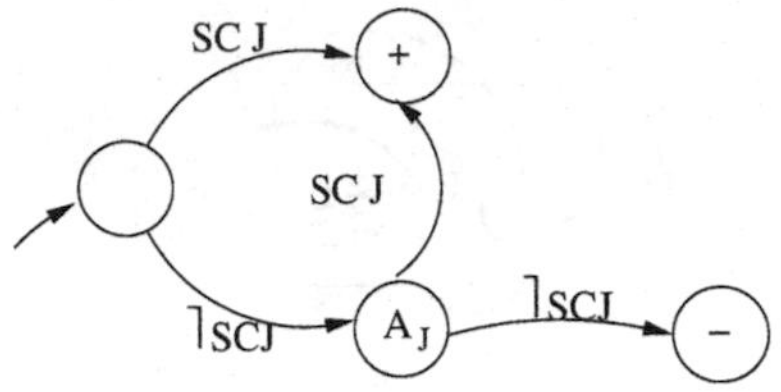


**Fig. 9.** Automaton for $(J, SCJ, 1, 0, 1, A_J)$

**Fig. 10.** Automaton for $(K, SCK, 1, 1, 0, A_K)$

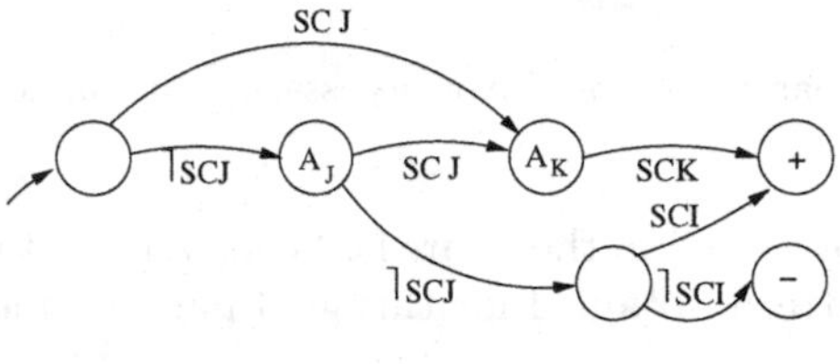


**Fig. 11.** Intermediate automaton

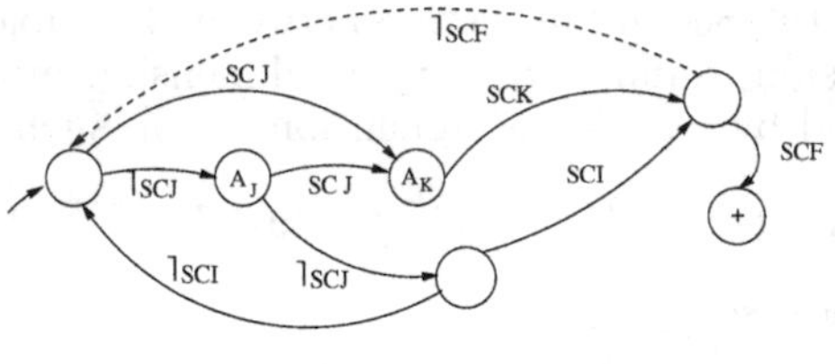


**Fig. 12.** Final automaton

When composed with the SyncSeqAnd operator, using its composition pattern (Figure 4), we obtain the automaton given in Figure 11. Starting from this last automaton, using the Iter composition pattern, we obtain the final automaton of Figure 12.

Notice that starting from elementary linear representations, and then by successive applications of matrix products compositions corresponding to successive operators, the result would give the linear representation of the automaton of Figure 12.

We can now give the set of all possible behaviours of the agent whose GDT is given in Figure 2. Let $Y = (\rceil SCJ \cdot SCJ \cdot SCK) \cup (SCJ \cdot SCK) \cup (\rceil SCJ \cdot \rceil SCJ \cdot SCI)$, and let $X = (\rceil SCJ \cdot \rceil SCJ \cdot \rceil SCI)^* \cdot Y$. Then the expression $X \cdot (\rceil SCF \cdot$

$X)^* \cdot SCF$ represents all possible successive tests of logical conditions made by the agent associated to the goal $F$. It clearly ends with the value *true* for the $SCF$ logical condition (indeed, the goal $F$ is a necessarily satisfiable one).

# 4 Conclusion

This paper presents parts of a global MAS design process which are focused on tools to specify and implement validated agents behaviours. The behaviour is specified by a verifiable GDT which can be automatically translated into an automaton allowing to obtain a validated implementation of the agent. One of the advantages of the automaton representation is the possible use of classical rational operations. Minimization methods [3] can also be applied. Then, the resulting automaton can be reduced, which allows to obtain, by reverse operation, a reduced GDT (if there were intermediate goals that could be eliminated). Moreover, the behaviour expression obtained from these behaviour automaton can be easily and directly used whatever the MAS development platform used is. Last but not least, behaviour automata are goal oriented. This allows us to keep, during program progress, information about the goals of the agents.

# References


1. R.H. Bordini, M. Fisher, W. Visser, and M. Wooldridge. Verifiable multi-agent programs. In M. Dastani, J. Dix, and A. El Fallah Seghrouchni, editors, *ProMAS*, 2003.
2. P. Caron and M. Flouret. From Glushkov WFAs to rational expressions. In *Proceeding of DLT'2003*, volume 2710 of *Lecture Notes in Computer Science*, pages 373–385. Springer, 2003.
3. P. Caron and M. Flouret. Glushkov construction for series: The non commutative case. *Int. J. Comput. Math.*, 4(80):457–472, 2003.
4. Scott A. Deloach Clint H. Sparkman and Athie L. Self. Automated derivation of complex agent architectures from analysis specifications. In *AOSE'01,Montréal*, 2001.
5. K. Culik and J. Kari. Image compression using weighted finite automata. In G. Rozenberg and A. Salomaa, editors, *Handbook of formal languages*, pages 599–616. Springer, 1997.
6. S.A. Deloach, M.F. Wood, and C.H. Sparkman. Multiagent systems engineering. *International Journal of Software Engineering and Knowledge Engineering*, 11(3):231–258, 2001.
7. J. Ferber. *Les systèmes multi-agents*. InterEditions, 1995.
8. D. Fournier M.Flouret G. Simon, B. Mermet. The provable Goal Decomposition Tree: a behaviour model of an agent. Technical report, LIH - Univ. of Le Havre, 2005.
9. L. P. Kaelbling. Goals as parallel program specifications. In *Proceedings, AAAI-88,St Paul, MN*, pages 60–65, 1988.
10. L. Lamport. The temporal logic of actions. *ACM Transactions on Programming Languages and Systems*, 1994.

11. H-D. Burkhard M. Lötzsch, J. Bach and M. Jüngel. Designing agent behavior with the extensible agent behavior specification language XABSL. In Springer, editor, *Proceedings RoboCup 2003*, 2004.
12. B. Mermet and D. Fournier. Variant extensions to prove MAS behaviours. In *Artificial Intelligence: Methods, Systems and Applications (AIMSA'04)*, 2004.
13. B. Mermet, G. Simon, D. Fournier, and M. Flouret. SPACE: A method to increase tracability in MAS Development. In *Programming Multi-agent systems*, volume 3067. LNAI, 2004.
14. M.B. van Riemsdijk, M. Dastani, F. Dignum, and J.-J.Ch. Meyer. Dynamics of declarative goals in agent programming. In *Proceedings of Declarative Agent Languages and Technologies (DALT'04)*, 2004.
15. M.Y. Vardi and P. Wolper. An automata-theoretic approach to automatic program verification. In *Symposium on Logics In Computer Science (LICS'86)*, pages 332–344, 1986.
16. R. Vincent, B. Horling, and V. Lesser. An agent infrastructure to build and evaluate multi-agent systems: the java agent framework and multi-agent system simulator. In *Infrastructure for Agents, Multi-Agent Systems, and Scalable Multi-Agent Systems*, 2001.
17. M. Winikoff, L. Padham, J. Harland, and J. Thamgarajah. Declarative & procedural goals in intelligent agent systems. In *Proceedings of the Eighth International Conference on Principles of Knowledge Representation and Reasoning (KR2002)*, 2003.
18. M. Wooldridge, N. R. Jennings, and D. Kinny. The Gaia methodology for agent-oriented analysis and design. *Journal of Autonomous Agents and Multi-Agent Systems*, 3(3):285–312, 2000.

# Dynamically Generated User-Specified MAS

Glenn Jayaputera, Arkady Zaslavsky, and Seng Loke

School of Computer Science and Software Engineeing,
Monash University,
900 Dandenong Road, Caulfield East, Victoria 3145, Australia
{Glenn.Jayaputera, Arkady.Zaslavsky, Seng.Loke}@infotech.monash.edu.au

**Abstract.** This paper presents an innovative multi-agent system development approach called mission-based on-demand agent generation. This approach allows agents to be dynamically composed at run-time and most importantly, only when needed. Such an approach is different from the conventional one, where agents are generally composed at design time. Our model of a mission allows the MAS to be suspended and resumed at later stage at the same or different location. We present the formal model of the mission, the strategy to execute the mission and the architecture of the prototype system called eHermes. Finally, we report the experimental results that shows that eHermes handles the load satisfactorily and performs the run-time optimization well.

## 1 Introduction

Researchers and developers realize that constructing multi-agent systems (including the individual agents and their coordination) is generally arduous. Many agent development tools such as ZEUS [1], JADE [2] and PAUL [3] were developed to address such issues. While such tools have addressed the issues to some degree, we argue that they are only useful for agent developers because those tools require the users to have detailed knowledge about agent technology. For instance, ZEUS requires the users to have knowledge about ontology, role modeling and coordination model before they can start any development.

In this paper we present an innovative approach which not only address such requirements but also introduces a new paradigm in Multi-Agent System (MAS) development and usage. Like any software system, MAS is created to address specific challenge. However, unlike in conventional software system, in MAS agent developers employ (multiple) agents as the key abstraction. Agents in MAS are specifically created to play certain roles. For instance, in a supply-chain application domain, there are some agents whose roles are to maintaining the stock level, to marketing the products, etc. When thinking at the level of individual agents, agent developers might need to very much focus on and fine-tune individual agents concerns (such as how each agent might communicate or cooperate with another, how it might negotiate or coordinate, learn, etc.), instead of focusing on the task or problem level semantics (e.g., the business logic, etc.) for the application. While this might be needed at times, we propose a different approach which:

J.P. Müller and F. Zambonelli (Eds.): AOSE 2005, LNCS 3950, pp. 139 – 153, 2006.

1. Adds a new level of abstraction; focusing on the purpose of the application rather than individual agents.
2. Emphasizes on the automatic generation of agents (as oppose to explicitly programming them). Our *mission-based on-demand agent generation* approach is analogous to a chief architect who concentrates on the overall design as opposed to wondering about who is going to do the plumbing, how good they are and so on. For the architect, once the design is complete a builder will be called in to build the house, and is not concerned with subcontractors for brick layering, plumbing, painting, and so on.

In our approach, given a mission, a set of agents are dynamically created at run-time and when they are needed to execute a task(s), thereby alleviating the need to think in terms of individual agents' details. Naturally, these agents are removed from the system once their service is no longer needed. The on-demand agent generation notion was first introduced in [4] while the mission concept was introduced in [5]. These new notions are the results of the following observations:

1. Many agent systems require the designer to estimate the number of agents needed at the design time. While such strategy is acceptable for a small system, it might soon become apparent that flexibility is needed due to the unpredictable nature of the run-time environment and the complexity of the task. Without the flexibility there could be a situation where there are not enough agents of the right capability to perform the task or even too many agents. Having inadequate number of agents can cause delays in reaching the goal, whilst too many agents do not necessarily mean that the goal can be reached faster or better results can be obtained. To use a classical example, having 100 plumbers to fix a broken pipe might not be any faster or yield better result than using only two.
2. Agents exist are to play specific roles, hence they are specialized to those roles throughout their life-cycle. Specialized means fixed in functionalities, and hence, when the problem domain changed then they cannot be used anymore. Furthermore, if we want to use those agents in a variant of the original problem domain then these agents need to be substantially modified and re-tested before they can be re-deployed. Such situation contradict to the spirit of component-based software engineering because we suspect that across such problem domain variations there would be common semantics as such that the reuse of logic and functionality is likely.
3. Specialized agents are acceptable only when the run-time condition is static or closely matched to the presumptions made at design time. However, when they are not, then this will force the execution to be aborted or failures to occur. For a simple illustration imagine a set of agents that were developed to operate on a SQL-based database have been deployed. However, if the database is changed then the whole monolithic MAS might need to be stopped and cannot the continued until the relevant agents are modified to accommodate this change.

Based on the observations above, we propose the mission-based on-demand agent generation as an alternative approach to construct MAS. Our objectives are as follows:

1. To be able to generate (the appropriate number of) agents (of the right functionality) when needed, given a description of the overall purpose of the application. Hence, depending on the complexity of the mission, the number of agents generated (and their functionality) is varied; complex mission might require more agents than simple ones.
2. To minimize the chance of aborting the mission execution unnecessarily. If the environmental conditions have changed during execution and the available agents are not suitable, then the execution should not be completely aborted, rather continued by generating the appropriate agents to replace the unsuitable ones (i.e., when there is an error, we avoid returning to the full cycle of code, compile, test and deploy). Also, the plan should be modifiable at run-time.
3. To be able to maintain the state and data of the mission so that it can be suspended and resumed at later stage as well as moved to different location at any time. Furthermore, by maintaining the execution history; the planner can use such knowledge in future planning.

The rest of this paper is divided into the following sections. Section 2 presents the theoretical work on the mission in particular its formal definition and the optimization strategy the system uses at run-time. Section 3 illustrates the implementation of our prototype system called eHermes and discusses time complexity of mission execution. Section 4 shows the experimental results, demonstrating the feasibility of our approach. Finally the conclusion and future work is presented in Section 5.

## 2 Mission: The Starting Point

Agents are created because they are needed to perform some actions; hence they have a "mission" to do. As well as the on-demand agent generation concept, *Mission* is one of the corner-stones of our approach. A mission exists if there is a goal and optionally a (partial) plan on how to achieve the goal. Given a mission, a set of agents (mobile and/or stationary) are created to work on the mission.

During the mission execution, the system monitors the number of tasks in hand and the number of available agents. Agents are created only when required and subsequently removed when they are not. This scalability is to ensure that there are no "jobless" agents in the system, either because of (i) lack of tasks to do, or (ii) waiting for a resource(s) to become available. The mission is modeled as a tuple of the form $M = (o, P, A, Z)$, where $o$ is goal of the mission as in string, *P* is a set of plans, *A* is a set of mobile and/or stationary agents working on the mission and finally, *Z* is a set of mission states.

Given a mission, the agents work to achieve the goal $o$ based on the current plan $p$ where $p \in P$. Hence, $p$ sets out the tasks that need to be executed. A task is defined as a tuple of the form $(u, n, y, s, o)$, where:

- $u \in U$, where $U$ is a set of unique IDs,
- $n \in N$, where $N$ is a set of locations at which tasks are executed,
- $y \in Y$, where *Y={primitive, compound}* denotes the set of task types,

- $s \in S$, where *S={completed, pending, inprogress, failed, aborted, assigned}* denotes the task status,
- $o \in O$, where *O* is a set of functions and/or logic calculations that must be performed.

From the definition above, there are two types of task, they are: *primitive* and *compound*. The primitive type is used to indicate that the task is the lowest level of task and hence cannot be decomposed further. Primitive tasks are directly executable. The compound type is used to indicate that (i) the task is complex and comprises of several compound and/or primitive sub-tasks, and (ii) the task may contain complex operational constructs. Each task has a status and this status represent the status of that task at any given point in time. For instance, the *completed* tag is used to indicate that the task has successfully executed, the *pending* tag indicates the task has not been executed and is waiting to be assigned to an agent, the *inprogress* tag indicates that the task is in the middle of execution, the *failed* tag indicates that the task has failed, the *aborted* tag indicates that the task has been aborted (but not failed) and finally the *assigned* tag indicates that the task has been allocated to an agent that is yet to start executing. Hence, as the tasks are executed their statuses are changed.

Tasks are interrelated to each other and they are represented by links. Links has two purposes, they are: (i) to convey the task decomposition structure information and (ii) to set the priori between the tasks (partial ordering). A link in a TDG is defined as a tuple of the form $(t_i, t_j, q)$ where $t \in T, i \in \mathbb{Z}^+, j \in \mathbb{Z}^+, q \in Q$ and *Q={includes, dependson}* is a set of link attributes. The *includes* attribute is used to capture the inclusion relationship between tasks. The *dependson* attribute is used to describe the dependency between tasks. For instance, a tuple $(t_a, t_b, dependson)$ means that $t_a$ depends on $t_b$ and hence $t_b$ must be executed and completed first before $t_a$ can start. This relationship dictates the dependencies between tasks in the plan and must be honored during execution.

A plan is represented in a DAG-based structure called *Task Decomposition Graph (TDG)* which is formally defined as follows:

*Given a function* $f_{type} : T \rightarrow Y$ *which returns the type of a given task, a TDG is a pair* $TDG = (T, L)$ *where T is a non-empty set of tasks, L is a non-empty set of links and has the following properties:*

$$\begin{aligned}
&\text{(i)} \quad \forall (t_i, t_j, q) \in L, \ \text{s.t. } f_{type}(t_i) \neq primitive \\
&\text{(ii)} \quad \forall (t_i, t_j, q) \in L \text{ s.t. if } q = includes \text{ then } f_{type}(t_i) = compound \\
&\text{(iii)} \quad \forall (t_i, t_j, q) \in L \text{ s.t. if } f_{type}(t_j) = compound \text{ then } \exists (t_j, t_k, q') \in L
\end{aligned} \tag{1}$$

*where* $t_i, t_j, t_k \in T, q, q' \in Q$ and $i, j, k \in \mathbb{Z}^+$.

The first property specifies that a primitive task cannot be a source node and hence primitive tasks are always at the leaf nodes. This property also specifies that a primitive task cannot depend on any other tasks. The second property specifies that when the link is an *includes* link then the source node must be a compound task, hence it indirectly specifies that a primitive task cannot be decomposed further. The third property specifies that a compound task cannot be at the leaf node.

When a mission is executed, the system actually executes the current plan specified within the mission.

*Given a function* $f_{status} : T \rightarrow S$ *which reports the status of a given task, a mission if said to be accomplished if all the tasks in the mission has been completed or aborted, and hence:* (2)

$$\forall t \in T \text{ s.t. } f_{status}(t) = completed \vee f_{status}(t) = aborted$$

A TDG can be potentially large in size; hence it is necessary to avoid exhaustive graph searching each time the system tries to find the next batch of tasks to be carried out. To answer this challenge we put the following policies:

- Only executes the primitive tasks.
- Disallow dependencies between primitive tasks as imposed by the TDG's property.
- Convert a compound task into a primitive according to the following rule:

  *A compound task* $t = (u, n, Compound, s, o)$ *can be converted into a primitive task if and only if all task t's sub-tasks are completed or aborted, and hence:* (3)

  $$L_c = \{(t_j, t_k, q) \in L \mid t_j = t_i\}$$

  $$\forall (t_j, t_k, q) \in L_c \text{ s.t. } f_{status}(t_k) = completed \vee f_{status}(t_k) = aborted$$

Run-time mission execution support is regarded as another key issue that must be address in order to increase the possibility to successfully carry out a mission. In our approach the supports provided include the mechanisms where data exchange can be carried out, the state and data of the mission are captured and maintained for later use and finally the mechanism to change the plan at run-time efficiently.

When the tasks are executed, they may or may not produce results/output. Subsequently, these results may or may not be required by other agents. Acknowledging this condition, we design a placeholder for the agents to exchange data and call this placeholder *Mission Data Space (MDS)*. The idea behind MDS is similar to that of JavaSpace™ except MDS is local to a mission. MDS is made local to a mission because: (i) MDS contains intermediate results and hence they should be exposed, (ii) localizing MDS means smaller size and hence easier to manage, and finally, (iii) security concern, we cannot permit agents from other systems or missions looking at the MDS of another mission. MDS is formally defined as follows:

*Mission Data Space (MDS) is a set of tuples of the form* $(u_t, r, t_s)$ *where* $u_t$ *is a unique ID of task* $t \in T$, $r \in R$ *and R is a set of results/output, and finally* $t_s$ *is the timestamp at which r was produced.* (4)

Besides identifying the importance of having a space for the agents to exchange their data, we also recognize the significance of capturing and preserving the mission execution history. In our concept, preserving the mission execution history means maintaining the state and data of the mission. Hence, the structure of the plan and the state and data of the tasks have to be captured. The benefits of capturing the execution history are: (i) the ability to suspend and resume the mission execution at the same or a different location, and (ii) execution history provides valuable knowledge for the mission planner to use in its learning process so that it can generate better plans in the future. The formal definition of the mission state is defined as follows

*Let* $E = \{e', e'', e''', \ldots\}$ *be the finite set of events that can trigger transitions and* $MS = \{ms_1, ms_2, \ldots\}$ *be a set of mission states, then a mission execution ME is a sequence of interleaved mission states and events such that:*

$$ME : ms_1 \xrightarrow{e'} ms_2 \xrightarrow{e''} ms_3 \xrightarrow{e'''} \ldots.$$

*A mission state* $z \in Z$ *is a snapshot of the state and data of the mission, and is defined as a tuple of the form (p, mds, e,* $t_s$ *) where* $p \in P$ *is the current plan,* $mds \in MDS$ *is the snapshot of the MDS,* $e \in E$ *is the event that trigger the state transition, E={Suspend, Stop, Resume, Start, ChangePlan} and finally* $t_s$ *is the timestamp at which the mission state is generated.* (5)

It is important and crucial for a mission to have the ability to modify its plan at run-time. This is because the plan can be partially complete initially or only represents the best plan that a planner can produce at a point in time. There is no absolute guarantee in general that, at the point of creation, the plan can succeed when executed. The success or failure of the plan can only be determined when it is executed. Providing alternative plans before run-time also does not necessarily solve the problem because there is a possibility that none of those plans can succeed. Furthermore, carrying those alternative plans can be impractical due the size of each plan can be quite big. Our approach to address this issue is to modify the plan dynamically at run-time.

Modifying a plan can be a complex task if the representation model itself is complex. Hence it is important (for our purpose) to have a lightweight, simple and dynamic plan representation. Since TDG is a DAG, modifying it is a simple operation of adding and/or deleting nodes and/or links. The operation of modifying the TDG is formally specified as follows:

*Let* $\Delta = \delta_T \cup \delta_L$ *be a set of tasks and nodes to be added/removed from the a plan p=(T,L), where* $\delta_T$ *is a non-empty set of tasks that need to be added/removed from p and* $\delta_L$ *is a non-empty set of links that need to be added/removed from p. Then* $\Delta$ *can be easily applied to p with the following operations* (6)

$$(T \cup \delta_T) \setminus (T \cap \delta_T)$$
$$(L \cup \delta_L) \setminus (L \cap \delta_L)$$

As previously mentioned, only primitive tasks are executed. Given a current plan *p=(T,L)*, a group of primitive tasks is called *stratum* and is formally defined as:

$$ST = \{t \in T \mid f_{type}(t) = primitive \wedge f_{status}(t) = pending\} \quad (7)$$

A stratum is not the same as the leveling concept that can be found in general graph theory where the depth of a node is used as to determine its level. Figure 1 shows the difference between the level and stratum.

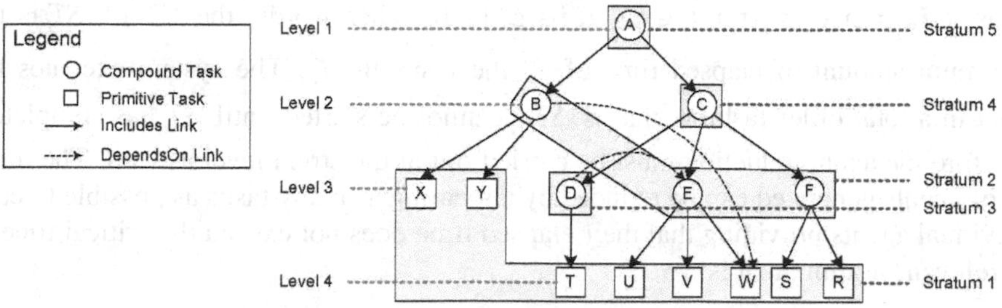


**Fig. 1.** The difference between graph level and strata. The first stratum is $ST_1 = \{X, Y, T, U, V, W, S, R\}$. Assuming that all the tasks in $ST_1$ are completed, then the second stratum is $ST_2 = \{B, E, F\}$. Note that, task *D* was not included in $ST_2$ because it depends on task *E*. The subsequent strata are: $ST_3 = \{D\}, ST_4 = \{C\}, ST_5 = \{A\}$.

Tasks are not executed directly by the system but rather through a set of agents. Depending on the location at which the task must be executed, mobile/stationary agents are created accordingly. The easiest and perhaps a naive approach is to create an agent for each of the task in the TDG. However, such a simplistic approach is too expensive to be used because it represents the worst case scenario where the total number of agents created will be equal to $|T|$, the total number of tasks in the current plan. In search for a better alternative, we decided to add some intelligence to the agent that controls the execution of the mission so that it can determine the cost and benefit of creating agents. Equipped with this capability, the controlling agent will try to minimize the cost of executing the mission without compromising the goal of the mission itself. Let the cost for executing a task be the cost for creating an agent to carry out the task plus the cost for executing the task, defined as follows:

$$f_{cost}(t) = f_{cost}(createAgent(t)) + f_{cost}(exec(t)) \quad (8)$$

Given a mission, then the cost for executing that mission can be easily defined as:

$$\sum_{i=1}^{|T|} f_{cost}(t_i) \text{ , where } \forall t_i \in T \quad (9)$$

A Critical Time (*CT*) of a mission is defined as *the minimum amount of time required to complete the mission*. Similarly the CT of a stratum is the minimum amount of time required to complete all the tasks in that stratum. We assume that the cost for executing a task is the same everywhere, ignoring the computing power and locality of the host. Hence, due to this assumption, the $f_{cost}(exec(t))$ of definition (7) above will become constant and thus ignored. This means that the cost of mission execution can be reduced by minimizing the number of agents generated. However, the reduction of the number of agents for a mission must be done adequately so that the mission completion time is not affected for, otherwise, we will end up with the situation where the benefit is also reduced as we reduce cost.

The tasks in a stratum are executed concurrently. Given $f_{\Theta}(t) = \mathbb{Z}^+$ where $t \in T$, a function that returns the elapsed time for task $t$ execution, then the CT of stratum $ST_i$ is $CT_{ST_i} = \max\{f_{\Theta}(t_j) \mid t_j \in ST_i, i, j \in \mathbb{Z}^+\}$. In other words, the CT of $ST_i$ is the maximum amount of elapsed time of all the tasks in $ST_i$. The system executes the strata in a total order fashion, that is $ST_{i+1}$ cannot be started until $ST_i$ has completed, therefore the agent reduction must be carried out at the strata level as well. The number of agents generated can be reduced by allocating as many tasks as possible to each individual agents providing that their elapsed time does not exceed the critical time of the relevant stratum, that is:

$$\sum_{j=1}^{n} f_{\Theta}(t_j) \leq CT_{ST_i} \text{ where } n = |ST_i|, t_j \in ST_i, i, j \in \mathbb{Z}^+ \tag{10}$$

Optimizing task allocation to the agents is an off-line bin packing problem and hence finding the optimal solutions to this problem would be NP-Hard. However, there are a number of near optimal solutions have been proposed and one of the best ones is FFD (First-Fit Decreasing) [6]. Using FFD algorithm, the tasks in each stratum are sorted in decreasing order according to their $f_{\Theta}$ values. Hence, the task that needs the longest time to complete will be the first and the shortest will be last. The size of the bin is then the value of $f_{\Theta}$ of the first task ($f_{\Theta}(t_1)$). The tasks from this stratum are then grouped into clusters where the sum of $f_{\Theta}$ of each clusters is less than or equal to $f_{\Theta}(t_1)$. Given $n$ as the total number of items to be bin-packed, FFD can be easily implemented in $O(n \log n)$ time [6].

## 3 eHermes: The Generator

eHermes is the prototype system that implements the concepts previously described. Its architecture is shown in Figure 2. Requests that are coming to the eHermes system are first handled by the mission generator. The mission generator is in charge of creating a mission object. This includes interpreting the request and converting it into a form that the mission planner can understand and finally wrapping the output from the planner into an object. The mission planner is the module which is in charge of generating the plan for a given request. Finding the best planning algorithm is beyond the scope of our project, however, we noted that a HTN-based planner [7] can accommodate such requirement.

During planning, the planner checks for the existing plans in the mission repository, and will utilize any similar plan if exists. The planner also uses domain knowledge from the ontology in order to avoid misinterpretation of the request. Once the planner has completed its task, it sends the plan it has just created to the mission generator. Then, the mission generator constructs a mission object from this plan. At this point, it is said that the mission is ready to be carried out.

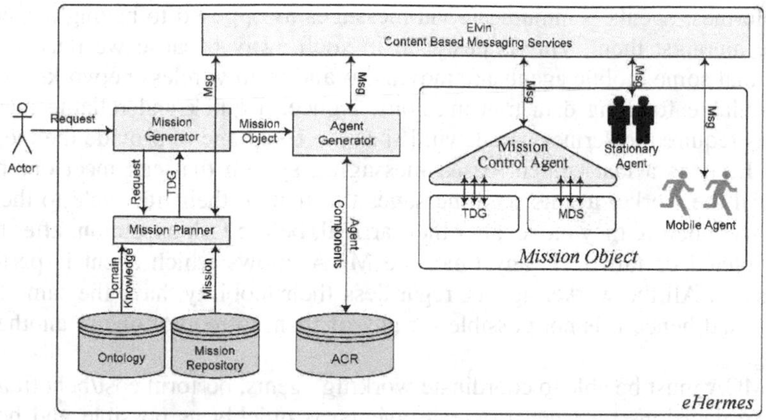


**Fig. 2.** eHermes Architecture. The *Mission Generator, Mission Planner, Agent Generator* and *Elvin* are the four main components of eHermes.

The mission object is passed on to the agent generator, the module which in charge of generating agents on the fly. The first thing the agent generator would perform upon receiving the mission object is to create a special agent called the *Mission Control Agent* (*MCA*). The main task of the MCA is to manage the mission execution and liaise with the actor. The MCA keeps the actor up to date with the mission execution status all the time. The actor can control the state of the mission execution via the MCA. For instance, if the mission needs to be stopped, then the actor instructs the MCA to stop the execution. In fact, from the actor's point of view, there is only a single agent (i.e. the MCA) works on the mission

When executing the mission, the MCA executes the tasks specified in the TDG in the stratum by stratum fashion as explained previously. The MCA does not execute the task by itself, but rather relies on the assistance from a set of agents which are dynamically created. Tasks within each stratum are analyzed by the MCA. The cost and benefit of assigning them to an agent are calculated as specified according to rule (6) in the previous section. Once the task clustering is done, the task clusters are sent to the agent generator along with the specification of each agent which will be used to create those agents. During the construction, the agent generator uses the available agent component from the *Agent Component Repository (ACR)*. Each of the agents created (including the MCA) has a unique ID (UID), which is sent back to the MCA. This UID is crucial because it is used for the communication between them. Once the agents are created, the MCA sends a command to them to start executing the task(s) that have been assigned. The MCA does not instruct nor control the agents where to go or what task to perform first but rather lets those agents use their ability to decide and make the move themselves. In many instances, the mobile agents are hopping from one location to another and execute the tasks at each location. During this execution, the agents keep in touch with the MCA about their activities and location. For instance, if one of the tasks has failed to execute the agent sends a message to the MCA which then will make a decision either to change that task to something else or inform the actor about the situation. If the mission needs to be modified then the simple set operations explained previously will be employed.

In eHermes, agents communicate via messages as opposed to having a speech act dialogue amongst them. This is designed in such away because we must take into account that some mobile agents are moving to and from wireless networks which are not so reliable for long data transmissions. Hence, a quick and reliable messaging service is required. eHermes uses Elvin [8] as the backbone to provide the messaging service. Elvin is a fast content based messaging system that can meet our requirements. All the worker agents send messages throughout their life cycle to the MCA. For instance, before they move, after their arrival, before task execution, after the task has completed or failed. At any time, the MCA knows which agent is performing what task(s). All the worker agents, regardless their mobility, have the same level of authority and hence it is not possible for any of them to request one to another to do anything.

The MCA must be able to coordinate working agents, perform cost/benefit analysis and make decisions on when to create agents as quickly as possible and hence its algorithm must be efficient. Table 1 shows MCA's algorithm.

**Table 1.** The MCA algorithm

```
1   // Create a stratum to work with                         .......T(n)
2   for i=0 to count([A])-1 do                               .......c1n
3       if A[i] == primitive && A[i] == pending              .......c2n
4           B.add(A[i])                                      .......c3n
5
6   if (isEmpty([B]) == false) then                          .......c4
7   {
8       quickSort([B])                                       .......O(m log m)
9
10      // FDD_Optimization takes on [B] and produce [C]
11      FFD_Optimization([B])                                .......O(m log m)
12
13      for j=0 to count([C]) do                             .......c5p
14      {
15          Agent = createAgent(C[j])                        .......c6p
16          sendCommand( Agent, START_EXECUTION )            .......c7p
17      }
18  }
```

Once created the MCA begins its activity by creating a stratum. In Table 1, *[A]* denotes a set of tasks in the current plan, *[B]* is a stratum and *[C]* is a set of task-clusters. Lines 2-4 are used to create a stratum. Tasks that are primitive and pending are collected and put into *[B]*. If *[B]* is not empty, then the execution is continued by sorting the content of *[B]* using Quicksort, and then performs FFD bin-packing routine over the sorted *[B]*. The bin packing routine produces a set of task clusters which are then stored into *[C]*. From here on, the MCA calls *createAgent()* repeatedly to create an agent for each cluster. Once those agents are ready, they will be instructed to start the execution by executing the *sendCommand()*. The notation on the right hand column of the table denotes the time (*T(n)*) taken to execute the related line of codes, where *n* is the number of tasks in *[A]*. Constants $ci, i \in \mathbb{Z}^+$ denote the costs for executing lines of code, e.g. *c1*, *c2*, *c3*, etc. Note, from lines 2-4, $[B] \subseteq [A]$, and since *m* denotes the number of tasks in *[B]* and *n* denotes the number of tasks in *[A]*, then $m \leq n$. Using a similar explanation, we get $[C] \subseteq [B]$ and $p \leq m$. It should be noted that, in our implementation, we have a generic agent class which we simply load at run-time when *createAgent()* is called, hence the time complexity of lines 15 is simply *c6p*. Similar explanation goes to line 16. The total amount time to execute the algorithm in Table 1 is then:

$$T(n) = c1n + c2n + c3n + c4 + O(m \log m) + O(m \log m) + c5p + c6p + c7p$$

Since $m \leq n$ and $p \leq m$, and in the worst scenario, $p = m$ and $m = n$, hence $p = n$. Therefore, after removing the constants, insignificant values, and substituting *m* and *p* to *n*, the average complexity time of our algorithm is $O(n \log n)$. In the worst scenario, Quicksort's complexity time becomes $O(n^2)$, which also pushes our complexity time to $O(n^2)$.

Figure 3 shows a screenshot of the eHermes client. The top right-hand side window shows the TDG structure being executed. Compound tasks are represented by circle and primitive tasks are by rectangles. The color of these tasks represents their status visually. When status of a task is pending then it will be painted in white. The green color is to illustrate that the task has been completed successfully, yellow color to indicate that the task is being performed and finally red to represent that that task has failed. The top left-hand side window lists the tasks and links of the TDG. By clicking

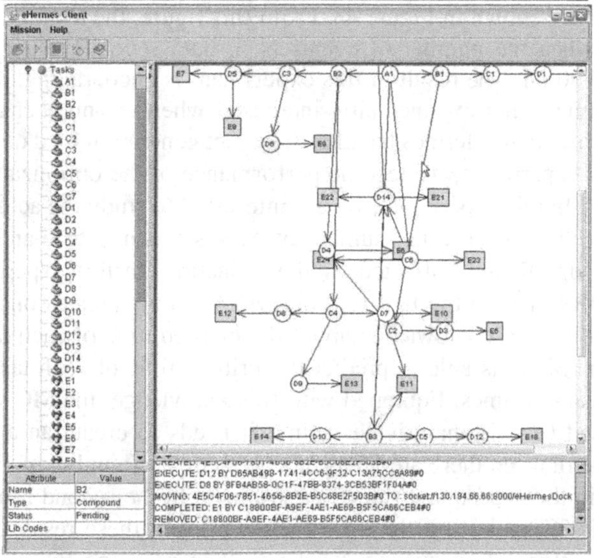


**Fig. 3.** The eHermes client screen snapshot. The square nodes represent the primitive tasks while the round nodes represent the compound tasks. The top left-hand side window shows the structural details of a mission. Clicking any of the items in this window will make the bottom left-hand window to display the details of that item. Finally, the bottom right-hand side window shows the log of the mission execution.

any of these items make the bottom left-hand side window to change its contents because this window shows the details of any highlighted task or link. The last window, the bottom right-hand window, shows the log of all the activities.

## 4 Experimental Results

The results of the experiments that have been conducted are reported in this section. The experiments were carried out on Pentium™ based machines running Microsoft™ Windows XP. Each machine has 512Mbytes of RAM and is connected through a 10/100 Mbps LAN with typical university loads. We use a Linux machine to host the Elvin message routing server and Grasshopper's Region Registry. The Region Registry is a directory service; it maintains the information of all the running agents.

Figure 4a shows the average performance of the system when the depth of the TDG and the number of tasks in the TDG increase. We set up a test case where the number of tasks in each level of the TDG is equivalent to $n^l$ where $n$ is the number of child nodes each parent node have and $l$ is the level number (counting from level 0 or the root). In this experiment, we use $n=4$ and $l=0,...6$. Hence, when $l=6$, the total number of tasks in the TDG is 5,461.

In the first experiment, we test how eHermes handles the load when it is given missions with various kinds of plan complexity. The simple plan consists of only five tasks while the most complex one contains 5,461 tasks. In this test we turn off the optimization strategy, thus we assign one task per agent. We calculate the average execution time by dividing the mission elapsed time with the number of agents generated. The results are shown in Figure 4a. From this figure, the average execution time is 1.4 seconds when the number of agents is 5, 0.95 seconds when the number of agents is 21 and so on. The result of this experiment is encouraging, in that the average execution time is not exponentially increased when the number of agents is increased. This shows that eHermes handles the agent generation load quite well.

In the second experiment, we test the performance of the optimization concept we presented earlier. In this experiment, we are interested to study the actual performance of the concept with respect to the number of agents it can reduce and if the mission elapsed time is significantly affected by the reduction. In this experiment the same mission is run 18 times. In the first run, the MCA simply creates one agent per task since it does not have any knowledge about the elapsed time of each task. In the subsequent runs, the MCA is able to predict the critical time of each task by averaging their previous elapsed times. Equipped with this knowledge, the MCA is able to perform the cost and benefit analysis each time it needs to create an agent. Figure 4b shows that in the first run there are 55 agents created. The number of agents is significantly reduced in the subsequent runs. For instance, in the second run the number of agents created is 37, and 38 in the third run, etc. From these results, it can be concluded that the optimization concept works well in reducing the number of agents needed to accomplish a mission. In this experiment, we have obtained as much as 40% agent reduction (run number 14). The graph in Figure 4b also shows the trend that after a number of runs the agent count cannot be reduced anymore.

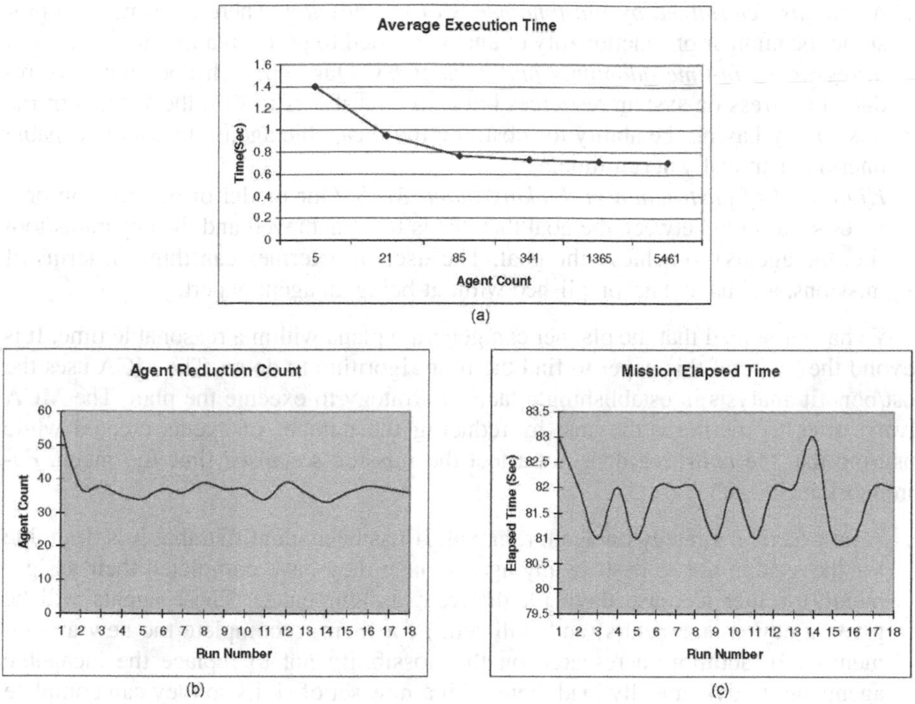


**Fig. 4.** The graphs that show the experimental results. The average execution time is shown in (a) while (b) shows the result of the cost/benefit analysis being applied.

While it has been demonstrated that the optimization concept can reduce the number of agents, we must also be ensured that the reduction does not affect the mission elapsed time significantly. Certainly it is not enviable to have a situation where the mission suddenly takes longer than anticipated although the cost to run it is cheaper. Therefore, for each of the run we conducted in this experiment, we also measured the elapsed time. The results are plotted as shown in Figure 4c. In the first run, where the optimization is not performed, it takes approximately 83 seconds to complete the mission. The graph in Figure 4c shows that the elapsed times of the subsequent runs are around the same as the first run. The best result obtained is on run number 14 where with the number of agent is reduced by 40%, yet the elapsed time is the same as there is no reduction at all. This experiments shows that the Cost/Benefit approach used in the optimization concept works well.

## 5 Conclusion and Future Work

We have presented the approach to dynamically generating agents from a mission. The notion of on-demand agent generation, the formal model of the mission, the prototype tool and experimental results are presented. Different from the traditional approach to creating MASs; we emphasize the dynamic and on-demand agent generation at run-time. The benefits of our approach are:

1. *Agents as determined by run-time needs of the mission.* There is no need to presume the number or functionality of agents needed to perform a mission.
2. *Integrated run-time adaptivity and robustness.* Our approach does not only reduce the stress on system resources but also contributes toward the success of the mission by having the ability to substitute the incapable agent(s) with the capable one(s) dynamically at run-time.
3. *High level of abstraction in thinking about MAS.* Our model of the mission provides separation between the goal that needs to be achieved and the apparatus/tool (i.e. the agents) to achieve the goal. The user of eHermes can think in terms of missions, and have it accomplished without being an agent expert.

We have assumed that the planner can generate plans within a reasonable time. It is beyond the scope of this paper to find the best algorithm to do so. The MCA uses the cost/benefit analysis in establishing a tactical strategy to execute the plan. The MCA always tries to minimize the cost by reducing the number of agents created while ensuring that the reduction does not affect the mission's elapsed time too much. Future work includes:

1. A new tactical strategy on agent removal. It has been identified that it is desirable for the system not to destroy any agents once they have completed their assignment(s), rather to reuse them for different assignment(s). These agents will be given a new assignment(s) and skill-set(s) for them to complete the new assignment(s). In addition, a research on the possibility not to replace the incapable agents but to dynamically load them with a new set of skills so they can complete the task(s) is needed.
2. The size of the TDG can potentially be large and hence it might be necessary to split it into several smaller sub-TDGs. The MCA then clones itself and assigns each clone with the sub-TDG. Research must be conducted to determine when the main MCA should clone itself and create sub-TDGs.
3. Using the average value of previous elapsed times is not too suitable to be used to estimate the critical time and hence other methods must be explored further.

## Acknowledgements

Support from the ARC Linkage Grant LPO211384 and Microsoft Research Asia is thankfully acknowledged.

## References

1. Nwana, H.S., et al. *ZEUS: A Toolkit and Approach for Building Distributed Multi-Agent Systems.* in *3rd International Conference on Autonomous Agents (Agents '99)*. 1999. Seattle, USA: ACM Press.
2. Bellifemine, F., et al., *JADE - A White Paper.* TILAB EXP, 2003. **3**(3): p. 6-19.
3. Ehrler, L. and S. Cranefield. *Executing Agent UML Diagrams.* in *3rd International Joint Conference on Autonomous Agents & Multi Agent Systems*. 2004. New York, USA: ACM Publishing.

4. Jayaputera, G.T., et al. *Assembling Agents On-Demand for Pervasive Wireless Services*. in *2nd International Workshop on Wireless Information Services (WIS 2003)*. 2003. Angers-France: ICEIS Press.
5. Jayaputera, G.T., S.W. Loke, and A. Zaslavsky. *Mission Impossible? Automatically Assembling Agents from High-Level Task Descriptions*. in *The 2003 IEEE/WIC International Conference on Intelligent Agent Technology (IAT 2003)*. 2003. Halifax, Canada: IEEE Computer Society.
6. Martello, S. and P. Toth, *Knapsack Problems: Algorithms and Computer Implementations*. 1990: John Wiley & Sons.
7. Russell, S.J. and P. Norvig, *Artificial Intelligence: A Modern Approach*. 1995: Prentice Hall.
8. Segall, B., et al. *Content Based Routing with Elvin4*. in *Australian UNIX and Open Systems User Group Conference 2000 (AUUG 2000)*. 2000. Canberra Australia.

# Supporting the Development of Multi-agent Interactions Via Roles

Giacomo Cabri, Luca Ferrari, and Letizia Leonardi

Dipartimento di Ingegneria dell'Informazione - Università di Modena e Reggio Emilia, Via Vignolese, 905 – 41100 Modena – Italy
{cabri.giacomo, ferrari.luca, leonardi.letizia}@unimo.it

**Abstract.** In the multi-agent scenario, interaction among agents is an issue that must be faced in an appropriate way. Modeling interactions by roles can simplify the development of the interactions in agent-based applications. The BRAIN framework proposes an interaction model based on roles, an XML notation to define roles, and interaction infrastructures based on the role model and notation. In this paper we explain how the BRAIN framework can be exploited in the different phases of the development of applications where agents play roles. The general advantage is that the development phases rely on the same information, adapted to different needs, granting coherence and continuity during the development.

## 1 Introduction

Multi-agent systems are gaining more and more ground in the development of complex applications [2]. The advent of agents raised the problem of dealing with interactions either in a cooperation or a competition way. In fact, one of the main features of agents is sociality, i.e., the capability of interacting with each other. This feature is exploited in Multi Agent Systems, where the main task is divided into small tasks, each one delegated to a single agent; agents belonging to the same application have to interact in order to carry out the main task [13]. Moreover, the diffusion of open systems, such as the Internet, has led to a scenario in which not only agents of the same application interact in a cooperative way, but also agents of different applications may interact in a competitive way, for example to use resources. The feature of mobility, which allows agents to change their execution environment, adds great flexibility at both conceptual and implementation levels, but also introduces peculiar issues in interaction that must be taken into account carefully [12].

Interactions are not an exclusive field of agent technology, and in fact, since the rising of distributed systems, interaction among entities has been an issue to be faced. Different approaches have been proposed, among which the most popular is message-passing [11, 22]; it enables the exchange of messages among entities, and it is simple and suits a wide range of application requirements. Another interaction approach that is worth being mentioned is Linda [1], which is based on an uncoupled coordination model and relies on shared dataspaces.

The above traditional approaches have been ported to the agent scenario [8], creating the "meeting point" abstractions [23], event-channels [3], and reactive tuple

J.P. Müller and F. Zambonelli (Eds.): AOSE 2005, LNCS 3950, pp. 154 – 166, 2006.

spaces [9]. Further approaches have been proposed, like the one adopted in Agentis [16], which models interactions in terms of services and tasks; such approach clearly points out the need of tailoring interactions on agent features.

In fact, approaches to agent interactions usually derive from adaptations of traditional models related to distributed systems, so they do not fit all the characteristics of the new scenario. Moreover, it is important to provide developers with appropriate tools to represent interactions and the way they happen [20, 19].

Recognizing the limitations of the traditional approaches, we have proposed BRAIN, a framework to deal with agent interactions based on *roles*. There are different advantages in modeling interaction by roles. First, it enables the separation of concerns between the algorithmic issues and the interaction issues in developing agent-based applications. Second, it permits the reuse of solutions and experiences; in fact, roles are related to a context (i.e., an execution environment), and designers can exploit previously defined roles for the context their application belongs; therefore roles can be seen as a sort of design patterns [2]: a set of related roles along with the definition of the way they interact can be considered as a solution to a well-defined problem, and reused in different similar situations. Finally, roles can be exploited to easily build agent-oriented interfaces of Internet sites [10]: in fact, roles can be bound to a specific site implementation and agents can exploit services of such site by assuming its roles.

The paper is organized as follows. Section 2 glances at the BRAIN framework, while section 3 explains how this framework can be exploited during the phases of the development process. Section 4 shows a simple example of application; section 5 reports some related work; and finally section 6 concludes the paper.

## 2 BRAIN

The BRAIN (Behavioural Roles for Agent INteractions) framework [5, 6] is based on the concept of *role* and aims at covering the agent-based application development at different phases. To this purpose, it provides for a *model of interactions* that is based on roles, an XML-based *notation* to describe the roles, and *interaction infrastructures* supporting agents in the management of roles. Such infrastructures are based on the adopted model and rely on the defined XML notation (see Fig. 1).

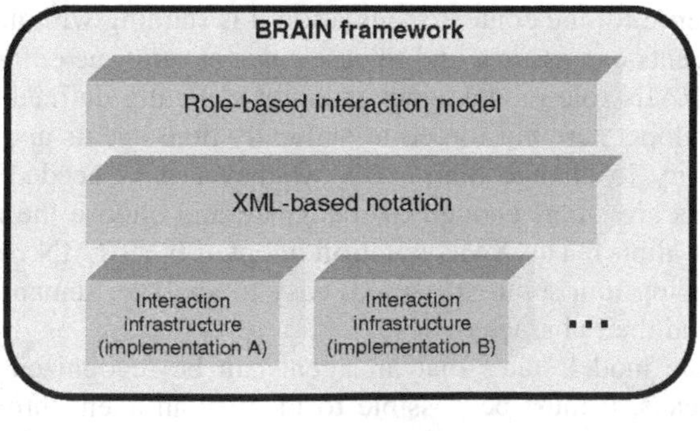


**Fig. 1.** The BRAIN framework

It is important to note that, since this framework is made by three layered levels, it can be easily adapted to different application scenarios and can evolve keeping a good modularity. For example, as shown in Fig. 1, BRAIN can support several interaction infrastructures, running under the same XML notation and role model. Moreover, thanks to its layered organization, the BRAIN framework is able to support the development of applications at all the main phases (i.e., analysis, design, implementation) and the runtime execution.

## 2.1 Role Model

In BRAIN, a role is defined as a *set of capabilities* and an *expected behavior*. The former is a set of *actions* that an agent playing such role can perform to achieve its task. The latter is a set of *events* that an agent is expected to manage in order to "behave" as requested by the role it plays. Interactions among agents are then represented by couples (action, event), which are dealt with by the underlying interaction system, part of the BRAIN infrastructure. Fig. 2 shows how an interaction between two agents occurs. This model of interactions is very simple and general, and well suits the main features of the agents: the actions can be seen as the concrete representation of agent *proactiveness* (i.e., the capability of carrying out their goals), while the events reify the agent *reactivity* (i.e., the capability of reacting to environment changes).

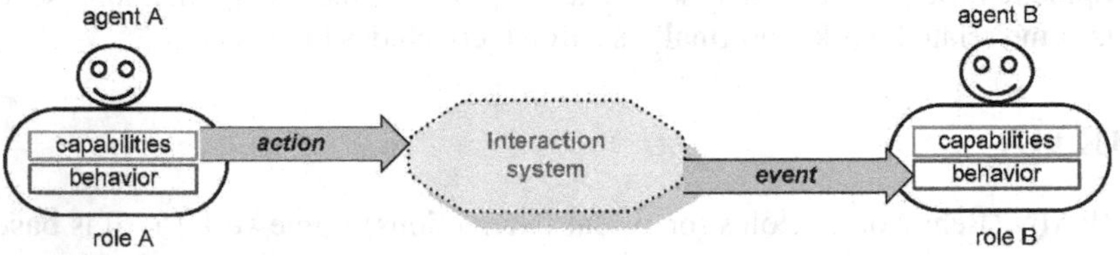


**Fig. 2.** The Interaction model in BRAIN

The role model proposed by BRAIN is flexible and dynamic, and in fact it must be noted that an agent is not tied to an unique role, but it can assume/release several roles during its entire life. Moreover, the same agent can play different roles at the same time, if it makes sense for the context/application it is running within.

The fact that agents can assume and release roles at run-time enforces the dynamic behavior of the BRAIN role model, since it is not statically defined. This means that designers and developers are not forced to statically bind agents and roles, leaving to agents the capability to change their roles whenever it is needed. Of course, this requires that agents are smart enough to recognize and choose the most appropriate role for its current aim(s). The XML notation adopted by BRAIN can be very useful to select roles, leading to a semi-structured, easy to analyze, semantically based way to describe roles and their characteristics.

The BRAIN role model states that an agent can be recognized by the role(s) it is playing, that means, it must be possible to identify an agent through the role it is playing. This is important due to two facts: (i) an agent can change the role it is playing dynamically, thus the agent/role mapping evolves and changes during the application life, (ii) since roles are used to model interactions, it is important that roles involved in the same interaction agree on the communication protocol, that means they must have been designed the one with regard to the others.

Due to this characteristic of the BRAIN role model other agents can search for and discover an agent playing a specific role(s) and thus providing specific capabilities and services.

## 2.2 XRole

The main aim of XRole is to support the management of the interactions among agents, at the different phases of the development of agent-based applications. XRole adopts the model of role of BRAIN, based on *actions* and *events* (see Fig. 2), exploiting the XML language.

XML, representing information in a tagged form, exhibits the well-appreciated feature of human-readability and platform-independence required for the Internet. This allows a high degree of interoperability and helps in dealing heterogeneous situations such as the ones of the Internet. In fact, the description of each role can be presented to people via an appropriate XSL sheet that transforms the information in a human-understandable document, for instance an HTML page with the needed pieces of information. This makes designers aware about the roles defined in a given context, and let them choose the representation of the information that better suits their requirements. In addition, programmers can exploit automatic tools to search for roles matching given keywords and which present the found results in a tailored way. A further advantage of XRole is that documents can be managed also by the agents themselves, which can be enabled to understand the content of XML documents and exploit or manipulate them without the need of the intervention of human people.

In XRole, roles are defined by XML documents that respect a specific XML schema [5]. The XML Schema for roles presents three main parts that have to be specified in the definition of a role, following the above-described model:

- *The basic information.* This part includes the pieces of information that are used to identify the role, and to specify a context for such role. Moreover, a high-level description and some keywords are supplied to let developers better understand the role functionalities.
- *The allowed actions.* Each role defines which the allowed actions are, i.e. the actions needed to carry out a task related to such role. An action is characterized by a name and a high-level description that can be useful for developers.
- *The recognized events.* These are events that the agent playing this role is expected to accept and manage. An event is characterized by a name and a high-level description that is useful to developers.

Fig. 3 shows an example of an XRole document for a game player role (see section 4 for further details), a role assumed by an agent that wants to participate to a gaming session. The description of the role, included between the <GenericRoleDescription> tags, includes a few information about the role (basic information) such as a description, the role name, the keywords, etc. Following that, it is possible to note the description of the askKind action (tag <OperationDescription>), which in particular allows the agent to ask to the game manager what kind of game is currently running. This operation will produce an incoming event (notifyKind), described in the <EventDescriptor> tags, that the agent should handle, since it represents the reply to the above question.

```
<?xml version='1.0'?>
<role xmlns="http://agentgroup.unimo.it/schema/BRAINSchema"
   xmlns:xsi="http://www.w3.org/2001/XMLSchema-instance"
   xsi:SchemaLocation="http://agentgroup.unimo.it/schema/BRAINSchema" >
 <GenericRoleDescription>
   <description>Game Player Role</description>
   <roleName>player</roleName>
   <!-- data useful to identify this role -->
   <keyword>game</keyword>
   <keyword>player</keyword>
   <keyword>make moves</keyword>
   <version>1</version>
   <!-- an operation of this role -->
   <OperationDescription>
     <name>askKind</name>
     <aim>get the kind of current game</aim>
     <keyword>kind</keyword>
     <keyword>request</keyword>
      ...
      <EventDescriptor>
         <name>notifyKind</name>
         <aim>Informs which kind of game is currently on</aim>
         . . .
         <ReceivingEvent>true</ReceivingEvent>
      </EventDescriptor>

    </OperationDescription>
   <!--  other role actions/operations here -->
   ...
   <!--  an event that can be received even without an action -->
   <EventDescriptor>
      <name>requestMove</name>
      <aim>Request the player to make a move</aim>
      . . .
      <ReceivingEvent>true</ReceivingEvent>
   </EventDescriptor>
 </GenericRoleDescription>
```

**Fig. 3.** An example of a XRole document for the game player role

It is important to note that, thanks to the XRole notation, a developer can easily understand what a role can do, and so how its assumption can be appropriate for the application context the agent is living in. Moreover, having a look at the <EventDescriptor> tag nested into an <OperationDescription>, it is possible to understand what consequences the execution of such operation will have on the surrounding environment and/or on other agents.

As shown in Fig. 3, one or more events are not strictly tied to a role action, that means an event can be delivered even if none role action has been executed yet. This is the case, for example, of the requestMove event, delivered to the player agent to inform that it must make a move to continue the game; there is not a correspondent previous action in the player role that accepts this event as a reply.

XRole documents can be used to construct role catalogues, that are collections of documents describing available roles, providing support for the choice of the right role to agents and their developers. Exploiting XRole to build role catalogues, grants advantages, such as the capability to use the same document to both describe the role and the operative use of it. Moreover, the advantage of exploiting the XML language is that this definition of role can be extended, to meet specific requirements that will arise in the future.

### 2.3 Interaction Infrastructures

BRAIN can adopt several interaction infrastructures, but they must rely on the XRole notation and must support the role model defined on the top of the BRAIN framework. These infrastructures can be developed using, for example, the Java language, that is a very exploited language in agent applications. Each interaction infrastructure must supply the interaction system that controls interactions and enforces local policies, such as allowing or denying interactions between agents playing given roles. Note that all policies applied to roles must be considered as additions to the programming language policy management, such as the Java security manager. This means that all policies applied into the BRAIN infrastructure can be applied in a separate way from the Java policy system, which can be kept enabled. Being able to change the interaction infrastructure allows BRAIN to adapt the role model depending on runtime constraints or parameters, choosing the most appropriate implementation for a specific scenario.

Currently, there are two interaction infrastructures compliant with BRAIN, both written in Java: RoleSystem [10] and RoleX [5]. Due to space limitation, this section briefly introduces only the latter one, RoleX, since it is more dynamic and adaptable of the other one; interested readers can found more details in [10]. RoleX exploits a combination of Java bytecode manipulation and dynamic class loading techniques in order to provide a very dynamic infrastructure to support the BRAIN role model. Thanks to its implementation, RoleX enables agents to assume/use/release roles, in a dynamic way, letting them evolving and adapting to the application they are living into. Moreover, RoleX supports the role *external visibility*, that means an agent can discover the role(s) played by another agent by means of natural Java language operators, like the `instanceof` one. Moreover, RoleX provides role catalogues (i.e., databases), supports search for agents through their role(s) and allows human administrator to interact with the system through the GUI shown in Fig. 4. Thanks to such GUI, an administrator can load new roles in the catalogues, making them available for agents, or can mark some of them as *incompatible*, that means an agent cannot assume them at the same time, etc.

All the above characteristics help developers dealing with the RoleX infrastructure, as well as they permit RoleX to support and to be compliant with the BRAIN role model described in section 2.1.

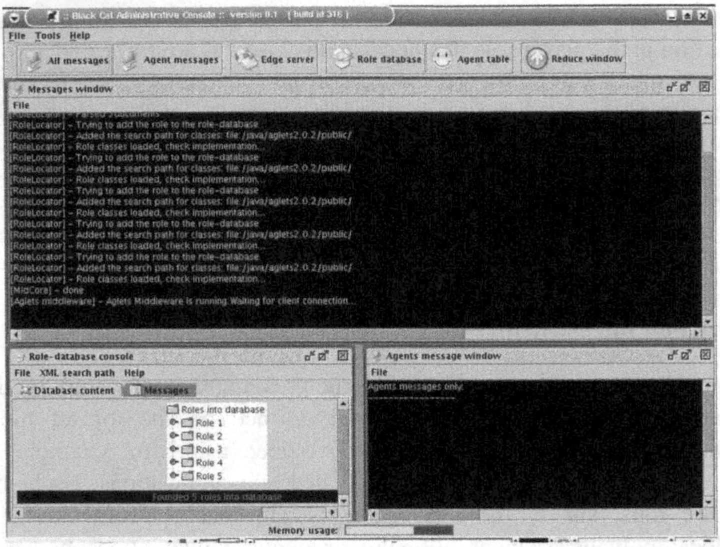


**Fig. 4.** The RoleX administrative GUI

# 3 Development Phases in BRAIN

In this section, we present the advantages that the BRAIN framework, and the XRole notation in particular, can provide in the three main phases of software development: analysis, design, implementation.

Is important to note that all phases related to the roles definition are independent from those that regard the agents definition, since the design and development of roles and agents can be done in different time and by different developers, while the exploitation of roles from agents is made possible by the BRAIN implementation.

## 3.1 Analysis

First of all, conceiving roles as first-class entities helps analysts in identifying common behaviors of the application agents, confining them into well-defined entities and associating the same roles to different agents that have some common behavior. Even if this is an advantage gained by the general role approach, in BRAIN the concept of roles as first-class entities is emphasized, thus leading analysts to reasoning consequently.

The BRAIN model helps analysts in identifying the requirements of roles. In fact, the model is based on actions and events, and analysts are required to find out which actions each (agent playing) role can perform, and which events each (agent playing) role must manage. More precisely, the proactive behavior of the agent is to be concretized into role actions, while the reactive behavior of the agent is to be translated into role events.

During the analysis, developers can exploit the XRole notation to speed up this phase. In fact, since XRole defines a structure for roles, it suggests developers what information is required to describe a role, with particular regard to actions and events. This leads developers to reason about the application not only with regard to its roles, but taking into account which actions a role can perform and what events it must handle. For example, a developer in charge of developing a bidder role for an auction, can analyze the seller and auction roles (maybe provided by another developer) in order to make his role compatible and interoperable with the above two. Moreover, the availability of XRole documents about already realized roles can help developers to analyze the existing solutions and, maybe, to reuse some of them.

## 3.2 Design

Depending on the set of roles and related actions/events, designers can write each role definition. The role definition implies the formalization of the set of allowed actions and events that the role can handle, providing also description about the role itself. Through such description, designers can place each role in the right application scenario.

In this phase, the exploitation of the XRole notation grants several advantages. First, being based on XML, XRole provides all advantages of this language, in terms of:

- Interoperability: notations derived by XML can be used in different platforms and applications;
- Manageability: there are different tools that helps in managing XML documents;
- Automation: since XML is a semi-structured language, its documents can be manipulated in an automatic way;
- Extensibility: XML documents can be extended depending on the application needs.

Then, the same XRole documents can be translated into HTML documents to suggest functionalities of the involved entities; applying different XSL sheets, the same information can be represented in different ways, adapting it to the needs of the readers.

As sketched before, a designer could decide to extend an existing role to produce a new role more suitable for its application. In this phase, advantages coming from the adoption of XML overtake the drawbacks of this language, such as the missing capability of dealing with inheritance [7].

## 3.3 Implementation

In the implementation phase, the model defined during the analysis and formalized during the design must become "real" and concretely usable. This phase is strictly tied to the interaction infrastructure the roles will be used on, since their implementation depends on the rules imposed by the bottom layer of the BRAIN framework. As already stated, there are two available interaction infrastructures for BRAIN, RoleSystem [10] and RoleX [5], both written in Java, and that provides a set of classes and facilities to support the implementation of roles and their reuse across agent systems. Actually, both the above implementations are available for the development and are respectively tied to the Jade [17] and Aglets [18] mobile agent platforms, even if it is quite simple to migrate them to other platforms.

It must be noted that, even in this phase, XRole can support and speed up the development: the same XRole documents can be exploited to obtain the code of the roles, or at least a structure of code that can be completed by programmers. For instance, appropriate XLS sheets can translate XRole documents into Java interfaces and classes that implement the role properties. The fact that this can be performed automatically, grants a fast and coherent development.

Thanks to both the facilities provided by the interaction infrastructures and the XRole notation, this phase can be successfully completed in a short time and without big efforts.

# 4 An Application Example

In this section, we briefly report a simple example related to the game world. In a game there are well-defined interactions, which occur in a given order, and follow the game-specific laws. Here we do not focus on a specific game, but we show roles and then the interactions of a generic game, which can be adapted to specific games by defining the appropriate laws.

## 4.1 Analysis

From the analysis we identify two roles in the applications: the *player* and the game *manager*. In each game, there is one manager and one or more players.

The main capability of the player is to play, but there are some collateral capabilities that are related to knowing which is the kind of the game and to leaving the game. The expected behavior concerns mainly to receive information about the game.

With regard to the manager role, the capabilities are related to notifying players about the game. On the other hand, a manager is expected to accept moves from the players, as well as reply to requests about the game situation.

## 4.2 Design

In the following, we report the actions and the events corresponding to the capabilities and the expected behaviors identified in the previous phase. These actions and events are coded into XRole documents like the one shown in Fig. 3.

### 4.2.1 The Player Role

Each agent that wants to participate to the game has to assume the role of *player*. The *actions* that can be performed by a player are:

- askKind. This action is used to ask the manager what kind of game it manages.
- reqPlay. The player requests the manager to play in the current game.
- move. By this action, the player tells the manager the willing of making a move. The action must contain also the description of the move.
- giveUp. It is used to notify the manager that the player leaves the current game.

The main *events* that a player must deal with are:

- notifyKind. By this event, the player is notified about the kind of the current game. This event is associated to a string that contains the actual game kind.
- requestMove. The player is requested by the manager to make a move.
- gameWon. The player is notified it is the winner of the game.
- gameOver. The player is told by the manager that the game is over.

#### 4.2.2 The Manager Role

Each game is ruled by an agent playing the role of *manager*. The main *actions* that can be performed by a manager are:

- notifyKind. The manager notifies a player about the kind of the current game.
- requestMove. The manager requests a player to make a move.
- gameWon. The manager tells a player it has won the game.
- gameOver. The manager tells a player that the game is over.

The main *events* that a manager must deal with are:

- askKind. The manager is notified that a player asks for the kind of game.
- reqPlay. The manager is notified that a player has requested for playing.
- move. The manager is notified about a move of a player.

Note that the actions of the player usually correspond to the events handled by the manager, and vice versa.

### 4.3 Implementation

For the implementation, we have derived Java interfaces from the XRole documents defined in the previous phase. With regard to the example of the player role and its XRole document (see Fig. 3), the Java interface of its role will be like the one reported in Fig. 5.

As shown in Fig. 5, the interface provides the method to request the kind of the game, and a couple of events. These static events are used to make possible for the agent/role to recognize all the notified events.

```
public interface player extends GenericRoleInterface{
  // the askKind action
  public void askKind();
  // the kind of recognized events
  public static GenericEvent notifyKind;
  public static GenericEvent requestMove;
   ...
}
```

**Fig. 5.** An example of role Java interface derived by a XRole document

## 5 Related Work

Since there have been different approaches for agents based on roles, this section briefly reports those similar to the BRAIN approach; interested readers can find more details in [6].

The Role/Interaction/Communicative Action (RICA) theory [21] aims to improve the FIPA systems [15] with support for social concepts. Similarly to BRAIN, the RICA theory defines a metamodel, that can be used as a language to define communicative entities (i.e., entities that can act in a social way, and thus can be aggregated into societies); its implementation is written in Java and it is called RICA-J. RICA models the behavior of agents through roles, thus an agent is nothing more than a role player. Moreover, RICA strongly uses social concepts, thus for each standard concept, it is possible to find out the correspondent social one (e.g., roles can be specialized in social roles, actions in social actions, and so on). From this point of view, BRAIN is more general, without explicitly distinguishing between social and non-social entities, since this separation strictly depends on the application context and is quite subjective.

AALAADIN [14] is a meta-model to define models of organizations. It is based on three core concepts: *agent*, *group* and *role*. Even if our approach is quite similar to the AALAADIN one, it differs for some reasons. First, we disregard the concept of *group*, while focusing on the interactions among agents and between agents and environments. Second, AALAADIN roles are tightly bound to the notion of agent, while our aim is to describe roles in a more independent way, both of applications and environments. Third, in AALAADIN, environments are mainly modeled by service agents, which is generally acceptable, but do not cover all real situations, where also agents that play roles of "pure clients" must be taken into account.

The ROPE project [4] recognizes the importance of defining roles as first-class entities, which can be assumed dynamically by agents. It proposes an integrate environment, called ROPE (Role Oriented Programming Environment), which can be exploit to develop applications composed by several cooperating agents. Rather than defining an integrated but *close* environment, we aim at proposing an *open* methodology to define agent roles. We address interoperability and also the dynamic use of roles. Moreover, our definition of roles can be exploit also for interactions among agents that do not belong to the same application (i.e., are competitive); this is a relevant aspect in the design of applications for wide-open environments, such as the Internet.

## 6 Conclusions and Future Work

The BRAIN framework proposes a role-based model for agent interactions, an XML notation and interaction infrastructures. This paper has explained how the BRAIN framework, and in particular the XRole notation, can be exploited in the different phases of the development of applications composed of different agents that play roles to interact.

We can state that the main advantage of using BRAIN is that the same information is used during the whole development process, granting coherence and continuity. The XRole notation, being based on the XML language, enables to present the same information in different ways, depending on the needs of people that read such information. Moreover, XRole documents can be manipulated by automatic tools for different purposes, and even understood by agents if needed. The chance of exploiting the information about roles at runtime well suits very dynamic environments.

Currently we are investigating security models to be embedded in BRAIN and in particular in its interaction infrastructure RoleX; these models include trust and security. We are also refining the role model to make it more suitable to open and dynamic environments, supporting for example an assumption driven by prerequisites.

The BRAIN framework and its interaction infrastructures are publicly available for download at the URL: http://www.agentgroup.ing.unimo.it/.

**Acknowledgements.** Work supported by the Italian MIUR and CNR within the project "IS-MANET, Infrastructures for Mobile ad-hoc Networks", by the CASCADAS European Project, and by the project L.A.I.C.A. (Laboratorio di Ambient Intelligence per una Città Amica), funded by the Regione Emilia-Romagna, Italy, under the initiative 1.1 "Programma per la ricerca su prodotti e servizi innovativi" of the development project "Piano telematico regionale".

## References

1. S. Ahuja, N. Carriero, and D. Gelernter, "Linda and Friends", IEEE Computer, Vol. 19, No. 8, pp. 26-34, August 1986.
2. Y. Aridor, D. Lange, "Agent Design Pattern: Elements of Agent Application design", International Conference on Autonomous Agents, ACM Press, 1998.
3. J. Baumann, F. Hohl, K. Rothermel, M. Straßer, "Mole - Concepts of a Mobile Agent System", The World Wide Web Journal, Vol. 1, No. 3, pp. 123-137, 1998.
4. M. Becht, T. Gurzki, J. Klarmann, M. Muscholl, "ROPE: Role Oriented Programming Environment for Multiagent Systems", The Fourth IFCIS Conference on Cooperative Information Systems (CoopIS'99), Edinburgh, Scotland, September 1999.
5. G. Cabri, L. Ferrari, L. Leonardi, "The RoleX Environment for Multi-Agent Cooperation", Eighth International Workshop CIA 2004 on Cooperative Information Agents, Erfurt, Germany, Lecture Notes in Artificial Intelligence N. 3191, September 2004
6. G. Cabri, L. Ferrari, L. Leonardi, "Agent Role-based Collaboration and Coordination: a Survey About Existing Approaches", The 2004 IEEE Systems, Man and Cybernetics Conference, The Hague, The Netherlands, October 2004.
7. G. Cabri, M. Iori, A. Salvarani, "Describing and Extending Classes with XMI: an Industrial Experience", Software Evolution with UML and XML (Idea Group, Inc., Hershey-USA), Hongji Yang Editor, ISBN: 1-59140-462-2, 2005.
8. G. Cabri, L. Leonardi, F. Zambonelli, "Mobile-Agent Coordination Models for Internet Applications", IEEE Computer, Vol. 33, No. 2, pp. 82-89, February 2000.
9. G. Cabri, L. Leonardi, F. Zambonelli, "MARS: a Programmable Coordination Architecture for Mobile Agents", IEEE Internet Computing, Vol. 4, N. 4, pp. 26-35, July-August 2000.
10. G. Cabri, L. Leonardi, F. Zambonelli, "Role-based Interaction Infrastructures for Internet Agents", IEICE Transactions on Information and Systems (Oxford University Press, Oxford-UK), Vol.E86-D, No.11, November 2003.
11. R. G. Chandras, "Distributed Message Passing Operating Systems", Operating Systems Review, Vol. 24, No. 1, pp. 7-17, 1990.
12. P. Domel, A. Lingnau, O. Drobnik, "Mobile Agent Interaction in Heterogeneous Environment", The 1st International Workshop on Mobile Agents, LNCS, Springer-Verlag (D), No. 1219, pp. 136-148, April 1997.

13. Amal El Fallah-Seghrouchni, Serge Haddad, Hamza Mazouzi, "Protocol Engineering for Multi-agent Interaction", The 9th European Workshop on Modelling Autonomous Agents in a Multi-Agent World (MAAMAW '99), Valencia, Spain, June 1999.
14. J. Ferber and O. Gutknecht, "AALAADIN: A meta-model for the analysis and design of organizations in multi-agent systems", The Third International Conference on Multi-Agent Systems (ICMAS), Cite des Sciences - La Villette, Paris, France, July 1998.
15. The Foundation for Intelligent Physical Agents (FIPA) web site: www.fipa.org
16. M. d'Inverno, D. Kinny, M. Luck, "Interaction Protocols in Agentis", The Third International Conference on Multi-Agent Systems (ICMAS), Cite des Sciences - La Villette, Paris, France, July 1998.
17. The Jade Agent Development Framework official web stie: http://jade.tilab.com/
18. D. B. Lange, M. Oshima, "Programming and Deploying Java™ Mobile Agents with Aglets™", Addison-Wesley, Reading (MA), 1998.
19. Jürgen Lind, "Specifying Agent Interaction Protocols with Standard UML", The 2nd International Workshop on Agent Oriented Software Engineering (AOSE), Montreal (C), May 2001.
20. James Odell, H. Van Dyke Parunak, Bernhard Bauer, "Representing Agent Interaction Protocols in UML", Agent Oriented Software Engineering, Paolo Ciancarini and Michael Wooldridge eds., Springer-Verlag, Berlin, pp. 121–140, 2001.
21. Jean Manuel Serrano, Sascha Ossowski, "On the Impact of Agent Communicative Languages on the Implementation of Agent Systems", Cooperative Information Agents VIII, M.Klush, S. Ossowski, V. Kashyap, R. Unland eds., Lecture Notes in Artificial Intelligence, ISSN 0302-9743, Springer, 2004
22. D. W. Walker, "The Design of a Standard Message Passing Interface for Distributed Memory Concurrent Computers", Parallel Computing Vol. 20, No. 4, pp. 657-673, 1994.
23. J. White, "Mobile Agents", in Software Agents, J. Bradshaw (Ed.), AAAI Press, pp. 437-472, 1997.

# Automating Model Transformations in Agent-Oriented Modelling

Anna Perini and Angelo Susi

ITC-irst, Via Sommarive, 18, I-38050 Trento-Povo, Italy
{perini, susi}@itc.it

**Abstract.** Current Agent-Oriented Software Engineering (AOSE) methodologies adopt a model-based approach for analysis and design, but, in order to become of practical use, they should include it in a clear and customizable software development process and provide CASE tools that support it.

In this regards, the Model-Driven Architecture (MDA) initiative of OMG is providing useful concepts and techniques. The MDA ultimate objective is that of improving quality and software maintainability by allowing for the reuse of models and mappings between models. It offers standards and techniques for model interoperability and for automating model transformations.

Our goal in this paper is to address the role of model transformations in AOSE by discussing a practical example, with reference to the *Tropos* methodology. In particular, we will focus on the automatic transformation of a *Tropos* plan decomposition into a UML 2.0 activity diagram.

We will show how to use the transformation technique to automate model mappings and describe how a CASE tool, based on a modular architecture, has been extended to automate models transformations.

## 1 Introduction

Modeling techniques are largely used in Agent-Oriented Software Engineering (AOSE). Current methodologies, like Gaia [24], PASSI [7], Prometheus [21], Adelfe [3], *Tropos* [4], propose their own conceptual modeling language and a set of diagrams (or views on the model) to support specific steps in the analysis and design of software. In order to become of practical use the following issues need to be addressed.

First, a model-driven software development process should be clearly defined by specifying the analysis and design steps, with their objectives, set of artifacts to be produced, guidelines and techniques to be exploited to build them.

Second, CASE tools should be provided, at support of the different tasks in model based design such as analysis and verification of models or automatic transformation from one specification language to another, in a transparent and simple manner. These latter aspects are at the core of the Model-Driven Architecture (MDA) initiative of OMG [19].

The ultimate goal of MDA is that of improving the quality of software products and of the development process, by allowing for the reuse of models and the mappings between models. Basically, MDA proposes an approach to software development based on modeling and on the automated mapping of source models to target models. Code

J.P. Müller and F. Zambonelli (Eds.): AOSE 2005, LNCS 3950, pp. 167–178, 2006.

can be seen as a target model as well. So, there is a lot of effort in MDA to develop model interoperability standards, as well as model-to-model transformation concepts and techniques for their automation.

The MDA initiative refers mainly to Object Oriented software development and proved to be effective in relevant application domain, such as web services (business process integration) [18]. Recently, a few proposals to exploit MDA ideas and techniques in Agent Oriented software engineering have been proposed [11, 15, 22].

We think that MDA standards and technological infrastructure are relevant to make AO methodologies usable by practitioners. In particular, adopting MDA standards for model interoperability and for model-to-model automatic transformation could, on one side, support a flexible and customizable software development process, on the other side, offer a complementary approach to the definition of a common metamodel[1].

In this paper we focus on model transformation concepts and techniques in an AO approach to software development, with reference to the *Tropos* methodology. In this methodology the concept of transformation has been introduced also in previous work. Here we will revise and discuss the role of automatic transformations in *Tropos* and describe a tool that supports them.

The paper is structured as follows. Section 2 recalls transformation concepts and techniques in MDA, previous work in *Tropos* and discuss the role of model transformations in *Tropos*. Section 3 and 4 present our approach, focusing on a particular type of transformation in *Tropos* (i.e. synthesis), and present a CASE tool, that supports it. Related works are discussed in Section 5. Finally, conclusion and future work are presented in Section 6.

## 2 MDA and Model Transformations in *Tropos*

The *Tropos* methodology [4] supports an agent-oriented approach to software development organized in five major phases or disciplines[2]. They are: *Early Requirements*, where a description of the application domain is produced; *Late Requirements*, in which the system-to-be is introduced in the domain and its impact within the environment is analyzed; *Architectural Design* where a representation of the internal architecture of the system is given in terms of subcomponents of the system and relationships among them; *Detailed Design* which focuses on the specification of agents capabilities and interaction; *Implementation*, i.e. the production of code from the detailed design specification, according to the established mapping between the implementation platform constructs and the detailed design notions.

For the first three disciplines *Tropos* adopts a modeling language that allows to represent intentional and social concepts, such as actor and goal, plan, resource, and a set of relationships between them, such as actor dependency, goal or plan decomposition, means-end and contribution relationships. While for the detailed design discipline the use of UML activity diagrams for the agent capabilities specification and of sequence

[1] A currently ongoing effort pursued by the AOSE Technical Forum Group of AgentLink [2].

[2] The term discipline is used according to the definition given in the Unified Process [14], namely a set of activities to be performed in order to produce a particular set of artifacts.

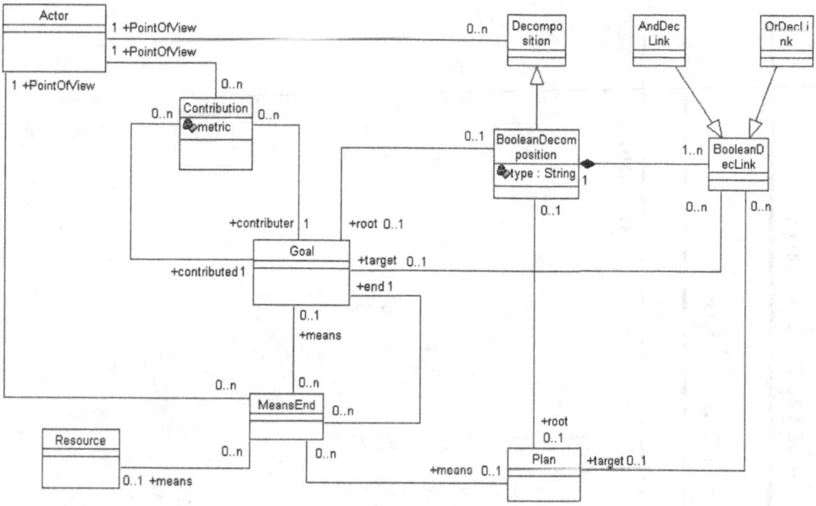


**Fig. 1.** An excerpt of the *Tropos* metamodel

diagrams for agent interactions specification have been proposed. In [4] a preliminary mapping to the JACK multi-agent platform was defined and applied to a case-study.

Modeling in *Tropos* has been conceived as an incremental process where an initial model is refined by adding new elements and properties by means of the analysis of each actor goals and plans. A description of this process in terms of a non deterministic concurrent algorithm has been given in [4]. Moreover, a first proposal to characterize it in terms of an iterative application of simple transformations has been described in [5].

In the following we will revise the role of transformations in the *Tropos* methodology in the light of the MDA framework. We will first recall the basic goals and concepts of MDA, then discuss how they can be adopted in CASE tools for supporting *Tropos*.

MDA considers models as corporate assets which can evolve independently of the relative code. Models can be partially reused or mixed with other models to generate a new system [19]. Models can be specified from different views and can be represented at different levels of abstractions.

Concerning model transformation, the basic idea proposed in MDA is that of defining the meta-models of source and target modeling languages according to a standard and to define mapping and transformation mechanisms between meta-model elements. The transformation of a source model into a target model will derive in a straightforward way from the transformation mechanisms defined at the meta-model level, since the models are instances of the correspondent language metamodel.

The MDA's meta-modeling standard is the Meta Object Facility (MOF) [16] which defines a set of modeling construct that allow to manage meta-models interoperability. For instance, it offers a standard mechanisms for automatically deriving a concrete syntax based on XML DTDs and/or schemas known as XML Model Interchange (XMI). An example of MOF compliant meta-model is illustrated in Figure 1 which depicts an excerpt of the *Tropos* modeling language metamodel.

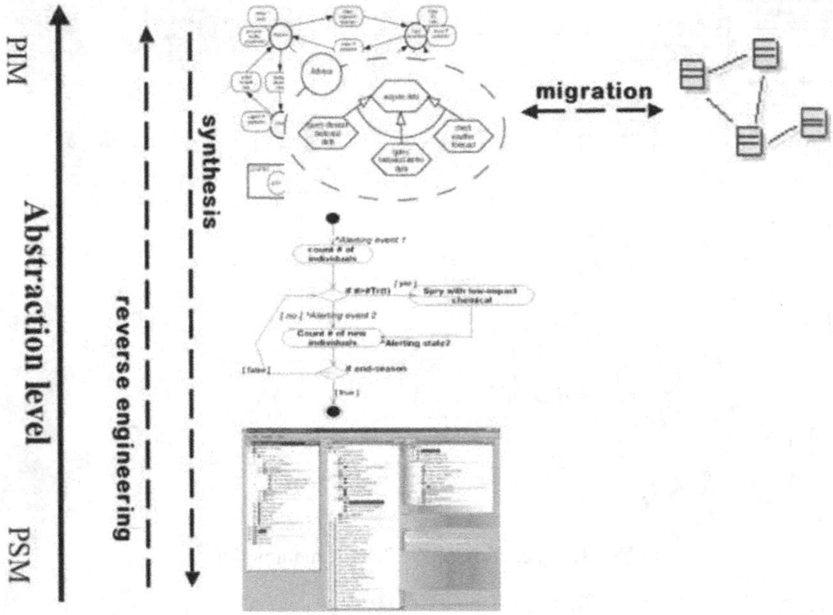


**Fig. 2.** Model Translation in MDA: an adaptation of the schema proposed in [18] to the *Tropos* methodology. The model abstraction level increases from Platform Specific Model (PSM), represented by JACK code, to Platform Independent Model (PIM), represented by UML and *Tropos* models.

A language for describing the generic transformation of any well formed model is not yet available in a standard form. A first step in the standardization process has been performed by OMG by issuing a request for proposal on Query/View/Transformation (MOF QVT [12]) which should take into account requirements such as that of defining a language for querying MOF models; giving a language for transformation definitions; allowing for the creation of views of a model. Several techniques for model transformation have already been proposed.

The role of transformations in *Tropos* can be discussed referring to a classification of QVT model transformations that have been proposed in [18], which uses the terminology introduced by Visser for program transformation [23]. Language *translation*, and language *rephrasing* are top level processes. Basically, in the former, a model is transformed into a model of a different language, and in the latter, a model is changed, in some way, into a same language model.

Figure 2 depicts the different translation processes in MDA, according to this classification. *Migration* is a type of translation in which a model is transformed to another one, or to a language dialect, at the same level of abstraction. For instance, if we intend to integrate *Tropos* architectural design with UML design we may need to migrate from actor diagrams to package / class diagrams. Another example of this type of transformation occurs when we need to specify behavioral properties of a model by temporal logic annotation (*FT*). An automatic transformation mechanism, from informal *Tropos* to *FT*, has been built adopting a visitor-based approach, as described in [22]. *Synthesis* is a type of translation in which a model is transformed to another one at a lower level of abstraction. This type of transformation in *Tropos* occurs when building the detail design model from the architectural design model, that is when we need to add specification of agent capabilities and of agent interactions. In this paper we will focus on this example considering, in particular how an actor (agent) plan decomposition can be automatically translated into a capability diagram (UML 2.0 activity diagram). *Reverse engineering* is the inverse transformation.

*Rephrasing* refers to different transformations that may occur when building and refining a model; *normalization* consists in a transformation of a model by reducing it to a sub-language; *refactoring*, concerns restructuring a model with the objective to improve it; *correction*, i.e. fixing possible model errors; and *adaptation* of a model in order to bring it up to date with new or modified requirements. The previously cited work [5] on defining the modeling process in terms of an incremental application of basic transformations was intended to support this type of transformation processes. Moreover, a first proposal of applying graph transformation techniques to its automation is described in [20].

We are currently interested in exploring the problem of transformation between two modeling languages defined by different metamodels, and in particular in maintaining the synchronization between the models. This is required in the *Tropos* methodology when we deal with the transition from a *Tropos* Architectural Design model, to a Detailed Design specification. Notice that the Architectural Design model is specified according to the *Tropos* metamodel as defined in [4], while for the second (which includes UML activity diagram, sequence diagram) we aim at exploiting the UML 2.0 metamodel and at maintaining the traceability between the models.

## 3 Automating *Tropos*-to-UML Model Transformation: An Example

Among the different approaches for model-to-model transformations that have been recently proposed, we focused on two of them namely: the Graph Transformation (GT) [13] and a Frame Logics [17]. In [20] we describe how to apply GT to *Tropos* model rephrasing transformation. Briefly GT approach is based on set of rules that represents the status of a certain sub-graph of the models before and after the application of the rule. In particular these rule's sub-graphs can be related respectively to the source and target metamodel. Some problem arises when we deal with GT specifications. In fact this framework introduces non determinism in at least two phases: in order to apply a rule we have first to choose it, and then we have to choose the sub-graph of the source model in which the rule has to be applied. The result of the transformation strictly depends on these choices. Some restrictions can be adopted in order to reduce this phenomenon: the next rule to be applied can be chosen on the basis of the rules applied before, or the application of the rules can be executed on the basis of a priority list. Another possible problem is the possibility to assure the termination of a sequence of rule application. Also in this case some hypothesis can be made in order to limit the problem.

We are exploiting a Frame Logics based approach described in [6] to deal with Metamodel transformation between the *Tropos* and the UML 2.0.

In particular this approach is based on the definition of some properties of the target model in terms of the source model, avoiding the specification of the process used to obtain the target, and it takes into account the mandatory requirements of the MOF QVT consortium related to the Query/View/Transformation framework. In particular the proposal defines a language for querying MOF-compliant models (or set of models) and a subset of this language can be used to specify transformation of MOF-compliant models. The transformations can be automated and views of models can be obtained via transformations. This approach leads to a simpler semantic model, respect, for example, to the GT techniques; this made easier the understanding of the transformation rule. Moreover it does not need any hypothesis related to the ordering in which the rules have to be applied or to the termination of the transformation.

The transformation language proposed in the approach consists of three major concepts: *pattern definitions*, *transformation rules*, *tracking relationships*. *Pattern definitions* are generated in order to identify structures that are used several times in a given transformation. *Transformation rules* allow to specify the target configuration in terms of the entities in the source configuration. *Tracking relationships* are used to associate the target elements with the source elements that lead to their creation allowing to maintain the traceability between source and target model instances entities. Moreover the work proposes a syntax for the rules composed by some clauses; some of them (e.g. the *Forall* and *Where*) are used by the rule to recognize some pattern in the instance of the source model, while other (e.g. *Make* and *Set*) are used to build the instance of the target model.

We will show how we applied it in *Tropos* showing an example of transformation from *Tropos* plan decomposition structure to a UML 2.0 Activity Diagrams.

A *Tropos* plan decomposition represents a graph describing a hierarchical relationship between the root plan and the sub-plans. Let us consider the case of an AND plan decomposition as the one represented in Figure 3 a).

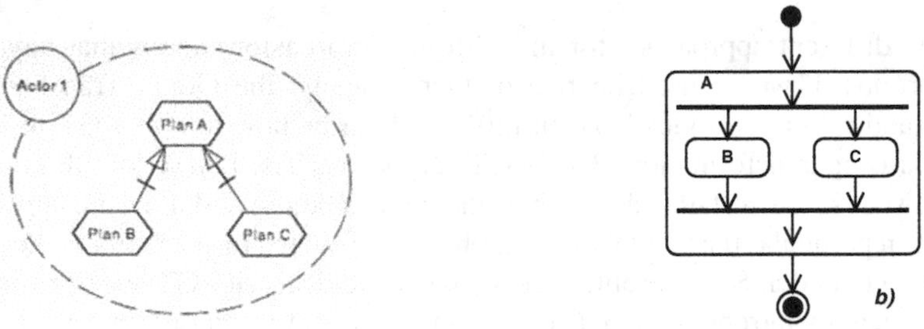


**Fig. 3.** A *Tropos* plan decomposition diagram for a given Actor and the corresponding UML 2.0 activity diagram

The meaning of the decomposition is: the root Plan A can be decomposed in the sub-plans Plan B and Plan C; both of them have to be executed in order to have the root plan executed. This hierarchy identifies a set of possible plans composed by the set of sub-plans. In particular nothing is specified about the order in which the set of sub-plans have to be executed.

```
TRANSFORMAI ION Tropos2UML: Tropos -> uml2

RULE PlanNoDec2Activity()
  FORALL Plan c
  WHERE NOT (c.booleanDecomposition=BooleanDecomposition)
     AND NOT (c.boolDecLink=BooleanDecLink)
  MAKE Action f, InitialNode Initial, Final Node Final, ControlFlow ToA, ControlFlow ToFin
  SET f.name="noDec", ToA.source=Initial, ToA.target=f, ToFin.target=Final, ToFin.source=f;

CLASS ActionForPlanDec {
  Plan pln;
  Action act;};

RULE PlanDec2Action(c,a,join,fork)
  FORALL Plan c
  WHERE Root(c)
  MAKE Action a, JoinNode join, ForkNode fork, InitialNode Initial,
     FinalNode Final, ControlFlow initToA, ControlFlow AToFin,
     ControlFlow AToFork, ControlFlow JoinToA
  SET a.name=c.name, a.redefinedElement=join, a.redefinedElement=fork,
     ......
LINKING ActionForPlanDec WITH act=a, pln=c;

RULE SubPlan(c,a,join,fork,d,b)
  EXTENDS PlanDec2Action(c,a,join,fork)
  FORALL Plan d
  WHERE ActionForPlanDec LINKS pln=c
     c=d.boolDecLink.BooleanDecomposition.rootPlan
  MAKE Action b, ControlFlow ForkToB, ControlFlow bToJoin
  SET b.name=d.name, a redefinedElement=b, ForkToB.name="ForkToB",
     ...

PATTERN Root(c)
  WHERE c.booleanDecomposition.type="and";
```

**Fig. 4.** The transformation specification defined in the grammar described in [6]

The plans in the *Tropos* plan diagram are translated into action nodes in the UML activity diagram; moreover from the structure of the plan decomposition it is possible to derive a basic structure for the resulting activity diagram.

In particular the assumption is that the Plan A can be mapped into an activity node, containing a structure composed by the activities corresponding to the plans B and C; moreover in the example the assumption is that the two plans has to be executed in parallel since no information is given about the sequence of the plans in the *Tropos* plan diagram. Figure 3 b) shows the resulting activity diagram.

The transformation shown in Figure 4 is specified via a subset of the grammar described in [6]. In the transformation definition it is possible to distinguish Rules and Pattern used to specify in a declarative way the transformation. The RULE *PlanNoDec2Activity* is for the transformation of the plan decomposition leaves, not decomposed, to an activity in the UML activity diagram. The role is composed by clauses. In the *PlanNoDec2Activity* rule, the clauses FORALL and WHERE retrieve the set of plans that are not decomposed; the clauses MAKE and SET are in charge to build the structure of the corresponding activity diagram, creating a new activity for every retrieved plan, and the links to other activities and control flow components in the diagram. The RULE *PlanDec2Activity* refers to decomposed plans and transforms them into UML actions that can then be further decomposed in other actions and control structures. In particular in our case fork and join control structures are added together with the action derived from the hierarchy root plan A. The RULE *SubPlan* redefine the rule for the decomposable actions in order to incrementally add new sub-actions in the activity diagram.

In the example the directive PATTERN recognizes the kind of decomposition the transformation has to face with; in this case the pattern recognizes the root of an "and" decomposition, a typical structure in the *Tropos* plan decomposition diagram.

For the sake of clearness, we described the simplest case of a plan and-decomposition structure. Typical cases require to deal with plan or-decomposition or temporal relationships [22] between sub-plans as the one shown in Figure 5. In this case a few additional rules can be defined within a limited effort.

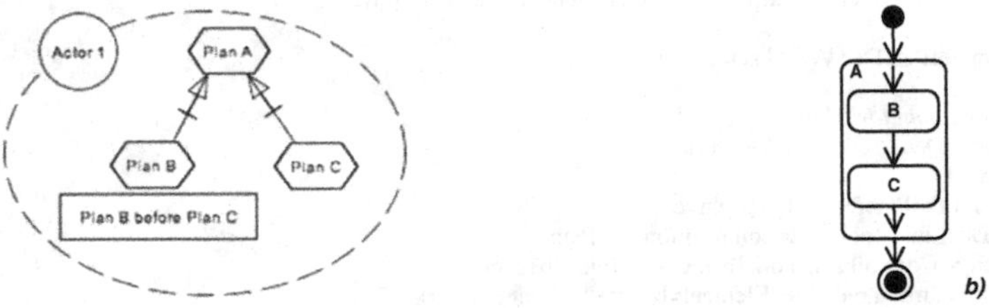


**Fig. 5.** A *Tropos* plan AND-decomposition diagram with temporal annotation for a given Actor and the corresponding UML 2.0 activity diagram

As described above a relevant issue for us is the possibility of having the synchronization between models and the reversibility of a transformation. The declarative transformations approach shown in [6] partially supports synchronization and reversibility in an automatic way. In general the reverse transformations has to be explicitly defined.

## 4 A CASE Tool

In this section we focus on the description of a set of tools for supporting the use of the *Tropos* methodology according to the MDA perspective. This requires, first to adopt MOF compliant modeling tools (i.e. whose respective modeling languages' metamodels are specified according to the MOF standard), second, to define model transformations in terms of mapping between the metamodels of the source and the target specification languages.

For instance, a CASE tool at support of the *Tropos* process discussed in the previous section should allow the analyst to build a *Tropos* model (in our case a plan decomposition diagram) using a modeler which includes the *Tropos* metamodel. Part of the model should be automatically translated into a UML model which should be editable by a UML modeler (which includes the UML metamodel). Modifications performed on the UML model should be automatically reflected into the *Tropos* model.

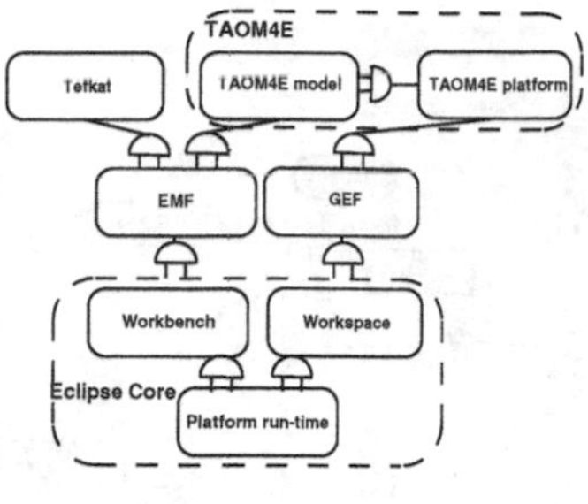


**Fig. 6.** The architecture of TAOM4e

A *Tropos* modeler called TAOM compliant with MDA metamodel interoperability standards has been described in [22]. The need of a higher flexible architecture which allow to easily extend it induced us to consider the opportunity to re-engineering this tool in the Eclipse Platform [1] that offers a flexible and (economically) convenient solution to the problem of component integration. The Eclipse Platform is an open source initiative that offers a "reusable and extensible framework for creating IDE-oriented tools" [10]. New tools are integrated into the platform through plug-ins that provide new functionalities to the environment. A plug-in is the smallest unit of function in Eclipse. The Eclipse Platform itself is organized as a set of subsystems (implemented in one or more plug-ins) built on the top of a small runtime engine, as depicted in Figure 6. Plug-ins define extension points for adding behaviors to the platform, that is a public declaration of the plug-in extensibility. More precisely, a "plug-in manifest" file specifies the extensions it uses and the extension points it defines.

Figure 6 depicts the architecture of the new modeler (called TAOM4e) and of how it has been extended with a model transformation plug-in. In particular, TAOM4e has been built on top of two existing plug-ins. First, the Graphical Editing Framework (GEF) plug-in[3] that allows developers to create a rich graphical editor from an existing application model. The functionality of the GEF plug-in helps covering one of the most essential requirements of the modeler, that is supporting visual development of Tropos model by providing some standard features like drag & drop, undo-redo, copy & paste and other.

Second, the EMF plug-in[4] which offers a modeling framework and code generation facility for building tools and other applications based on a structured data model. From a model specification described in XMI, EMF provides tools and runtime support to produce a set of Java classes for the model. Most important of all, EMF provides the foundation for interoperability with other EMF-based tools and applications.

The TAOM4e component consists of two plug-ins, as depicted in Figure 6, namely, the *TAOM4e model* which implements the Tropos meta-model extending the EMF plug-in and the *TAOM4e platform* which implement the modeler functions needed for building and managing a Tropos Model. It extends the GEF plug-in and the *TAOM4e model* plug-in.

[3] http://www.eclipse.org/gef/
[4] http://www.eclipse.org/emf/

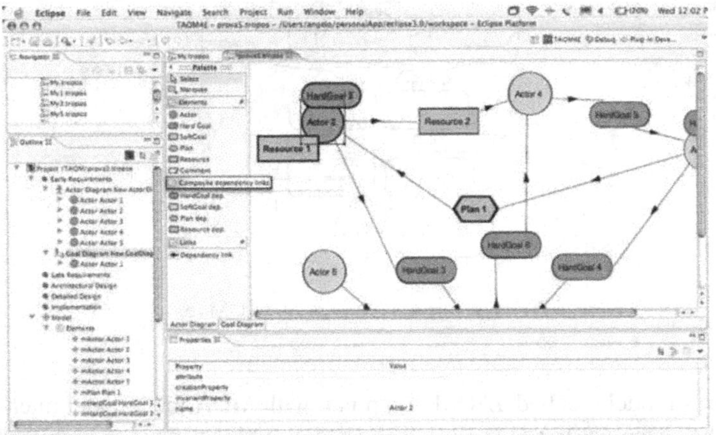


**Fig. 7.** A snapshot of the TAOM4e Graphic User Interface

The transformation plug-in we used is a model transformation engine called Tefkat[5] that implements a subset of the requirements and of the transformation language described in the DSTC proposal for MOF QVT as in [6]. The tool consists of a set of Eclipse plug-ins based on EMF. Tefkat allow to specify transformations between metamodels that are specified via an XMI compliant notation used by the EMF for the definition of metamodels. Moreover, due to the plug-in structure, Tefkat can easily interact with other Eclipse plug-ins devoted to model definition and management.

## 5 Related Work

Several works related to Agent-Oriented Software Engineering dealt with the concept of transformation as already pointed out in the first two sections [3, 7, 21]. In particular in [5] a transformational approach to support the analyst during the *Tropos* software development process has been proposed and in [20] Graph Transformation were applied to support the analyst in choosing and/or validating possible model refinement actions. A first proposal to use Graph Transformation in AOSE is given in [11] where this technique is adopted both to capture agent-specific aspects and to define a formal semantics in the definition of an agent-oriented modeling technique. In [15] a work which applies the MDA idea of transform a Platform Independent Model to a Platform Specific Model is proposed; in that case the Platform Specific Model refers to the JACK platform.

More generally QVT proposals are of particular interest for our work. An interesting classification of them can be found in [9]. Moreover interesting ideas on how to apply the MDA framework to a specific domain is given in [18]. In this work automatic transformations between source and target models are proposed in the case of busi-

[5] Tefkat is part of Pegamento project of the DSTC in the University of Queensland http://www.dstc.edu.au/Research/Projects/Pegamento/tefkat/index.html

ness process integration, when dealing with the complexity of large business processes mapping from visual languages to code.

## 6 Conclusion and Future Work

In this paper we focused on the role of model transformations in an agent-oriented software development by adopting concepts and techniques that are proposed in the MDA initiative by OMG [19].

MDA offers a meta-modeling standard, the Meta Object Facility (MOF) [16], which allows model and meta-model interoperability and is managing the standardization process of model transformations which should be compliant with the so called Query/View/Transformation (MOF QVT [12]) requirements. Several techniques have been already proposed. Although MDA refers mainly to Object Oriented software development its concepts and techniques may be adopted Agent Oriented software engineering as well [8, 11, 15, 22].

In particular, in Section 2 we considered different types of model transformations that can support software development in the *Tropos* methodology and revised how the concept of transformations have been addressed in previous works. We think that most of the considerations can be applied also to other AOSE methodologies.

We presented a (simple) practical example concerning the automatic transformation of a *Tropos* plan decomposition into a UML 2.0 activity diagram (a transformation type called *synthesis* in Section 2), by adopting a declarative transformation language proposed in [6] and we pointed out critical issues such as model synchronization. This type of transformation supports the transition between architectural design and detailed design in *Tropos*, but we may consider to adopt it also for supporting translation between *Tropos* models and UML models referring to a same level abstraction (for instance during architectural design).

We showed also how we are extending a CASE tool implemented in the ECLIPSE platform which offers a highly modular and flexible architecture, to include automatic model transformations.

## References


1. *ECLIPSE Platform Technical Overview*, object technology international edition, July 2001. http://www.eclipse.org.
2. C. Bernon, M. Cossentino, M. P. Gleizes, P. Turci, and F. Zambonelli. A Study of Some Multi-agent Meta-models. In *Agent-Oriented Software Engineering V: 5th International Workshop, AOSE 2004*, volume 3382 of *Lecture Notes in Computer Science*, pages 62 – 77, New York, USA, NY, July 2004.
3. C. Bernon, M. Gleizes, S. Peyruqueou, and G. Picard. ADELFE, a Methodology for Adaptive Multi-Agent Systems Engineering. In *Third International Workshop Engineering Societies in the Agents World (ESAW-2002)*, Madrid, Spain, 2002.
4. P. Bresciani, P. Giorgini, F. Giunchiglia, J. Mylopoulos, and A. Perini. Tropos: An Agent-Oriented Software Development Methodology. *Autonomous Agents and Multi-Agent Systems*, 8(3):203–236, July 2004.

5. P. Bresciani, A. Perini, P. Giorgini, F. Giunchiglia, and J. Mylopoulos. Modeling early requirements in Tropos: a transformation based approach. In M. Wooldridge, P. Ciancarini, and G. Weiss, editors, *Agent-Oriented Software Engineering II*, volume 2222 of *LNCS*, pages 151–168. Springer-Verlag, 2001.
6. CBOP, DSTC, and IBM. MOF Query/Views/Transformations, 2nd Revised Submission. Technical report, 2004.
7. M. Cossentino. Different perspectives in designing multi-agent systems. In *Proc. of AGES '02*, Erfurt, Germany, 2002.
8. M. Cossentino, P. Burrafato, S. Lombardo, and L. Sabatucci. Introducing Pattern Reuse in the Design of Multi-agent Systems. In *Agent Technologies, Infrastructures, Tools, and Applications for E-Services 2002*, pages 107 – 120, 2002.
9. K. Czarnecki and S. Halsen. Classification of Model Transformation Approaches. In *OOPSLA'03 Worshop on Generative in Context of Model-Driven Architecture*, 2003.
10. J. D'Anjou, S. Fairbrother, D. Kehn, J. Kellerman, and P. McCarty. *The Java developers guide to Eclipse*. Addison-Wesley, 2004.
11. R. Depke, R. Heckel, and J. M. Küster. Agent-Oriented Modeling with Graph Transformation. In P. Ciancarini and M. Wooldridge, editors, *AOSE*, volume 1957 of *Lecture Notes in Computer Science*, pages 150 – 120. Springer, 2001.
12. T. Gardner, C. Griffin, J. Koehler, and R. Hauser. A review of OMG MOF 2.0 Query / Views / Transformations Submissions and Recommendations towards the final Standar. In *MetaModelling for MDA Workshop*, York, England, 2003.
13. S. Gyapay and D. Varró. Automatic Algorithm Generation for Visual Control Structure. Technical report, Dept. of Measurement and Information System, Budapest University of Technology and Economics, Hungary, 2000.
14. I. Jacobson, G. Booch, and J. Rumbaugh. *The Unified Software Development Process*. Addison-Wesley, 1999.
15. G. B. Jayatilleke, L. Padgham, and M. Winikoff. Towards a Component-Based Development Framework for Agents. In G. Lindemann, J. Denzinger, I. Timm, and R. Unland, editors, *Multiagent System Technologies, Proceedings of the Second German Conference, MATES 2004*, number 3187 in LNAI, pages 183 – 197. Springer-Verlag, 2004.
16. S. R. Judson, R. B. France, and D. L. Carver. Specifying Model Transformations at the Metamodel Level, 2004. http://www.omg.org.
17. M. Kifer, G. Lausen, and J. Wu. Logical Foundations of Object-Oriented and Frame-Based Languages. *Journal of ACM*, 42(4):741 – 843, 1995.
18. J. Koehler, R. Hauser, S. Sendall, and M. Wahler. Declarative techniques for model-driven business process integration. *IBM Systems Journal*, 44(1), 2005.
19. S. J. Mellor, K. Scott, A. Uhl, and D. Weise. *MDA Distilled*. Addison-Wesley, 2004.
20. A. Novikau, A. Perini, and M. Pistore. Graph Rewriting for Agent Oriented Visual Modeling. In *In Proc. of the International Workshop on Graph Transformation and Visual Modeling Techniques, in ETAPS 2004 Conference*, Barcelona, Spain, 2004.
21. L. Padgham and M. Winikoff. Prometheus: a methodology for developing intelligent agents. In *AAMAS*, pages 37–38, 2002.
22. A. Perini and A. Susi. Developing Tools for Agent-Oriented Visual Modeling. In G. Lindemann, J. Denzinger, I. Timm, and R. Unland, editors, *Multiagent System Technologies, Proceedings of the Second German Conference, MATES 2004*, number 3187 in LNAI, pages 169–182. Springer-Verlag, 2004.
23. E. Visser. A survey of strategies in program transformation systems. *Electr. Notes Theor. Comput. Sci.*, 57, 2001.
24. F. Zambonelli, N. R. Jennings, and M. Wooldridge. Developing Multiagent Systems: The Gaia Methodology. *ACM Transactions on Software Engineering and Methodology*, 12(3):317 – 370, July 2003.

# Paving the Way for Implementing Multiagent Systems: Integrating Gaia with Agent-UML

Juan C. García-Ojeda[1], Alvaro E. Arenas[2], and José de Jesús Pérez-Alcázar[3]

[1] Laboratorio de Cómputo Especializado, Universidad Autónoma de Bucaramanga, Calle 48 No 39-234, El Jardín. Bucaramanga, Santander - Colombia
jgarciao@unab.edu.co
[2] CCLRC Rutherford Appleton Laboratory, Chilton-Didcot OX11 0QX, Oxfordshire - United Kingdom
a.e.arenas@rl.ac.uk
[3] EACH, Universidade de São Paulo, Avenida Arlindo Bettio, 1000 - Hermelindo Matarazzo. São Paulo - Brazil
jperez@usp.br

**Abstract.** This paper describes how to refine a Gaia design by applying agent-oriented extensions of UML. First, we show how the Gaia Interaction model can be improved by applying the first two layers of the Agent Interaction Protocol (AIP) of AUML. Second, Gaia Agent and Service models are refined by applying the AIP's third layer combined with Extended UML Class Diagrams. Third, Gaia Organisational Structure is enriched by applying the Aalaadin model. The final aim of the whole process is to obtain a more concrete design closer to implementation. We demonstrate how the refinement process can be applied to the development of an agent-based system for conference management.

## 1 Introduction

Several methodologies for developing MAS have been proposed in the literature, for instance [7, 8, 15, 18], but there is not a methodology that has secured industrial acceptance. It has been identified that one way of increasing industrial acceptance of a new technology is to present it as an incremental extension of known and trusted methods. This paper describes how to integrate Gaia [18], a methodology for developing MAS that is gaining acceptance within the agent community, with agent-oriented extensions of the standard *de-facto* UML. The outcome of the Gaia process is a semi-formal, and somehow abstract, specification that could be implemented using agent-based or object-oriented frameworks. However, the road toward implementation is a difficult one, and developers need guidelines in order to produce detailed designs close to implementation. This paper contributes to closing such gap by providing an approach to refine Gaia output by applying the Agent Interaction Protocol (AIP) of Agent-UML (AUML) [11, 12], taking into consideration agent-oriented extensions to UML class diagrams [2] and the representation of social structures in UML [14]. Section 2 gives an overview of our approach and of the technologies applied when integrating Gaia and UML. The core of the paper is section 3 that describes how to refine a Gaia design using AUML, Extended UML Class Diagrams (ECD) and the

J.P. Müller and F. Zambonelli (Eds.): AOSE 2005, LNCS 3950, pp. 179 – 189, 2006.

Aalaadin model. Section 4 shows the usefulness of our approach by applying it to a case study. Finally, section 5 presents concluding remarks, compares our work with other approaches ,and highlights future work.

## 2 Overview

To represent the integration between Gaia and AUML, we use the Software Process Engineering Metamodel (SPEM) [13], a specification adopted by the Object Management Group to describe software-development processes. Figure 1 lists some useful stereotypes defined by SPEM to represent possible outcomes of a development process. For example, the element *WorkProduct* represents any artefact produced, consumed or modified by a process like an *UMLModel* or *Document*; the *Phase* element represents the work performed in a process; the *MASElement* represent an element of a MAS model, such as a protocol or a role.

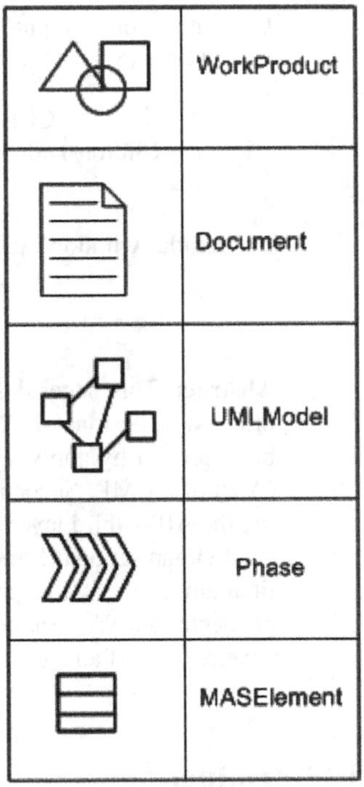


**Fig. 1.** SPEM notation

The Gaia methodology uses an organisational view to construct MAS [18]. It starts with an analysis phase, which aims at organising the collected specifications and requirements of the system into the following: an environmental model, an abstract computational representation of the environment in which the MAS will be situated; a preliminary role model, which identifies the basic skills required by the organisation; a preliminary interaction model -identifying the basic interactions required to accomplish the preliminary roles; and a set of organisational rules that the organisation should respect and enforce in its global behaviour. The next step in the methodology is the design phase, consisting of an architectural design and detailed design phases. The goal of the architectural design is to identify an efficient and reliable way to structure the MAS organisation, completing accordingly the preliminary roles and interactions models. The detailed design phase is responsible for eventually identifying the agent model and the services model which, in turn, act as guidelines for the actual implementation of agents and their activities.

Figure 2 shows the overall Gaia design phase in SPEM and our integration proposal. Our approach is built on top of our previous work on integrating Gaia and AUML [1, 6], taking into consideration the new proposal of Gaia [18], the extended UML class diagram (ECD) for agents [2], and representation of organisational/social structures such as the Aalaadin Model[5] and its extension for UML [14].

The AIP is composed by three layers: the first layer represents the overall protocol, defining communications patterns by means of aggregations concepts as packages and templates; the second layer represents the interactions among agents by means of sequence, collaboration, activities or statecharts diagrams; the third layer models the internal process of an agent by means of activity or statecharts diagrams for represent such internal process. We have exploited the AIP in several ways: Gaia Interaction model is refined using the first layer of AIP; the Agent and Service models are refined in the third layer of AIP, using state machine for representing the internal behaviour of agents.

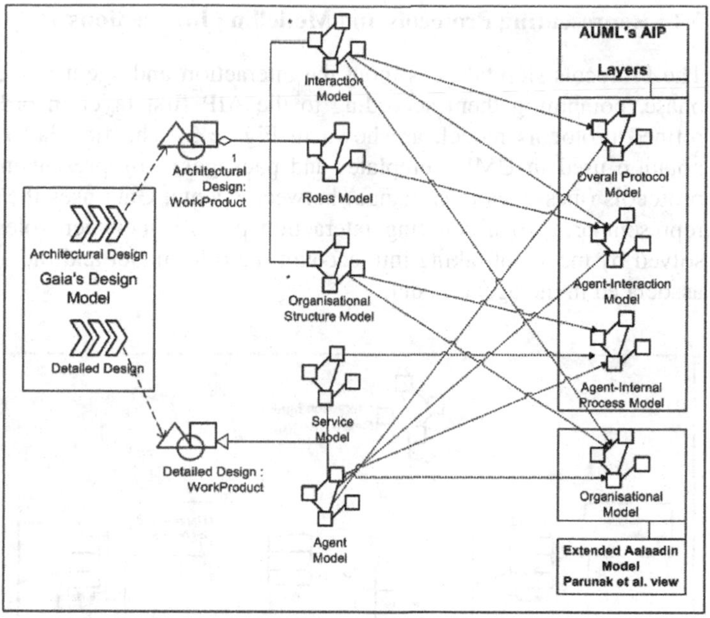


**Fig. 2.** Combining Gaia and AUML

The work of Bauer in [2] extends the traditional UML class diagrams in the context of agent-oriented development. It defines a ECD as a class that includes: an agent head part, dealing with the goals, states, etc of an agent; an agent body, representing the pure actions of an agent; and a communicator part, representing the agent communication by means of communication acts. We have exploited Bauer's work by refining an agent into an extended UML agent class.

An important abstraction in agent development is to model agent societies using concepts such as groups, roles and structures. Such an abstraction is the base of Aalaadin [5], a meta-model of artificial organisation by which one can build MAS with different structures AUML such as market-like and hierarchical organisations. We have exploited UML extended Aalaadin model (EAM) [14] to represent the roles and organisational structure models. The next section explains in more detail the whole integration process between Gaia and UML.

## 3 Refining Gaia with AUML

Our process to refine Gaia with AUML follows a top-down approach, taking as input the Gaia models, which are then enriched by including AIP models. Following the AIP structure, the process is composed by three steps: Protocols and Interactions, Agents and Organisations. Each step takes as input a model or set of models obtained form Gaia's design phase and produces AIP models.

### 3.1 Representing Protocols and Modelling Interactions

The Protocols step takes as input the interaction and agent models from Gaia design phase, combining them according to the AIP first layer in order to obtain a more refined protocols model, as shown in Figure 3. The first layer of AIP extends the notation used in UML (templates and packages) to represent in a concrete way the protocols (messages interchange) between agents. Gaia uses the interaction model to represent protocols, denoting interaction patterns between roles. This difference is solved by means of taking into account the role model and the agent to which it was associated in the agent model.

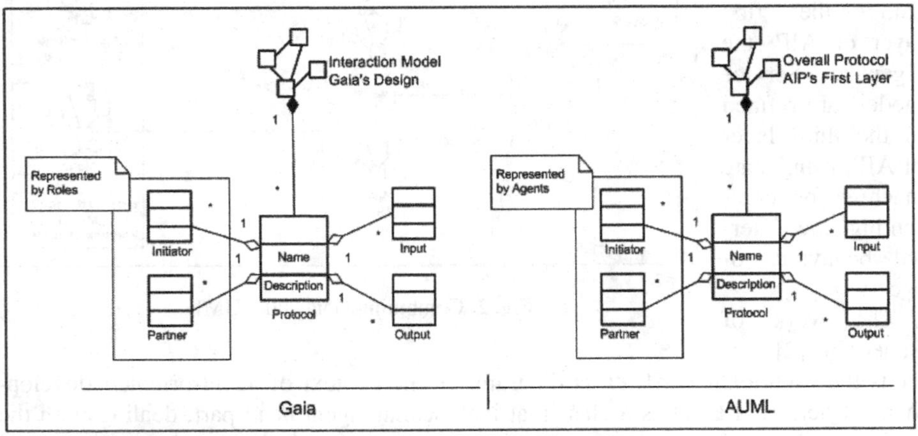


**Fig. 3.** Relation between Protocols in Gaia and AUML (SPEM notation)

The interaction between agents can be further refined using the second layer of AIP, which represents interaction between agents. This can be done in a similar way to the previous step, taking as input the Interaction, Roles and Agent models from Gaia's design phase.

### 3.2 Representing Agents

Once the interactive part between roles and agents of the system is refined, we proceed to further refine the agents and the services they realise. In order to do so, we take as inputs the Roles, Agent and Service models from Gaia and combine them with the ECD. The ECD is composed of seven major sections. The first section is Agent Class Description and Roles, which associates roles to the agent classes, in a similar way as carried out in Gaia Agent model. The second section makes reference to the state description, dealing with all formal descriptions of a state, similar to the Liveness Properties in Gaia. The third section defines the actions that the agent or role must take (this could be active or reactive). In the fourth section, methods are defined. In the fifth section, capabilities of the role or agents are specified. The sixth section defines the restrictions to which the role will be subdued, similar to the safety properties of the roles schema in Gaia. The last section is one of the most important of the ECD from our point of view, since it allows us to model each one of the communication acts in which the role or agent intervenes. An important aspect when modelling this section is the Agent-Head-Automata that can be modelled with the most internal layer of the AIP model (representing internal agent processing). With this, we can describe the incoming messages and its relation with the internal state of the agent, actions and the outgoing messages. It is worth noticing that these activities or internal processing derive from Gaia's model of services.

### 3.3 Representing the Organisational Structure

As mentioned before, Gaia follows an organisational view for developing MAS. In this final phase, we propose to represent the organisational structure making use of the Aalaadin model [5] and others concepts associated to the representation of social structures [14]. In Figure 4, we can observe our model to represent the organisational structure for the specific case of Gaia. We have marked with a single line the three main concepts used by Aalaadin: agent, role and group. Within the Aalaadin model, an agent is seen as an active communicating entity; a group as is a set of agents; and a role is an abstract representation of an agent function. Following [9], a MAS consists of three main concepts: environment, agent-roles and interactions; the relation among these concepts has been strengthened by Parunak *et al.* [14] by integrating the environment into the Aalaadin model. This extension is marked with a dotted line in Figure 4. Furthermore, we have added others elements to the model, such as the organisational rules, the abstract computational resources and the organisation. With

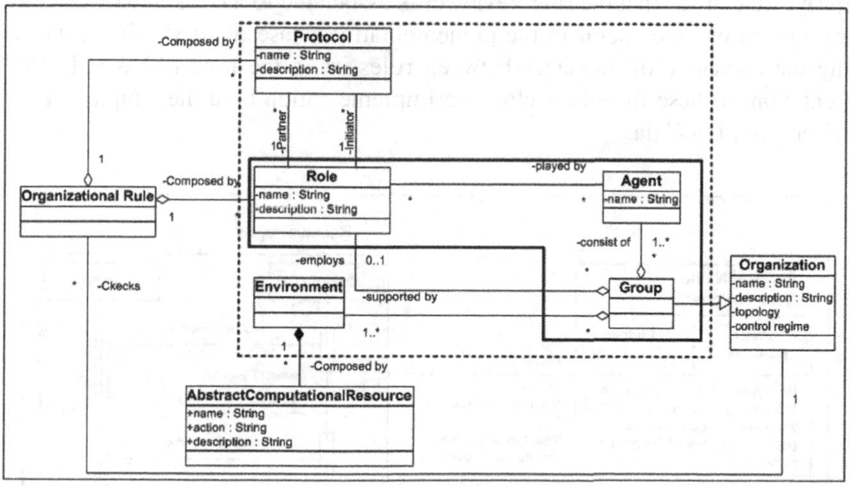


Fig. 4. Organisational Structure Model

this model we can obtain a more concrete model to implement the organisational structure of the MAS, allowing in this way to join together all the fundamental aspect treated by Gaia into a meta-model view.

## 4 A Case Study: Refining a Conference Management System

To illustrate our proposal of integration we have taken as case study the development of an agent-based system for conference management (This case study is borrowed from [18]). The proposed problem could be summarised as follows. During the submission phase, authors send papers; authors are then informed that their papers have been received and have been assigned a submission number. In the review phase, the program committee (PC) has to handle the review of the papers: contacting potential referees and asking them to review a number of papers. Eventually, reviews come in and are used to decide about the acceptance or rejection of the submission. In the final phase, authors need to be notified of these decisions and, in case of acceptance, must be asked to produce a revised version of their paper. The publisher has to collect these final versions and print the proceedings.

### 4.1 Representing Protocols and Modelling Interactions

Taking as example the *ReceivePaper* protocol ([18], p.348), we have represented that protocol in Figure 5. This protocol is initiated by the role PC-Chair who wants to know whether a potential evaluator of an article that has reached the organisation of the conference can evaluate it or not. In Figure 5, we have also modelled the *ReceivePaper* protocol using the first layer proposed by the AIP (Overall Protocol). In that sense, we have associated the PC-Chair Role to a class of agents called PC-Chair; similarly, we can see that the role Reviewer is associated to a class of Reviewer agent. These annotations are useful in the implementation phase of MAS. For instance, by adding the exchange of messages between roles using the note FIPA-ACL, the implementation of these models is closer to implementation than the simple interaction model proposed in Gaia.

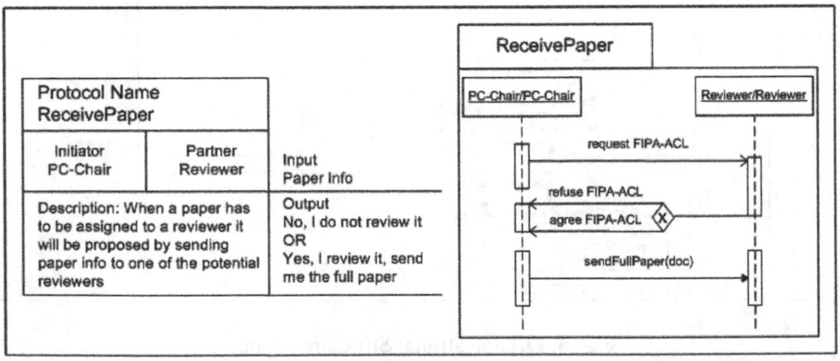


**Fig. 5.** Protocol Definition in Gaia and AUML (real notation)

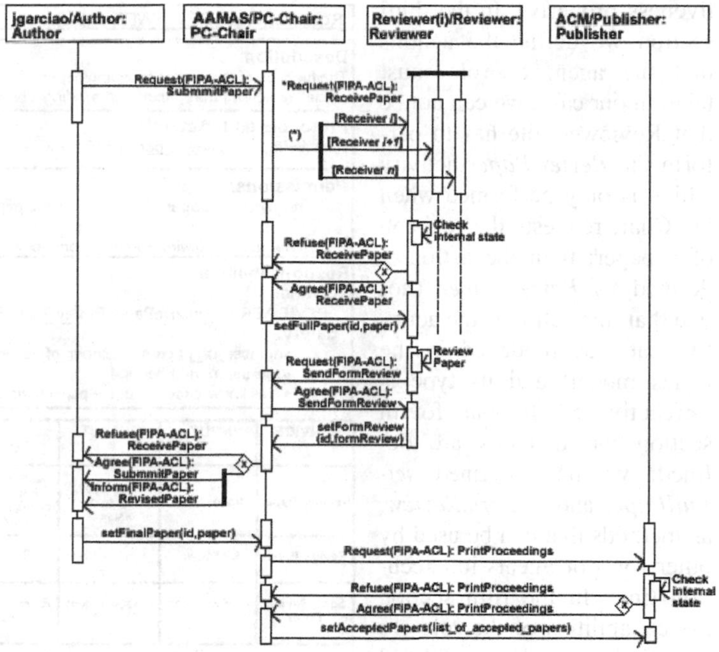


**Fig. 6.** Representing the Interactions between Agents

Figure 6 gives a view of the interactions in our case study. As it can be noted, the Author sends a request to the PC-Chair so that it evaluates his article; PC-Chair then proceeds to send the request to the possible Reviewers of the article for the revision (notice that given the rules of the organisation, PC-Chair might send in a concurrent way to three potential Reviewers); if they accept, PC-Chair sends the document. The Reviewers then will proceed to evaluate the article and send to PC-Chair the corresponding evaluations. Once analysed, PC-Chair will decide whether it accepts or rejects the article sent by an author. In the case the article is accepted, it sends the Author an acceptance message and informs him of the revised version he must submit. Once the Author delivers the revised version to PC-Chair, it will proceed to request the Publisher if he is available to print the proceedings; if he accepts, then PC-Chair will send a file with the articles accepted for publishing.

## 4.2 Representing Agents

Once the interactive part between roles and agents of the system is represented, we proceed to refine the Roles model (in our case, Reviewer Role, generated in [18], p. 347) combined with the Service model associated to Reviewer agent (see Figure 7). In order to do so, we make use of the extended vision of Bauer's Class Diagrams[2]. We have modelled each one of the main characteristics of the Reviewer role. As we mentioned in section 3, the extended vision of Bauer splits a conventional UML class diagram in seven major sections (see Figure 8). In the first section we associate the role to the agent class to which it belongs; in our case study the Reviewer role belongs to the Reviewer agent class (Reviewer/Reviewer). In the second section we need to represent the state description, for that reason we make use of the expression $REVIEWER=(ReceivePaper.\underline{ReviewPaper}.SendReview)^{maximum\_number}$ (Reviewer role liveness property). In the third section we define the actions that the agent or role must take; in our case, we can notice that Reviewer role has to perform the *ReviewPaper* activity which is only performed when PC-Chair requests the revision of a paper; then the action is defined as *ReviewPaper* (notice that this action is the activity that was modelled in the Roles model) and its type is <<reactive>>. In the fourth section the methods are defined; we have defined *setFullPaper* and *fillFormReview*, as methods that can be used by other roles or agents in execution time. In the fifth section the capabilities of the role are specified; we have defined three general features in our Reviewer role: (i)Capabilities: knowledge about the papers' topic, (ii) Service Description: Receive Paper, Review paper and Send Review Forms (Notice that this feature is similar in the role schema proposed in Gaia in the protocol and activities section) and (iii) Supported Protocols: *ReceivePaper* and *SendReview*. In the sixth section we have defined two restrictions: one of social type and another of variable type, the first is related to the group to which the role or agent belongs, and the second to internal control of the role or agent. In the last section we have modelled all the internal agent processing. We can notice that the Reviewer role participates in two protocols called *ReviewPaper* and *SendReviewForm*, likewise the types of message that it can transmit (Agree, Refuse and Request) and the ones that can receive (Request and Agree). An important aspect when modelling this section is the Agent-Head-Automata that can be modelled with the third layer of AIP. In our case, we have modelled the internal processing of the Reviewer role using an activities diagram, and the states by which the role transits together with the messages that it has to receive or send according to the states or activities to perform. It is worth noticing that these activities or internal processing derive from Gaia's model of services.

**Role Scheme:** REVIEWER (REV)

**Description:**
The function of this role is receiving papers for review from some conference official, reviewing that paper, and sending it back a completed review form.

**Protocols and Activities:**
ReceivePaper,ReviewPaper,SendReview

**Permissions:**
reads papers // all the papers it receives
changes ReviewForms //one for each of the papers

**Responsabilities**
**Liveness:**
REVIEWER = (ReceivePaper,ReviewPaper,SendReview)$^{maximum\_number}$
**Safety:**
- number_of_papers = number_of_reviewforms
- maximum_number < 4
- Has knowledge about the paper's topic

| SERVICE | INPUT | OUTPUT | PRE-CONDITION | POST-CONDITION |
|---|---|---|---|---|
| Receive Paper | Paper Info | message: agree or disagree | maximum_number < 4 && Paper is Avalible for reading && Has knowlede about paper's topic | message <> null |
| Review Paper | full Paper | Review_Form | full Paper is complete | Review_Form is complete |
| Send Review Form | Review_Form | messge: request | Review_Form is complete | receive an agree message |

**Fig. 7.** Roles and Service Models Generated

### 4.3 Representing the Organisational Structure

As it can be noted in Figure 9, our MAS is formed by a central structure called group, which is composed by the Author, Pc-Chair, Reviewer and Publisher agents; besides the agents are related to the roles they can play (i.e. PC-Chair plays *ReviewCatcher* and *ReviewCollector*, see [18], p 358) and the environment where it exists. The model thus presented may be considered as a pattern in the modelling of the organizational structure of any MAS (taking into consideration the protocols and organisationals rules).

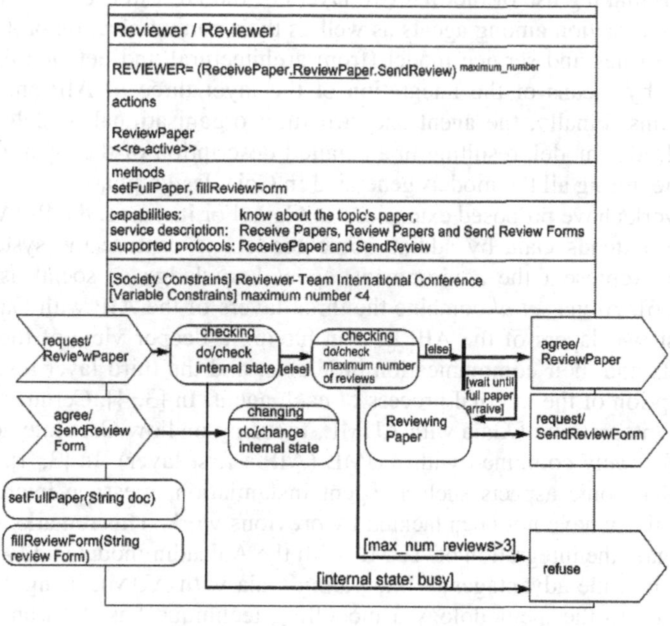


Fig. 8. Extended View of an Agent Model

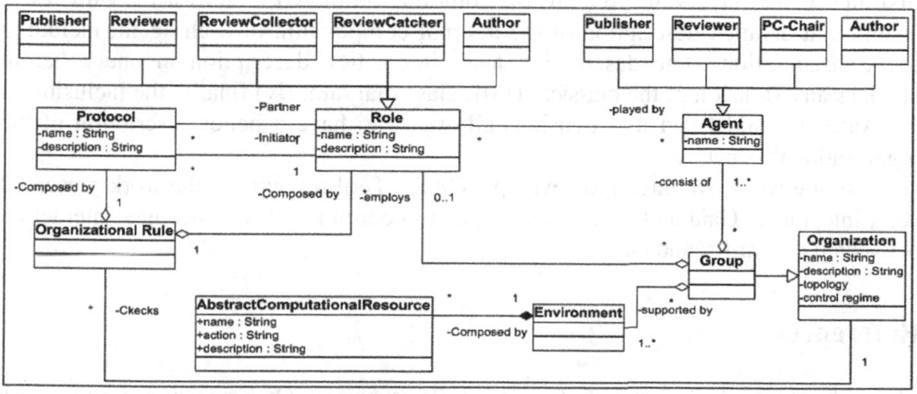


Fig. 9. Representing the Organisational Structure of the MAS

## 5 Conclusions and Future Work

Gaia is an agent-oriented methodology gaining acceptance in the agent community. This paper has shown how to further refine a Gaia design with extensions to UML. The main motivation for this work is to obtain a more concrete design by applying techniques of UML, a standard de-facto. The refinement process consists of three steps, taking as input the models generated in Gaia design phase (both Architectural and Detailed) In the first step we refine the interaction model (from architectural design phase) making use of the first two layers of the AIP, in order to have a deeper view on the interaction among agents as well as their communication protocols. Next, we refine the roles and service model (from architectural and detailed design phase respectively) by means of the integration of the layer three of AIP and the extend Class Diagrams. Finally, the agent and structural organisational models are refined with the Aalaadin model, resulting in a detailed description of the agent organisation structure (integrating all the models generated in Gaia design phase).

Several works have proposed extensions to Gaia. For instance, the ROADMAP[10] methodology extends Gaia by adding some models to capture the system requirements and to represent the environment, agent knowledge or social aspect of the MAS. In [1, 6], Arenas *et al* combine the three layers of the AIP with Gaia, showing how the first two layers of the AIP help in having a deeper view of the interaction among agents and their communication protocols, and the third layer results in a detailed description of the internal process of each agent. In [3, 4], Cernuzzi *et al.* have proposed an integration of Gaia with AUML, focusing on how Gaia interaction model could be effectively combined with AUML (AIP's first layer). In [3, 4], the authors mentioned that some aspects such as agent instantiation, message interactions, and agent interactivity have not been tackled by previous work. This remarks has inspired us to investigate the integration of AUML with the Aalaadin model and ECD.

Summarising, the advantages of integrating Gaia with AUML using our approach are: (i) it adds to the methodology a modelling technique based on an standard *de facto* as UML, this fact could make Gaia more attractive to the industry; (ii) the interaction model proposed by Gaia is quite abstract, this can be improved by using the first and second layers of AIP; (iii) the combination of AIP's third layer with ECD results in a detailed description of the internal composition of each agent; including agent instantiation, state description, and interaction description in one coherent block as an extension of the classical UML class diagram; (iv) finally, the inclusion of the Aalaadin model and its extensions allows us to have a better description of the organisational structures.

As future work, we intend to develop a CASE-Tool for support the work presented here, integrating Gaia and UML features, with the aim to allow a stronger interaction between the industry and Gaia.

## References

1. A. E. Arenas, J. C. García-Ojeda, and J. J. Pérez-Alcázar. On Combining Organizational Modelling and Graphical Languages for the Development of Multiagent Systems. Journal of Integrated Computer-Aided Engineering, 11(2):151–163, 2004.
2. B. Bauer. UML Class Diagrams Revisited in the Context of Agent-Based Systems. In Proceedings of the Second International Workshop on Agent Oriented Software Engineering (AOSE'01), 101–118, 2001.
3. L. Cernuzzi, T. Juan, L. Sterling, and F. Zambonelli. The Gaia Methodology: Basic Concepts and Extensions. In Methodologies and Software Engineering for Agent Systems. Kluwer Academic Publisher, 2004.

4. L. Cernuzzi and F. Zambonelli. Experiencing AUML in the Gaia Methodology. In Proceedings of the Sixth International Conference on Enterprise Information Systems (ICEIS'04), Kluwer Academic Publisher, 283–288, 2004.
5. J. Ferber, and O. Gutknecht. A Meta-Model for the Analysis and Design of Organizations in Multiagent Systems, In Proceedings of the Third International Conference on Multi-Agent Systems (ICMAS'98), IEEE Computer Society, 128-135, 1998.
6. J. C. García-Ojeda, J. J. Pérez-Alcázar, and A. E. Arenas. Appliying Gaia and AUML to the Selective Dissemination of Information on the Web. In Proceedings of the Fourth Iberoamerican Workshop on Multi-Agent Systems at IBERAMIA'02, 2002.
7. P. Bresciani, P. Giorgini, F. Giunchiglia, J. Mylopoulos and A. Perini. TROPOS: An Agent-Oriented Software Development Methodology. In Journal of Autonomous Agents and Multi-Agent Systems, Kluwer Academic Publishers, 8(3):203-236,2004.
8. C. A. Iglesias, M. Garijo, J. C. Gonzalez, and J. R. Velasco. Analysis and Design of Multiagent Systems using MAS-CommonKADS. In Proceedings of the Fourth Workshop on Agents, Technologies, Architectures and Languages(ATAL'97), 313–327, 1997.
9. N. R. Jennings. On Agent-Based Software Engineering. Artificial Intelligence, 117(2):277–296, 2000.
10. T. Juan, A. Pearce, and L. Sterling. ROADMAP: Extending the Gaia Methodology for Complex Open Systems. In Proceedings of the First International Joint Conference on Autonomous Agents and Multi-Agent Systems (AAMAS'02), ACM, 3-10, 2002.
11. J. Odell, V. D. Parunak, and B. Bauer. Extending UML for Agents. In G. Wagner. In Proceedings of the Second Workshop on Agent-Oriented Information Systems (AOIS'00), iCue Publishing, 3–17, 2000.
12. J. Odell, V. D. Parunak, and B. Bauer. Representing Agent Interactions Protocols in UML. In Proceedings of the First International Workshop on Agent-Oriented Software Engineering (AOSE'01), Springer Verlag, 121–140, 2001.
13. OMG. Software Process Engineering Metamodel Specification. (available at http://www.omg.org/cgi-bin/apps/doc?formal/05-01-06.pdf), January 2005.
14. H. V. Parunak, and J. Odell. Representing Social Structures in UML. In Proceedings of the Second International Workshop on Agent-Oriented Software Engineering (AOSE'02), Springer Verlag, 1–16, 2002.
15. J. Pavón, and J. Gómez-Sanz. Agent Oriented Software Engineering with INGENIAS. In Proceedings of the Third International Central and Eastern European Conference on Multi-Agent Systems (CEEMAS'03), Springer Verlag, 394-403, 2003.
16. F. Zambonelli, N. Jennings, A. Omicini, and M. Wooldridge. Coordination of Internet Agents, In Agent-Oriented Software Engineering for Internet Applications. Springer-Verlag, 2001.
17. F. Zambonelli, N. R. Jennings, and M. Wooldridge. Organizational Abstractions for the Analysis and Design of Multi-Agent Systems In Agent-Oriented Software Engineering. Springer-Verlag, 2001.
18. F. Zambonelli, N. R. Jennings, and M. Wooldridge. Developing Multiagent Systems: The Gaia Methodology. ACM Transactions on Software Engineering and Methodology, 12(3):317–370, 2003.

# Applying Multi-agent Concepts to Dynamic Plug-In Architectures

Lawrence Cabac, Michael Duvigneau, Daniel Moldt, and Heiko Rölke

University of Hamburg, Department of Computer Science,
Vogt-Kölln-Str. 30, D-22527 Hamburg
http://www.informatik.uni-hamburg.de/TGI/

**Abstract.** In this work we present the basic concepts for a dynamic plug-in-based software architecture using concepts from the Petri net-based MAS framework MULAN. By transferring the concepts of agent-orientation to a plug-in-based architecture we are able to design our application and the plug-in-based system on an abstract level. Moreover, general problems that evolve from a highly dynamic and configurable architecture have been solved by basing the conceptual design on multi-agent principles. In this paper we discuss the general properties of extensible systems and the benefits that can be achieved when applying the multi-agent view to their architecture.

In addition to the conceptual modeling of such architectures, we provide a practical example where the concept has been successfully applied in the development of the latest release of RENEW. Through the introduction of the multi-agent concepts, the new architecture is now – at runtime – dynamically extensible by registering plug-ins with the management system.

**Keywords:** Components, dynamic software architectures, high-level Petri nets, modeling, MULAN, multi-agent systems, nets-within-nets, plug-in architectures, reference nets, RENEW.

## 1 Introduction

Today's application software has to be adaptable, configurable and customizable to fulfill the needs of the users. Many system developers approach this challenge by introducing extensible systems as plug-in systems to extend or alter the functionality of these applications. Some systems are augmented with simple plug-in mechanisms, others reorganize the architecture of the application towards a system that consists exclusively of plug-ins. While applications of the first category usually resort to simple designs with extremely restrained possibilities of extending, the applications of the second category have to face many challenges to assure consistency and interoperability of plug-in components.

Plug-in frameworks like those of Eclipse [5] or NetBeans [12] provide elaborated plug-in features in their practical environment. However, a conceptual model of a plug-in is not discussed in this context.

J.P. Müller and F. Zambonelli (Eds.): AOSE 2005, LNCS 3950, pp. 190–204, 2006.

By examining plug-in systems from the agent-oriented perspective, restrictions and problems of current systems can be discovered and attacked. Moreover, by basing the architectures of plug-in systems on agent-oriented principles, the designs of the application architectures adopt the advantages of multi-agent systems. These advantages are the handling of problems such as concurrency, conflicting functionality, service dependencies, locality and privacy, compatibility and dynamic extensibility. Challenges of plug-in systems can then be addressed in a more general way in Multi-agent systems. One of the foremost benefits is, that the plug-in architecture becomes dynamically extensible i.e. functionality can be altered, added or removed at runtime without the need to restart the application. For example, Bergenti and Huhns discuss and formally define the aspect of reusability when using agents as components in [1, pp. 19–32].

In this paper we benefit from the expressiveness of our Petri net based model of multi-agent systems. Based on agent-oriented Petri nets [8] and the FIPA-compliant MAS framework Capa (see [4]) we present a conceptual model for plug-in based systems. The idea is to structure and improve such systems using important concepts from the agent-oriented area, along with a visual representation.

In the following Section 2 we give an introduction for the Petri net-based multi-agent reference architecture Mulan. Mulan, the conceptual basis for Capa, uses the formalism of reference nets, a high-level Petri net formalism to handle concurrency, distributedness and localities. The focus lies on the concepts in the MAS, which are used in the design of our concept model of a general plug-in architecture. In Section 3 we present our agent-oriented concept model for a dynamic plug-in architecture. After a short sketch of a specialized concept model for a plug-in system in Section 4, we discuss in Section 5 the realization of the concept model in Renew and discuss some pragmatic design decisions.

Note that the Petri net IDE Renew is portraited here in two different ways. First, it is used to act as modeling tool and virtual engine for the abstract and the functional Mulan models. Second, it is used as the application, which architecture is examined and presented as a realization of the concept model of a general plug-in architecture. A similar manifold object of discussion is the agent platform Capa which is realized as a plug-in for Renew, but also used in the development of the concept model.

## 2 Agent System Architecture

In this section we will introduce the agent system architecture Mulan together with the Capa extension. Mulan is implemented using the reference net formalism (and Java) so we start with an overview on reference nets.

### 2.1 Reference Nets

Reference nets [9] are expressive high-level Petri nets that allow nets to be nested within nets in dynamical structures (nets-within-nets [17]). In contrast to ordinary Petri nets, where tokens are passive elements, tokens in nets-within-nets are active elements, i.e. Petri nets. In general we distinguish between two different kinds of token semantics: value semantics and reference semantics. In value semantics tokens can be seen as direct representations of nets. This allows for nested nets that are structured in a hierarchical order because nets can only be located at one location. In reference semantics arbitrary structures of net-nesting can be achieved because tokens represent references to nets. These structures can be hierarchical, acyclic or even cyclic.

Reference nets may be modelled and executed using the Petri net-IDE RENEW [10] (see Section 5).

Reference nets are object-oriented nets. Similar to objects in object-oriented programming languages, where objects are instantiations of classes, net instances are instantiations of net templates. Net templates define the structure and behavior of nets just like classes define the structure and methods of objects. While the net instance has a marking that determines its status, the net template determines only the behavior and initial marking that is common to all net instances of one type.

Communication between different nets (net instances) is possible via synchronous channels. Synchronous channels resemble method calls in object-oriented programming languages, but they are more powerful. They temporarily fuse two (or more) transitions and allow the passing of arguments in either directions. Furthermore, the enabledness of the channel is determined by all participating transitions, not only by one caller.

## 2.2 The Multi-Agent System MULAN

Today, agents and multi-agent systems (MAS) are one of the most important structuring concepts for complex software systems. By including attributes like autonomy, cooperation, adaptability and mobility, agents go well beyond the concept of objects and object-oriented software development.

The multi-agent system architecture MULAN [8] is based on the nets-within-nets paradigm, which is used to describe the natural hierarchies in an agent system. MULAN is implemented in reference nets using RENEW [10]. MULAN has the general structure as depicted in Figure 1: Each box describes one level

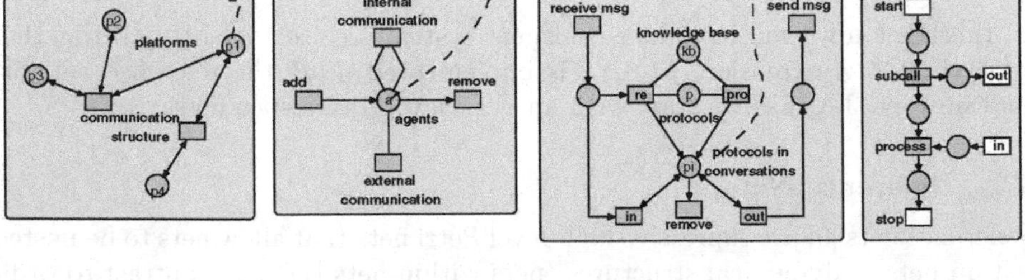


**Fig. 1.** Agent system as nets-within-nets

of abstraction in terms of the net hierarchy. Each upper level net contains net tokens, whose structures are made visible by the ZOOM lines.[1] The figure shows a simplified version of MULAN, since for example several inscriptions and all synchronous channels are omitted. Nevertheless, MULAN is an executable model. In Figure 1 each box can be seen as a specific view on the multi-agent system.

**The Multi-Agent System View.** The net in the far left of Figure 1 describes an agent system, whose places contain agent platforms as tokens. The transitions describe communication or mobility channels that build up the infrastructure. The multi-agent system net shown in the figure is just an illustrating example, the number of places and transitions or the interconnections have no further meaning.

**The Platform View.** By zooming into the platform token on place p1, the structure of a platform becomes visible, shown in the second box. The central place agents hosts all agents that currently reside on this platform. Each platform offers services to the agents, some of which are indicated in the figure.[2] Agents can be created (transition add) or destroyed (transition remove). Agents can communicate by message exchange. Two agents of the same platform can communicate by the transition internal communication, which binds two agents, the sender and the receiver, to pass one message over a synchronous channel. Transition external communication only binds one agent, since the other agent is bound on a second platform somewhere else in the agent system. Also mobility facilities are provided on a platform: agents can leave the platform (via the transition new) or enter the platform (via the transition destroy).

In the diagram some details of the platform are hidden for the reason of simplicity. An important feature that cannot be seen is that a platform may itself act as an agent. By this means, arbitrary hierarchies of agents and platforms are possible, in particular a platform is able to encapsulate its agents from the outside world.

**The Agent View.** An agent is a message processing entity. It must be able to receive messages, possibly process them and generate messages of its own. Each agent consists of exactly one *agent net* that is its interface to the outside world (third box in Figure 1) and an arbitrary number of *protocols* (last box) defining its behavior. The agent may exchange messages with other agents via the platform. This is done using the transitions receive message and send message. These two transitions are the only interconnection of the agent to the rest of the (multi-) agent system, so the agent is a strongly encapsulated entity. Please note, that communication of agents is asynchronous even though synchronous channels are utilized for this cause.

The central point of activity of such an agent is the selection of protocols and therewith the commencement of conversations. The protocol selection can

[1] This zooming into net tokens should not to be confused with place refinement.

[2] Note that only mandatory services are mentioned here. A typical platform will offer more and specialized services, for example implemented by special service agents.

basically be performed pro-actively (the agent itself starts a conversation) or re-actively (protocol selection based on a conversation activated by another agent). In the case of the pro-active protocol selection, the place knowledge base is the main enabling condition, the protocols are a side condition.

**The Interaction View.** The activities of an agent are modeled as protocol Petri nets (or short: protocols) – an example is given in the far right box of the figure. The variety of protocols ranges from simple linear step-by-step plans to complex dynamic workflows. Petri nets are well suited for the modeling of procedures or process flows, which can be seen by their wide-spread use in the area of (business) process modeling [18].

### 2.3 Agents as Platforms

As stated before, platforms in a full featured MULAN system may act like agents and encapsulate the hosted agents. It is therefore no problem to implement e.g. a holonic MAS using MULAN agents. The logical consequence of this approach is to exclusively use these "platform agents" as agents in the MAS. Following this idea leads to a dynamically reconfigurable MAS structure, i.e. a new hierarchy level may be introduced at run-time simply by creating a new (platform) agent and migrating other agents into it.

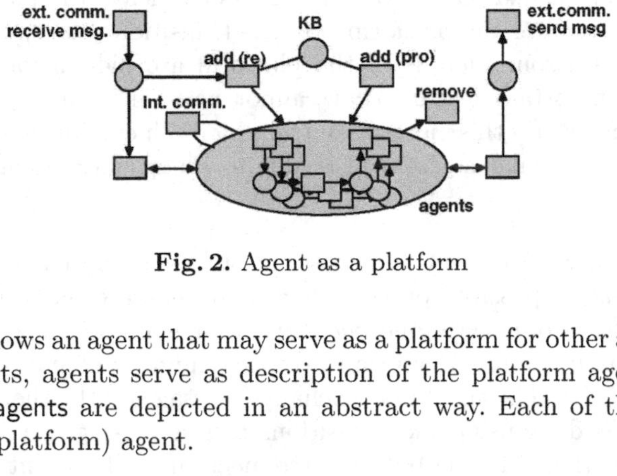


**Fig. 2.** Agent as a platform

Figure 2 shows an agent that may serve as a platform for other agents. Instead of protocol nets, agents serve as description of the platform agent's behavior. The internal agents are depicted in an abstract way. Each of them may be a full-featured (platform) agent.

### 2.4 CAPA

CAPA (Concurrent Agent Platform Architecture) [4] is a partial re-implementation of the MULAN framework. CAPA ensures the compatibility of the MULAN framework to the FIPA specifications [6]. The internal structure of the agents and the possibilities sketched above are not changed by CAPA.

Part of the compliance to the FIPA specifications concerns the management of an agent platform. In particular, an agent management system (AMS) and a directory facilitator (DF) have to be provided. This is done by placing special agents on each platform that offer the mandatory services. Additional services may be offered by agents residing on the platform. Agents migrating to a platform may offer new services previously lacking on this platform.

This migration idea may serve as a basis for the conceptualization of plug-in architectures. This will be demonstrated in the next chapter.

## 3 Concept Model for a Dynamic Plug-In Architecture

A dynamic architecture is characterized by extensibility and adaptability. We sketch some general concepts of plug-in systems and map these concepts to agent-oriented concepts. In this work we conceive extensibility as a recursive feature. We apply the idea of nested platform agents to our concept, which leads to recursive extensibility. A system is extended by components, which again are extended by plug-ins, which are (specialized) components. Finally, we show that the recursive agent-oriented plug-in model is a full-fledged plug-in system that allows for dynamic configuration. The realization of this concept in Renew 2.0 is described in Section 5.

### 3.1 Extensibility

To construct extensible systems it is useful to get a notion of what is meant by extensibility. In software engineering, components have been introduced as units of extensibility. Sametinger gives a definition of a component:

**Definition 1.** *Component [13, p. 68]*
*Reusable software components are self-contained, clearly identifiable artifacts that describe and/or perform specific functions and have clear interfaces, appropriate documentation and a defined reuse status.*

Likewise, extensibility in the agent-oriented view is a first-order concept. An agent system is extended by creating or migrating agents onto a platform. These agents provide additional functionality to all other agents in the system as long as they exist within the system. Removing the agent subtracts its provided functionality from the system.

Obviously we can map the concepts of components on the concepts of agents. Agents are encapsulated (self-contained, clearly identifiable) artifacts. They have the capability of action and reaction (specific functions). In FIPA-compliant platforms, the service directory, communication languages and ontologies provide clear interfaces and documentation. MULAN agents are composed of reusable protocols.

The platform net in Figure 1 visualizes the idea of extensibility: Net tokens that provide functionality – agents – can be put onto and removed from the central place of this net. These primitive platform services provide the component management of the software system. In the platform net of Figure 1 we are able to say that the system is extensible on one level. This notion of *one-level extensibility* [15] expresses the fact that new components can be introduced to the system but these components can not be extended themselves. The possibility to extend the components leads us to a notion for a recursively extensible system.

The extended agent model shown in Figure 2 already provides recursive extensibility. Every agent can serve as a platform for an arbitrary number of agents, which can be platforms again. Components that recursively extend other components are plug-ins. We take the following definition from Schumacher:

**Definition 2.** *Plug-in [14, p. 34]*
*Plug-ins are components that change the behavior of one or more other components in the system. This is done by using the provided interface of the components.*

Up to now, we have a hierarchical structure of the system. The extension relation is strongly tree-structured. The use of reference semantics enables us to relax this condition. With reference nets we would be able to create arbitrary structured extension relations, e.g. acyclic graphs. This would also be desirable for a plug-in system, however, as long as we regard the containment relation of agents within agents as a physical relationship, one agent cannot be located at two platforms at the same time. Nevertheless, the logical platform concept allows an agent to be residing at multiple platforms. Von Lüde et. al. [16] stress the necessity of the use of multiple memberships of agents in platforms from a sociological viewpoint in analogy to the membership of humans in communities.

### 3.2 Communication Between Components

In a multi-agent system, communication between agents is always carried out through messages. These are transported horizontally by the platforms – this is a basic platform service. In addition, the nesting of agent platforms introduces vertical message passing as depicted in Figure 2 (ext. comm.).

In fact, the communication services provided by each platform allow us to see the functionality of all agents inside that platform as functionality of that platform, including the management services of that platform and its children. Thus, the distinction between management and functionality that we made earlier can be dropped now.

One of the advantages of the component-orientation is the re-usability (cf. [13, p. 68]). This means for instance that the functionality that is offered by the plug-in can be utilized by all components that need this functionality. Therefore, a component has to be able to address another component / plug-in. For this we need the notion of services that are offered by components. Services have to be published and made accessible for other components. The service directory provided by the directory facilitator (DF) of FIPA-compliant platforms serves that purpose. If the DF is modeled as an agent, we can provide its service at any platform in the hierarchy. However, for a software system it is more practical to have one global service directory. Therefore, we require a DF only at the top-level platform. Likewise, we demand for our system that every component (agent) is a direct member of the top level platform. Although this is an enormous restriction of our general model it simplifies the management of the plug-in system. If each extensible component declares its extension management interface as a public accessible service, potential plug-ins can query the platform for that service and register themselves directly.

We enforce a life cycle for all plug-ins within the platform. The communication protocols induced by the life cycle enables the plug-in/agent to participate during migration by reacting to migration requests issued by third parties. Also the exact time of extension registration and configuration is determined by the life cycle.

The participation of a plug-in can be realized by simply adding a synchronous channel request to the add and remove transitions of a platform. These channel requests must be confirmed by the added / removed plug-ins. This ensures that the services of a plug-in cannot be used by components before the plug-in has been properly initialized.

It should be noted that each containment relationship is accompanied by its own life cycle. In this view we can map the agent life cycle, as standardized by the FIPA [7], onto the life cycle of the plug-in on the top-level platform. The life cycles in each containing sub-level should be handled by interaction protocols, defined by the extended component.

A multi-agent system already defines per definition an extensible system. By mapping some of the multi-agents concepts back to the model of a plug-in architecture we are able to design a system that offers extensibility as first-order concept. In addition, an agent-based view also takes into account that extensible systems have to deal with conflicts, concurrency, redundant functionality and also missing functionality. We have shown in this section that a concept model for a dynamic plug-in system architecture can be developed on the basis of multi-agent principles. We have achieved a formalization of plug-in systems that enables plug-ins to be loaded dynamically at runtime. In the following section we demonstrate the feasibility of our concepts in a real-world example.

## 4 Specialized Plug-In Model

In [2], we explain how we model the Renew plug-in system using reference nets. Although that model uses different notations and communication mechanisms, it is rather similar to the one presented in the previous section. We refer to it because it is more visual and helps to understand the agent based model. Also there exists an executable version of the model that proves the feasability of our concepts.

### 4.1 Reference Net Based Model of the Plug-In System

We start with a simple abstract reference net model of extensibility, as shown in Figure 3. The upper grey colored elements of the net define the extension management part of the system. The net shows the system as reference net in which the central place acts as the container for extensions. Functionality is

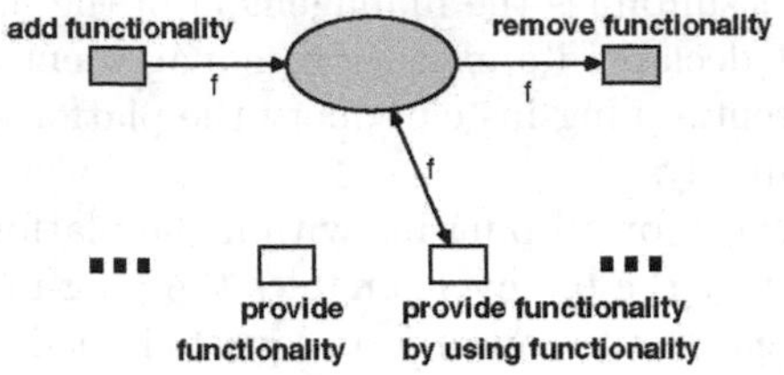


**Fig. 3.** Extensibility (from [2])

added to the system by a synchronous channel at the transition labeled `add functionality` and then put on the central container place. Functionality is removed by the transition labeled `remove functionality`.

The white transitions in the lower part are representatives for the available domain-specific functionality of the system. Some of the functionality may incorporate the functionality provided by extensions that lie in the central container place. All elements `f` that are extending the system are net instances again, according to the nets-within-nets paradigm.

In the paper [2], we refine the abstract model further until we obtain executable reference nets, thereby introducing all concepts explained in Section 3 like recursive extensibility, a service directory, a component lifecycle and a top-level net called `PluginManager`. The refined model of a component is shown in Figure 4.

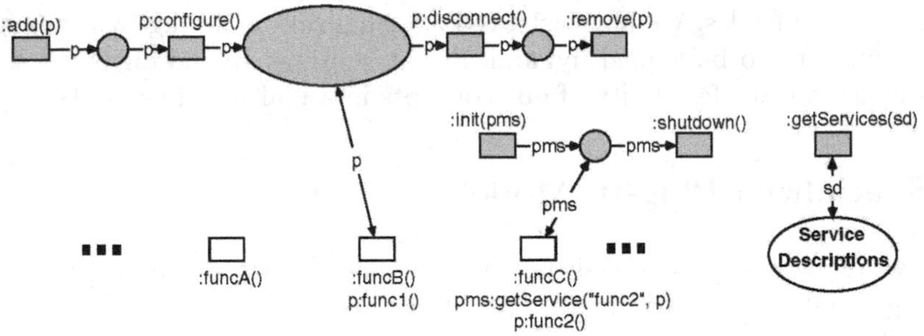


**Fig. 4.** Refined component model (from [2])

### 4.2 Mapping Between Both Models

A mapping between the agent-based model in this paper and the net model in [2] is established easily. The agent platform of the MULAN model (see Figure 1) has obviously the same `add` and `remove` channels as the basic concept of extensibility shown in Figure 3. The internal and external communication channels of the platform are not needed in the plug-in system because nested plug-ins use vertical communication. To allow horizontal communication, the plug-in manager provides the service directory where plug-ins can obtain direct references to other plug-ins. In the agent system, these references are agent-identifiers and reference-based horizontal communication is the normal case.

The agent net in Figure 2 is more generic than the component net, allowing any message to enter and leave the agent, while the plug-in net only accepts other plug-ins. The `init` and `shutdown` channels of the component net implement the life-cycle of the plug-in inside the plug-in management system. In the FIPA architecture, the life-cycle is implemented by message-based communication with the AMS agent, adhering to standardized interaction protocols. Analogously, the service lookup channels in the plug-in model are mapped onto message-based communication with the DF agent.

In the reference net model of plug-ins, we use white transitions to indicate domain-specific functionality of the plug-in. Such functionality is not directly visible in the agent net of the agent model because a MULAN agent implements such functionality by protocol nets on its lower layer.

The similarities between both models are not surprising given the fact that we already thought of an agent-based design when we designed the reference net-based model. It should be noted that the agent model of the plug-in system is more generic and thus more flexible, while the reference net model is specialized for the intended purpose. Therefore, the reference net model is more visual than the agent model, the nets show more application-specific details that are hidden in nested, dynamically changable protocols in the agent model.

Both models handle the same set of concepts and use similar means to acheive the intended functionality. Besides the different notations and message passing mechanisms, both models are the same. Both models are in fact agent-based models. They use the key concepts of multi-agent system, namely encapsulation, autonomy, cooperation, adaptability and mobility (although the latter is not discussed extensively in this paper, plug-ins can surely move from one container to another in our reference net model). But both models also restrict features like autonomy at a certain level in order to obtain a predictable, well-organized software system.

## 5 RENEW Plug-In Architecture

We use our tool RENEW for a case study where the plug-in concept is applied. RENEW (the **Re**ference **N**et **W**orkshop) is an open source IDE for Petri nets [10]. Its main functionality is provided by a simulation engine, which is accompanied by a graphical editor for Petri nets. The transformation from graphical nets to simulation code is realized as an abstract compiler interface so that the tool can be extended to handle arbitrary Petri net formalisms. The tool is shipped with a reference net compiler that provides the formalism sketched in Section 2.1.

The RENEW tool has grown enormously since its first release in 1999, and many application-specific extensions have been created in the meantime. These extensions, like a workflow engine, an agent platform or an editor for UML interaction diagrams, are themselves already grown to applications with their own extensions. Up to RENEW 1.6, all extensions were compiled into one large application. Some sets of functionality could be selected by specifying a mode at startup, but mode switching at runtime was not possible. However, a user would normally not need all extensions at the same time, but possibly in arbitrary combinations. Altogether, RENEW is very well suited as a case study for a dynamic, recursive plug-in system.

The plug-in system along with the decomposed application has been released as RENEW 2.0 and presented from the user's point of view in [11]. In this section we want to show how the concepts developed in Section 3 are applied to the RENEW plug-in system. Please note that our concepts have been modeled with the reference net formalism provided by RENEW, so that we have a cyclic relation between model and tool.

### 5.1 Functional Decomposition

From the user's point of view, RENEW comprises two main components: the simulation engine and the graphical net editor. Already in the first release it has been stated that RENEW supports multiple formalisms, since new formalisms could easily be added by implementing the appropriate compiler. Clearly it is desirable to separate each formalism into its own plug-in.

Figure 5 shows some plug-ins of the current decomposition.[3] At the bottom, there are some unnamed class libraries that are used by many or all plug-ins. Some of these libraries are integrated into the application as a plug-in of their own, but they do not provide any extension interfaces. At the right there is the main plug-in of RENEW, the simulation engine.

The graphical editor comprises two plug-ins: JHotDraw and Gui. The Gui plug-in enhances the JHotDraw application by Petri net specific figures and control commands for the token game.

The management of formalisms is divided into two plug-ins, and an analogous partitioning is suggested for each individual formalism as well as each other extension to the simulation engine: One plug-in extends the simulation engine and/or formalism management components. It provides the pure functionality extension without graphical adornments, e.g. the formalism management, or a compiler. The second component is a plug-in of the editor component and provides additional menu entries, graphical representations of net structure and tokens, formalism-specific tools, etc. to the user.

The two white plug-ins show the integration of the agent platform CAPA into the system. It extends the simulation engine to set up additional services when a simulation is started. Capa is also a plug-in of the Gui plug-in, it adds some menus and graphical adornments for agent nets. The NetComponents plug-in extends the graphical editor by toolbars of commonly used net patterns. Such a toolbar is defined by the MulanComponents plug-in, these patterns have been presented in [3].

[3] It has to be noted that the decomposition of an existing application with approximately 900 classes in 30 packages into several components is not unique and therefore some functionalities might be reassigned between components in future releases. The refactoring of RENEW is still work-in-progress.

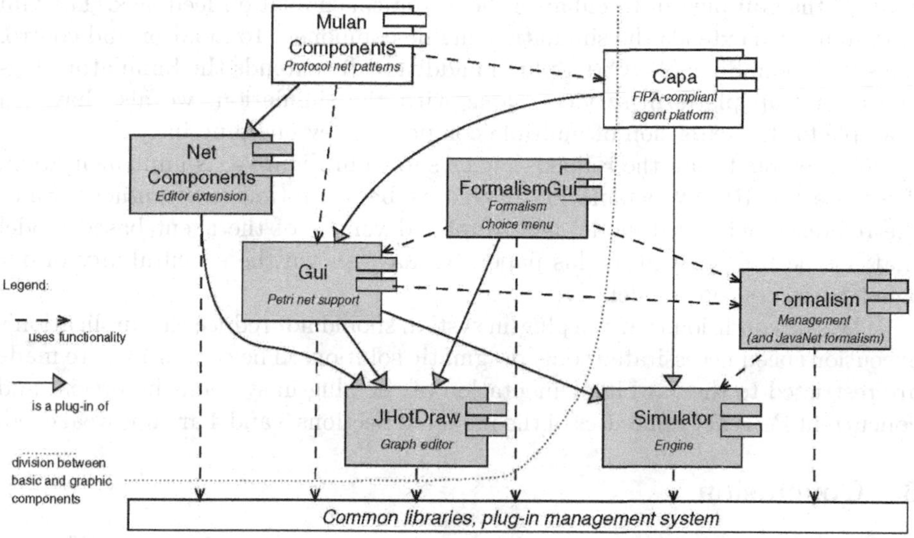


**Fig. 5.** Plug-ins and their dependencies as of RENEW 2.0

### 5.2 Applied Concepts

The RENEW plug-in system is implemented along the concepts developed in Section 3. In the system there exists a `PluginManager` that acts like the platform net shown in Figure 1. There is no distinction between components and plug-ins because any component may also act as a plug-in to any other component.

Plug-ins can enter the system in two ways. At startup, a plug-in finder looks at specific locations for pre-installed plug-ins, and during runtime plug-ins can be loaded dynamically by supplying an URL to the plug-in loader. Analogously, all plug-ins are unloaded when the system shuts down. The removal of components can also be initiated at runtime through an `unload` command.

The maintenance of the service directory is automated: Each plug-in is accompanied by a description of its provided services, the `PluginManager` maintains the directory during the initialization and shutdown transitions.

Optionally, the `PluginManager` may enforce dependencies between plug-ins. If a plug-in is also accompanied by a description of required services, the `PluginManager` will not include it in the system unless the required services are available. This mechanism delegates some commonly needed autonomous decisions of the plug-in to the `PluginManager` to simplify the plug-in development process. Likewise, the unloading of a plug-in is prohibited as long as another plug-in requires a service provided by the plug-in to remove. Of course, this dependency enforcement only works for static service requirements—but this is exactly what a *Java* programmer needs to ensure the availability of required class definitions.

Recursive extensibility (as introduced in Section 3.1) is included in the system as a chain of component extensions. An example is the CAPA plug-in, which extends the Gui plug-in to enhance the graphical simulation feedback. The Gui plug-in in turn extends the simulation engine component to monitor and control the simulation. Since the CAPA plug-in additionally extends the Simulator plug-in to start up platform services along with the simulation, we also have an example for the extension of multiple components by one plug-in.

We are able to use the refined nets as shown in Figure 4 as implementation, if we use the RENEW simulation engine as basic runtime environment. Since the reference net based model is a simplified version of the agent based model that has been developed in this paper, we have shown the executability of our agent-based concept model.

The side condition that the plug-in system should not reduce the application's execution speed necessitated some pragmatic solutions. The concessions we made are restricted to the *Java* implementation of the plug-in system, the precise and concurrent Petri net semantics of the model in Sections 3 and 4 are not weakened.

## 6 Conclusion

MULAN is an expressive modeling framework, based on the reference net formalism, that is capable of modeling dynamic system architectures. Models that are built with MULAN agents can profit from the multi-agent architecture, which among other benefits provide the ability to construct arbitrary and dynamic structures. The agent/platform model allows to express extensibility and dependency relationships of system components. Furthermore, the possibility to concretize the model by refinement leading to a functional model is of great advantage when designing, discussing, prototyping and (re-)designing a system.

The presented generic – reference net multi-agent based – concept model for a dynamic architecture proves to be an approach that is both, sufficiently abstract for expressive modeling and sufficiently concrete to be able to transfer it to a real-world application. Moreover, it is the only modeling technique – to our knowledge – that is able to represent a flexible, adaptable and dynamic design of an application architecture. The level of abstractness is a benefit to the general design decisions. The level of concreteness helps the architect and developer to experiment and evaluate the model prior to the implementation.

The concept model comes with an explicit top-level net, the platform respectively plug-in management system. Furthermore, the similarity of structures on the top level and all other levels allows for the introduction of independent service and extension management units on every level. Our model is capable of describing a pluggable plug-in mechanism. Such a model is useful to merge multiple systems with independent management architectures.

The Petri net IDE RENEW has undergone major refactorings and this process is still in progress. However, the preliminary results are promising. It is safe to say that the decision to refactor the system was the right way to go. We achieved a lean and flexible plug-in mechanism that permits arbitrarily nested plug-ins.

Beside just another plug-in mechanism with specific features that are very valuable in the context of our research and development, a visual modeling concept for plug-ins has been presented. In fact, currently well-established modeling techniques are highly elaborated and powerful but also oriented towards static architecture design and very resistant against paradigm shifts. In order to improve modern architecture design many dynamic aspects have to be included as first-order concepts. Extensibility is one of them. Our model can cope with extensibility because it roots as well in the multi-agent as in the nets-within-nets paradigm.

We are looking forward to unleashing the full power of our architecture model by supporting an interleaved multi-formalism simulation support. Thereby, several advantages of different formalisms can be combined to the advantage of the designed model.

## References


1. Federico Bergenti, Marie Gleizes-Pierre, and Franco Zambonelli, editors. *Methodologies and software engineering for agent systems: the agent-oriented software engineering handbook.* Multiagent systems, artificial societies, and simulated organizations. Kluwer Academic, Boston [u.a.], 2004.
2. Lawrence Cabac, Michael Duvigneau, Daniel Moldt, and Heiko Rölke. Modeling dynamic architectures using nets-within-nets. In Gianfranco Ciardo and Philippe Darondeau, editors, *Applications and Theory of Petri Nets 2005: 26th International Conference, ICATPN 2005, Miami, USA, June 2005. Proceedings*, volume 3536 of *LNCS*, pages 148–167, Berlin, 2005. Springer Verlag.
3. Lawrence Cabac, Daniel Moldt, and Heiko Rölke. A proposal for structuring Petri net-based agent interaction protocols. In W.M.P. van der Aalst and E. Best, editors, *Lecture Notes in Computer Science: 24th International Conference on Application and Theory of Petri Nets, ICATPN 2003, Netherlands, Eindhoven*, volume 2679, pages 102–120, Berlin: Springer, June 2003.
4. M. Duvigneau, D. Moldt, and H. Rölke. Concurrent architecture for a multi-agent platform. In Fausto Giunchiglia, James Odell, and Gerhard Weiß, editors, *Third International Workshop, AOSE 2002, Bologna, Italy, July 15, 2002, Revised Papers and Invited Contributions*, volume 2585 of *LNCS*, Berlin, 2003. Springer Verlag.
5. Eclipse Homepage. `http://www.eclipse.org`, 2005.
6. FIPA. Foundation for Intelligent Physical Agents. `http://www.fipa.org`, October 2005.
7. Foundation for Intelligent Physical Agents. *FIPA Agent Management Spec.*, 2005.
8. Michael Köhler, Daniel Moldt, and Heiko Rölke. Modelling the structure and behaviour of Petri net agents. In *Proc. of 22nd International Conf. on Applications and Theory of Petri Nets 2001 (ICATPN 2001) / J.-M. Colom, M. Koutny (Eds.), Newcastle upon Tyne, UK*, pages 224–242. Lecture Notes in Computer Science 2075, edited by G. Goos, J. Hartmanis and J. van Leuwen, Springer, June 2001.
9. Olaf Kummer. *Referenznetze.* Logos-Verlag, Berlin, 2002.
10. Olaf Kummer, Frank Wienberg, and Michael Duvigneau. Renew – The Reference Net Workshop. `http://www.renew.de`, October 2005. Release 2.0.
11. Olaf Kummer, Frank Wienberg, Michael Duvigneau, Jörn Schumacher, Michael Köhler, Daniel Moldt, Heiko Rölke, and Rüdiger Valk. An extensible editor and simulation engine for Petri nets: Renew. In Jordi Cortadella and Wolfgang Reisig, editors, *Applications and Theory of Petri Nets 2004: 25th International Conference, ICATPN 2004, Bologna, Italy, June 2004. Proceedings*, volume 3099 of *LNCS*, pages 484–493, Berlin, 2004. Springer Verlag.

12. NetBeans Homepage. `http://www.netbeans.com`, 2005.
13. J. Sametinger. *Software Engineering with Reusable Components.* Springer Verlag, Berlin, 1997.
14. Jörn Schumacher. Eine Plug-in-Architektur für Renew: Konzepte, Methoden, Umsetzung. Diplomarbeit, University of Hamburg, Department of Computer Science, October 2003.
15. Clemens Szyperski. *Component software: beyond object-oriented programming.* ACM Press books. Addison-Wesley, 2. edition, 2002.
16. R. v. Lüde, D. Moldt, and R. Valk. *Sozionik: Modellierung soziologischer Theorie*, volume 2 of *Reihe: Wirtschaft – Arbeit – Technik.* Lit-Verlag, Münster - Hamburg - London, 2003.
17. Rüdiger Valk. Petri Nets as Token Objects - An Introduction to Elementary Object Nets. In J. Desel and M. Silva, editors, *19th International Conference on Application and Theory of Petri nets, Lisbon, Portugal*, volume 1420 of *LNCS*, pages 1–25, Berlin, 1998. Springer Verlag.
18. Wil van der Aalst, Jörg Desel, and Andreas Oberweis, editors. *Business Process Management: Models, Techniques, and Empirical Studies*, volume 1806 of *LNCS.* Springer-Verlag Berlin, 2000.

# Using the Analytic Hierarchy Process for Evaluating Multi-Agent System Architecture Candidates

Paul Davidsson, Stefan Johansson, and Mikael Svahnberg

Department of Systems and Software Engineering,
Blekinge Institute of Technology,
Soft Center, 372 25 Ronneby, Sweden
{pdv, sja, msv}@bth.se

**Abstract.** Although much effort has been spent on suggesting and implementing new architectures of Multi-Agent Systems (MAS), the evaluation and comparison of these has often been done in a rather ad-hoc fashion. We believe that the time has come to start doing this in a more systematic way using established methods. For instance, we argue that it is important to evaluate the architecture candidates for a particular application according to several quality attributes relevant to that application. The architecture that provides the most appropriate balance between these attributes should then be selected. As a case study we investigate the problem of load balancing and overload control of Intelligent Networks and present four MAS architectures that can be used to handle this task. We instantiate each of these and define metrics for the selected quality attributes. The instantiations are studied in simulation experiments and measurements of the metrics are recorded. The measurements are then analyzed using the Analytic Hierarchy Process, which is a basic approach to select the most suitable alternative from a number of alternatives evaluated with respect to several criteria. We illustrate how such analyzes can be used for deciding which architecture candidate is the most appropriate in different situations.

## 1 Introduction

Much effort has been spent on suggesting and implementing new architectures of Multi-Agent Systems (MAS). However, less work has been done in studying how these architectures should be evaluated and compared. Most evaluations and comparisons have been carried out in a quite unstructured way. For instance, when a (group of) researcher(s) invents a new architecture and applies it to a particular domain and concludes that it seems to be appropriate for this domain. Often this new architecture is not even compared to any existing MAS architecture. Also, the selection between candidate architectures for a particular application is typically done in a rather *ad hoc* fashion. We believe that this area has now reached the level of maturity when it is appropriate to compare and evaluate MAS architectures in a more systematic manner. We show how an established method from Management Science can be used to achieve this, e.g., by taking into account several quality attributes and weighting them according to the requirements of the application at hand.

J.P. Müller and F. Zambonelli (Eds.): AOSE 2005, LNCS 3950, pp. 205–217, 2006.

Of course, there is no single MAS architecture that is the most suitable for all applications. Since agent technology has shown to be successful for *dynamic resource allocation*, e.g. power load management [19] and cellular phone bandwidth allocation [4], we have chosen a concrete example of this domain for a case study. The purpose of the case study is to show how the evaluation method can be applied, and the application concerns load balancing and overload control in *Intelligent Networks*, a type of telecommunication system.

The remainder of this article is organised as follows. In Section 2 we present the proposed methodology for evaluating software candidates based on a selection of quality attributes. In Section 3 we present an illustration of the evaluation method. The methodology is discussed in Section 4, and our results are concluded in Section 5.

## 2 Software Architecture Evaluation Methodology

Typically, an architecture constitutes a balance between different quality attributes, just as different applications may require a specific balance or trade-off between quality attributes. Hence, to select the most suitable architecture for a particular application require knowledge about relevant attributes and how different MAS architectures support them.

It is probably impossible to find a MAS architecture that is optimal with respect to all the attributes relevant for a certain application. Rather, there is typically a trade-off between these attributes and different architectures balance this trade-off in various ways. Different applications, on the other hand, often require different balancing of this trade-off. Thus, in order to choose the right architecture for a particular application, knowledge about relevant attributes and how different MAS architectures support them is essential. We thus need a methodology that enables us to assess and compare different quality attributes with each other, and then compare different architecture candidates against this blend of quality attributes to assess which candidate that is the most suitable for the application in question.

The Analytic Hierarchy Process (AHP) [14, 15] is a multi-criteria decision support method from Management Science [1] that has previously been tried in various and similar software engineering settings (e.g. [10, 11, 17, 18]). One of the cornerstones in AHP is to evaluate a set of alternatives based on a particular blend of criteria, i.e. considering a specific trade-off situation. The AHP can quantify subjective assessments through a process of pair-wise comparisons or use data that is e.g. collected from a simulation. Most uses of AHP focus on the subjective assessments, which are easy to understand and relatively easy to use to gather data. In this article, however, we use the ability of AHP to mix subjective assessments and measured data (Saaty uses the expression *tangible data* [14, 15]. As we will see, this poses some additional challenges.

The AHP-based architecture evaluation methodology is based on a number of different steps, described below.

*The first step* in AHP is to set up a hierarchy of the criteria that are being evaluated. This means that one criterion can be broken down into several sub-criteria, and the evaluation of the different alternatives is done by weighing in all levels of this decision support hierarchy. For example, the case study described in Section 3 uses the hierarchy

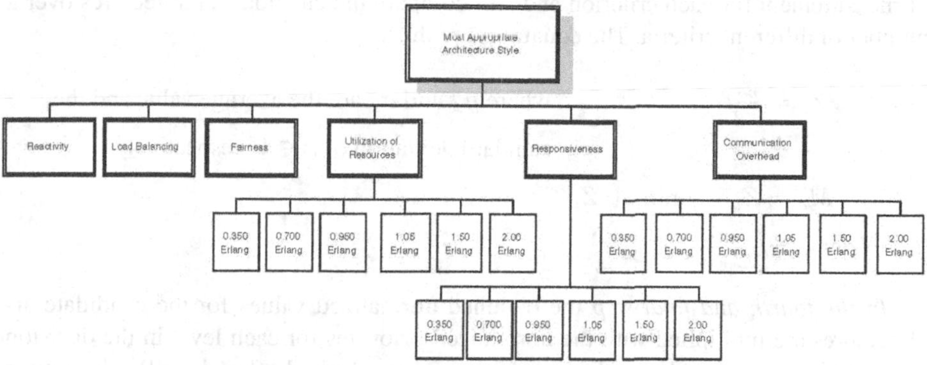


**Fig. 1.** AHP Decision Support Hierarchy

outlined in Fig. 1. In this hierarchy, the top-level goal is *Most Appropriate Architectural Candidate*. Below this top-node in the hierarchy the different evaluation criteria are listed, in our case *Reactivity*, *Load Balancing*, *Fairness*, *Utilization of Resources*, *Responsiveness*, and *Communication Overhead*. For three of these criteria a further specialization is necessary, namely the expected load of the target system. Hence, under the criteria Utilization of Resources, Responsiveness, and Communication Overhead, we add as criteria different levels of offered loads, i.e. *0.350, 0.700, 0.950, 1.05, 1.50,* and *2.00* Erlang[1].

*The second step* is to prioritize the criteria in accordance with how desired they are for the system. This prioritization is done both for the different loads and the aforementioned quality attributes, and can be done using e.g. the pair-wise comparison process provided in the AHP method or by means of any other prioritization method. For future use, we also at this stage make sure that the priorities on a particular level in the decision tree are normalized so that they sum up to one.

*The third step* is to use this decision support hierarchy in conjunction with the different alternatives (the candidate architectures in the particular domain) as follows. For each of the leaf nodes in the decision support hierarchy we compare each of the candidate architectures (described in Section 3) with the other candidate architectures. This can be done by using a pair-wise comparison process or by providing measured data. In this study, we use data measured from a simulation (further described below).

When using measured data, it is not advisable to compare different measured data sets with each other directly, since AHP uses data on a ratio scale (compare e.g. the ratio between 1001 and 1010, and between 101 and 110). Hence we need to add a sub-step to ensure that different measurements are comparable. This sub-step consists of calculating the so called Z-score, $Z_v$, of the measurements $v \in V$. Z-score ensures that the values are normalized to be distributed around zero [7]. We then "move" these values so that the smallest value is zero, and then divide all values with the sum of the values. Ultimately, the values for a particular measurement are thus normalized so that their total sum $\sum_{i \in V} Norm_i = 1$. This process enables us to take data using any unit

[1] 1.0 Erlang correspond to 100% load.

of measurement for each criterion and still compare the candidate architectures over a number of different criteria. The equations are thus:

$$Z_v = \frac{v-\mu_x}{\sigma_x} \quad \text{where } \mu_x \text{ and } \sigma_x \text{ are the average value and the standard deviation of } x \in V \text{ respectively}$$

$$M_v = Z_v + |\min_{i \in V} Z_i|$$

$$Norm_v = \frac{M_v}{\sum_{i \in V} M_i}$$

*In the fourth and final step* the obtained normalized values for the candidate architectures are multiplied with the normalized priorities for each level in the decision support hierarchy (i.e. the quality attributes and the desired offered load). The results of these multiplications are summed for each candidate architectural style. These sums represent the suitability of each alternative *in relation to the other alternatives*. It is thus not absolute numbers but a ratio compared to the other alternatives that is obtained.

# 3 Case Study: Load Balancing in Intelligent Networks

One important area in which the dynamic resource allocation problem is present is telecommunications. The Intelligent Network (IN) concept was developed in order to enable operators of telecommunication networks to create and maintain new types of services [12]. Two important entities of an IN are the Service Switching Points (SSPs) and the Service Control Points (SCPs). The SSPs continuously receive requests of services which they cannot serve without the help of the SCPs where all service software resides. Thus, the SCPs are providers and the SSPs are customers. The SSPs and SCPs communicate via a signaling network.

It is assumed that a small part of the available bandwidth of this network is reserved for the resource allocation, i.e., the communication overhead caused by agent communication (and transportation). It is assumed that all SCPs support the same set of service classes and that all service requests can be directed by a SSP to any SCP.

## 3.1 Multi-Agent System Architectures

Common for the four architectures are the use of three different types of agents: *quantifiers, allocators,* and *distributors* [2]. A quantifier acts on behalf of a provider of the resources, an allocator acts on behalf of a customer, and a distributor decides the allocation of some (or even all) available resources. Although these three types of agents have similar roles in all the four multi-agent system architectures, the actual implementation may be rather different (in particular this holds for the distributors). The reason, of course, is that different system architectures may put different demands on the agents.

**The Centralized Auction Architecture.** The *Centralized Auction* (CA) architecture is an example of a synchronous, centralized architecture. Arvidsson et al. [2] suggested an approach where the resource allocation is carried out by means of tokens (cf. market-based control [5]). Each token represents a service request and is consumed when the request is accepted by a provider. The three types of agents have the following functionality:

- The quantifiers try to *sell* the amount of tokens that corresponds to the load that the provider is able to *serve* between two auctions.
- The allocators try to *buy* the amount of tokens corresponding to the resources they predict their customers will receive during the time to the next auction.
- The distributor receives bids from the quantifiers corresponding the available capacity at their providers (and the *prices*), and bids from the allocators with the expected needs for resources. The distributor then carries out the auction so that the common good is maximized and sends messages about the result to the involved agents.

An allocator maintains a pool of tokens for each provider and type of resource. Each time the allocator feeds a provider with a request for a particular type of resource, one token is removed from the associated pool. If all pools associated with a particular resource type are empty, the customer cannot accept more requests. The pools are refilled at the auctions that take place at fixed time intervals. In order to avoid spending all tokens immediately during high loads (which would lead to excessive delays caused by long queues at the providers), percentage thinning is used so that the probability of buying a certain type of resource is never higher than the number of remaining tokens over the number of expected needs during the reminder of the interval. For more details we refer to Arvidsson et al. [2].

**The Hierarchical Auction-Based Architecture.** One possible implementation of a distributed, synchronous system is the *hierarchical auction* (HA) architecture [19]. The idea is to partition the set of allocators and to use one distributor for aggregating bids and holding auctions for each partition. These distributors then connect to higher order distributors in a hierarchical manner until the total demand can be matched against the amount of available resources offered by the quantifiers.

**The Centralized Leaky Bucket Architecture.** The centralized asynchronous architecture chosen is based upon an asynchronous approach called *Leaky bucket* [3].

The basic idea is that each provider is equipped with a Leaky bucket that feeds requests to the provider at an even and optimal rate. This is done by inserting the incoming requests from the customers in a queue in the Leaky bucket. These requests are then dequeued at a rate corresponding to the maximum capacity of that provider. If the queue is full, the requests are rejected. To get a *centralized* architecture, the *centralized leaky bucket* (CLB) [9] is introduced, in which there is just one central distributor, common for all allocators and quantifiers.

The allocators send all requests to this distributor, a common leaky bucket for queuing the requests. It also has a router that continuously dequeues requests at a rate corresponding to the total capacity of the providers and then forwards the requests evenly to the providers in proportion to their capacity. If the bucket is full, the request is returned to the allocator where it is rejected.

**The Mobile Broker Architecture.** As an example of a distributed, asynchronous system, a *mobile broker* (MB) architecture [9] is selected. In this architecture, the distributors are implemented as mobile brokers (one for each provider) that sequentially visit each (or a subset) of the allocators offering the resources currently available at the corresponding provider.

The allocator then *requests* the resources it needs for the moment (or rather, predicts it will need in the near future). If possible, the broker gives this amount of resources to the allocator. Otherwise, it gives as much as is currently available at the provider.

However, there are two problems with this naive approach:

- If an allocator demands all the available resources, the broker will give them to that allocator. Thus, the broker will not be able to hand out any more resources for a while, which would not be fair.
- If the overall load is low or moderate, the allocators are given just as much resources as they demand. However, if an allocator need slightly more resources than it asked for (predicted), it will have to turn down requests, even though the provider has lots of surplus capacity.

In order to solve these problems, a broker mechanism is used that strive to give out all the available resources and give each allocator resources in proportion to their part of the total current demand (of the allocators in the route). For the details of this approach we refer to Johansson et al. [9].

If an allocator is visited by several brokers it may be that some of the brokers' SCPs are carrying a higher load than the others. To deal with this problem an additional balancing function is used, making the allocators try to move load from those SCPs with higher load to those with lower load. The allocator calculates the load of a broker from the quotient between what it asked for and what is was given by the broker.

### 3.2 Metrics

It is possible to evaluate MAS architecture candidates with respect to several different quality attributes [6]. Some of these attributes are domain independent and some are specific for each set of applications, e.g., performance-related attributes. We have identified the following important performance-related attributes to dynamic resource allocation (together with the metrics collected for each of the quality attributes):

- Reactivity is measured by how fast the MAS is able to re-allocate the available SCP processing time when there are sudden changes of offered loads by the SSPs. We measure the number of time steps it takes in the simulation between the rise in requested load from 0.35 Erlang to 0.70 Erlang and the time step when the offered load meets the requested load again.
- Load balancing is measured by the standard deviation between the carried load of the SCPs. We measure the average of the standard deviations for 500 time units.
- Fairness is measured by the standard deviation of accepted calls divided by the generated calls between the SSPs, i.e., the acceptance rates. The acceptance rates are measured for all SSPs and the standard deviation of these rates $s_{ssp}$ is calculated. $1 - s_{ssp}$ is then finally our fairness measure.
- The utilization of resources is measured by how close the carried load is to the target load, or offered load if the offered load is less than the target load. SCP load

levels should be as close to the target load (e.g., 0.9 Erlang, corresponding to 90% of its capacity) as possible but not exceed it. If an overload situation is approaching, the SSPs should throttle new requests. This is measured by taking the actual average carried load of the system.
- Responsiveness is measured by the time it takes for the SSPs to get response from an SCP.
- Communication overhead is measured by the bandwidth (in terms of number of messages per time unit) necessary for the MAS to perform the reallocation.

In addition, there are a number of more general software architecture quality attributes [13] that could be addressed, e.g. Robustness and Modifiability. Although these softer quality factors are important when building real systems, we choose not to include them in this evaluation, since they are difficult to measure in quantitative terms. It is, however, possible to mix subjective pair-wise assessments for these quality attributes with measured data for the aforelisted quality attributes.

### 3.3 Experimental Setup and Results

The four concrete architectures have been evaluated in simulations consisting of 8 SCPs and 32 SSPs. Here we use refined data from a large series of simulation experiments that provides estimations of the performance measures of the architecture candidates. Complete descriptions of the simulation results can be found in Johansson et al. [9] where all the technical details of the experiments are thoroughly described. Considering the limited space available, and as the aim here is to explain the use of an AHP-based architecture evaluation methodology, we leave out most of the technical details.

We have now constructed a decision support hierarchy (Fig. 1) and defined metrics for the quality attributes (Section3.2). We have also defined a set of architecture candidates (Section 3.1) to evaluate. We are thus ready to move on with steps two, three and four of the architecture evaluation methodology.

*For step two*, we assign priorities to the quality attributes. In this illustration, we include two different priorities (Table 1) in order to show how changes in priorities may change the results. It should be noted that these are *examples* of priorities (just as the resource allocation in IN is an example of a domain) and as such they are of course of limited interest in a general meaning. The actual priorities should be set for the specific system considered. These two cases corresponds to one scenario where the (potential) system bottleneck lies in the communication network ($P_c$) and one where

**Table 1.** Priorities of the various properties in the case of a restricted communication ($P_c$) and limited resources ($P_u$)

| Property | Reactivity | Load Balancing | Fairness | Utilization | Responsiveness | Comm. |
|---|---|---|---|---|---|---|
| Priority $P_c$ | 0.10 | 0.10 | 0.10 | 0.10 | 0.10 | 0.50 |
| Priority $P_u$ | 0.20 | 0.20 | 0.10 | 0.30 | 0.20 | 0 |

**Table 2.** Weights of the six different levels of loads

| Load $l$ | 0.35 | 0.70 | 0.95 | 1.05 | 1.50 | 2.0 |
|---|---|---|---|---|---|---|
| Weight $w_l$ | 0.10 | 0.15 | 0.25 | 0.25 | 0.15 | 0.10 |

**Table 3.** The raw data $v$ and the z-score normalization, $Norm_v$, of each of the properties of the four architectures

| | | Raw values | | | | $Norm_v$ | | | |
|---|---|---|---|---|---|---|---|---|---|
| | | CA | HA | CLB | MB | CA | HA | CLB | MB |
| Reactivity | | 12.12 | 12.12 | 2.02 | 4.04 | 0 | 0 | 0.5556 | 0.4444 |
| Load Bal. | | 0.04937 | 0.04888 | 0.03539 | 0.2111 | 0.3237 | 0.3247 | 0.3517 | 0 |
| Fairness | | 0.98243 | 0.98052 | 1 | 0.99260 | 0.1280 | 0 | 0.4958 | 0.3762 |
| Utilization of resources | 0.35 | 0.3484 | 0.3492 | 0.3507 | 0.3500 | 0 | 0.1709 | 0.4904 | 0.3387 |
| | 0.70 | 0.6993 | 0.6922 | 0.7000 | 0.6902 | 0.4368 | 0.0957 | 0.4675 | 0 |
| | 0.95 | 0.8575 | 0.8372 | 0.9005 | 0.8324 | 0.2562 | 0.0488 | 0.6950 | 0 |
| | 1.05 | 0.8598 | 0.8544 | 0.8997 | 0.8503 | 0.1500 | 0.0650 | 0.7850 | 0 |
| | 1.50 | 0.8760 | 0.8664 | 0.8998 | 0.8829 | 0.1608 | 0 | 0.5617 | 0.2775 |
| | 2.0 | 0.8948 | 0.8666 | 0.9003 | 0.8980 | 0.3021 | 0 | 0.3615 | 0.3364 |
| Responsiveness | 0.35 | 0.006403 | 0.006330 | 0.006409 | 0.006482 | 0.2614 | 0.2409 | 0.4977 | 0 |
| | 0.70 | 0.01010 | 0.00979 | 0.00847 | 0.01150 | 0.2283 | 0.2784 | 0.4933 | 0 |
| | 0.95 | 0.01886 | 0.01510 | 0.1604 | 0.02775 | 0.3374 | 0.3463 | 0 | 0.3162 |
| | 1.05 | 0.01849 | 0.01680 | 0.1627 | 0.03251 | 0.3431 | 0.3471 | 0 | 0.3097 |
| | 1.50 | 0.01882 | 0.01857 | 0.1636 | 0.06193 | 0.3698 | 0.3705 | 0 | 0.2597 |
| | 2.0 | 0.02257 | 0.01839 | 0.1637 | 0.07656 | 0.3778 | 0.3890 | 0 | 0.2332 |
| Communication overhead | 0.35 | 72 | 80 | 1010 | 85 | 0.3358 | 0.3330 | 0 | 0.3312 |
| | 0.70 | 72 | 80 | 2020 | 85 | 0.3345 | 0.3332 | 0 | 0.3323 |
| | 0.95 | 72 | 80 | 2740 | 85 | 0.3342 | 0.3332 | 0 | 0.3326 |
| | 1.05 | 72 | 80 | 3029 | 85 | 0.3341 | 0.3332 | 0 | 0.3327 |
| | 1.50 | 72 | 80 | 4328 | 85 | 0.3339 | 0.3333 | 0 | 0.3329 |
| | 2.0 | 72 | 80 | 5771 | 85 | 0.3337 | 0.3333 | 0 | 0.3330 |

**Table 4.** Results of the AHP given the two priorities $P_c$ and $P_u$

| $P_c$ | |
|---|---|
| MB | 0.281 |
| CA | 0.267 |
| HA | 0.238 |
| CLB | 0.214 |

| $P_u$ | |
|---|---|
| CLB | 0.439 |
| CA | 0.209 |
| MB | 0.203 |
| HA | 0.150 |

the resources (the SCPs) are the limiting factor ($P_u$). In the first case it is important to keep communication overhead at a low level, whereas in the second case it is not. Instead, utilization of the resources is prioritized. For three of the attributes (Utilization of resources, Responsiveness, and Communication overhead) we also need to weigh in the desired offered load, using the example values presented in Table 2. We use the same desired offered load in both example cases.

*In step three* we compare the architecture candidates with each other. In our case, this consists of collecting the metrics discussed ealier. These data are used to populate table 3. In this table, we see each of the architecture candidates as one column (under "raw values"), and the metrics gathered for each of the quality attributes and each architecture candidate. This data is then normalized as described in Section 2. During this normalization we also take into account that for many metrics a low value is more desirable than a high value. We do this by multiplying the normalized $Z_v$ score with $-1$ before shifting and re-normalizing the values. The raw values are inverted for all quality attributes except Fairness and Utilization of resources.

*The fourth step* is to calculate which of the architecture candidates that best meet the desired blend of quality attributes. For each of the two cases we take the product of the priorities of the quality attributes and desired load, and multiply this with the corresponding normalized value, $Norm_v$, for each candidate architectural style. The result of this is then summed for each candidate architectural style, and presented in Table 4. As can be seen, in the first case $P_c$, with restricted communication abilities, the MB architecture is the most suitable, followed by CA, HA and CLB. In the second case $P_u$, with restricted computing resources, the CLB architecture is more than twice as good as its nearest competitors CA and MB, and almost three times as good as HA.

# 4 Discussion

Naturally, there are limitations to the proposed evaluation method. Firstly, it only evaluates the *potential* of different architecture candidates. A good implementation may achieve this potential, and a bad implementation may not reach the potential at all. When developing a software system, the potential of the chosen architecture is one important influence of the resulting system, but there are others. For example, familiarity with a particular architectural style, development organization, and coding standards may also influence the final result.

Secondly, which architecture candidate the evaluation framework proposes is strongly dependent on the priorities of the quality attributes and the desired load that is fed into the framework. Hence, care must be taken when prioritizing the needs of the system so that the priorities are in fact truly representing the needs for the target system.

Thirdly, the quantitative suggestion that the framework produces should be seen as one input among many to the decision process. Other inputs may include e.g. previous experiences or intuition.

In this study we implement the candidate architectures for a particular application domain and instrument the AHP decision support hierarchy with measurements gathered from this simulation. A potential shortcoming of this approach is that we are using simulated data and therefore may get simulated results. However, this is often the best we can do, as it may be very expensive, and sometimes even impossible, to actually fully implement all the candidate architectures and measure the performance of the deployed system. Although we use simulated data, we argue that the suggested approach is a step forward compared to the *ad hoc* and subjective choice between candidate architectures that is currently often the case.

To gather empirical data from simulation experiments is possible for some quality attributes that have easily defined metrics. However, there are many quality attributes that are not as easily measured. For example, in Section 3.2 we list the attributes Robustness and Modifiability as being of interest in a MAS setting. For these quality attributes a possible extension of the evaluation method outlined in this article would be to make use of AHP's ability to deal with a mixture of tangible data and subjective judgments (successfully used in other studies, e.g. [18]).

An interesting question concerns whether is it possible to draw any more general conclusions from the type experiments presented here on concrete MAS architectures in a concrete domain. An obvious possibility is generalization though abstraction. If we start with the domain, it can be argued that we have studied an instance of a class of application domain, namely dynamic resource allocation. Basically, this class of problems concerns allocation of resources between a number of *customers*, given a number of *providers*. The dynamics of the problem lie in that the needs of the customers, as well as the amount of resources made available by the providers, vary over time. The needs and available resources not only vary on an individual level, but also the total needs and available resources within the system may vary over time. Moreover, the resources cannot be buffered, i.e., they have to be consumed immediately, and the cost of communication (and transportation of resources) between any customer-provider pair is equal. However, we cannot draw the conclusion that the studied MAS architectures will perform in the same way as in our experiments in all instances of this more general class of problem domains. But it give us the opportunity to formulate qualified hypotheses concerning their performance that can be used to make more informed decisions when selecting MAS architectures for other instances of dynamic resource allocation.

Concerning generalization with respect to architectures, we argue that it is useful to study classes of MAS architectures, corresponding to *architectural styles* [16]. These may describe abstractions of software entities of varying abstraction levels such as enterprise architectures, system architectures, subsystem architectures, or the architecture within a particular component.

**Table 5.** The four different multi-agent system architectures classified in terms of architectural style

| | *centralized* | *distributed* |
|---|---|---|
| *synchronous* | Centralized auctions (CA) | Hierarchical auctions (HA) |
| *asynchronous* | Centralized leaky bucket (CLB) | Mobile brokers (MB) |

We have focused on a particular abstraction level were it is possible to characterize MAS architectural styles according to two properties: the type of control used (from fully centralized to fully distributed), and the type of coordination (synchronous vs. asynchronous). Thus, we may say that we have compared four MAS architectural styles for dynamic resource allocation: centralized synchronous architectures, centralized asynchronous architectures, distributed synchronous architectures, and distributed asynchronous architectures. (See Table 5.) The issue of evaluating MAS architectural styles is further elaborated in [8].

## 5 Conclusions and Future Work

We have described an approach based on AHP for multi-criteria evaluation of different MAS architecture candidates. It was applied to in an experimental study of implementations of four architecture candidates for load balancing and overload control in Intelligent Networks.

Previous work indicated that asynchronous architectures react faster than synchronous, and that centralized asynchronous architectures better utilize the available resources, although having larger delays and consume more bandwidth when the load is high [9]. With the proposed use of AHP, however, we are not only able to test hypothesis as the ones we just described. We are also able to:

- Quantify the differences in goodness of the candidate architectures according to the desired balance between quality attributes.
- Weight the different scenarios continuously.
- Easily add new instrumentations to increase the granularity of the evaluation.
- Easily add new architectures to evaluate.
- Easily add new evaluation criteria.

The results of the case study are, not very surprisingly, that different architectures excel in different dimensions. The choice of MAS architecture for a particular application should hence be based on a trade-off between the dimensions (e.g. the involved quality attributes) that is optimal for that application. We believe that if the systematic approach suggested here is widely adopted, such choices can be more informed than is currently the practice. Our plans for future work include:

- Further experimental validation of the approach by applying it to other domains.
- Further develop the application of the AHP method in MAS settings, e.g. to include qualitative measures of factors such as robustness and maintainability.

- Investigating to what extent the implementations of the individual agents influence system performance.
- Further development of the concept of architectural styles for characterizing MAS.

## Acknowledgements

The authors would like to thank the Swedish Knowledge Foundation and Blekinge Institute of Technology for funding this work.

## References

1. D. R. Anderson, D. J. Sweeney, and T. A. Williams. *An Introduction to Management Science: Quantitative Approaches to Decision Making*. South Western College Publishing, Cincinnati Ohio, 2000.
2. A. Arvidsson, B. Jennings, L. Angelin, and M. Svensson. On the use of agent technology for IN load control. In *Proceedings of the 16th International Teletraffic Congress*. Elsevier Science, 1999.
3. A. Berger. Comparison of call gapping and percent blocking for overload control in distributed switching systems and telecommunication networks. *IEEE Trans. Commun.*, 39:574–580, 1991.
4. E. Bodanese and L. Cuthbert. An intelligent channel allocation scheme for mobile networks: An application of agent technology. In *Proceedings of the 2nd International Conference on Intelligent Agent Technology*, pages 322–333. World Scientific Press, 2001.
5. S. Clearwater, editor. *Market-Based Control: Some early lessons*. World Scientific, 1996.
6. P. Clements, R. Kazman, and M. Klein. *Evaluating Software Architectures*. Addison Wesley, 2002.
7. P. R. Cohen. *Empirical Methods for Artificial Intelligence*. MIT Press, Cambridge MA, 1995.
8. P. Davidsson, S. Johansson, and M. Svahnberg. Characterization and evaluation of multi-agent system architectural styles. In *Software Engineering for Multi-Agent Systems IV*, Lecture Notes in Computer Science. Springer Verlag, 2006. To appear.
9. S. Johansson, P. Davidsson, and M. Kristell. Four architectures for dynamic resource allocation. In A. Karmouch, T. Magedanz, and J. Delgado, editors, *Mobile Agents for Telecommunication Applications*, volume 2521 of *LNAI*, pages 239–248. Springer Verlag, 2002.
10. J. Karlsson and K. Ryan. A cost-value approach for prioritizing requirements. *IEEE Software*, 14(5):67–74, 1997.
11. J. Karlsson, C. Wohlin, and B. Regnell. An evaluation of methods for prioritizing software requirements. *Information and Software Technology*, 39(14-15):938–947, 1998.
12. T. Magedanz and R. Popescu-Zeletin. *Intelligent Networks*. International Thomson Computer Press, 1996.
13. J. McCall. *Encyclopedia of Software Engineering*, chapter Quality Factors, pages 959–969. John Wiley & Sons Inc., 1994.
14. T. L. Saaty. *The Analytic Hierarchy Process*. McGraw Hill, Inc., New York NY, 1980.
15. T. L. Saaty and L. G. Vargas. *Models, Methods, Concepts & Applications of the Analytic Hierarchy Process*. Kluwer Academic Publisher, Dordrecht the Netherlands, 2001.
16. M. Shaw and D. Garlan. *Software Architecture - Perspectives on an Emergin Discipline*. Prentice Hall, Upper Saddle River NJ, 1996.

17. M. Shepperd, S. Barker, and M. Aylett. The analytic hierarchy process and almost dataless prediction. In R. J. Kuster, A. Cowderoy, F. Heemstra, and E. P. van Veenendaal, editors, *Project Control for Software Quality - Proceedings of ESCOM-SCOPE 99*, Maastricht the Netherlands, 1999. Shaker Publishing BV.
18. M. Svahnberg. An industrial study on building consensus around software architectures and quality attributes. *Journal of Information and Software Technology*, 46(12):805–818, 2004.
19. F. Ygge. *Market-Oriented Programming and its Application to Power Load Management*. PhD thesis, Lund University, Sweden, 1998.

# Estimating Costs for Agent Oriented Software*

Jorge J. Gómez-Sanz[1], Juan Pavón[1], and Francisco Garijo[2]

[1] Universidad Complutense Madrid, Dep. Sistemas Informáticos y Programación, 28040 Madrid, Spain
{jjgomez, jpavon}@sip.ucm.es
http://grasia.fdi.ucm.es
[2] Telefónica I+D, Emilio Vargas 6, 28043 Madrid, Spain
fgarijo@tid.es

**Abstract.** Despite the progress in agent oriented software engineering, there is still a long way before achieving maturity. Among others, there is a lack of shared experience in evaluating the cost when developing software using the agent paradigm. This paper provides some results on this issue. It collects data from real agent based projects and gives hints for the application of existing software cost estimation models and what would be appropriate metrics for an agent based software development.

## 1 Introduction

When trying to convince industry of the benefits of the agent approach, so far, most arguments have been of the type *agents are X and objects do not, hence agents are better*, where *X* can be one or many of the following: autonomous, intelligent, adaptive, social, etc. To proof these arguments, we build applications that demonstrate agent capabilities, though their size and complexity, in most cases, does not go beyond toy examples.

Building complex agent oriented applications will serve as proof of concept for us, researchers in the area, and may draw attention from industry, but we wonder whether this is enough to convince. Our opinion is that we still need to answer an important question: *how much does it cost to build a concrete application with an agent-oriented approach?* This information is fundamental in order to integrate agent technology into industrial software engineering practices. There is no exact answer to this question, though.

Conventional software engineering has faced a similar problem and has invested an important effort in studying methods to foresee how much it would cost to build a software system. This estimation is made, initially, knowing in advance what this system should do and without coding anything at all. Such studies are generally referred as *software economics*. There are well-known prediction models such as COCOMO and COCOMO II, or Putnam [2]. These models take the experience on previous developments to predict the cost of similar developments. With this

* This work has been funded in part by the Spanish Council for Science and Technology under grant TIC2002-04516-C03-03.

J.P. Müller and F. Zambonelli (Eds.): AOSE 2005, LNCS 3950, pp. 218–230, 2006.

experience, software managers can build estimations of cost, taking into account variables like average expertise of programmers, complexity of the problem, source lines of code, precedentness, and many more.

In order to do the same with agent oriented applications we need:

1. *Source code of agent oriented applications to make measurements.* Known applications of agents do not usually make public their code, so it is difficult to get a collection of applications to base on.
2. *Adaptation of software engineering methods.* Conventional metrics consider some aspects, like encapsulation or complexity of interfaces, which are different from how we understand an agent oriented development, where learning features or problem solving methods attract more attention. This means that estimations of the effort may not be accurate for our domain.

In this paper we mainly address these two issues. To get measurements on the costs of developing a multi-agent system, we contribute with our experience in three European research projects where we have developed multi-agent systems of reasonable size. With respect the definition of metrics for agent oriented software, we consider a list of agent features that are implemented into these projects and integrate them into a well-known estimation model, COCOMO II [1]. To evaluate the resulting costs in terms of development time and human resources, we have used three tools: Eclipse Metrics Plugin [5], CodeCount [4], and USC COCOMO II v2000 program [9] (v1999 gives slightly different results). More information about the experiments can be found at http://grasia.fdi.ucm.es/gschool.

These results can assist agent developers to elaborate tentative estimations of how much effort they should dedicate to their projects and, with this data, determine their costs. To evaluate our results, we have used the knowledge of how much did it really cost against how much our estimation says it should cost.

The rest of the paper is structured as follows. The next section introduces the projects we have participated into, which are going to be the base for this study. This is followed by some basic concepts about cost estimation. Then, we introduce our cost indicators, adapted for agent-oriented developments. Afterwards, we present a summary of the costs we have faced so far. This serves as starting point for some cost estimations in the next section, and the base for obtaining metrics for agent related concepts. Finally, we present some discussion on the results and the conclusions we draw from these.

## 2 Domain Problem

As source of knowledge, we consider three European research projects. Their nature is not exactly the same as industrial projects, since budget and time cannot be modified and it is not expected that the products of the project are finally commercialised (therefore, maintenance costs are not normally assumed). But our role here was similar to a consulting company, since we had to implement the system with time and budget constraints, and deliver a product with some quality requirements. Moreover, though the first two are more research oriented, the third had closer resemblance to an industrial project. In all of them, the outcome of the project was an application that had to be used in a real environment with real end users. The first two had as purpose demonstrating the maturity of agent technology. Therefore, the quality of the result was not as important as the proof of concept. To give an accurate idea of each project, we describe briefly the purpose of each one, and provide some references to publications of relevant results:

- Eurescom P815. *Communications Management Process Integration Using Software Agents* (1999-2000) [7]. This project was concerned with the use of agents to improve workflow management applications. Our part in the project was the specification and implementation of agents that assisted users in the management of a proprietary Intelligent Network Service Creation Environment. The main issues in this system were interface agents interacting with users and interoperability with an existing system. We finally implemented two types of agents: the personal manager agent (PMA), for assistance to a project manager, and the personal developer agent (PDA), for developers in a project. A BDI architecture was considered for agent control, which was implemented with Java and JESS (Java Expert System Shell). Agent communications with other agents or with the existing system was based on CORBA. Code for P815 is available at http://www.eurescom.de/public/projects/P800-series/P815 (IN SCE Case Study prototype).
- Eurescom P907. *MESSAGE: Methodology for Engineering Systems of Software AGEnts* (2000-2002) [3]. The main result of this project was the definition of the MESSAGE/UML methodology. To test MESSAGE/UML, we developed a Travel Assistant service. In this implementation, there were three types of agents: a Personal Assistant that represents the user in the system, an Information Finder agent with the responsibility of looking for information sources related with airports, and the InfoAENA agent that wrapped an airport information source. The service implemented in this case study was the notification of flights incidences. User-Personal Assistant interaction was web based and implemented with servlets. Servlets communicated user's orders to the Personal Assistant through Java RMI. Inter-agent communication was implemented with JADE. The behaviour of the Personal Agent was BDI based, whereas the other agents were reactive. Code for P907 is available at http://www.eurescom.de/~public-webspace/P900-series/P907 (implementation of the UPA4T case study).
- PSI3. Personalized Service Integration Using Software Agents (2001-2003) [6]. This was an IST project where we implemented an agent based collaborative information filtering system. The system tried to form virtual communities of users where every registered user received only interesting information. Each user was represented in the system by an agent that knew user's current interests and learned new ones. We named these agents Personal Agents. They got together into one or many virtual communities, represented with a Community Agent. The challenge here was to evolve communities' topics, managed by Community Agents, as user interests were shifting, and how Personal Agents could learn new topics from the user. Also, whether Community Agents and Personal Agents together could prevent unwanted behaviours like information spam. This system is more complex

than the previous. It was made with an undetermined number of agents (we tested the system with up to three hundred heavy agents) and was rather scalable (new computers could be added to increase the number of agents registered). Agents were implemented with CORBA communications and a JESS control. This time it was not a BDI control, but a more conventional session oriented control.

These three projects make together an excellent data repository to extract conclusions upon. Their size is beyond toy applications since the average of time per project was more than a year involving at least two developers at the same time. Readers interested in knowing more about these projects can consult suggested links or http://grasia.fdi.ucm.es, where we have grouped together links to demos and more information.

## 3 Basic Concepts About Project Management and Metrics in COCOMO II

Estimation of how much a software project will cost is commonly measured in terms of size, human resources and time. The estimation model we use, COCOMO II [1], starts expressing the size of the application in different ways:

- *Source Lines of Code (SLOC).* A line of code refers to the smallest piece of code a programmer can produce. However, there are some elements that are not a SLOC, like a breakline character, a comment, or a compiler directive. There is a list of conditions elaborated by the Software Engineering Institute that is implemented into CodeCount [4].
- *Unadjusted Function Points (UFP).* They represent the amount of functionality in a software project and a set of individual project factors. They can be used at the beginning of a project when no source code is available yet to determine what the expected size of the system is. UFP are usually translated into SLOC. COCOMO II counts the ways an application communicates with the user or environment by categorizing into: External input (EI), External output (EO), Internal Logical File (ILF), External Interfaces File (EIF), or External Inquiry (EQ). Each instance of these function types is then classified by complexity level. The complexity level determines a set of weights, which are applied to their corresponding function counts to determine the UFP value.
- *Application Point (AP).* An application point is another way of expressing the functionality to implement. An application point can be a screen of the application, a report or a 3GL component. There is some ongoing work on this topic in COCOMO II, though, so far, there are not enough projects measured this way.

COCOMO II uses several formulas where these factors are weighted with the experience obtained in previous developments. To these variables, each estimation model adds additional elements to be considered: degree of reuse, automatically generated lines of code, experience of the staff involved, complexity of the development, existence of previous similar developments, etc.

## 4 Agent Specific Implementation Elements

In COCOMO II, a main element that affects the final cost is the estimated size of the development expressed in SLOC or UFP. These elements do not work properly for predicting the cost of an agent-oriented application, as we will see in the next section. Nevertheless, accounting only SLOC associated to key agent specific indicators lead to better cost estimations. There were many candidates for indicators, but we mention here those we found more relevant for the developments we were involved into.

In the projects under consideration in this study, we have used regularly some agent-oriented features:

- A BDI control. Using BDI means that there are *goals* and that these goals are to be satisfied by *tasks*. To make it work, there must be information structures that interrelate different goals and that describe what to do on goal failure or satisfaction conditions. Besides, there has to be some management infrastructure to deal with decisions referring to which goal to focus at the moment and how to do so.
- Session based control. Agents should have infrastructures to handle conversations (that is, instances of protocols) with other agents or human users. A common way to do this in the telecommunications domain is the *session management* scheme. There is a session manager responsible of creating, destroying, and monitoring ongoing sessions (conversations). Sessions can be used also to model reactive behaviours in communications and they are usually implemented as state machines.
- Perception of the environment. Defining proper system boundaries is one of the first tasks when designing a system. With agents, system boundaries are determined by the allocation of agent *sensors*. Sensors produce information that is later processed by agents.
- Abstract Communications. In our projects we did not stick to a concrete middleware technology, since the agent interaction concept is technology independent. To abstract from the different technologies, agents were built over a resource layer, which was responsible of implementing technology specific communication artefacts, and offering upwards a homogeneous interface.

To gather information about these aspects, we have defined several variables:

- *Sociability.* We try to estimate how social an agent is. We measure this aspect as the count of interaction specific elements such as:
  - *Interactions.* Being one interaction, for instance, the capability of an agent to engage into one conversation with another agent. Usually, we identify the number of interactions with the number of protocols that an agent is able to understand and follow.
  - *Messages.* This gives an idea of the complexity of the conversations used by the agent. By message, we mean a prototype of information that it is intended to be exchanged along a conversation. Messages sent within loops, for instance, would not count as many messages, since each message would have the same format with subtly different data.

- *Behaviour.* Taking into account that agents can contain either reactive or deliberative behaviours, we tried to select elements that would be shared by most implementations:
  - *Task.* This element informs of the capabilities of an agent. If, in the agent architecture, the task is a method or a procedure, then we would count the number of such methods. In general, it is more probable to find tasks identified with isolated structures, such as modules, scripts, or classes.
  - *Rules.* Most agents implement their control with rules. Here we would count general rules directly, without taking care of the purpose of the rule.
  - *Goal Management rules.* These would be rules whose responsibility is to control the lifecycle of goals in the agent. These rules tell what to do when the goal has been achieved or when it has failed. They also may tell which goal to focus on next. Of course, they make sense when the control of the agent is goal oriented.
  - *State Machines.* It is another classic way of implementing agent control. By counting the number of different state machines and the states they consider, we have an initial idea of the complexity of the behaviour of the agent.
- *Information.* Here, we try to know how the agent perceives the world, and how he manages to take decisions.
  - *Mental entities.* This counter is related with cognitive agents having a mental state. By counting mental entities, we obtain an integrated numeric representation of how the agent represents its environment and how precise is the control of the agent. This serves also as a generalization of the counting of events and goals, which are more specific measures that may not be applied in concrete representations.
  - *Events.* It refers to the perception of the agent. We assume that whatever information that is perceived from the environment takes the form of events, once the agent start processing it. Here, depending on the paradigm, we may find events implemented as predicates in a knowledge base, specialised classes, or, perhaps, only as strings.
  - *Goals.* Goals are special mental entities that are dedicated to control purposes in most cognitive agents. Counting them gives an estimation of how complex is the control of a cognitive agent.

Developers are expected to elaborate descriptions of their systems and count the elements mentioned before. With this data, the developer can apply the COCOMO II model as section 6 indicates in order to obtain the manpower and the expected time for a given project.

## 5 Some Numbers

We have inspected the three projects (P815, P907, and PSI3) in two ways. First with a conventional tool, the Eclipse metrics module [5], and then, manually, inspecting the resulting code. Since we are facing projects of different nature, we had to differentiate

**Table 1.** Statistical data about the implementation of projects P815, P907, and PSI3. Data extracted from project sources excluding generated files such as RMI/CORBA skeletons or stubs. Tools for obtaining the data were CodeCount and Eclipse Plugin Metrics. The account of declarative parts is omitted here but mentioned on Table 2. The programming language was JAVA in all cases.

| | P815 | P907 | PSI3 |
|---|---|---|---|
| Number of classes | 482 | 172 | 130 |
| Number of packages | 45 | 31 | 23 |
| Average methods per class | 5.17 | 4.09 | 5.3 |
| **SLOC Logical lines** | 15843 | 5393 | 9862 |
| **SLOC Physical lines** | 20009 | 7007 | 13102 |

**Table 2.** Statistical data common to all projects. Data refer to elements commonly associated with agents whose control is expressed with rules.

| | P815 | P907 | PSI3 |
|---|---|---|---|
| Total number of Interactions with other agents | 3 | 5 | 4 |
| Total number of messages interchanged | 15 | 19 | 11 |
| Total number of events considered | 61 | 10 | 10 |
| Total number of rules | 198 | 48 | 39 |
| Total number of tasks | 71 | 9 | 39 |
| Total number of state machines applied | 5 | 10 | 8 |
| Total number of states in every state machine | 13 | 46 | 37 |

**Table 3.** Statistical data about BDI behaviour. Some elements were duplicated into each agent. The numbers here are obtained after eliminating duplicates.

| | P815 | P907 |
|---|---|---|
| Total number of types of mental entities (F=Facts, G=Goals, E=Events) | 8F+135G+61E= 204 | 3F+29G+10E= 42 |
| Total number of Goals | 135 | 29 |
| Rules dedicated to management of mental entities | 190 | 46 |
| Events | 61 | 10 |

between conventional statistics, related with the object oriented implementation, and agent statistics, related with agent oriented topics, as reviewed in the previous section. These data will be used in the next section to evaluate COCOMO II models and check their results.

These data were used to adjust the different variables and make them fit with the actual costs of the project. As readers can see, P815 and PSI3 are more complex than P907. The main reason is that P907 had less effort allocated for development than the other two. P907 main goal was producing the MESSAGE methodology and not a prototype of an agent system.

## 6 Applying Estimation Models

The application of COCOMO II *Early Design Development* model is configured with the following considerations:

- Each project is structured as a single module representing the whole system. This module has a size in SLOC determined by the logical SLOC row in Table 1.
- Time for each project is strictly limited by the time assigned in the respective project plan. To weight the effort, we adjusted the man power invested in order to have a more realistic view of what effort it required.
- We do not take into account maintenance effort since project prototypes did not have to be maintained. Also, for the sake of simplicity, we assume a waterfall development process.
- We use scale factors shown in Table 4, though *Effort Adjustment Factor* (EAF) is modified to fit each project concrete domain problem and experience, see Table 5. Values are extracted from the tables presented in the COCOMO II software modelling manual [9]. We encourage reading this manual since it illustrates the ratings of some sections which may not seem logical. Values from Table 5, for instance, are obtained by adding the values of, at least, two other factors and applying a conversion table.

**Table 4.** Scale factors applied to each project

| | **P815** | **P907** | **PSI3** |
|---|---|---|---|
| Precedentness | Nominal | High | High |
| Development Flexibility | High | High | Nominal |
| Architecture/ Risk resolution | Extra High | Extra High | Nominal |
| Team Cohesion | Hi | Very High | Very High |
| Process Maturity | Low | Nominal | Nominal |

In Table 4, *Precedentness* grows as we gain experience in the development. *Flexibility* was high in P815 and P907 projects since the prototypes were made only by our team. In PSI3 there was a considerable integration effort and this implied defining strict interfaces and integration tasks. *Architecture and risk* factors were under control in P815 and P907, since no functionality was considered hard to be solved. Therefore, we chose an extra high. In PSI3 there was an uncertainty about a part of the project that depended on document classifiers, so we labelled this time as nominal the value. *Team cohesion* was high at the beginning, and very high at the end, as the development team gained knowledge and confidence. *Process maturity* refers to the Capability Maturity Model questionnaire, and, at the beginning, we were in the Level 1 which is equivalent to Low at the beginning, and Nominal in the others, since we were able to repeat the development process.

Several factors that contribute to adjust effort values are indicated in Table 5. RCPX depends on the size of the data managed, the reliability associated to the system, and the kind of operations it makes. P815 made interpolation operations, had several protocols implemented, and managed a data base of project tasks of moderated size. This means for us a High value overall. P907 performed simple

**Table 5.** Effort Adjustment Factor (EAF) applied to each project

| | **P815** | **P907** | **PSI3** |
|---|---|---|---|
| Product Reliability and Complexity (RCPX) | High | Nominal | Very High |
| Reusability (RUSE) | Very High | Very High | Nominal |
| Platform Difficulty (PDIF) | High | Very High | High |
| Personnel Capability (PERS) | Nominal | Nominal | Nominal |
| Personnel Experience (PREX) | Low | Nominal | High |
| Facilities (FCIL) | Nominal | High | High |
| Required Development Schedule (SCED) | Nominal | Nominal | Nominal |

operations, had also many protocols between different agents, and the data handled referred to airplanes and departures, what makes an overall of nominal. PSI3 had to perform complex operations to classify documents and learn user interests, the interactions where also many, and the database size was the largest since we handled part of the Reuters news collection.

RUSE measures the effort in building reusable components. In P815 the effort was very high as in P907, since we produced goal management facilities, communication facilities, and the agent architecture. In PSI3 the effort was nominal since there was interest in obtaining reusable components, but it was not a primary goal.

PDIF combines consumption of time during execution, platform volatility, and main storage constraints. In all projects, platforms were rather stable, with changes between 6 months and 12 months. Only PSI3 had some time execution constraint, in order to share the processor with other applications. P815 consumed around 50% of CPU and P907 around 95%. Percentage of use of storage resources in all projects was very low but all of existing resources were dedicated to the developed applications.

PERS measures the skills of analysts and programmers and their continuity in the company. The core of the development team along the three projects was rather stable, with some particular contributions for P907 and PSI3, so we consider that this factor can be considered in the nominal category.

PREX refers to the experience in the application, languages/tools, and platform experience. With respect the platform, P815 used CORBA and JESS. The first was rather well known, but the second was not so. P907 had similar problem. We used JADE for the first time, and ILOG JRules for the first time as well. PSI3 used again CORBA, which we knew, JESS, now well known, and Rainbow (a text mining library), which was completely new for us. All developments used JAVA and CASE tools for modelling, in which we had more than three years of experience. With respect to the application, P815 was our first agent system, P907 the second, and PSI3 the third, apart of some academic projects.

FCIL combines the use of software tools and multi-siteness, that is, if members of the project were working remotely and, if so, in what degree. In P815, we used IDEs for development and CASE tools for modelling, but independently. In P907 and PSI3 we tried to integrate more, but still had to reach maturity. With respect multi-siteness, P815 was performed within the same city, where as PSI3 and P907 were in the same building with occasional meetings with companies.

SCED measures acceleration of the project in order to eliminate risks. In all projects there was none. This is expressed as a nominal value.

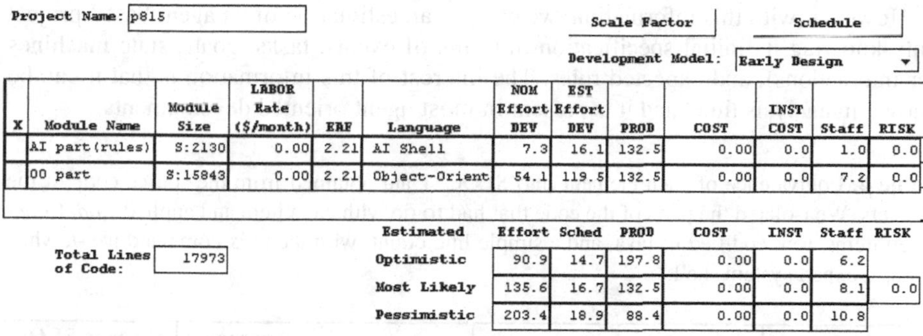
Project Name: p815
Scale Factor
Schedule
Development Model: Early Design
X
Module Name
Module Size
LABOR Rate ($/month)
EAF
Language
NOM Effort DEV
EST Effort DEV
PROD
COST
INST COST
Staff
RISK
AI part(rules)
S:2130
0.00
2.21
AI Shell
7.3
16.1
132.5
0.00
0.0
1.0
0.0
OO part
S:15843
0.00
2.21
Object-Orient
54.1
119.5
132.5
0.00
0.0
7.2
0.0
Total Lines of Code:
17973
Estimated
Effort
Sched
PROD
COST
INST
Staff
RISK
Optimistic
90.9
14.7
197.8
0.00
0.0
6.2
Most Likely
135.6
16.7
132.5
0.00
0.0
8.1
0.0
Pessimistic
203.4
18.9
88.4
0.00
0.0
10.8

**Fig. 1.** Snapshot of the P815 project estimation obtained from COCOMO II 2000

With this configuration, and using the estimation tool, we found out that effort in projects P907 and P815 had been overestimated in more than 500%. In the case of PSI3, there was a depreciation of the effort close to 10% (Table 7), which is not a bad result. These values only tell us that agent-oriented developments are different from conventional developments, and that the effort is not invested into the elements that the standard COCOMO II considers. Hence, the estimation should study only those elements related with the construction of the agent, discarding the other ones as non relevant.

As an experiment, we selected a set of concepts from the list presented in section 4, and measured their implementation cost in SLOC, as Table 6 shows. We recalculated the cost for all projects and obtained the column B in Table 7, as illustrated in Fig. 2. The results were better with P907 and P815, but not with PSI3. Besides, we wanted to have an estimation of the cost of implementing each one of the concepts from section 4. That is the reason why we tried another experiment.

Our next step was obtaining an equivalence of average SLOC per task, state machine, event, and so on. We omitted interactions on purpose because they usually appear as state machines. Also, we omitted messages and states considered by machines, since in the projects we study, there is some redundancy due to dependencies among the number of states and the number of messages.

With results from Table 6 we recalculate again the models, applying this time the values from *Average SLOC per item* multiplied by the number of events, state machines, and so on, of each project. As a consequence, we obtain the data presented in Table 7 column C. As it can be seen with values in column B and C, the results are more accurate that those of column A, which correspond to the COCOMO II applied directly over the total SLOC, the one shown in Table 1.

With the new estimation parameters, we got worse results for project PSI3. This could be explained because of the management and debugging facilities that we had to implement in order to deal with scalability, and that we removed in order to make this study. If we consider that code as tasks to be executed by the system, the new estimation is better 19.5 PM and 9 months, but not as good as the one generated by pure COCOMO II. As we will comment in the next section, this could be a proof that we still need more knowledge from more agent oriented developments.

However, with this information, we can get an estimation of an agent based project only knowing its initial specification in terms of events, tasks, goals, state machines (or interactions), and expected rules. The interest of this information is that it can be known in analysis time, and it is present in most agent oriented developments.

**Table 6.** Equivalence of each element into SLOC. Data obtained from the source code of the projects. We isolated the parts of the code that had to do with each item and applied *CodeCount* when items were codified in Java, and a simple line count, with the unix command *wc -l*, when it was a expert system shell.

| Element | SLOC P815 | SLOC P907 | SLOC PSI3 | Average SLOC | Average SLOC per item |
|---|---|---|---|---|---|
| Event | 443 | 86 | 172 | 233.66 | 11.02 |
| Rule | 2130 | 923 | 1047 | 1366.66 | 18.94 |
| Goal | 1581 | 110 | | 845.5 | 7.75 |
| Task | 793 | 520 | 303 | 627 | 76.17 |
| State machines | 142 | 691 | 1048 | 233.66 | 11.02 |

**Table 7.** Comparison of values obtained with pure COCOMO II (A), pure COCOMO II with the data obtained from Table 6 (B), and COCOMO II using average SLOC count per item (C). (B) and (C) where calculated with nominal values in EAF. PM stands for Personnel Month, and represents the effort of one programmer in one month. Column A is obtained from the most likely estimation. Real months refers to the length of the project according to signed contracts. Real PM refers to all the people who participated into each project.

| Project | Real cost PM/months | (A) PM/months | (B) PM/months | (C) PM/months |
|---|---|---|---|---|
| P907 | 6 / 5 | 34.4 / 10.6 | 7.2 / 6 | 6.8 / 6.6 |
| P815 | 18 / 9 | 135.6 / 16.7 | 16.3 / 8.7 | 25 / 9 |
| PSI3 | 69 / 18 | 63.7 / 13.4 | 7.6 / 6.8 | 7.3 / 6.7 |

Project Name: p815    Scale Factor    Schedule

Development Model: Early Design

| X | Module Name | Module Size | LABOR Rate ($/month) | EAF | Language | NOM Effort DEV | EST Effort DEV | PROD | COST | INST COST | Staff | RISK |
|---|---|---|---|---|---|---|---|---|---|---|---|---|
| | tasks | S:793 | 0.00 | 1.00 | Object-Orient | 2.5 | 2.5 | 312.6 | 0.00 | 0.0 | 0.3 | 0.0 |
| | goals | S:1581 | 0.00 | 1.00 | AI Shell | 5.1 | 5.1 | 312.6 | 0.00 | 0.0 | 0.6 | 0.0 |
| | state machines | S:142 | 0.00 | 1.00 | Object-Orient | 0.5 | 0.5 | 312.6 | 0.00 | 0.0 | 0.1 | 0.0 |
| | rules | S:2130 | 0.00 | 1.00 | AI Shell | 6.8 | 6.8 | 312.6 | 0.00 | 0.0 | 0.8 | 0.0 |
| | events | S:443 | 0.00 | 1.00 | Object-Orient | 1.4 | 1.4 | 312.6 | 0.00 | 0.0 | 0.2 | 0.0 |

Total Lines of Code: 5089

| Estimated | Effort | Sched | PROD | COST | INST | Staff | RISK |
|---|---|---|---|---|---|---|---|
| Optimistic | 10.9 | 7.7 | 466.6 | 0.00 | 0.0 | 1.4 | |
| Most Likely | 16.3 | 8.7 | 312.6 | 0.00 | 0.0 | 1.9 | 0.0 |
| Pessimistic | 24.4 | 9.8 | 208.4 | 0.00 | 0.0 | 2.5 | |

**Fig. 2.** P815 estimation using only elements chosen from Table 6 and data from SLOC p815 column. All EAF values are set to nominal.

## 7 Evaluating the Results

Software estimation is not an exact science. Obtaining more accurate estimations is a matter of choosing the best indicators for a problem domain and choosing the adequate estimation model and values for the terms involved in the equations of software economics. COCOMO II was not completely explored. Therefore this paper should be understood as preliminary work that could be improved.

One of our decisions was applying an early design model, a model we could associate with the initial stages of an agent-oriented development. Indeed, an immediate improvement could be applying a Post Architecture COCOMO II model, which considers more parameters than those we have chosen. But, again, we wanted to include our experience to provide some prediction at the analysis stage for the development of a multi-agent system. Also, another improvement could be using application points instead of the SLOC approach we took. Though the theory behind application points indicates that they could be a better estimate than UFPs and SLOCs, we thought that SLOCs were a more feasible integration point for agent concepts.

With the values we have obtained, it is possible for us to foresee the cost in man power and lines of code by using only an agent based specification. However, the data collected is not enough yet for accurate estimations. We still need to gather data from more projects in order to have a database of costs associated to each project and obtain more accurate measures. With COCOMO II is possible to obtain more accurate estimations by means of recalibration of the scale factors it considers (the different weight associated to each variable in the effort and schedule formulae). Hence, the more data about projects exist, the better we can foresee the cost of new multi-agent systems.

However, increasing the amount of data is a hard goal to achieve, since it implies either a common effort in sharing the results of the projects we, agent researchers, have been involved into, or promoting the development of multi-agent systems and making its implementation public. So far, this effort has been quite limited.

Some readers may argue that these results are not applicable to any agent-oriented developments. This is true in part. Developments with conventional software engineering can be as diverse as those based on agents. We can find very different system architectures and technologies in each one, and, yet, COCOMO II holds. There are not exact measures, but error is usually within 20% of the real cost, which may be considered as a good estimation. Whether the same estimations work the same for agents is something to be proven beyond any doubt, and, in that sense, this paper is a first step.

## 8 Conclusions

The goal of this paper is to establish some alternatives that facilitate the transition from agent research experience in the development of prototypes to common software engineering practices. In concrete, we have addressed the cost estimation problem, an issue that has not been studied in depth in our area, yet.

Our contribution to the agent community in this issue starts with statistical data about three projects where we have been involved, an estimation of SLOC required for each element present in our implementations, and its inclusion into a COCOMO II model.

There is much work to do, still. As we pointed out before, we need more data and further experimentation with COCOMO II models, to identify more concrete agent features that influence the development. Also, we need to perform similar studies to this one but centred in the area of Rapid Application Development, since our main line of research in the INGENIAS methodology [8] deals with automatic code generation from specifications. Also, we need to identify the influence of the reuse of code from previous developments and existing libraries.

In the near future, the adapted COCOMO II for agents will be implemented as a module of the INGENIAS Development Kit, so that agent researchers can estimate in analysis/design time how much effort an agent oriented development may take.

Interested readers can check and download the data used to elaborate this paper at http://grasia.fdi.ucm.es/gschool.

## References


1. Boehm, B.W., Sullivan, K.J.: Software Cost Estimation with COCOMO II. Prentice Hall (2000)
2. Boehm, B.W., Sullivan, K.J.: Software economics: a roadmap. In: Proceedings of the Conference on The future of Software Engineering. ACM Press (2000) 319-343
3. Caire G., Evans R. Massonet P., Coulier W., Garijo F.J., Gomez J., Pavón J., Leal F., Chainho P., Kearney P.E., Stark J.: Agent Oriented Analysis using MESSAGE/UML. In: The Second International Workshop on Agent-Oriented Software Engineering (AOSE 2001). Lecture Notes in Computer Science, Vol. 2222, Springer-Verlag (2002) 119-135
4. CodeCount. http://sunset.usc.edu/research/CODECOUNT/index.html
5. Eclipse Metrics Plugin. http://metrics.sourceforge.net
6. Gómez-Sanz, J., Pavón, J., Díaz Carrasco, A.: The PSI3 Agent Recommender System. International Conference on Web Engineering (ICWE 2003). Lecture Notes in Computer Science, Vol. 2722. Springer-Verlag (2003) 30-39
7. Gómez-Sanz, J., Pavón, J., Garijo, F.: Intelligent Interface Agents Behaviour Modelling. MICAI 2000: Advances in Artificial Intelligence. Lecture Notes in Computer Science, Vol. 1793. Springer Verlag (2001) 598-609
8. Pavón J., Gómez-Sanz J. and Fuentes, R. The INGENIAS Methodology and Tools. In Henderson-Sellers, B. and Giorgini, P. (editors), *Agent-Oriented Methodologies.* Idea Group Publishing, 2005, chapter IX, 236-276
9. USC COCOMOII application v2000. Available only from the support CDROM of 1. V 1999 available from http://sunset.usc.edu/available_tools/index.html

# Aspects in Agent-Oriented Software Engineering: Lessons Learned

Alessandro Garcia[1], Uirá Kulesza[2], Cláudio Sant'Anna[2], Christina Chavez[3], and Carlos J.P. de Lucena[2]

[1] Lancaster University, Computing Department, InfoLab 21, Lancaster - United Kingdom
a.garcia@lancaster.ac.uk
[2] PUC-Rio, Computer Science Department, LES, Rio de Janeiro - Brazil
{uira, claudio, lucena}@les.inf.puc-rio.br
[3] Federal University of Bahia (UFBA), Computer Science Department, Salvador - Brazil
flach@im.ufba.br

**Abstract.** Several concerns in the development of multi-agent systems (MASs) cannot be represented in a modular fashion. In general, they inherently affect several system modules and cannot be explicitly captured based on existing software engineering abstractions. These crosscutting concerns encompass internal agent properties and systemic properties, such as learning, code mobility, error handling, and context-awareness. In this context, it is important to systematically verify whether emerging development paradigms support improved modularization of the crosscutting concerns relative to MASs. This paper reports some lessons learned based on our experience in using aspect-oriented techniques and methods to address these problems. In the light of these lessons, related work and a set of future research directions are also discussed.

## 1 Introduction

Software engineering of large multi-agent systems (MASs) involves a number of concerns, including autonomy, roles, learning, mobility, error handling, fault tolerance, and context-awareness. The modeling, design, and implementation of many of these concerns are challenging because they are inherently crosscutting as the system complexity increases. In other words, these concerns crosscut several agent actions and plans, which implement the agents' basic functionality and other agent concerns. Several system quality attributes, such as reusability and maintainability, depend largely on the ability of software engineering techniques and methods to support the explicit separation of MAS concerns throughout the design and implementation stages.

Existing modeling languages [8, 20] and design and implementation approaches [6, 9, 11, 20] are not able to provide explicit support for the separation of crosscutting MAS-related concerns. In this context, it is important to systematically verify whether emerging development paradigms support improved modularization of the

J.P. Müller and F. Zambonelli (Eds.): AOSE 2005, LNCS 3950, pp. 231 – 247, 2006.

crosscutting concerns relative to MASs. Aspect-oriented software development (AOSD) [12] is a promising paradigm to promote improved separation of concerns, leading to the production of software systems that are easier to maintain and reuse. AOSD is centered on the aspect notion as an abstraction aimed to modularize crosscutting concerns throughout the software lifecycle. Hence, aspect-oriented approaches are candidates to address the crosscutting property of some concerns in multi-agent systems. However, up to now AOSD research has focused on trivial or well-known crosscutting concerns, such as logging, tracing, distribution, and persistence. There are very few reported experiences involving aspects in the MAS domain. For example, Kendall et al focus on the use of aspects for enabling improved modularization of agent roles [10].

There is a pressing need for understanding the interplay between agent-oriented software engineering (AOSE) and AOSD. This paper reports some lessons learned based on our experience in applying both aspect-oriented techniques and methods to the construction of MASs. We have developed and applied aspect-oriented approaches to specify [22], architect [21], design [6], and implement [23] multi-agent systems. We have also conducted some qualitative [7] and quantitative [24] empirical studies. Our lessons learned are related to four different inter-related dimensions of software engineering, which are captured in the following research questions:

(i) What are the main motivations to use AOSD techniques for MAS development?
(ii) What are the MAS-related concerns which were well modularized (or not) with aspects according to our experimental settings?
(iii) What are the limitations of existing aspect-oriented techniques, methods and tools to address crosscutting concerns in MASs?
(iv) What are some future directions that naturally emerged from the practical exploration of AOSD in the context of MASs?

The lessons learned presented here provide a clear understanding of important strengths and weaknesses of the investigated aspect-oriented approaches as well as their compatibility and divergences. The results are important sources towards a potential integration of AOSD and AOSE. They are also useful for engineers of realistic MASs who need to model, design and implement their systems in the presence of crosscutting concerns. The conclusions may also be of interest to agent-oriented methodologists since they may decide to incorporate solutions for problems detected in our experiences directly as part of their methodologies.

The remainder of this paper is organized as follows. Section 2 presents some typical examples of crosscutting concerns in MASs. Section 3 introduces relevant AOSD terminology and overviews our aspect-oriented approach to support the modularization of MASs. Section 4 presents the lessons learned. Section 5 discusses related work. Section 6 includes some concluding remarks and directions for future work.

## 2 Crosscutting Concerns in MASs

Several authors have identified that some agent properties are often crosscutting, such as mobility [25], interaction [23, 24], learning [26], autonomy [27, 28], and collaboration

[10, 25]. Some empirical studies confirm their findings [7, 15, 24]. This section presents some examples of crosscutting concerns in MAS development. A concern is some part of a MAS that we want to treat as a single conceptual unit. Concerns are modularized throughout software development using different abstractions provided by techniques, methods, and tools.

Fig. 1 shows a partial representation of a multi-agent system, which was modeled with an agent-oriented extension to UML (based on stereotypes), and implemented using the Java programming language. The modeled system is a multi-agent application that supports the management of the reviewing process for research conferences [23]. This system will be herein referred to as Expert Committee (EC). In this system development, the JADE platform was also used to support inter-agent collaborations and agent mobility. Machine learning techniques were designed and implemented to address the learning-related requirements of this application. Role modeling was used to structure the collaborative capabilities of the agents. Each set of classes, surrounded by a gray rectangle, has the main purpose of modularizing a specific agent concern, namely interaction, environment, basic concerns, learning, and collaboration. This MAS includes other MAS concerns, such as mobility and error handling, which are not represented in the figure for simplicity purposes.

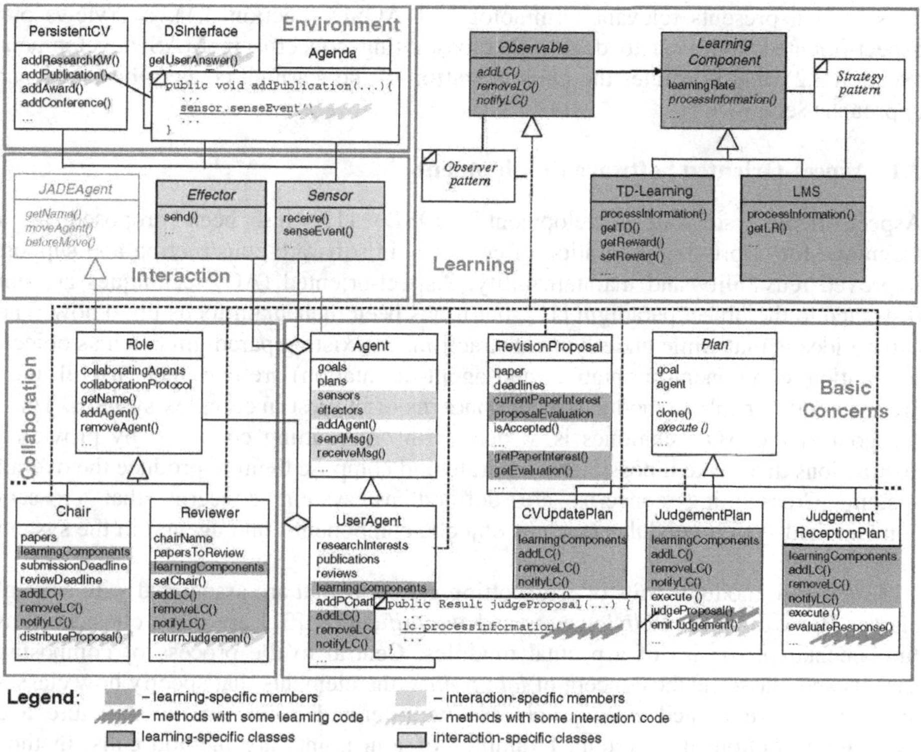


**Fig. 1.** Crosscutting Agent Concerns

Note that, for example, the learning concern crosscuts several agent actions and plans implementing other agent concerns; it has a huge impact on the basic agent structure and the collaboration design. Although part of the learning concern is localized in the classes of the Strategy and Observer patterns, learning-specific code replicates and spreads across several class hierarchies of a software agent. Several participants have to implement the observation mechanism and the gathering information and, as a consequence, have learning code in them. Some classes also have learning-specific knowledge. For example, the attributes currentPaperInterest and proposalEvaluation are elements which were introduced to the class RevisionProposal only due to learning purposes.

As a result, adding or removing the learning code from system modules requires invasive changes in those classes. Note that even if we try to refactor the design solution presented in Fig. 1, we cannot find a more modular solution. This problem happens because learning is a crosscutting concern independently of the system decomposition used [30]. Fig. 1 also illustrates similar problems for the interaction concern, which is usually crosscutting.

## 3 Modularizing Multi-Agent Systems with Aspects

This section presents relevant terminology of AOSD (Section 3.1), overviews our aspect-oriented approach to deal with crosscutting concerns in MAS development (Section 3.2), and illustrates the modularization of the learning concern based on our approach (Section 3.3).

### 3.1 Aspect-Oriented Software Development

Aspect-oriented software development (AOSD) [12] has been proposed as a technique for improving separation of concerns in software construction and support improved reusability and maintainability. Aspect-oriented (AO) techniques are not restricted to the object paradigm [12], but it has been their main focus up to now. The central idea is that while underlying abstractions of existing paradigm (such as object-orientation, component-orientation, and agent-orientation) are extremely useful, they are inherently unable to modularize all concerns of interest in complex systems. Thus, the goal of the AO techniques is to deal with crosscutting concerns, by providing abstractions that make it possible to separate and compose them to produce the overall system. Crosscutting concerns are defined as system concerns that crosscut conventional system modules (such as objects, components, and agents) in the system development.

*Aspects* are modular units of crosscutting concerns that are associated with a set of classes (for example). *Obliviousness* and *quantification* [32] are often considered as fundamental properties of aspectual modules. Central to the process of composing aspects and classes is the concept of *join points*, the elements that specify how classes and aspects are related. Join points are well-defined points in the structure and dynamic execution of a system. Examples of join points are method calls, method executions, and field sets and reads. An aspect defines sets of join points and advice. *Advice* is a special method-like construct attached to join points. *Weaver* is the mechanism responsible for composing the classes and aspects.

AspectJ [13] is a practical aspect-oriented extension to the Java programming language. AspectJ supports the definition of aspects, advices, join points, and pointcuts. *Pointcuts* are collections of join points and are used in advice definitions. AspectJ also supports *inter-type declarations* that either specify new members (attributes or methods) to the classes to which the aspect is attached, or change the inheritance relationship between classes. Nowadays there are several AO techniques [44, 45] to support the separation of crosscutting concerns beyond programming. However, such techniques are rarely dedicated to AOSE; the existing AOSD approaches have been limited to addess crosscutting concerns in the object-oriented and component-oriented paradigms.

### 3.2 Aspect-Oriented Modeling, Design and Implementation of MASs

The basic idea of our approach is the use of aspect-oriented abstractions to enable improved separation of crosscutting concerns in the software engineering artifacts associated with MASs. Aspects are used as unifying abstractions to capture the agent concerns that are hard to modularize with both existing agent-oriented high-level notations and object-oriented design and implementation techniques. These aspects are supported from high-level specifications and architecture design to the detailed design and implementation. The goal is to obtain untangled software artifacts and promote enhanced reuse and evolvability in MAS development. The proposed approach is independent of MAS implementation frameworks, such as JADE [1] and ZEUS [14].

Our approach supports MAS developers with four main elements. The first element of our approach is a domain-specific language (DSL) [22], called Agent-DSL, that supports the high-level modeling of the MAS at hand. Agent-DSL supports the modeling of fundamental abstractions in AOSE, such as agents, plans, actions, and goals, as well as the modeling of crosscutting agent-related features as separate modules, i.e. aspects. Aspects are used to explicitly capture concerns like mobility, learning, roles, and adaptation.

The second element of our approach is an aspect-oriented software architecture [21] for structuring the basic internal modules of a software agent. Since the agents have been specified using our DSL, the internal architecture of each agent type in the system needs to be defined. As the system specification is refined, new crosscutting concerns manifest and must be modularized at the architectural stage. Our architecture provides a set of constraints to support the modularization of crosscutting agent-related concerns as architectural aspects. This aspectual agent architecture is flexible to support different compositions of agent concerns for heterogeneous agent types [21]. In addition, our approach provides a set of guidelines [6, 31] to refine the specification of aspectual agent architectures in terms of detailed design.

The third element is a language of design patterns that provides solutions for the detailed design of crosscutting MAS-related concerns, such as mobility [29], learning [30], roles [36], interaction [37], autonomy [23], and adaptation [23]. The patterns can be directly mapped into implementation elements. The proposed design patterns have been implemented in AspectJ. In this context, the fourth element of our approach is an implementation framework [23, 22], called AspectT, which materializes those design patterns in AspectJ and provides support for the implementation of the crosscutting MAS concerns with a set reusable classes and aspects. Finally, we have a set of prototype tools [22] to support the DSL-based modeling of the multi-agent system and the partial code generation of this system based on those provided models.

### 3.3 An Example

This section illustrates how the use of our aspect-oriented approach supports the modularization of the learning concern (Section 2). Due to space limitations, in this work, we focus on the *detailed design* of the learning concern. A more detailed description for the other MAS concerns and other development stages, the reader should refer to the publications described in Section 3.2. In fact, the full description of our approach is outside the scope of this paper. Fig. 2 illustrates the design aspectization of the learning property in the EC system (Section 2).

The design notation in Fig. 2 is based on an aspect-oriented modeling language [2]. This language extends UML with notations for representing aspects. The notations provide a detailed description of the aspect elements. In this modeling language, an aspect is represented by a diamond; it is composed of internal structure and crosscutting interfaces. The internal structure declares the internal attributes and methods. A crosscutting interface specifies when and how the aspect affects one or more classes [2]. Each crosscutting interface is presented using the rectangle symbol with compartments, as indicated in Fig. 2. A crosscutting interface is composed of advices and inter-type declarations (Section 3.1) The notation uses a dashed arrow to represent the crosscutting relationship, which relates one aspect to affected classes and/or aspects. Such classes and aspects affected by the learning aspects are represented in gray.

Fig. 2 shows that learning aspects encapsulate the entire implementation of the learning concern, including the learning-specific knowledge and the information gathering. The aspectual modules separate the learning protocol from the modules with the purpose of implementing other agent concerns, including: (i) classes representing the agent types (e.g. UserAgent class), (ii) classes implementing agent actions and plans (e.g. JudgementPlan class), and (iii) other aspects, such as the Reviewer aspect..

The Learning aspects connect the execution points (join points) on different agent classes with the corresponding learning components, making it transparent to the agent's basic functionality the particularities of the learning algorithms in use. These aspects are able to crosscut join points in the dynamics of other agent modules in order to enhance those modules with learning-specific behavior, from where learning algorithms are invoked. These points include the change of a knowledge element, execution of actions on plans, roles, and agent types, or still some thrown exceptions. The aspects gather information at those well-defined join points which is relevant for learning purposes, without impacting the internal design of other agent modules.

Auxiliary classes are used to implement different learning techniques. The learning process in the EC system is indirect because the agent will build its knowledge through the results of the inter-agent negotiations. Machine learning is used to address the knowledge acquisition. Distinct learning techniques are used in the EC system: Temporal Difference Learning (TD-Learning) [23] and Least Mean Squares (LMS) [23]. LMS is used by the reviewer role in order to learn the user preferences in the subjects he/she likes to review. TD-Learning is used in the context of the user agent type to learn about some general user preferences in terms of research topics. Note that the scattering and tangling relative to the learning concern presented in Fig. 1 is overcome in the aspect-oriented solution (Fig. 2).

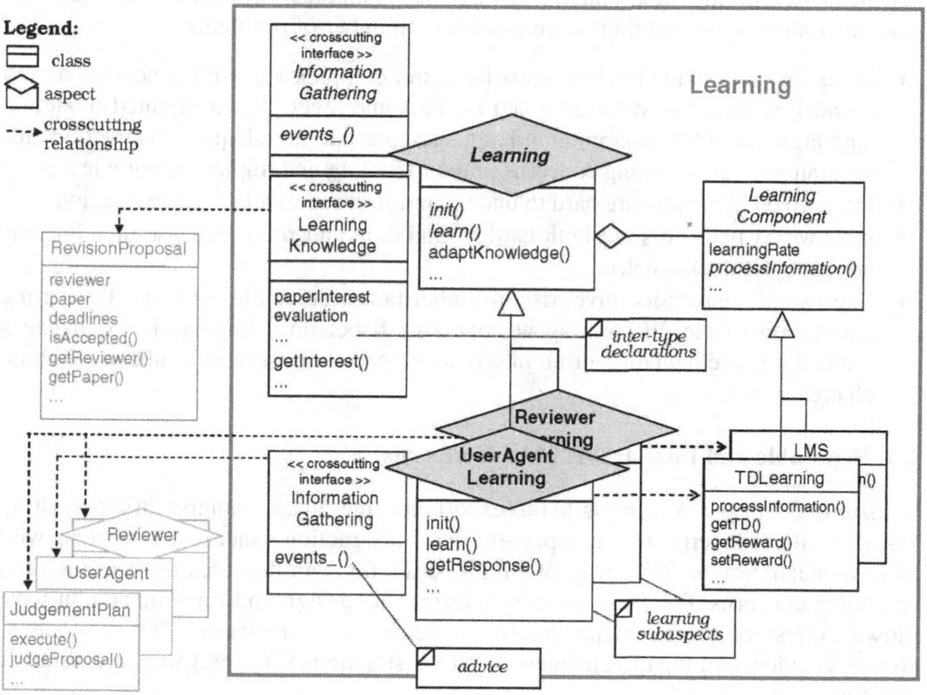


**Fig. 2.** The Detailed Design of the Learning Aspects

## 4 Lessons Learned

We discuss below important benefits and pitfalls in using AO techniques for the development of MASs. Our lessons learned are related to four different inter-related dimensions of software engineering, which are presented in the following subsections.

### 4.1 Motivation for AOSD in MAS Development

The main motivation for using AOSD techniques is the increasing complexity of today's agent-based applications. The advent of novel and innovative networking technologies makes it necessary for software systems to incorporate and deal with an ever greater variety of agent-specific concerns such as mobility, adaptation, and learning. Underlying all of these special purpose concerns is the basic concern responsible for the basic functionality of the system. According to our experience [4, 23, 24], the agent properties are typically overlapping and crosscut the agent's basic functionality. The basic functionalities of agents already are quite complicated, and so agent properties should be designed separately from the agents' basic behaviors [31].

With MASs growing in size and complexity, the separation of their concerns throughout the different development phases is crucial to MAS engineers. Separation of crosscutting concerns is an important principle in software engineering to achieve improved reusability and maintainability of complex systems. The lack of modularization of crosscutting concerns raises a number of problems:

- Designing intertwined behaviors is hard and complex since all concerns have to be dealt with at the same time and at the same level. Agent-oriented modeling languages and OO programming languages provide no adequate abstractions for separation of crosscutting concerns in the modeling and implementation levels.
- Intertwined behaviors are hard to understand because of a lack of abstraction.
- Intertwined behaviors are both hard to maintain and reuse because the concerns are strongly amalgamated.
- Intertwined behaviors give rise to inheritance anomalies due to the strong connection of the different agent concerns. It becomes impossible to change a method's implementation or an intertwined special concern in a subclass without changing both.

## 4.2 Separable and Inseparable MAS Concerns

*Separable Concerns.* According to our experience, there was a number of crosscutting MAS-specific concerns which aspect-oriented abstractions succeeded to cope with their modularization. This was often the case for mobility, learning, roles, and autonomy concerns. For these agent properties, the design and implementation have shown expressive improvements in terms of separation of concerns. This observation provides evidence of the effectiveness of AO abstractions for segregating crosscutting structures.

The use of aspects in these cases was also useful to reduce the coupling between the design modules for these concerns and increase their cohesion, since the aspect-oriented mechisms enabled the modularization of all the behaviours relative to these agent concerns. We have captured a common characteristic of these aspects: they exhibit a high connection between the internal elements of these aspects, i.e. a high interaction between internal aspect attributes, methods, inter-type declarations and advices, which is fundamental to improve their cohesion and minimize the system coupling.

*Aspects Emerging in the Software Lifecycle.* Many agent properties in a MAS will likely not be designed from scratch as aspects. Rather, many crosscutting concerns will emerge as a MAS evolves. An assessment framework based on a metrics suite [17], for instance, could help the detection of crosscutting concerns in the MAS at hand. Capturing such agent concerns as aspects sometimes also requires restructuring of the classes and methods implementing the agents' basic functionality and other agent aspects to expose suitable join points (Section 4.3).

*Inseparable Concerns.* There were also some crosscutting concerns, which aspect-oriented solutions failed to improve their modularization. For example, the Interaction aspects do not modularize the message assembling from different plans or roles; the message needs to be prepared within a method on plan classes or on role aspects because its assembling is very coupled to the role or plan context of the respective agent. One solution would be to separate the message assembling with aspects, but it would result in higher complexity.

The design of the adaptation concern, for example, also sounds to be natural in the OO fashion, and it does not seem reasonable or even possible to isolate the adaptation behavior into aspects. The AO design of the adaptation aspects somewhat improved the concern locality, but the differences in terms of coupling and cohesion are not significant. In fact, an additional interesting observation in our studies is that sometimes the crosscutting MAS concerns can be expressed separately as aspects, but it remains non-trivial to specify how these separate aspects should be recombined into a simple manner. A lot of effort is required to compose the participant classes and the aspects that modularize the agent concern. Hence, there are some cases where the separation of the agent-related concerns leads to more complex solutions.

*Inter-aspect Relationships.* Many aspects are orthogonal and interact with each other. For example, code mobility affects not only the agent kernel, but also other important agent concerns such as roles, interaction, and learning. Since the mobility concern is related to these concerns, the presence of sophisticated composition mechanisms is important to specify the relationships between the mobility aspects and these other agent aspects.

*Complex Structure for Simple Agents.* We have often found that the choice between using aspects or not depends highly on the complexity of the crosscutting concern in the specific agent-oriented application at hand. For example, we have decided to use aspects for modularizing the autonomy property of software agents in a reactive MAS. However, some simple reactive agents do not require thread control, react only to few events, make very simple decisions, and do not have proactive behavior. In this case, the autonomy code tends to be localized in fewer methods. The use of aspects in this specific situation can increase rather than decrease the agent design's complexity.

*Overlapping Concerns.* There were some concerns that have shown themselves as overlapping. For example, adaptation and learning are a classical example of overlapping concerns. The implementation of the learning aspects includes the same behaviors already implemented by the adaptation aspects. In order to avoid code duplication, we have exposed this common behavior as part of the interface of the adaptation aspects so that the learning aspects can access them.

*Aspects as 'Glue' between Agents' Basic Concerns and MAS Frameworks.* Several of our agent aspects at the detailed design level achieved a common structure: the aspect behavior forms the glue between the OO structure implementing the agents' basic functionality and the specific MAS frameworks used to support some concerns. For instance, the Learning aspects [30] work as a glue between the hierarchy of agent types and the hierarchy of modules implementing the learning strategies. This design structure is beneficial because it allows to express the agent's basic functionality in its own object structure and to use an aspect to inject that agent property into the basic functionality in a way that is transparent. In our case studies, the same design solution was also applied to glue the basic agent structure and the mobility frameworks and platforms.

*Incremental Process vs. Iterative Process.* During our case studies [7, 23, 24], we have tried to "incrementally" deal with agent concerns at the specification (using Agent-DSL mentioned in Section 3.2), architectural, design and implementation stages. We have found that, as the MASs increases in complexity, the boundary between increments is not as transparent as expected. For example, the design and implementation of the mobility aspects required the creation of new pointcuts in the interaction aspects previously defined. In this way, we mostly had to follow an iterative process rather than an incremental approach in order to specify and implement the aspect-oriented agent architectures.

*Mastering Aspects Complexity.* In the design and implementation of the agent aspects, we have observed that it is easier to build an aspect-oriented system when the interface between aspects and classes is narrow and unidirectional. *Unidirectional* means that the aspect code refers to the classes but not vice versa, although many AO solutions do not follow this constraint. In fact, central to the quality achieved in our MAS is the notion of structuring crosscutting concerns separately from the "primary" agent concerns, using aspects that cannot be referenced back by the objects. Narrow means that the aspect code has a well-defined effect on particular points in the code.

### 4.3 Limitations of Existing Aspect-Oriented Techniques to MAS Development

*Inter-aspect Conflicts.* As mentioned previously, we have used AspectJ to implement the agent aspects. The modularization of some agent concerns with AspectJ caused aspectual conflicts. For example, roles were implemented as AspectJ aspects in our case studies. Each role aspect introduces the role behavior to the respective classes that represent the agents playing that role. This behavior introduction was implemented as AspectJ inter-type declarations. However, some of the roles encompassed similar structural and behavioral elements due to their very nature. Hence, this property of roles imposed conflicts in their AspectJ implementations. As an agent can play more than a role, those attributes and methods had to be renamed and changed so that two or more conflicting role aspects could be added to the same agent class.

*Lack of Obliviousness.* As mentioned previously, capturing agent concerns as aspects sometimes required restructuring of the classes and methods implementing the agents' basic functionality and other aspects to expose suitable join points. For instance, we have extracted code from existing methods of a plan class into a new method to expose a method-level join point so that a *role aspect* could intercept it. In these cases, the aspect obliviousness is not complete, although many AOSD researchers (e.g. [32]) argue that obliviousness is a fundamental property of AOSD. In this context, intimacy has been defined as the additional effort required to prepare the classes and methods for the incorporation of aspects into the system [32].

*Repetitive and Time-Consuming Definitions.* We have modularized the interaction concern (Section 3.3) as aspects using both Agent-DSL and AspectJ. As part of the aspectization process of the interaction concern at the implementation level, all the message senders of the system must be specified in the pointcut inside the Interaction aspects. This might indeed be repetitive and tedious, suggesting that AspectJ, the language used in our studies, should have more powerful metaprogramming constructs. However, this is not an unsolvable problem because code-generation tools can assist MAS engineers in this development step (Section 4.4). In addition, we can establish a naming convention and use wildcards supported by most aspect-oriented languages. The initial implementation of our case studies used naming conventions.

*Naming Conflicts.* The use of AspectJ and existing MAS frameworks/platforms to implement the aspect-oriented agent architectures have led to some design mismatches. For example, we have used JADE to support code mobility in our case studies. The JADE architecture imposes on the application developers the extension of the jade.Agent class to make the application agents (or specific roles) mobile. This abstract class provides a number of mobility services, such as a method getName() which is responsible for generating an unique name for the mobile agent instances in a distributed context. However, we have previously defined a Agent class in the agent architectures that implement the agents' basic services, such as a method getName() with a different purpose. As we have used AspectJ aspects to implement the mobility concern, we used inter-type declarations to specify this extension in the aspects and inject the implementation of the jade.Agent class in the Agent class in our application. This architectural mismatch caused by the AspectJ mechanism required the renaming of this method and changes in the respective callers.

*Implementation Limitations.* In addition, some AspectJ restrictions complicated the materialization of some architectural and design solutions. For example, each agent instance must often have its own mobility aspect. As a consequence, mobility aspects must be instantiated per Agent instance (or Role instance). The current version of AspectJ supports the specification of per-object aspects. We could describe the instantiation of the Mobility aspect using the `perthis` mechanism, such as:

```
public abstract aspect Mobility perthis(Agent) {…}
```

However, the use of `perthis` restricts the scope of the aspect. When one AspectJ aspect is declared to be singleton or static, its scope is the whole system and the aspect can crosscut all system classes. Per-object aspects can only crosscut the object with which it is associated. Since the mobility protocol crosscuts several classes, not only the Agent class or the Role class, the perthis clause cannot be used in this context. As a result, we have to declare mobility aspects as singletons and introduce the methods and attributes to the Agent and Role classes. The use of inter-type declarations complicates the design of the Mobility aspect since it requires the agent or role instance to be exposed as a parameter in each advice of the Mobility aspect.

### 4.4 Research Directions

*Need for Improved Traceability.* According to our experience, there is a need for handling aspects in a uniform way throughout the different development stages. In our approach, agent aspects were represented as first-class elements in the system specification (using the Agent-DSL), in the detailed design and in the implementation level (using AspectJ). However, we missed some support for describing the agent aspects in intermediary modeling languages, such as agent-oriented design languages in order to support a better traceability between the software artifacts.

*Code Generation.* The definition of some agent aspects involves some time-consuming tasks, such as extensive description of pointcuts. Tools should be developed to maximize the automatic generation of the pointcuts and overcome this time-consuming task. We are improving a generative approach [22] that supports the code generation of the agent aspects. The idea is to support our methodology (Section 3.2) with an additional number of tools and wizards that automate the code generation in AspectJ.

*Aspects in Agent-Oriented Modeling.* According to the experience of this research, there are some crosscutting concerns even at the agent-oriented modeling level, such as coordination, exception handling, and context awareness. In addition, many of the agent properties, such as those ones discussed in this paper, have a broadly-scoped effect in agent-oriented design models; they affect a consistent number of goals and actions representing other MAS concerns, and often also have implications over different agent-oriented modeling views. Our work has been more concerned with an architectural and design approach. There is a need to extend existing AOSE meta-models (e.g. TAO [33]) and agent-oriented modeling languages (e.g. Gaia [19]) with aspect-oriented abstractions to support the representation of crosscutting concerns in agent-oriented models.

*Integration with Another Development Methods.* With the growing and dissemination of the use of agent technology in the development of software systems, it is also important to adapt current methods of agent-oriented software engineering to be integrated with existing development methods. In this sense, we have particular interest in how we can integrate our approach with other Web modeling and design methods, such as, OOHDM [34] and WebML [35], in order to introduce software agents in web-based information systems.

## 5 Related Work

Dealing with several crosscutting agent concerns, such as mobility and learning, has been recognized as a serious problem that has not received enough attention [15, 25]. However, research in agent-oriented software engineering has concentrated on high-level methodologies and modeling languages [20], without giving enough attention to the role of aspects in the context of AOSE. In addition, implementation frameworks [1, 14] provide object-oriented APIs for MAS development, without providing guidelines for the modularization of crosscutting agent concerns.

Some researchers have recognized these problems for some single agent concerns, such as roles [26] and mobility [25], and have proposed techniques for dealing with these concerns. However, such techniques are for separating only these individual concerns. In addition, most of them are focused only on the implementation stage and do not provide explicit support for the separation of crosscutting concerns at early development stages.

Pace et al [15] have developed the Smartweaver approach. Their approach provides assistance for the development of MAS applications by means of integration of agent-oriented and aspect-oriented frameworks. It consists of two components: (i) Bubble [42] – an agent-oriented framework used to the implementation of reactive agents; and (ii) Aspect-Moderator [39] – an AO framework that supports the coordination between functional components and aspects. Aspect-Moderator is used to capture typical crosscutting concerns, such as concurrency, logging, and event handling. The Smartweaver approach addresses the incorporation of aspects in agent models. However, the code generation is limited and it does not support essential agent concerns, including autonomy, interaction, and adaptation.

Amor et al [40] investigate how the gap between agent-oriented methodologies and implementation frameworks can be addressed. They analyze how this process can be automated in a way that is independent from the methodology and the framework adopted. The authors use the concepts, models, and mechanisms defined in the Model Driven Architecture (MDA) specification [41] to provide a mapping between abstractions in agent-oriented methodologies and elements in implementation frameworks. Malaca, a platform-neutral agent architecture proposed by the authors, is used as an intermediate representation to simplify this task of mapping. The Malaca architecture specifies separately the agent functionality from the concerns related with the agent platform adopted, such as, agent interaction, and distribution/codification of FIPA ACL messages. Although these concerns are not implemented using any aspect-oriented language, this separated specification enables the reuse of the agent functionality and the dynamic reconfiguration of the agent behavior. There is a strong connection between these concerns in Malaca architecture and the Interaction and Role aspects in our aspect-oriented software architecture.

Cossentino et al [38] have proposed PASSI (Process for Agent Societies Specification and Implementation), a methodology to specify, design and implement MASs. This methodology proposes the organization of the MAS development process in different phases from the requirements specification through to system deployment. Each phase focuses on the definition or refinement of a system model. Many PASSI models are adaptations of UML standard models, such as use-case, class, and activity diagrams, which incorporate agent-oriented abstractions. The use of class diagrams in the design of MASs brings the facility to generate the skeletons of many classes of the system. The authors have also explored the reuse of recurring agent design patterns to improve the quantity and quality of code generated. However, the PASSI approach does not support the systematic modularization and generation of code relative to crosscutting agent concerns.

Tropos provides to some extent abstractions for expressing crosscutting concerns [42]. However, the focus is on the representation of inter-goal influences in the early and late requirements development phases. It provides a very-high level set of abstractions (goals and soft-goals), which allow the description of positive and negative contributions between goals representing functional and non-functional MAS properties. Soft goals can be viewed as MAS aspects at the requirements level. Although the goal models could be refined in late development stages, Tropos does not provide a complete modularization framework to design and implementation stages as supported in our approach. As pointed out in Section 2, crosscutting relationships naturally emerge in several development stages beyond inter-goal relationships. In fact, we believe our agent-oriented design framework is complementary to the Tropos notations.

Another approach that shows interesting aspect-oriented ideas incorporated in a modeling language is [43]. This approach focuses on representing the system-to-be according to several different perspectives; each one of them promoting an abstract representation of the system. Nevertheless, it only sketches the characteristics of an autonomy perspective for MAS specification. In addition, it does not address a comprehensive concern-independent framework for modularizing crosscutting structure and behavior in agent-oriented software development.

## 6 Conclusions and Ongoing Work

Aspect-oriented software development is gaining wide attention both in research environments and in industry. AOSD is a promising paradigm to promote improved separation of concerns, leading to the production of software systems that are easier to maintain and reuse. The separation of MAS concerns is essential to software engineers since they may decide to extend and modify such concerns as the system evolves. Hence it is important to systematically verify whether emerging development paradigms support improved modularization of the crosscutting concerns relative to MASs. More generally speaking, there is a need for understanding the relationships between aspect- and agent-oriented abstractions.

This paper has presented some lessons learned with the use of aspect-oriented techniques and methods to develop some multi-agent systems. This paper complements our previous work on empirical studies [7, 23, 24] by focusing on more generic software engineering questions. Our aspect-oriented approach has been evaluated using representative systems from different domains. An initial quantitative study [24] has provided evidences of the benefits of the aspect-oriented approach. Although experimental studies are time-consuming, it is necessary to replicate this study with a variety of agent applications and with different heterogeneity facets. These replicated studies would build an improved body of knowledge about the interplay among aspects and MAS concerns. For example, it would be desirable to conduct quantitative studies with the application of AI techniques in a large-scale fashion in order to understand how the aspect-oriented approach scales in this context.

**Acknowledgements.** This work has been supported by European Commission grant IST-2-004349: European Network of Excellence on Aspect-Oriented Software Development (AOSD-Europe), 2004-2008. This work has also been supported by CNPq under grant No. 140252/2003-7 for Uirá and grant No. 140214/04-6 for Cláudio. The authors were also supported by the ESSMA Project under grant 552068/02-0.

## References

1. Bellifemine, F., Poggi, A., Rimassi, G. “JADE: A FIPA-Compliant agent framework”. Proc. Practical Applications of Intelligent Agents and Multi-Agents, April 1999, pp. 97-108.
2. Chavez, C., Lucena, C. “Design Support for Aspect-oriented Software Development”. Doctoral Symposium at OOPSLA’2001, Tampa Bay, USA, October 2001, pp. 14-18.

3. Finin, T. et al. "KQML as an Agent Communication Language", Proc. of the 3rd Intl. Conference on Information and Knowledgc Management, ACM Press, 1994, pp. 456-463.
4. FIPA Specifications. "FIPA ACL Message Structure Specification". http://www.fipa.org/specs/fipa00061/
5. Gamma, E. et al. "Design Patterns: Elements of Reusable Object-Oriented Software". Addison-Wesley, Reading, 1995.
6. Garcia, A., Lucena, C., Cowan, D. "Agents in Object-Oriented Software Engineering". Software: Practice and Experience, Elsevier, April 2004.
7. Garcia, A., Silva,V., Chavez, C., Lucena, C. "Engineering Multi-Agent Systems with Aspects and Patterns". Journal of the Brazilian Computer Society, July 2002, v. 8, no. 1, pp. 57-72.
8. Iglesias, C. et al. "A Survey of Agent-Oriented Methodologies", Proceedings of the ATAL-98, Paris, France, July 1998, pp. 317-330.
9. Jennings, N., Wooldridge, M. "Agent-Oriented Software Engineering". In: J. Bradshaw (Ed). "Handbook of Agent Technology". AAAI/MIT Press, 2000.
10. Kendall, E. "Role Model Designs and Implementations with Aspect-oriented Programming". OOPSLA 1999, pp. 353-369.
11. Kendall, E et al. "A Framework for Agent Systems", In: Fayad, M. et al (Eds), "Implementing Applications Frameworks: Object Oriented Frameworks at Work". John Wiley & Sons, 1999.
12. Kiczales, G. et al. "Aspect-Oriented Programming". European Conference on Object-Oriented Programming (ECOOP), LNCS (1241), Springer-Verlag, Finland., June 1997.
13. Kiczales, G. et al. "Getting Started with AspectJ". Communication of the ACM, vol. 44, no. 10, October 2001, pp. 59-65
14. Nwana, H., Ndumu, D., Lee, L. "ZEUS: An advanced Toolkit for Engineering Distributed Multi-Agent Systems", Proceedings of PAAM'98, 1998, pp. 377-391.
15. Pace, A., Trilnik, F., Campo, M. "Assisting the Development of Aspect-based MAS using the SmartWeaver Approach". In: Garcia, A. et al (Eds). "Software Engineering for Large-Scale Multi-Agent Systems". Springer-Verlag, LNCS 2603, April 2003.
16. Rashid, A. "A Hybrid Approach to Separation of Concerns: The Story of SADES". Proceedings of the Reflection 2001, LNCS 2192, pp. 231-249.
17. Sant'Anna, C., Garcia, A., Chavez, C., Lucena, C., Staa, A. "On the Reuse and Maintenance of Aspect-Oriented Software: An Assessment Framework". Proc. of the XVII Brazilian Symposium on Software Engineering, Manaus, Brazil, October 2003, pp. 19-34.
18. Sycara, K., Paolucci, M., Velsen, M., Giampapa J. "The RETSINA MAS Infrastructure." Journal of Autonomous Agents and Multi-Agent Systems, v. 7, n. 1/2, July/September 2003.
19. Wooldridge, M., Jennings, N., Kinny, D. "The Gaia Methodology for Agent-Oriented Analysis and Design". Journal of Autonomous Agents and MAS, 3:3, 2000, pp. 285-312.
20. Bergenti, F., Gleizes, M.-P., Zambonelli, F. (Eds.). "Methodologies and Software Engineering for Agent Systems: The Agent-Oriented Software Engineering Handbook". Springer, 2004.
21. Garcia, A., Lucena, C. "Taming Heterogeneous Agent Architectures with Aspects". Communications of the ACM, March 2005. (submitted)
22. Kulesza, U., Garcia, A., Lucena, C. "A Generative Approach for Multi-Agent System Development". "Software Engineering for Multi-Agent Systems III", Springer, LNCS 3390, December 2004, pp. 52-69.

23. Garcia, A. From Objects to Agents: An Aspect-Oriented Approach. PhD Thesis, Computer Science Department, PUC-Rio, Brazil, April 2004.
24. Garcia, A et al. Separation of Concerns in Multi-Agent Systems: An Empirical Study. In: "Software Engineering for Multi-Agent Systems II". Springer, LNCS 2940, February 2004.
25. Ubayashi, N., Tamai, T. "Separation of Concerns in Mobile Agent Applications". Proc. of the 3rd Conference Reflection 2001, LNCS 2192, Kyoto, September 2001, pp. 89-109.
26. D'Hondt, M., Gybels, K., Jonckers, V. "Seamless Integration of Rule-Based Knowledge and Object-Oriented Functionality with Linguistic Symbiosis". Proceedings of the 19th Annual ACM Symposium on Applied Computing (SAC 2004), Nicosia, Cyprus, March 2004.
27. Guessoum, Z., Briot, J. From Active Objects to Autonomous Agents. IEEE Concurrency, Special Series on Actors and Agents, Vol. 7, N. 3, 1999, pp. 68-76.
28. Amandi, A., Price, A. Building Object-Agents from a Software Meta-Architecture. In: Advances in Artificial Intelligence, LNAI, vol. 1515, Springer-Verlag, 1998.
29. Garcia, A. et al. "The Mobility Aspect Pattern". Proc. of the 4th Latin-American Conference on Pattern Languages of Programming, SugarLoafPLoP'04. August, 2004, Fortaleza, Brazil.
30. Garcia, A. et al. "The Learning Aspect Pattern". Proc. of the 11th Conference on Pattern Languages of Programs (PLoP2004), September 2004, Monticello, USA.
31. Garcia, A., Kulesza, U., Lucena, C. "Aspectizing Multi-Agent Systems: From Architecture to Implementation." "Software Engineering for Multi-Agent Systems III". Springer-Verlag, LNCS 3390, December 2004, pp. 121-143.
32. Filman, R. "What Is Aspect-Oriented Programming, Revisited". Proceedings of the Workshop on Advanced Separation of Concerns at ECOOP'01, June 2001.
33. Silva, V. et al. "Taming Agents and Objects in Software Engineering". In: "Software Engineering for Large-Scale Multi-Agent Systems", Springer, LNCS 2603, March 2003.
34. Ceri, S., Fraternali, P. "Web Modeling Language (WebML): A Modeling Language for Designing Web Sites". Proc. of the 9th. Intl. World Wide Web Conference, 2000, pp 137-157.
35. Schwabe, D., Rossi, G. "An Object-Oriented Approach to Web-based Application Design". Theory and Practice of Object Systems, v. 4, pp.207-225, October, 1998.
36. Garcia, A., Chavez, C., Kulesza, U., Lucena, C. "The Role Aspect Pattern". Proc. of the 10th European Conf. on Pattern Languages of Programs (EuroPLoP'05), July 2005, Irsee, Germany.
37. Garcia, A., Kulesza, U., Chavez, C., Lucena, C. The Interaction Aspect Pattern. Proc. of the 10th European Conf. Pattern Languages of Programs (EuroPLoP), July 2005, Irsee, Germany..
38. Cossentino, M., Potts, M. "A CASE Tool Supported Methodology for the Design of MASs." Proc.. of the Intl. Conf. on Soft. Eng. Research and Practice (SERP'02), Las Vegas, June 2002.
39. Constantinides, C., Bader, A., Elrad, T., Fayad, M. "Designing an Aspect-Oriented Framework". ACM Computing Surveys, 32:41, 2000.
40. Amor, M., Fuentes, L., Vallecillo, A. "Bridging the Gap Between Agent-Oriented Design and Implementation Using MDA". Proceedings of 5th International Workshop on Agent-Oriented Software Engineering, AOSE 2004, Springer, LNCS 3382, July 2004, pp. 93-108.
41. OMG. "Model Driven Architecture - A Technical Perspective". Object Management Group, OMG Document ab/2001-01-01, 2001. Available from www.omg.org.

42. Castro, J., Kolp, M., Mylopoulos, J. "Towards Requirements-Driven Information Systems Engineering: the Tropos Project". Information Systems 27(6), 2002, p. 365–389.
43. Cossentino, M., Zambonelli, F. "Agent Design from the Autonomy Perspective". LNCS 2969) Springer, p. 140-150, 2004.
44. Filman, R. et al. "Aspect-Oriented Software Development". Addison-Wesley, 2005.
45. Chitchyan, R. et al. "Survey of Aspect-Oriented Analysis and Design". AOSD-Europe Project Deliverable No: AOSD-Europe-ULANC-9. www.aosd-europe.net

# Author Index

# Lecture Notes in Computer Science

For information about Vols. 1–3861

please contact your bookseller or Springer

Vol. 3987: M. Hazas, J. Krumm, T. Strang (Eds.), Location- and Context-Awareness. X, 289 pages. 2006.

Vol. 3968: K.P. Fishkin, B. Schiele, P. Nixon, A. Quigley (Eds.), Pervasive Computing. XV, 402 pages. 2006.

Vol. 3959: J.-Y. Cai, S. B. Cooper, A. Li (Eds.), Theory and Applications of Models of Computation. XV, 794 pages. 2006.

Vol. 3958: M. Yung, Y. Dodis, A. Kiayias, T. Malkin (Eds.), Public Key Cryptography - PKC 2006. XIV, 543 pages. 2006.

Vol. 3956: G. Barthe, B. Gregoire, M. Huisman, J.-L. Lanet (Eds.), Construction and Analysis of Safe, Secure, and Interoperable Smart Devices. IX, 175 pages. 2006.

Vol. 3955: G. Antoniou, G. Potamias, C. Spyropoulos, D. Plexousakis (Eds.), Advances in Artificial Intelligence. XVII, 611 pages. 2006. (Sublibrary LNAI).

Vol. 3954: A. Leonardis, H. Bischof, A. Pinz (Eds.), Computer Vision – ECCV 2006, Part IV. XVII, 613 pages. 2006.

Vol. 3953: A. Leonardis, H. Bischof, A. Pinz (Eds.), Computer Vision – ECCV 2006, Part III. XVII, 649 pages. 2006.

Vol. 3952: A. Leonardis, H. Bischof, A. Pinz (Eds.), Computer Vision – ECCV 2006, Part II. XVII, 661 pages. 2006.

Vol. 3951: A. Leonardis, H. Bischof, A. Pinz (Eds.), Computer Vision – ECCV 2006, Part I. XXXV, 639 pages. 2006.

Vol. 3950: J.P. Müller, F. Zambonelli (Eds.), Agent-Oriented Software Engineering VI. XVI, 249 pages. 2006.

Vol. 3947: Y.-C. Chung, J.E. Moreira (Eds.), Advances in Grid and Pervasive Computing. XXI, 667 pages. 2006.

Vol. 3946: T.R. Roth-Berghofer, S. Schulz, D.B. Leake (Eds.), Modeling and Retrieval of Context. XI, 149 pages. 2006. (Sublibrary LNAI).

Vol. 3945: M. Hagiya, P. Wadler (Eds.), Functional and Logic Programming. X, 295 pages. 2006.

Vol. 3944: J. Quiñonero-Candela, I. Dagan, B. Magnini, F. d'Alché-Buc (Eds.), Machine Learning Challenges. XIII, 462 pages. 2006. (Sublibrary LNAI).

Vol. 3942: Z. Pan, R. Aylett, H. Diener, X. Jin, S. Göbel, L. Li (Eds.), Technologies for E-Learning and Digital Entertainment. XXV, 1396 pages. 2006.

Vol. 3939: C. Priami, L. Cardelli, S. Emmott (Eds.), Transactions on Computational Systems Biology IV. VII, 141 pages. 2006. (Sublibrary LNBI).

Vol. 3936: M. Lalmas, A. MacFarlane, S. Rüger, A. Tombros, T. Tsikrika, A. Yavlinsky (Eds.), Advances in Information Retrieval. XIX, 584 pages. 2006.

Vol. 3935: D. Won, S. Kim (Eds.), Information Security and Cryptology - ICISC 2005. XIV, 458 pages. 2006.

Vol. 3934: J.A. Clark, R.F. Paige, F.A. C. Polack, P.J. Brooke (Eds.), Security in Pervasive Computing. X, 243 pages. 2006.

Vol. 3933: F. Bonchi, J.-F. Boulicaut (Eds.), Knowledge Discovery in Inductive Databases. VIII, 251 pages. 2006.

Vol. 3931: B. Apolloni, M. Marinaro, G. Nicosia, R. Tagliaferri (Eds.), Neural Nets. XIII, 370 pages. 2006.

Vol. 3930: D.S. Yeung, Z.-Q. Liu, X.-Z. Wang, H. Yan (Eds.), Advances in Machine Learning and Cybernetics. XXI, 1110 pages. 2006. (Sublibrary LNAI).

Vol. 3929: W. MacCaull, M. Winter, I. Düntsch (Eds.), Relational Methods in Computer Science. VIII, 263 pages. 2006.

Vol. 3928: J. Domingo-Ferrer, J. Posegga, D. Schreckling (Eds.), Smart Card Research and Advanced Applications. XI, 359 pages. 2006.

Vol. 3927: J. Hespanha, A. Tiwari (Eds.), Hybrid Systems: Computation and Control. XII, 584 pages. 2006.

Vol. 3925: A. Valmari (Ed.), Model Checking Software. X, 307 pages. 2006.

Vol. 3924: P. Sestoft (Ed.), Programming Languages and Systems. XII, 343 pages. 2006.

Vol. 3923: A. Mycroft, A. Zeller (Eds.), Compiler Construction. XIII, 277 pages. 2006.

Vol. 3922: L. Baresi, R. Heckel (Eds.), Fundamental Approaches to Software Engineering. XIII, 427 pages. 2006.

Vol. 3921: L. Aceto, A. Ingólfsdóttir (Eds.), Foundations of Software Science and Computation Structures. XV, 447 pages. 2006.

Vol. 3920: H. Hermanns, J. Palsberg (Eds.), Tools and Algorithms for the Construction and Analysis of Systems. XIV, 506 pages. 2006.

Vol. 3918: W.K. Ng, M. Kitsuregawa, J. Li, K. Chang (Eds.), Advances in Knowledge Discovery and Data Mining. XXIV, 879 pages. 2006. (Sublibrary LNAI).

Vol. 3917: H. Chen, F.Y. Wang, C.C. Yang, D. Zeng, M. Chau, K. Chang (Eds.), Intelligence and Security Informatics. XII, 186 pages. 2006.

Vol. 3916: J. Li, Q. Yang, A.-H. Tan (Eds.), Data Mining for Biomedical Applications. VIII, 155 pages. 2006. (Sublibrary LNBI).

Vol. 3915: R. Nayak, M.J. Zaki (Eds.), Knowledge Discovery from XML Documents. VIII, 105 pages. 2006.

Vol. 3914: A. Garcia, R. Choren, C. Lucena, P. Giorgini, T. Holvoet, A. Romanovsky (Eds.), Software Engineering for Multi-Agent Systems IV. XIV, 255 pages. 2006.

Vol. 3910: S.A. Brueckner, G.D.M. Serugendo, D. Hales, F. Zambonelli (Eds.), Engineering Self-Organising Systems. XII, 245 pages. 2006. (Sublibrary LNAI).

Vol. 3909: A. Apostolico, C. Guerra, S. Istrail, P. Pevzner, M. Waterman (Eds.), Research in Computational Molecular Biology. XVII, 612 pages. 2006. (Sublibrary LNBI).

Vol. 3908: A. Bui, M. Bui, T. Böhme, H. Unger (Eds.), Innovative Internet Community Systems. VIII, 207 pages. 2006.

Vol. 3907: F. Rothlauf, J. Branke, S. Cagnoni, E. Costa, C. Cotta, R. Drechsler, E. Lutton, P. Machado, J.H. Moore, J. Romero, G.D. Smith, G. Squillero, H. Takagi (Eds.), Applications of Evolutionary Computing. XXIV, 813 pages. 2006.

Vol. 3906: J. Gottlieb, G.R. Raidl (Eds.), Evolutionary Computation in Combinatorial Optimization. XI, 293 pages. 2006.

Vol. 3905: P. Collet, M. Tomassini, M. Ebner, S. Gustafson, A. Ekárt (Eds.), Genetic Programming. XI, 361 pages. 2006.

Vol. 3904: M. Baldoni, U. Endriss, A. Omicini, P. Torroni (Eds.), Declarative Agent Languages and Technologies III. XII, 245 pages. 2006. (Sublibrary LNAI).

Vol. 3903: K. Chen, R. Deng, X. Lai, J. Zhou (Eds.), Information Security Practice and Experience. XIV, 392 pages. 2006.

Vol. 3901: P.M. Hill (Ed.), Logic Based Program Synthesis and Transformation. X, 179 pages. 2006.

Vol. 3900: F. Toni, P. Torroni (Eds.), Computational Logic in Multi-Agent Systems. XVII, 427 pages. 2006. (Sublibrary LNAI).

Vol. 3899: S. Frintrop, VOCUS: A Visual Attention System for Object Detection and Goal-Directed Search. XIV, 216 pages. 2006. (Sublibrary LNAI).

Vol. 3898: K. Tuyls, P.J. 't Hoen, K. Verbeeck, S. Sen (Eds.), Learning and Adaption in Multi-Agent Systems. X, 217 pages. 2006. (Sublibrary LNAI).

Vol. 3897: B. Preneel, S. Tavares (Eds.), Selected Areas in Cryptography. XI, 371 pages. 2006.

Vol. 3896: Y. Ioannidis, M.H. Scholl, J.W. Schmidt, F. Matthes, M. Hatzopoulos, K. Boehm, A. Kemper, T. Grust, C. Boehm (Eds.), Advances in Database Technology - EDBT 2006. XIV, 1208 pages. 2006.

Vol. 3895: O. Goldreich, A.L. Rosenberg, A.L. Selman (Eds.), Theoretical Computer Science. XII, 399 pages. 2006.

Vol. 3894: W. Grass, B. Sick, K. Waldschmidt (Eds.), Architecture of Computing Systems - ARCS 2006. XII, 496 pages. 2006.

Vol. 3893: L. Atzori, D.D. Giusto, R. Leonardi, F. Pereira (Eds.), Visual Content Processing and Representation. IX, 224 pages. 2006.

Vol. 3891: J.S. Sichman, L. Antunes (Eds.), Multi-Agent-Based Simulation VI. X, 191 pages. 2006. (Sublibrary LNAI).

Vol. 3890: S.G. Thompson, R. Ghanea-Hercock (Eds.), Defence Applications of Multi-Agent Systems. XII, 141 pages. 2006. (Sublibrary LNAI).

Vol. 3889: J. Rosca, D. Erdogmus, J.C. Príncipe, S. Haykin (Eds.), Independent Component Analysis and Blind Signal Separation. XXI, 980 pages. 2006.

Vol. 3888: D. Draheim, G. Weber (Eds.), Trends in Enterprise Application Architecture. IX, 145 pages. 2006.

Vol. 3887: J.R. Correa, A. Hevia, M. Kiwi (Eds.), LATIN 2006: Theoretical Informatics. XVI, 814 pages. 2006.

Vol. 3886: E.G. Bremer, J. Hakenberg, E.-H.(S.) Han, D. Berrar, W. Dubitzky (Eds.), Knowledge Discovery in Life Science Literature. XIV, 147 pages. 2006. (Sublibrary LNBI).

Vol. 3885: V. Torra, Y. Narukawa, A. Valls, J. Domingo-Ferrer (Eds.), Modeling Decisions for Artificial Intelligence. XII, 374 pages. 2006. (Sublibrary LNAI).

Vol. 3884: B. Durand, W. Thomas (Eds.), STACS 2006. XIV, 714 pages. 2006.

Vol. 3882: M.L. Lee, K.-L. Tan, V. Wuwongse (Eds.), Database Systems for Advanced Applications. XIX, 923 pages. 2006.

Vol. 3881: S. Gibet, N. Courty, J.-F. Kamp (Eds.), Gesture in Human-Computer Interaction and Simulation. XIII, 344 pages. 2006. (Sublibrary LNAI).

Vol. 3880: A. Rashid, M. Aksit (Eds.), Transactions on Aspect-Oriented Software Development I. IX, 335 pages. 2006.

Vol. 3879: T. Erlebach, G. Persinao (Eds.), Approximation and Online Algorithms. X, 349 pages. 2006.

Vol. 3878: A. Gelbukh (Ed.), Computational Linguistics and Intelligent Text Processing. XVII, 589 pages. 2006.

Vol. 3877: M. Detyniecki, J.M. Jose, A. Nürnberger, C. J. '. van Rijsbergen (Eds.), Adaptive Multimedia Retrieval: User, Context, and Feedback. XI, 279 pages. 2006.

Vol. 3876: S. Halevi, T. Rabin (Eds.), Theory of Cryptography. XI, 617 pages. 2006.

Vol. 3875: S. Ur, E. Bin, Y. Wolfsthal (Eds.), Hardware and Software, Verification and Testing. X, 265 pages. 2006.

Vol. 3874: R. Missaoui, J. Schmidt (Eds.), Formal Concept Analysis. X, 309 pages. 2006. (Sublibrary LNAI).

Vol. 3873: L. Maicher, J. Park (Eds.), Charting the Topic Maps Research and Applications Landscape. VIII, 281 pages. 2006. (Sublibrary LNAI).

Vol. 3872: H. Bunke, A. L. Spitz (Eds.), Document Analysis Systems VII. XIII, 630 pages. 2006.

Vol. 3871: E.-G. Talbi, P. Liardet, P. Collet, E. Lutton, M. Schoenauer (Eds.), Artificial Evolution. XI, 310 pages. 2006.

Vol. 3870: S. Spaccapietra, P. Atzeni, W.W. Chu, T. Catarci, K.P. Sycara (Eds.), Journal on Data Semantics V. XIII, 237 pages. 2006.

Vol. 3869: S. Renals, S. Bengio (Eds.), Machine Learning for Multimodal Interaction. XIII, 490 pages. 2006.

Vol. 3868: K. Römer, H. Karl, F. Mattern (Eds.), Wireless Sensor Networks. XI, 342 pages. 2006.

Vol. 3866: T. Dimitrakos, F. Martinelli, P.Y.A. Ryan, S. Schneider (Eds.), Formal Aspects in Security and Trust. X, 259 pages. 2006.

Vol. 3865: W. Shen, K.-M. Chao, Z. Lin, J.-P.A. Barthès, A. James (Eds.), Computer Supported Cooperative Work in Design II. XII, 659 pages. 2006.

Vol. 3863: M. Kohlhase (Ed.), Mathematical Knowledge Management. XI, 405 pages. 2006. (Sublibrary LNAI).

Vol. 3862: R.H. Bordini, M. Dastani, J. Dix, A.E.F. Seghrouchni (Eds.), Programming Multi-Agent Systems. XIV, 267 pages. 2006. (Sublibrary LNAI).